"That They All May Be One . . ."

**Studies on Unity, Freedom, and Authority
in the Body of Christ**

By

Walton Weaver

**Including a response to the leading arguments in
the book, *Free in Christ*, by Cecil Hook**

ISBN 1-58427-027-6

Guardian of Truth Foundation
P.O. Box 9670
Bowling Green, Kentucky 42102

Table of Contents

Part Three: Other Areas Of Concern Today

Part Four: Appendix

Foreword
L.A. Stauffer

Unity and *restoration* were the twin themes of the Restoration Movement in America. Thomas Campbell highlighted both ideas in his *Declaration and Address,* a document first printed in the fall of 1809. Campbell stressed again and again the need to remove the "rubbish of the ages" — his expression for the traditions of men — and to find a "thus saith the Lord" for every belief and practice. Oneness in the religious world can exist in any generation, he contended, if believers establish in every city the church Jesus built. Campbell also noted in a sermon that summer before the *Declaration* was published that unity and restoration will come only when disciples "speak where the Bible speaks and remain silent where the Bible is silent."

The history of the Restoration Movement reveals the difficulty of attaining and maintaining unity through restoration. Campbell's own son, Alexander, pressed these themes early on in his writings and preaching, but was one of the first to promote ideas and projects in the 1830s and 1840s which disrupted the oneness of the movement. From these decades forward two different approaches to authority and unity dogged efforts toward the restoration of first-century Christianity. Innovations, modernism, denominationalism, and sectarianism returned time after time to rob proponents of these grand goals.

So it can be said of our own times since the 1950s. Institutionalism, sponsoring churches, church supported recreation, and other innovations grew out of thinking in the late 1940s and divided churches in the 50s and 60s. Amidst this division arose another movement of particular significance that was popularized by W. Carl Ketcherside, who penned his "Thoughts on Fellowship" in 1957. In an effort to promulgate principles that he believed would unite all brethren of the restoration heritage, Ketcherside published this series of articles in his monthly paper, *Mission Messenger.* This charismatic and itinerant evangelist moved freely among churches of Christ and Christian Churches for some thirty years to promote his thoughts on the fellowship of all believers. He also arranged and conducted unity meetings and workshops in most major cities to bring brethren together for discussions and debate on oneness in Christ and fellowship among brethren.

Ketcherside's views, as those who followed his writings can testify, took him much farther than he could have imagined in those early days, and left in his wake three decades or so later a host of disciples and imitators. A number of these men through a variety of publications soon parroted his views, and found *their* solution to unity and fellowship in the Reformation theology of salvation by grace through faith alone. They fought hard all those who were committed to biblical authority, calling them "legalists," opposing strenuously the view that the silence of the Scriptures forbids, and rejecting the idea of a New Testament pattern for the Lord's church. That brethren, including Ketcherside, came to reject the essentiality of baptism for salvation should be a red flag to any generation of disciples. It should warn brethren everywhere that something went awry over the past 50 to 60 years.

Walton Weaver has rendered a service to the present generation in the work that is now before us. *That They All May Be One* is at once a history of restoration thought, a study of hermeneutics, a biblical exposition of pertinent passages that deal with both unity and fellowship, and a review of distortions of plain Bible teaching. It, I must warn, is a book to be studied, not merely read.

Weaver begins his work with "The Biblical Framework" in which he examines minutely all the major Bible passages that call for unity and peace and condemn division. This section is a series of textual studies that are preparatory and absolutely essential to understanding where the "grace-faith only-fellowship" approach to unity has jumped track. Here the book outlines in five chapters God's demand and plan for oneness — taking an in-depth look at 1 Corinthians 1:10-13, Philippians 2:1-4, Ephesians 4:1-6, and key passages on the one body. He concludes in a sixth chapter with an appeal to the authority of the Scriptures. Brethren must grasp these principles.

Weaver proceeds over the next several chapters to develop analytically and persuasively a response to *Free in Christ,* a book written by Cecil Hook in 1984 and now in its ninth printing. Hook affirms the standard line that following a biblical pattern is legalistic and destroys the liberty that disciples have in Christ. Weaver follows Hook's reasoning and thoroughly analyzes the relationship and compatibility of "law" to "grace," "love," "commands," and "liberty." He also drives home the need for authority in "amoral" commands as surely as in "moral" principles. This includes a detailed examination of the "lawyer-like approach" to Scriptures that is so anathama to Hook, and demonstrates its hermeneutical soundness. And, finally, he illustrates his rejection of Hook's approach to Scripture with an analysis of New Testament teaching about worship.

Weaver concludes his work with two sections: "Other Areas of Concern" and an "Appendix" of questions relating to his thesis. He looks at "Faith, Opinion and Romans 14," but the most notable discussion in the final part of the book is the detailed study of the issue of "silence." The author gives a significant amount of space to the principle of silence and to the arguments from a book by George F. Beals entitled, *How Implications Bind and Silence Forbids: Studies in Biblical Hermeneutics.* This may be the most explicit and most minute examination of this important idea that I have read. It, at times, is technical and demands study, but will pay valuable dividends to those who have the patience to follow it through. This is must reading. If brethren do not grasp the principle of silence and how it limits what men believe and practice, the church can never maintain its biblical purity and its distinctive character in the religious world.

Our thanks to Walton Weaver for a comprehensive study of vital issues that have divided brethren in the past fifty years and threaten to destroy what remains of a brotherhood that is devoted to the original ideals of the restoration movement — oneness in Christ through the pattern of sound words revealed in Scripture. We commend the author for tackling what he himself admits are tough topics. He makes no pretence of simplicity, but acknowledges that these issues are difficult though understandable. This book, if both read and studied, will educate serious Bible students and prepare leaders to convict gainsayers and to protect God's flock from grievous wolves that parade among them in sheep's clothing (see Tit. 1:9; Matt 7:15-20; Acts 20:28-30).

Introduction

"Behold how good and how pleasant it is for brethren to dwell together in unity!" (Ps. 133:1). Jesus prayed to the Father, "I do not pray for these alone, but also for those who will believe in Me *through their word*; that they all may be one, as You Father, are in Me, and I in You; that they also may be one in Us, that the world may believe that You sent Me" (John 17:20-21, emphasis added). Much of the unity proposed today fails to take seriously the proper place for the word of God in establishing and maintaining unity.

There have been many in the last forty years who have advocated a unity in diversity that goes far beyond the kind of diversity we find allowed in the New Testament. Much has been written on the need for a "new hermeneutic," and many have attempted to make a difference between gospel and doctrine, all for the purpose of finding a broader basis for unity than the word of God.

When we first began writing this book it was our sole intent to provide a response to the central arguments advanced by Cecil Hook in his book, *Free in Christ*. As we went along, however, it appeared to us that it would be better if we would begin with a brief study of the teaching of Paul on the subject of unity and allow this to serve as a foundation for what had been planned in our response to Cecil Hook. So we decided to begin our study of unity by examining the key unity passages from the hand of the beloved apostle Paul. These passages provide what we call "The Biblical Framework" for our study of this subject. Paul has more to say on the subject of unity than any other New Testament writer. By a careful study of these passages, one should be able to see how far afield many present day unity advocates have gone from the New Testament pattern for unity.

Why did we choose to respond to Cecil Hook? Many have written on this subject, and we could have chosen to follow the lines of argument that are being advanced today by a number of different men, but we decided instead to limit our study in Part Two to what has been written by Cecil

Hook in his book *Free in Christ*. There were three main reasons for this decision.

First, the number of copies of this book that have been printed and distributed seemed to dictate that we do so. With the 1998 printing we are informed that 40,000 copies of this book had been put in print, and that tens of thousands of copies have been distributed around the world free of charge.

Second, I have personally known of people who have been influenced by the teaching of this book to leave conservative churches, and I have known of others who have witnessed the same thing.

Finally, the candor with which Hook presents his case, and the underlying principles in his arguments as they are expressed throughout — as well as his terrible fear of what he calls "legalism," and his apparent revulsion for traditional ways of establishing divine authority that is so apparent on almost every page — appear to this writer to offer the best opportunity to deal with what he considers to be the heart of the issue. In answering Hook we answer every other proponent of the type of unity-in-diversity he advocates. They all are of one mind in their attitude toward the Scripture, and most, if not all, of them believe that the only thing that matters is the principle in a command, not the specifics of a command. They all alike are adamant in their opposition to what they call "legalism." And this basically is the subject we wanted to give emphasis to in this part of our book.

Even though this was our major concern as we began this study, it became apparent that more was needed. There are problems we have encountered through the years that must be addressed. It is a matter of simple, observable fact that these problems keep recurring with each new generation. Every major division the churches of Christ have experienced since the beginning of the restoration movement in America has centered upon the matters of "opinions," faith, and the silence of Scripture. Such subjects seem to lie at the heart of the problem of unity and division of the church on the local level. Until we are right (biblically) in our manner of treating these subjects we can never hope to be successful at being able to maintain "the unity of the Spirit in the bond of peace" as Paul requires. With this fact in mind we decided to give some attention to these subjects in Part Three.

Our final section (Part Four) is an attempt to raise and answer some questions that seem to us to be pertinent to our subject. These are matters we have not sufficiently addressed in the preceding part of our study. The list of questions we have included are far from being an exhaustive list of the kinds of questions that could be raised on the general subject of unity, but they do touch on a variety of subjects that come within the scope of our purpose in writing this book.

It is our ardent desire that only good will come from this effort. If through this means God may find a way to lead some others to give more serious and prayerful thought to this profound and important subject of the unity of the church, our efforts will be sufficiently rewarded.

Walton Weaver
September 11, 2003

Part One:
The Biblical Framework

Chapter 1

One Body Yet Many Members

The New Testament uses several metaphors to help one understand certain truths about the church. The ones best known are those of a kingdom (Matt. 16:18-19; Col. 1:13; Heb. 12:28), a house (Heb. 3:3-6; 1 Tim. 3:15), a building or temple (1 Cor. 3:16-17; Eph. 3:21), and a body (Rom. 12:4-5; 1 Cor. 12:12ff.; Eph.1:22-23; Col. 1:18). The figure Paul uses the most is the church as the body of Christ. This metaphor more than any other tells us about who we are as Christians.

This figure reveals that Christians are those who have been baptized into one body (1 Cor. 12:13), those who make up one body in Christ (Rom. 12:5), those who are the body of Christ (1 Cor. 12:27), those who are members of the body of Christ (Eph. 5:30; 1 Cor. 6:15), those who are members one of another (Rom. 12:5; Eph. 4:25), and those who have been called into the one body (Col. 3:15). In these and other ways Paul teaches that the church is the body of Christ (Eph. 2:22-23; Col. 2:24), and that Christ is the head of that body (Eph. 1:22-23; 5:22-23; cf. Col. 1:18 and 2:19 with Eph. 4:15-16).

The "one body" of Ephesians 4:4 is clearly the body of Christ, though Paul does not add "of Christ" when he affirms in this passage that there is one body. What other body is there? There is only one body and we are members of his body, the church (Eph. 5:29-30). Paul gives a fuller treatment of this subject in 1 Corinthians 12, and toward the end of the discussion says, "Now ye are the body of Christ, and severally members thereof" (v. 27).

In What Sense?
But in what sense is the church the body of Christ? In a study of the unity of the church this question is important because the Scriptures represent the church as a body having many members and yet being "one body in Christ" (Rom. 12:5). In 1 Corinthians 12 Paul says, "for as the body is

one, and hath many members, and all the members of the body, being many, are one body; so also is Christ" (v. 12).

As one moves from Romans and 1 Corinthians to Ephesians and Colossians he notices a difference in emphasis. The earlier letters represent the church as the whole body, while the later letters portray the body as distinct from the head. Also in the earlier letters the metaphor emphasizes the closeness of the church's union with Christ and how the Spirit operates through the members in various ways (by supplying differing spiritual gifts), but the later letters stress the Lordship of Christ and his devotion to and care for the church.

But exactly what do these terms mean? In what way is the church the body of Christ? Is the term "the body of Christ" as applied to the church meant to be taken literally or metaphorically? Since the body is the body of Christ, are the members of the body "in literal fact the risen organism of Christ's person in all its concrete reality," as John A.T. Robinson claims in his book, *The Body* (51)? He identifies the church with Christ's person. For him the word "body" is applied to the church and means "something *not concrete but corporal*. It directs the mind to a person; it did not of itself suggest a social group. . . . Consequently, one must be wary of speaking of 'the metaphor' of the body of Christ. Paul uses the analogy of the human body to elucidate his teaching that Christians form Christ's body. But the analogy holds because they are in literal fact the risen organism of Christ's person in all its concrete reality" (51).

Ernest Best, in his book, *One Body in Christ*, writes an extensive response to Robinson's view that the term "the body" when applied to the church should not be taken as a metaphor. Though Best concedes that "there is a strand of thought in Paul, which tends to identify Christ with the Church" (195), he contends that "Paul wishes to evade the identification of Christ and the Church" (100); and, even more strongly, he declares that "the Church is not really and ontologically the body of Christ," but only "metaphorically" (112). We agree with Best on this point. The term "body of Christ" suggests only certain likenesses and no more. Would not the many different ways in which Paul uses this term lead one to this conclusion? Note, for example, the following:

• The head is an ordinary member of the body (1 Cor. 12:21)
• The head is Christ (Col. 1:18; 2:19)

How can both be true in "reality"? When one looks at the other ways in which Paul describes the church, the point becomes ever more clear that in using such terms he could not be speaking literally. Not only is it the body of Christ, for example, but it is also a "pure virgin" (2 Cor. 11:2; see Eph. 5:22ff.) and "a temple of God" (1 Cor. 3:16). But "can the church be really and ontologically all these at one and the same time?"(99), Best asks. "The Church can in certain respects," he points out, "resemble each of them — Body of Christ, bride, temple. . . . In a certain sense we can say it is each of these, but not finally and completely to the exclusion of the others" (99).

The Seven Ones of Ephesians 4

It is interesting to notice that the grounds of Paul's exhortations to unity (the name of Christ, our calling, and our experience as Christians, all to be considered in a later chapter) are closely related, if not parallel to, his description in Ephesians 4:4-6 of the unity that exists among all Christians. The seven factors named as the basis of Christian unity also serve as motives to remain united in Christ. Since the same may be said of the grounds upon which Paul's exhortations for unity are based, the grounds and motives would perhaps be expected to overlap. And this is exactly what occurs.

There appears to be a rhetorical character in Ephesians 4:4-6 which is meant to be argumentative, didactic, and parenetic. Hanson argues this point because, for him, this is the only way he can make sense of the relation of Paul's formula given in vv. 4-6 with his plea to preserve unity which he makes in v. 3. So he connects v. 3 with vv. 4-6 in the following way: "The author admonishes the congregation to keep the unity of the Spirit (v. 3), and after that he enumerates his arguments: 'It is, you know, one Body . . .,'" etc. (*The Unity of the Church in the New Testament* 150-51). He further sees each of the components listed as directly connected with baptism: "In Eph. 4:4-6 we seem to be confronted with a parenesis of baptism, or in any case a traditional formula in some way connected with baptism" (151).

This helps explain why other important elements of unity, such as the Lord's supper, are not mentioned. Everything listed has an obvious relation to baptism. Other things which do not, but are a part of the unity of the church, are not included in the list. But of the seven items, faith, he believes, is central, because everything else depends on it.

In an article on "The Unity of the Church in Paul" (*Restoration Quarterly* II, 4 [1958]: 187-96), Abraham J. Malherbe studies three passages (Eph. 4, 1 Cor. 1, Col. 2) which deal particularly with unity. He sees the main elements of unity in all three of these passages as "one Lord, one faith, one baptism" from Ephesians 4:5. In 1 Corinthians 1, for example, Paul is concerned with three things which are parallel to the "one Lord, one faith, one baptism" statement: the person of Christ, baptism, and the message that he preached, to which faith was the response. In Colossians 2:6-12 "it is the person of Christ whom one puts on by baptism as an act of faith that is opposed to the beguiling philosophies" (188).

1. One Body and One Spirit. The body of Christ, the church, is one. This obviously refers to what Paul has already demonstrated in Ephesians. In speaking of bringing together Jew and Gentile, he said, "For he [Christ] is our peace, who made both [Jew and Gentile] one, and brake down the middle wall of partition . . . that he might create in himself of the two [Jew and Gentile] one new man, so making peace; and might reconcile them both in one body unto God through the cross" (Eph. 2:14-16). So there are not two rival communities, for the body with its members is yet one even though it consists of different peoples with entirely different backgrounds.

The one Spirit of God dwells in the one body. This refers to the Holy Spirit. The one body and one Spirit references belong together because of what Paul says in 1 Corinthians 12:13: "For by one Spirit are we all baptized into one body, whether we be Jews or Gentiles, whether we be bond or free; and have been all made to drink into one Spirit." The one Spirit through one baptism creates unity by bringing each person into the one body, and it is the same Spirit who preserves unity as each member continues to drink of him. The latter point is supported by Paul's statement, "for through him [Christ]," Paul says, "we both [Jew and Gentile] have access by one Spirit unto the Father" (Eph. 2:18). All Christians by right of their baptism into Christ (see also Rom. 6:3-4 and Gal. 3:26-27), and by right of the one Spirit who dwells in them, are one in Christ.

2. One Hope. In addition to the one body and one Spirit, Paul says, "even as also ye were called in one hope of your calling." The first two words "even as" are likely meant to introduce illustrative proof of the statement just made. So our being called into one hope illustrates the fact that there is one body and one Spirit. How is the hope of the Christian "one"? It has one object which is the glory placed before us ("Christ in you, the hope of glory," Col. 1:27) and one foundation which is Christ (1 Cor. 3:11). The call of the Ephesians had brought them into the possession of this hope. "In one hope" represents the accompanying element in which the calling took place, for it is "one hope of your calling." The Christian's calling holds out the hope of eternal salvation for him.

3. One Lord, One Faith, One Baptism. After Paul speaks of the one body which is formed of living members, of the one Spirit which dwells in each member, and the common hope held by all, he turns to the very beginning of unity and speaks of its fundamental principles. These factors of unity, which already exist among the Ephesians, describe how each came by one Spirit into the one body where he enjoys the one hope. The one Lord is Christ, the Lord of all. He is central and paramount, and there is only "one" over against what Paul elsewhere calls "lords many" (1 Cor. 8:5-6).

The fact that there is one Lord makes unity possible and necessary. The relationship Christians sustain to the one Lord also necessitates one faith. In Paul the word "faith" may be used subjectively to mean confidence or assurance, plus conviction (see Rom. 10:9-10, 17 with Heb. 11:6), or it may be used objectively to mean the body of doctrine, or the truth, that is to be believed (see. Gal. 1:23 and Rom. 1:5). Obviously subjective faith is not unrelated or independent of objective faith, since faith comes by hearing the word of God (Rom. 10:17).

Objective faith, the body of truth revealed and made known by God through the one Spirit (1 Cor. 2:6-13), remains important. God holds man accountable for how he handles his truth (1 Tim. 2:15). Dissensions frequently arise because false teachers do not serve Christ, and they sometimes have selfish motives (Rom. 16:17-18). Others, because they love controversy, dispute about words and produce envy, strife, railings, and evil surmising (1 Tim. 6:4). There is only one gospel (Gal. 1:6ff.), and Paul says the things he has taught are to be adhered to (2 Thess. 2:15). Christians were told to withdraw themselves from those who would not receive Paul's instructions (2 Thess. 3:14).

Yet, in the context of Ephesians 4:5 the "one faith" is probably subjective faith. If so, it is the faith that comes to the heart through the preaching of the crucified and resurrected Christ, the one Lord who is mentioned just before the one faith in Paul's statement. It is this faith that must be confessed with the mouth (Rom. 10:9-10). In Ephesians the word faith is often used in this way (Eph. 1:13, 15, 19; 2:8; 3:12, 17; 6:16, 23).

The "one baptism" brings the one faith and the one Lord together. Though faith comes from the word of God, it is directed toward the one God and the one Lord Jesus Christ (John 14:1; Heb. 11:6; John 8:24). Baptism is an act of faith. In obedience to the *one Lord*, motivated by the *one faith* in him, one is baptized into the *one body* by the *one Spirit*. Every person in the one body of Christ comes there by the instrumentality of the Holy Spirit (more on this subject at a later time) at the time he is baptized in water for the remission of sins (John 3:3-5; Acts 8:36f.; Eph. 5:26; Tit. 3:5; Acts 2:38; 22:16). At this point in one's obedience, he is brought into Jesus Christ (Rom. 6:3-4; Gal. 3:27; Col. 2:12-13) and into the one body of Christ (1 Cor. 12:13).

4. One God and Father of All. The one God and Father is the Father of the Lord Jesus Christ (Eph. 1:2-3, 17; 2:18; 3:14). He is also the God and Father of "all," but the reference does not appear to be to the whole universe but to all Christians. All, whether Jew or Gentile, male or female, have the same Father, having been begotten of him through the gospel (Jas. 1:18; 1 Pet. 1:22-24; see also 1 Cor. 4:15). The Father of all Christians is sovereign because he is "over all"; he is ever present and imminent because he is "through all" and "in all." These three prepositional phrases emphasize God's transcendence and sovereignty. They point out the greatness of the one Father of all the redeemed. All the redeemed are brothers and sisters in Christ because there is one God and Father over them all.

Many Members

In 1 Corinthians 12:12 Paul affirms that the human body is "one," yet he is quick to mention that even though it is one body, it has many members. He makes this point about the human body in order to make application to Christ and his body, the church: "so also is Christ." He repeats this point about many members in vv. 14, 19, and 20. First, he says, "for the body is not one member, but many," and, then, "and if they were all one member, where were the body? But now are they many members, yet but one body." Since Paul describes the body and its members to help us understand the relationship and responsibilities of members in a local church, at least two things may be concluded about the local church from this analogy.

1. The Church is a Diversified Unit. Some people become concerned when they hear others speak of "unity in diversity" when they are talking about the subject of unity, but there is a certain kind of unity in diversity being described in this passage of Scripture. The body is one, yet there are many members. That describes unity, but it also describes diversity. The local church is a diversified unit. There is, for example, diversity of nationalities (1 Cor. 12:13; Eph. 2:11; 3:6), of social classes (1 Cor. 12:13), and of spiritual gifts (1 Cor. 12:1-11; Rom. 12:6-8). Each member has his own function in the body, according to the gifts given to each.

Yet, there is unity in this diversity. There is *unity of origin* of these spiritual gifts. They all come from the same Spirit (1 Cor. 12:11), and God has placed each member in the body as it pleased him (1 Cor. 12:18). There is also *unity of heritage*: "that the Gentiles should be fellow-heirs, and of the same body, and partakers of his promise in Christ by the gospel" (Eph. 3:6). In fact, the whole range of things Christians hold in common may be listed here: redemption (Eph. 2:16), baptism into the one body (1 Cor. 12:13), and all the "ones" of Ephesians 4:3-6.

All this simply says that unity does not mean uniformity. Each member of the body of Christ (even those less esteemed members! 1 Cor. 12:22-24) has its specific and indispensable function. Just as it is with our own body, the local church fares better when each member performs its own function and not that of another.

2. The Church is a Unit of Relationships. It is from the head that all the members receive life and draw cohesion and unity. Each member depends upon the head for its life, health, and growth. The body as a whole is knit together by its various parts to form a harmonious structure. But even though God supplies what is needed for this progress, the growth of the body takes place when each organ fulfills its assigned function. In this manner all members contribute, in a spirit of love, to the organic growth of the body (Eph. 4:16).

There is organization of the various members lest anarchy result. Unity of the members cannot be maintained without the members being fitted together and united by every contributing part under the direction of the head, which is Christ. To maintain unity among the members of the body two things are required: (1) each member must remain united to Christ, and (2) members must maintain the proper relationship to each other under Christ's direction and control. Without either of these two ingredients the body cannot grow.

Why is holding on to Christ the head so important? Paul answers: Some had left Christ by failing to hold him as head. "And not holding the Head, from which all the body by joints and bands having nourishment ministered, and knit together, increaseth with the increase of God" (Col. 2:19). Once removed from the head one loses contact with the source of all spiritual life and growth of the body.

The words "knit together" show that the body coheres as a direct result of contact with the head. When the head is left behind, the life, growth, and cohesiveness of the body are all lost. Paul's point is that as each member receives such benefits from the head, those members in turn provide the same for the rest of the body so that the whole body benefits by the contribution of each part. The local church is indeed a unit of relationships.

Chapter 2

Paul's Plea For Unity

The problem of division in the form of a strong party spirit was a real threat to the church at Corinth; so much so that Paul immediately addresses the subject. The problem is so serious that he devotes the first four chapters of the epistle to it. There were no doubt actual divisions within the church. The use of words like "contentions" suggests this, and the fact that he uses the word "divisions" with the "to be" verb ("that there be no divisions") rather than the "to become" verb (he does not say, "that there may or will be no divisions") is ample support for this conclusion.

The question, "Is Christ divided?" is further evidence that there were already factions in the church. None of the parties had yet separated from the church, however. Undoubtedly, Paul hoped that he not only would be able to prevent them from separating, but that he would be able to help the Corinthians remove the carnal spirit which divided them. Brethren have "contentions" and "division" among themselves before they actually separate physically from each other.

Attitudes which cause this kind of disunity are just as sinful as when brethren actually pull away from one another and form separate and distinct groups which no longer work and worship together. The same words ("contentions" and "divisions") used here to describe their attitudes toward one another also appear in the catalogue of the works of the flesh in Galatians 5:19-21. Paul ends this list of sins by saying that "they who practice such things shall not inherit the kingdom of God." Sins of disposition are just as wrong and damnable as other works of the flesh.

The Basis For Paul's Appeal

At the very outset, Paul makes clear that the unity he calls for is a unity based on Christ, not a unity based on the essence of the church. "Is Christ divided?" he asks. The answer obviously is no; Christ is not divided; therefore, the church, if it really is the church, cannot be divided. The unity of the church is a unity between Christ and the church. This shows quite pointedly how serious the situation really is in Corinth. The problem of division is a problem of misplaced loyalty.

That Paul's appeal for unity is based on Christ is again made clear when he calls for oneness "through the name of our Lord Jesus Christ" (v.10). To point up the emphasis he has placed on Christ's name already, it should be noted that he names Jesus Christ nine times in the first nine verses of this chapter. To appeal for unity through Christ's name is to call for it on the basis of all that he is and all that he has been revealed to be to every Christian. Christ has been given "the name which is above every name" (Phil. 2:9). Only in his name is there salvation (Acts 4:12). Paul's exhortation, therefore, rests upon the knowledge which the Corinthians have of the person and work of the Lord Jesus Christ. The first nine verses give a summary of Christ's work among the Corinthians, and Christ's name will call up the memory of all the tender proofs of divine love displayed in him who bore the name.

Another appeal which shows the foolishness of the partisan spirit being displayed by the Corinthians is their own experience. Each of them belongs to Christ (not Paul, Apollos, or Cephas) because he is a sharer in a common calling (1 Cor. 1:9), and it is Christ who had been crucified for them, and it is into his name each of them had been baptized (1 Cor. 1:13). Paul shows a real concern in this chapter with the person of Christ, with baptism, and with the message that he preached. Through the preaching of the gospel one is called into the fellowship of Jesus Christ.

Fellowship is participation or communion. In this manner Paul speaks of the believer's participation in the life of Christ. This became a fact upon the baptism of each one into the name of Christ. To be baptized into Christ's name not only points to his authority (and therefore his claim to our allegiance), but "name" becomes synonymous with the person of Christ. This is parallel with Galatians 3:27 and Romans 6:3. Because of this common experience and life in the one Lord, the Corinthians ought to speak the same thing and be united in the same mind and judgment.

The Kind of Unity Demanded

The emphasis in 1 Corinthians 1:10ff. is on factionalism. This sin first manifests itself in a difference of speech. So Paul's first exhortation is "that ye all speak the same thing." Whether this difference in speech had developed beyond some claiming to belong to one leader, and some to another, one is unable to determine for certain. That Paul is rebuking party zeal at this place is clear. Other problems are dealt with in later chapters and corrections are called for in those areas as well.

Throughout the epistle the Corinthians are reminded that there is a divine standard by which each issue is to be settled. What Paul writes is "the commandment of the Lord" (1 Cor. 14:37). He is not simply telling them what he thinks, but he has "the mind of Christ" (1 Cor. 2:16). No person has the right to glory in men because their reasonings are vain (1 Cor. 3:20-21). Such glorying in men leads one beyond the things which are written, and this is forbidden (1 Cor. 4:6). Paul uses this same divine standard everywhere he goes; he teaches the same thing in every church (1 Cor. 4:17). It then becomes the business of every church to conform to that one divine standard. This is the first business of every church. Goudge (quoting C.P. Eden) states the case well:

> Our first work is — not to arrive at unity, but — to conform ourselves to the standard of Divine truth; just as the duty of a choir is not gained by each singer striving to keep in with his neighbor, but by all following the prescribed notes of music (*First Epistle to the Corinthians* 6).

A difference of speech is a clear sign of divisions, so Paul adds, "that there be no divisions among you." In the classical Greek the word translated "divisions" meant only an actual rent in material. In the New Testament it sometimes has this meaning (Matt. 9:16; Mark 2:21), but is used also in the sense of faction, discord (John 7:43; 9:16; 10:19). Instead of being divided into various factions due to misplaced loyalties, they should "be perfected together in the same mind and in the same judgment."

The word "perfected" may mean either "to restore" (Matt. 4:21; Gal. 6:1), or "to bring to completion" or "make perfect" (Luke 6:40). In the latter sense it sometimes means "the act of adjusting the pieces of a machine with a view to its normal action; hence the equipment of a workman for his work (Eph. 4:12)" (Godet, *Commentary on the First Epistle of St. Paul to the Corinthians* I:62-63). Both meanings may be intended here. Paul pleads for the various members to be reunited and thus equipped for the proper function of the body.

The unity called for consists of having the "same mind and the same judgment." The exhortation to oneness of mind is also a part of Paul's plea to the Philippians (Phil. 2:2-4), but a different Greek word is used in the two passages. In Philippians the meaning is equal to our word "sentiment," as the sequel in the passage indicates. Vincent rejects the words "to think" as expressing the meaning in that passage because the word "denotes rather a general disposition of the mind rather than a specific thought directed at a given point" (*Epistles to the Philippians and to Philemon* 8). In 1 Corinthians 1:10, however, the word is generally taken to refer to the thought originating in the mind. "Judgment" from yet another Greek word, denotes the way a particular thing is decided, or the conclusion arrived at by applying one's mind to a given point. Hence, Meyer says, "Through the fact, namely, that Christians in Corinth thought differently . . . on important matters, and in consequence of this difference of thinking, formed in a partisan spirit different opinions and judgments . . . and fought for these against each other, the . . . (same speech — *ww*) was wanting and . . . (factions — *ww*) prevailed" (*The Epistles to the Philippians and Colossians* 72).

Causes of Discord

If we look at the broader context (chapters 1-4), it will be possible for us to find in Paul's discussion certain causes of the factionalism which prevailed in the Corinthian church. Such causes are so common in churches of our own day where this same spirit exists that we cannot afford to overlook them.

1. False Wisdom. Paul finds *a false wisdom* in the church at Corinth. He identifies certain classes of men who are known for their intellectual pursuits (the wise man, the scribe, and the disputer of this world, 1:20). But the human wisdom they advance must be viewed as inadequate when it is seen to lead them to reject the wisdom of God as it is revealed in the cross of Christ. Human wisdom cannot serve as a basis for unity among Christians; in fact, it had proven to produce a spirit of rivalry among them, and contentions and divisions resulted. Such wisdom must be rejected as false because it cannot help one find God and the unity which the message of the cross produces.

In contrast to divine wisdom Paul describes the wisdom of the world as foolishness (1:18f). God's wisdom has to do with the "things of the Spirit of God" (2:14) and the "mind of Christ" (2:16). It is "not of this world, nor of the rulers of this world" (2:6). The word "world" means "age," and every age has its "rulers" ("the wise men after the flesh," 1:26), those who set the pattern or mold the character of a given age. They establish such standards according to their own wisdom, so how they think determines the "wisdom" of the age in which they live.

Because God's wisdom has to do with the things of the Spirit and the mind of Christ, it is a revealed wisdom (2:10) and points to the person of Christ and his redemptive work (1:24, 30). It is a wisdom that is higher, nobler, more powerful, everlasting, and redemptive. This wisdom, Paul claims, is the wisdom "we speak" (2:6a, 7a), and a wisdom that is "of God" (2:7a). It is different from the wisdom of man for the very reasons listed here.

Paul has been making this contrast between the wisdom of man and the wisdom of God to arrive at the following conclusion:

> Let no man deceive himself. If any man among you seemeth to be wise in this world, let him become a fool that he may be wise. For the wisdom of this world is foolishness with God. For it is written, He taketh the wise in their own craftiness. And again, The Lord knoweth the thoughts of the wise, that they are vain. Therefore let no man glory in men. For all things are yours; whether Paul, or Apollos, or Cephas, or the world, or life, or death, or things present, or things to come; all are yours; and ye are Christ's; and Christ is God's (3:18-23).

How foolish for Christians to divide over men or the wisdom of men. Yet it is ever the wisdom of man that divides them from each other. The rivalry in the church at Corinth over men was due to human wisdom, and the truth of God does not stand in the wisdom of man but in the wisdom of God. These brethren needed to learn "not to think of men above that which is written, that no one of you should be puffed up for one against another" (4:6). The only way they could do this was to receive Paul's teaching. He had the mind of Christ and was making known God's wisdom to them. This is the reason he can later say that the things he is writing to them "are the commandment of the Lord" (14:37). There is only one revelation from God, so Paul teaches the same things wherever he goes:

> I write not these things to shame you, but as my beloved sons I warn you. For though ye have ten thousand instructors in Christ, yet *have ye* not many fathers: for in Christ Jesus I have begotten you through the gospel. Wherefore I beseech you, be ye followers of me. For this cause have I sent unto you Timotheus, who is my beloved son, and faithful in the Lord, who shall bring you into remembrance of my ways which be in Christ, as I teach every where in every church (4:14-17).

2. Pride. *Pride* was one of the major causes of factionalism in the Corinthian church. One can just imagine one of the members of one of the parties in the church there standing with his thumb under his suspenders (to use a modern analogy) and his chin pitched high, crying out, "I belong to Paul," or "I belong to Apollos." Paul senses in these party slogans the boastful tone that must have pointed to the real problem of party pride which would have given rise to such slogans. So he tells them that "no flesh should glory before God" (1:29); "if any man thinketh that he is wise among you in the world, let him become a fool, that he may become wise" (3:18); and "that no one of you be puffed up for the one against the other" (4:6).

3. False Loyalty. *False loyalty to religious leaders* was a cause of factionalism. We have already seen Paul's response to this misplaced loyalty. The problem was not with Paul, or Apollos, or Cephas; the problem was with the Corinthians. Paul was not divided against Apollos, or Apollos against Cephas, etc., but the Corinthians were divided over them. When Paul says he is thankful that he only baptized a few in Corinth, and that God did not send him to baptize, but to preach the gospel (1:14, 17), he is still showing that unity is based on one's relation to Christ, not on one's relation to his teacher or any other human being.

How could the Paul party say they belonged to Paul when Christ, not Paul is the center of the gospel? This is made clear in Paul's argument in verse 13. For this very reason, Paul had avoided the practice of baptizing people himself; he left that to others. The fact that he had baptized so few in Corinth should prove beyond question that no one in Corinth had been baptized into Paul's name. So the point Paul makes is that the center of the gospel is not any man, but Jesus. He is not making a point about the importance of baptism or whether baptism is essential or not; he has already shown in verse 13 that in baptism one is identified with Christ and is incorporated into Christ. That's how important baptism is. Because baptism identifies one with Christ and brings one into Christ, baptism becomes absolutely essential if one is to belong to Christ.

Chapter 3

Maintaining Unity in the Bond of Peace

Paul begins his exhortations to unity in both 1 Corinthians 1 and Ephesians 4 with the word "beseech." Some prefer the word "exhort" in Ephesians. It is true that the Greek word may mean either "beseech" or "exhort" at different places in the New Testament, and at times it even means "comfort." But the probable meaning in both 1 Corinthians 1:10 and Ephesians 4:1 is "beseech." This is true because in both passages Paul's plea is based upon the profundity of his previous thoughts. It is an absolute duty to which he calls them. There is a mixture of entreaty and command in the word.

That Paul's plea is based upon the grandeur of his previous thoughts is brought out more clearly in the Ephesians passage than in 1 Corinthians. His use of "therefore" in Ephesians 4:1 necessarily points back to what has preceded. The word itself may be used in an inferential sense and be translated "therefore," "so," "consequently," or "then" (cf. John 3:23; 4:5, 12, 33, 40). At other times, however, the word has a transitional or continuative meaning. When this is its meaning it is usually rendered "then" or "now." A third way in which the word is used is with an emphatic or intensive particle, and in this case it is usually translated with such words as "be sure," "surely," "indeed," "certainly," "above all," and "in fact." Sometimes the word may have a responsive sense, meaning "in reply," "in response," or "in return." In spite of all these different possibilities, the inferential sense of "therefore" or "consequently" is likely the sense that Paul uses the term here in Ephesians 4:1.

There have been differences of opinion how far back the word "therefore" directs the reader. Salmond is probably correct that it is best to understand the word "as basing the exhortations which follow on the whole preceding statement of the great things done for the readers by God's grace — from chapter iii.6 onwards" (*Expositor's Greek Testament* 3:319).

The Diligence Required

The KJV says in verse 3, "Endeavouring to keep the unity of the Spirit." Other translations use the words "giving diligence" instead of "endeavouring." The reason for this is that the word "endeavouring" does not seem to convey the eagerness Paul expresses in the use of this Greek word. The word "diligence" is a better word here, since the Greek word means "to be zealous or eager, take pains, use every effort" (Arndt and Gingrich, *Greek-English Lexicon* 771). The idea of urgency, haste, and passion are all found here, but more than that is included in the word. Paul appeals to the whole man. Take pains, put forth every effort, he says; involve your will, your sentiment, your reason, your physical strength, and your total attitude.

Members in local churches where a divisive spirit has prevailed can appreciate the urgency with which Paul speaks. The words of the psalmist express the sentiment of the genuine Christian: "Behold, how good and how pleasant it is for brethren to dwell together in unity!" (Ps. 133:1). Division is so unpleasant to those who care about peace, harmony, and good-will between brethren that it is worth taking pains, putting forth every effort to maintain unity.

That is exactly what Paul urges Christians to do: "Giving diligence to maintain the unity of the Spirit." That the Ephesians are urged "to maintain" this unity of the Spirit is proof enough that the unity Paul calls for was already a reality among them. There is a difference between maintaining something and attaining something. Paul wants the Ephesians to maintain the unity they already have among themselves, and that will take the most diligent effort on the part of each member of the body.

What was the unity that already existed among the brethren of the church at Ephesus? A common calling, for one thing. One basis of Paul's exhortation in this passage is "the calling wherewith ye were called" (v. 1). The Christian must walk "worthily" of that calling. That is, he must let it be befitting or becoming. Equally balanced and becoming of what? The Christian calling.

Every person who is in Christ is in him because he has been called by God through the gospel of Jesus Christ (2 Thess. 2:14). The Ephesians, as all Christians, had heard through the gospel preached to them about the one Lord, had believed ("one faith") in the one Lord, and had been baptized ("one baptism") into the one Lord. Upon this initiation into Christ they were "sealed with the Holy Spirit" ("one Spirit") of promise (Eph.

1:13), and consequently became sharers in a "common salvation" (Jude 3) and the "one hope."

As each one was saved, the Lord added him to the "one body," the church (Acts 2:47), which is to say that he was added to the number of the saved. Ultimately, of course, "the one God and Father of all, who is over all, and through all, and in all" is the source of this unity. The seven "ones" in this passage are another reason Paul exhorts Christians to maintain the unity which the common experience suggested by these "ones" indicates already existed among them.

The Unity of the Spirit
Paul's appeal is that Christians maintain the unity "of the Spirit." The Bible nowhere calls for any other kind of unity. It is not real unity unless it is "of the Spirit." Every one of the Christians who made up the church at Ephesus were what they were in Christ because of what the Spirit had done for them. As the revealer of divine truth (John 16:13; 1 Cor. 2:10-13), the Holy Spirit used men like Paul and Apollos to preach the gospel in Corinth and Ephesus. These men became "ministers through whom ye believed" (I Cor. 3:5). Since belief comes of hearing, and hearing by the word of Christ (Rom. 10:17), we are not surprised to read that "many of the Corinthians hearing believed, and were baptized" (Acts 18:8), and that the Ephesians believed upon hearing the word of the truth (Eph. 1:13).

Through the truth that was revealed by the Holy Spirit and preached by Paul for the first time in Corinth and Ephesus, God's new society, the church, was created by the Spirit so that Paul could say that those who made up the church in Ephesus "are builded together for an habitation of God through the Spirit" (Eph. 2:20). The unity that exists as a result of initiation into Christ, or the body of Christ, upon one's belief in and baptism into Christ, is indeed a unity that is created by the Holy Spirit.

Everything the Christian has, he has because of his relation to Christ. Christian unity begins among Christians by the incorporation of each one into Christ through baptism (Rom. 6:3-4; Col. 2:12; Gal. 3:27). This act of initiation into the body of Christ serves as a reminder of the common salvation we share because of our relation to Christ. But this is not the sole ground of unity. The unity of the Spirit is well illustrated by this common experience, and this "calling wherewith ye were called" is a common denominator that demands a life consistent with that calling.

Only as Christians adhere to the requirements of their calling is it possible to *maintain* the unity of the Spirit. This unity of the Spirit, however, goes far beyond initial incorporation into Christ. True unity demands right doctrine insofar as God has clearly revealed his will to man, just as much as it requires a walk consistent with our calling. The statement of Francis Foulkes in the Tyndale series of commentaries (*Ephesians* 111) has captured this important truth:

> The apostle who was so concerned with the practical unity of Jews and Gentiles in the Church, and with the working together of all Christians, would surely have abhorred many of the divisions that we accept. Where differences in essential doctrine and contradictions in ethical teaching make such divisions, he would strive to know and uphold the way of Christ in every detail. Where differences are caused merely by superficial things or by the selfish individualism of members, he would toil and fight for a breaking down of barriers and the working out of genuine fellowship.

As Paul continues to define and describe the nature of the unity he calls for in this passage in Ephesians, he makes clear that there was agreement already on matters of faith and doctrine in the church at Ephesus. Some have suggested otherwise by contending that Paul says here that we are to have fellowship first, according to verse 3, and the agreement in doctrine is to come later, according to verse 13. According to this view, the Christian is to have fellowship with people who disagree with him on doctrinal matters and that through such fellowship one could hope to arrive ultimately at agreement on doctrine. But just the opposite is true. Paul argues that the Ephesians were already in agreement on doctrinal matters.

It is obvious that the people Paul refers to in verse 13 by the pronoun "we" are the same people he has been talking about earlier in this chapter: those defined in 1:12,13 as having believed and received the "gospel of salvation." These are the people who have already accepted the doctrine. In verse 13 Paul is describing a "perfecting" (v. 12) of something that already exists, when he says, "Till we all attain unto the unity of the faith, and of the knowledge of the Son of God." The faith they already had and the knowledge they already possessed would grow and develop according to the purpose God had in giving the gifts named in verse 11 so that ultimately they would be perfected, or brought to manhood, and would thus be equipped to do the work of ministering and building up the body of Christ. These brethren already had faith, and they had already accepted the faith, or gospel message, but they needed "full perfection" of faith; they already had knowledge but they needed "full knowledge" of the Son of God.

Christians are not to be "tossed to and fro and carried about with every wind of doctrine" (v. 14). To prevent this they must be brought to the "fulness of Christ," or become full-grown men in Christ. What these brethren already understood about the seven "ones" must be enlarged upon; they must be brought to a fuller understanding or else they run the risk of being led away from the truth. Not only must brethren make every effort to maintain the unity of the Spirit which they already have upon their initiation into Christ, but they must continue to move forward into a fuller perception and appreciation of the truth as it has been revealed by the Holy Spirit. The unity "of the Spirit" not only begins in the truth, but it must also find its completion in the truth.

This does not mean of course that fellowship is based upon *perfect* knowledge. The unity of the Spirit allows for the spiritual maturation of those without perfect understanding or perfect obedience to God's revelation. The fellowship of Christ is not conditioned on perfect understanding or perfect obedience.

Speaking Truth in Love
That truth is a necessary component in the unity that Paul describes in this passage is again made evident in verse 15 where Paul says, "but speaking truth in love, may grow up in all things into him, who is the head, even Christ." This statement is offered in contrast to the manner in which the false teachers of verse 14 are said to lead away the immature — "by the sleight of men, in craftiness, after the wiles of error." We are to speak the truth, not error, and we are to "deal truly" in speaking the truth, not in trickery or deceit. When our speaking the truth and dealing truly is prompted by love then such tactics as those employed by those who have wandered away from the truth, and who would take others with them by their scheming ways, will be avoided. Love is to govern both the speaking of the truth (v. 15) and our growth (v.16) in Jesus Christ. Without love we are nothing (1 Cor. 13:1-7).

It must be pointed out again for emphasis, that without the truth it is not possible either to attain or to maintain the unity of the Spirit. Nor is it possible to have the unity that God calls for without the truth being spoken in love. "Where there is no love, the truth revealed by God is denied. Equally, without 'truth' there may well be a 'conspiracy' that aims to subjugate men to human 'opinions', but no solid unity and community" (Markus Barth). The truth, or doctrine, is not to be minimized; it is not to be suppressed in the interest of love. But neither is the truth to be preached without love for the one who needs the truth. We are to speak the truth in love.

It must be admitted, however, that some who seem to be interested in unity first and truth second, as though true unity can exist in the absence of the truth, have totally missed the meaning of what it is to speak the truth in love. Some years ago the following statement was printed in a church bulletin and attributed to R.L. Whiteside (the location of the statement was not noted, but it sounds like brother Whiteside). It is a perceptive comment on this subject, and worthy of note:

> Much is said about preaching the truth in love, and so it should be preached. But in love of what? The preacher should so love the truth that he will not sacrifice any of it nor pervert it; and he should so love people that he will not withhold from them even an unpleasant truth. He that does either of these things loves neither the truth nor the people. We frequently fool ourselves; we think we do thus and so to spare the feelings of others, when it is our own feelings that prompt us. "Preach the word; be urgent in season, out of season; reprove, rebuke, exhort, with all longsuffering and teaching."

Read the language of Paul to one who was a perverter of the right ways of the Lord, in Acts 13:10, and then ask yourself how it was that the very man who charged us to speak the truth in love could use such language. Does it not follow that love sometimes demands that strong language be used. The Lord himself did the same thing on some occasions (Matt. 23:1-36). No doubt that there is much softness prevalent in many local churches today. It is entirely likely that in some congregations this language would be considered a bit strong; and were Paul present and attempted to speak in such fashion, he would be charged with being a "hard preacher." False teachers are deserving of no mercy and should be exposed and refuted. They are the world's greatest threat.

Elymas was seeking "to turn aside the procounsul from the faith" (Acts 13:8), or attempting to keep some from obeying the gospel preached by Paul. Are those who keep some out of the kingdom today by teaching that one does not have to do what Jesus himself teaches one must do to be saved any less false teachers than was Elymas? In view of Paul's strong opposition to Elymas as an opposer of the faith, what is to be said of gospel preachers today who fraternize with such false teachers, associate with them and enjoy their fellowship, join their alliances, and cooperate with them? What is to be said of gospel preachers who are at this present time doing this same thing with those who have introduced unscriptural practices into the worship and work of the church? Where are the stalwart preachers in our day who will "contend earnestly for the faith which was once for all delivered unto the saints" (Jude 3) by dealing with false teachers in a way that is deserving of all opposers of the faith?

The only way to preach the truth in love is to handle a given case with the severity it deserves. Not every case is to be handled alike. But at no time is truth to be compromised in the name of love. Love demands that truth be taught no matter what the cost. "Buy the truth, and sell it not; also wisdom, and instruction, and understanding" (Prov. 23:23).

Only by speaking the truth in love is it possible for each member in the body to "grow up in all things in him, who is the head, even Christ" (v. 15b). This again emphasizes the necessity of obedience to Christ, the very embodiment of truth, and the only source of life for the Christian, if each member is to be healthy and strong and is to grow up into full-grown men and women in him. The members must continue to be under his direction, they must be obedient to his control. This introduces the same thought Paul made to the Corinthians, when he asked, "Is Christ divided?"

Paul shows by this question that the unity of the church is a unity between Christ and the church, because it suggests that since Christ is not divided, the church, if it really is the church, cannot be divided. It will always be true that whenever and wherever there is division in the church there is a problem of misplaced loyalty on the part of some members. In such cases Christ is no longer received as head; and this holds true whether the differences are over matters of truth, or opinions, or personalities.

Growth in Love

The final verse in this discussion (v. 16) shows the function of each individual part in the building up or edifying of the whole body. The leading point seems to be on the edifying of the whole body, rather than the growth of the individual members. Each member is to be interested in the building up of the whole, not simply in his own progress, and he is to work toward that end. The particular area in which the spiritual growth of the whole body is to be seen when each member is working for the good of the whole is in love.

Without the contribution made by each member the growth of the whole body would not be possible. As each member is subject to Christ as Head, and as each supplies what the body needs, the whole body makes increase and is built up in love. This kind of disinterested service cannot help but engender a feeling of love and respect among the members and therefore make a valuable contribution toward maintaining unity among them. Love binds everything together. It is the secret to maintaining the unity of the Spirit "in the bond of peace." What is the "bond of peace"? It is the realm or sphere in which this unity is to be enjoyed. Christians should be bound together in the sentiments and affection of peace. The unity of the Spirit is a unity in the truth, but it is more than this. There is also unity of love, joy, and peace.

This side of unity is equally important with the demand that brethren be united in the truth of God. Paul began his appeal to maintain unity by calling for a walk consistent with "the calling wherewith ye were called, with all lowliness and meekness, with longsuffering, forbearing one another in love" (Eph. 4:1a-21). Unity is maintained only so far as brethren are at peace with one another, and the way to be a peacemaker is to walk in the manner described here.

After giving a more lengthy list of prerequisites to unity in Colossians 3:12-13, Paul adds, "And above all these things put on love, which is the bond of perfectness" (v. 14). When each member lives in relation to every other member as these prerequisites demand, the "bond of perfectness" will be created. That is to say, there will be "increase of the body unto the building up of itself in love," and unity will be maintained in the "bond of peace."

Chapter 4

The Grounds of Paul's Appeals for Unity

Paul's plea for unity is not one without a basis or foundation. There are many grounds upon which his exhortations are built. These grounds may be grouped under four headings: the name of Christ, the Christian calling, the oneness of Christ, and common Christian experiences.

The Name of Christ

Paul's first appeal for unity is based upon the name of Christ: "Now I beseech you, brethren, by the name of our Lord Jesus Christ . . ." (1 Cor. 1:10). There is no higher ground for Paul's appeal for unity among Christians than the name of Christ. He has barely begun his discussion of this subject and yet he has already named the name of Christ nine times in the first nine verses of this chapter. This certainly points up the emphasis he wishes to give to Christ's name in relation to this subject.

The word translated "by" in this statement means, as Edwards suggests, "by making mention of," and, as he goes on to point out, by mentioning Christ's name so much in this connection Paul is appealing to "the fundamental Christian position of union with Christ" (*The First Epistle to the Corinthians* 15). It is an appeal that is based upon all that Christ is in himself and all that he is revealed to be to the Christian. Christ is our mediator, intercessor, king, priest, and perfect example. All these truths about him, and the positions he occupies with regard to them, come into view every time reference is made to Christ's "name." Paul could have no higher authority upon which to base his appeal for unity than the "name" of Christ.

Christ has been given the "name which is above every name" (Phil. 2:9), and only in this name is there salvation (Acts 4:12). Paul's exhortation, in fact, rests upon the knowledge which the Corinthians have of the person and work of the Lord Jesus Christ. The word "Lord" is the name given to

Christ in Philippians 2:9, and it brings out the fact of his authority. With the words "Jesus Christ" being added, Paul, in the use of these words, "calls up the memory of all the tender proofs of Divine love displayed in Him who bore the name" (Godet I:62), as mentioned in chapter 3. As Elliott points out, "the name of the common Lord is in itself a call to unity" (*St Paul's First Letter to the Corinthians* 12).

The Christian Calling

In Ephesians, one basis for Paul's exhortation to unity is "the vocation where-with ye were called" (Eph. 4:1). The word "vocation" is rendered "calling" in all of the other standard versions. By repeating the root word for "call" two times in this verse Paul combines the words in such a way as to call for a consistent life on the part of the brethren in Ephesus. By beginning his appeal with the connective "therefore" he appeals for a consistent life with the whole plan of salvation in view at least from 3:6 forward. Yet, the whole picture of this scheme of redemption takes in the first three chapters of the letter, and it is possible that the connective takes the reader back to this entire section.

What is this "calling," and what is the "call" that brought these brethren into this "calling"? First, consider the word "calling." This word describes the whole of the life of the Christian, especially as it pertains to his bless-ings and responsibilities in relation to salvation. The Ephesians had been abundantly blessed, as Paul has enumerated in the first three chapters of the letter. And blessings pertaining to salvation bring responsibilities. That the "calling" Paul mentions is our lives as Christians as it pertains to our blessings and responsibilities is reinforced by the way Paul uses the word "walk" in connection with this word. The word "walk" often is used meta-phorically "of living, passing one's life, conducting oneself" (Abbott-Smith, *A Manual Greek Lexicon of the New Testament* 356). Our conduct, or way of life, is to be consistent with our calling, or our life as it pertains to our salvation with all its benefits and responsibilities.

Second, notice how the word "call" is used in connection with this call-ing. To describe the Christian life as a "calling" gives our lives as Chris-tians a special significance, but to add the fact that we have been called to this calling (i.e., into a life of blessings and responsibilities as Christians) concerning the matter of our salvation, raises its significance to an even higher level. Not only do we have a "calling," but we have been called to it — "the calling with which you were called" (NKJV). They had come to be in this calling through a call of God.

God calls men through the preaching of the gospel (2 Thess. 2:14). The Ephesians had "heard the word of the truth, the gospel of your salvation,

— in whom, having also believed, ye were sealed with the Holy Spirit of promise" (Eph. 1:13, ASV). The order of hearing, believing, and baptism is the pattern in Acts (8:12; 16:14-15; 18:8). In Ephesians 1:13, however, "sealed" takes the place of baptism when compared with the other cases of conversion. But we read of the baptism of the Ephesians in Acts 19:1-7, so we know that the one is not actually taking the place of the other. The Ephesians were both baptized and "sealed with the Holy Spirit of promise." This sealing with the Holy Spirit probably is the same as "and you shall receive gift of the Holy Spirit" of Acts 2:38. It is in receiving the gift of the Holy Spirit that one is sealed by the Spirit. To be "sealed" is to be authenticated and marked. The received Spirit serves as a mark of authentication that one belongs to God (see also 2 Cor. 1:22).

The Ephesians had heard the truth of the gospel. When the gospel was preached they learned of God's plan to sum up all things in Christ, the one in whom are found all spiritual blessings (Eph. 1:10 and 1:3). These spiritual blessings include election (1:4), sonship (1:5), redemption (1:7), forgiveness (1:7), knowledge (1:9), the Spirit (1:13), and the inheritance of Christians (1:14). They believed the message, were baptized, and were sealed with the Spirit of promise. This was God's way of calling them to the calling they were in at the time Paul pens this letter. Because of this high calling, Paul urges them to walk worthy of it (4:1) — in all lowliness, meekness, longsuffering (4:2), "giving diligence to keep the unity of the Spirit in the bond of peace" (4:3, ASV).

The Oneness of Christ

The unity Paul calls for in 1 Corinthians 1:12-13 is a unity between Christ and the church. His question, "Is Christ divided?" demands a negative answer, so his plea for those in the church at Corinth to be one is based upon the oneness of Christ. Christ is one, therefore they should be one. Since they each belong to Christ as a result of a common calling (see v. 2, "called to be saints," and v. 9, "called unto the fellowship of his Son Jesus Christ our Lord"), they are all one in him. This is the same point Paul makes when he affirms that there is "one Lord." But notice that when Paul contends for unity on the basis of the oneness of Christ he does not base his argument on the essence of the church, but on Christ himself. Since Christ is not divided, the church, if it really is the church, cannot be divided. The unity Paul contends for is a unity between Christ and the church.

The idea of unity based upon the oneness of Christ is presented in different ways in Paul's letters. Two of these ways are given here when he asks two additional questions in connection with his initial question, "Is Christ divided?" Others appear later in this letter, and still others are taken up at other places. We will now turn our attention to some of these, but we will be brief in our treatment of them.

1. Christ's Death. The peace that Christians enjoy in the body of Christ is due to the oneness of Christ and the oneness of Christ's body because of its relation to Christ. It is significant that right after Paul asked the Corinthians, "Is Christ divided?" he asked, "Was Paul crucified for you?" (1 Cor. 1:13), thereby connecting Christ's death with his oneness. All of those who made up the church at Corinth belonged to Christ because Christ had died for them. His death for each and every one of them argues for oneness among them and makes their divisions absurd. Paul also brings the oneness of Christ and Christ's death together in the book of Ephesians. It is best explained in the following passage:

> But now in Christ Jesus ye who sometimes were far off are made nigh by the blood of Christ. For he is our peace, who hath made both one, and hath broken down the middle wall of partition *between us;* Having abolished in his flesh the enmity, *even* the law of commandments *contained* in ordinances; for to make in himself of twain one new man, *so* making peace; And that he might reconcile both unto God in one body by the cross, having slain the enmity thereby: And came and preached peace to you which were afar off, and to them that were nigh. For through him we both have access by one Spirit unto the Father. Now therefore ye are no more strangers and foreigners, but fellowcitizens with the saints, and of the household of God; And are built upon the foundation of the apostles and prophets, Jesus Christ himself being the chief corner *stone;* In whom all the building fitly framed together groweth unto an holy temple in the Lord: In whom ye also are builded together for an habitation of God through the Spirit (2:13-22).

First, notice that the theme of *oneness* runs throughout the entire statement. The reconciliation of Jews and Gentiles is "in one body" (v. 16). Another way this thought is expressed is that of the two groups this reconciliation has "made both one" (v. 14). Or to put it another way, by removing the law that separated the Jews and Gentiles, Paul says that Christ removed the law "to make in himself of twain one new man, so making peace" (v. 15). "One new man" refers to humanity, so Christ brought together into one body the two races thus creating a new humanity composed of all races of men. "There is neither Jew nor Greek, there is neither bond nor free, there is neither male nor female: for ye are all one in Christ Jesus" (Gal. 3:28).

Second, this reconciliation was made possible *through Christ's death*. Jew and Gentile were reconciled to each other, but they were also reconciled to God. It took Christ's death to accomplish this reconciliation. Paul keeps repeating this fact: "by the blood of Christ" (v. 13), "in his flesh" (v. 15), "by the cross" (v. 16). All of these statements refer to Christ's sacrifice for us, how in his death he shed his blood to make redemption and reconciliation possible. Since Christ had died for the Corinthians, *how could they claim to belong to another?* The divisions in Corinth were not consistent with the common salvation they all enjoyed, a salvation made possible through the death of Christ. Just as Christ is one, they too are one in him because of what they hold in common in relation to him — salvation through his death on the cross.

2. Baptism into Christ's Name. When Paul asks, "Were ye baptized in Paul's name?" (1 Cor. 1:13), he introduces a second thing that illustrates Christ's oneness and the oneness of the Corinthians in him. Just as Christ's death was something they all held in common and shows that each of them belonged to Christ, not to Paul, Apollos, or Peter, the baptism each of them had experienced also proves that each of them belonged to Christ. T.C. Edwards states the case well when he says, "To baptize, therefore, into the name of Paul would be a confession in act that Paul was the source of our spiritual life through a redemptive death" (21).

The preposition Paul uses is *eis* and is better rendered "into," as the above comment has suggested. None of the Corinthians had been baptized into Paul's name, so why would he say he belongs to Paul? To be baptized *into* the name of another brings one into a new relationship with that person. It is essentially the same as to say that one is baptized into that person, or that one enters into union with that person. The New Testament clearly teaches that one is baptized into Christ, the one who died for us (Rom. 6:1-11; Gal. 3:26-28). In being baptized into Christ we become "united" with him (Rom. 6:5, ASV, NASB, NKJV).

The two questions following the first question, "Is Christ divided?" show how one knows he belongs to Christ, and not to a Paul, or an Apollos, or a Cephas, or Christ party. If Christ was crucified for you and you have been baptized into the name of Christ, you belong to Christ.

3. The One Bread. The concept of the oneness of Christ and our oneness in him is brought up again by Paul when he discusses the one bread later in 1 Corinthians: "For we being many are one bread, and one body: for we are all partakers of that one bread" (10:17). The wording in the KJV is subject to being misunderstood and thereby leading one to a wrong conclusion. Those who eat the bread do not become the bread. The NASB conveys the true thought by rendering the verse, "Since there is one bread, we who are many are one body; for we all partake of one bread." Those who partake of the one bread become one with all others who partake of the same bread. Paul has just stated that those who eat the bread and drink the fruit of the vine have communion with the blood and body of Christ in their eating and drinking of these elements (10:16). This joint participation with Christ carries over into communion or joint participation with all those who partake of the Lord's supper. Paul uses the fact that there is only one bread of which we all partake to make this point.

Paul's main point here is not on unity *per se*, but in making his point about having communion with Christ and with one another in eating the Lord's supper, he describes a certain oneness that exists between Christ and those who partake. He also describes a oneness that exists between the participants as they each partake of the one bread. We are one body because we partake of the one bread. Knowing that we are made one body by eating of the one bread in the Lord's supper should make the appeals Paul makes for unity more meaningful for us.

4. Baptized into One Body. In 1 Corinthians 12:13 Paul says, "For by one Spirit are we all baptized into one body, whether we be Jews or Gentiles, whether we be bond or free; and have been all made to drink into one Spirit." Again, the oneness theme is clear. Paul mentions both the "one body" and the "one Spirit" of Ephesians 4:4. Would he not also have in mind the "one baptism" of Ephesians 4:5 when he says, "for by one Spirit are we all baptized into one body"? The "one Lord" of Ephesians 4:5 would also be in view since elsewhere we are told that we are baptized into Christ (Rom. 6:3-4; Gal. 3:27). What brings one into Christ also causes him to become a part of the one body of Christ.

What baptism is meant? Is it the baptism of the Holy Spirit or baptism in water as directed and instructed by the Spirit? This is too large a subject to discuss it in any length here, so we will be content to make a couple of points on the matter. The reader should be aware that not only in the KJV, but in many others as well, the word rendered "in" in some translations is rendered "by" in many others. For example, in addition to the KJV, the word is rendered "by" in the RSV, NASB, NKJV, Moffatt, Phillips, and others. This means that the word *en* as used here may have instrumental or agency significance (see J. W. Roberts, "Instrumental EN in the New Testament," *Restoration Quarterly* VI [1962]: 146), as it does in many other places in Scripture.

Another point to consider is the fact that the last part of the verse says that all who are baptized "by one Spirit" are "made to drink of one Spirit."

How likely is it that the latter statement would have been made if the first statement means Holy Spirit baptism? Godet makes the point that "made to drink of one Spirit" cannot be the same as "by one Spirit are we all baptized," for if this were the case, he says, "there would be an asyndeton" (II: 211). He goes on to say, however, that "baptized by one Spirit" means *baptized into the same Spirit which fused them into one body!* But the passage does not say "baptized into one body," it says "baptized by one Spirit into one body." How can one say it says baptized into the Spirit when it says baptized into one body by the Spirit?

J.W. McGarvey also argued that "in Spirit" is frequently used by the apostles to express what is done "by" the Spirit, and that it may be rendered "by the Spirit" whenever it is more suitable to the context, or to the nature of the subject under discussion in a particular passage. After presenting the evidence for this conclusion he affirmed he had established three propositions:

> 1. That to render the passage in question, "we were all immersed 'in' one Spirit into one body," would be a mislocation of the apostles words, and untrue in fact.

> 2. That it would be equally untrue to render it, "'in' one Spirit we were all immersed into one body"; meaning thereby that we were first in the Spirit, and afterwards immersed into one body.

> 3. That the passage may be rendered, so far as grammatical propriety is concerned, "'by' one Spirit were all immersed into one body." This last rendering being entirely consistent with the New Testament usage, and the only alternative if the first two are rejected ("Immersion in the Holy Spirit," *Lard's Quarterly* I June [1864]: 434-435).

In his commentary on 1 Corinthians, McGarvey says that the one Spirit "acting through the apostles and other evangelists and ministers (1 Thess. 1:5), had begotten people of different races and nationalities and conditions (John 3:5), and had caused them to be baptized into the one church, and had bestowed itself upon them after they had been thus baptized (Acts 2:38)" (*Thessalonians, Corinthians, Galatians, and Romans* 124).

In this statement McGarvey takes the second reference to the Spirit in 1 Corinthians 12:13 to be the same as the "gift of the Holy Spirit" in Acts 2:38. He defends his conclusion on "by one Spirit were we all baptized" by his conclusion reached on the meaning of "and were all made to drink into one Spirit":

If we are right in thus understanding the last clause of the sentence; we are right in our interpretation of the first clause. For after saying that "we were all *immersed in one Spirit* into one body," it would be but a useless repetition to add, "and we were all made to drink into one Spirit." The reception of the Spirit is the thing affirmed in the last clause, and it is presented as something additional to what was said in the first; but if the reception of the Spirit is what was said in the first, the last is not an additional fact, but a repetition. We conclude, therefore, that the first clause does not refer to the reception of the Spirit at all. On the contrary, it declares that it was by the Holy Spirit that we were induced to be immersed and become one body; while the last clause declares the additional fact that we all then became partakers of the refreshing influence of the Spirit within us ("Immersion in the Holy Spirit" 438-439).

The idea of oneness expressed in the verse is the thing of significance for our purpose. "Baptized into one body" may mean either "so as to be united to one body," or "so as to form one body." In the above statement McGarvey expresses the latter view when he says, "it was by the Holy Spirit that we were induced to be immersed and become one body." The language seems to support this conclusion. Edwards points out that if Paul had meant to say that baptism unites those who are thus baptized to one body he would have used *en* following *eis* in the statement (325). It is probably best to take the preposition *eis* ("unto," or "into") as conveying the idea of result, and meaning, "so as to constitute one body."

5. Called into the Fellowship of Jesus Christ. Paul shows that the Corinthians had been called "unto the fellowship of his Son Jesus Christ our Lord" (1 Cor. 1:9). Immediately after this reminder of their calling into the fellowship of Christ, Paul launches his exhortation to unity.

It is characteristic of Paul to point his readers to what they have as well as to point out what they lack and what they must yet seek. What the Corinthians lacked was oneness of mind and speech; what they held in common was that each of them shared in Christ's death, and by one Spirit they had been baptized into Christ's name and body. To state these common privileges in the terms Paul used in writing to the Ephesians, they shared in a common calling of which they must walk worthily. In the words of 1 Corinthians 1:9, they all had been called by God into the fellowship of Christ.

Fellowship is joint participation or communion. In the case here, Paul speaks of the fellowship of Christ, or a participation of Christians in the life of Christ. This life which every Christian shares from a common Father is "in his Son," and "he that hath the Son hath the life; he that hath not the Son hath not the life" (1 John 5:11-12).

The "calling" itself would be the same as the initial calling one receives from God in becoming a Christian. This is the call one receives when he is called by the gospel (2 Thess. 2:14). The Corinthians had heard the gospel, believed it, and obeyed it (Acts 18:8). As we saw in the last point of the above section, their baptism was by one Spirit into one body (1 Cor. 12:13). Earlier we learned that it was also a baptism into the name of Jesus Christ (1 Cor. 1:13). Elsewhere we are told that baptism brings one into Christ (Rom. 6:3-4; Gal. 3:27). Being in Christ they now shared (had fellowship in) all the benefits one has in belonging to Christ; the kind of spiritual blessings one finds in Christ as enumerated by Paul in Ephesians 1:3-14, such as having been chosen by God, adoption into God's family, redemption, forgiveness of sins, and an eternal inheritance.

When Paul reminds the Corinthians of their calling into the fellowship of Christ, he wishes to impress them with this grand privilege and uses it as a ground to call them to unity. Because they have been called into the fellowship of Christ, they were "called saints" and Paul addresses them as "brethren" (1 Cor. 1:2, 10). They should, therefore, make every effort to have the same mind and judgment as called for in 1 Corinthians 1:10.

Common Experiences As Christians
Underlying the exhortation to oneness of mind in Philippians 2 are four grounds which underscore the deepest experience of Christians: "If there be therefore any consolation in Christ, if any consolation of love, if any fellowship of the Spirit, if any tender mercies and compassions, make full my joy, that ye be of the same mind" (vv. 1-2). This fourfold incentive behind Paul's appeal reaches out to the noblest impulses of the brethren at Philippi, and in view of their experience should move them to favorably respond to his plea. Paul does not use "if" in these statements to indicate any doubt as to whether the condition is really true, but simply to emphasize that since the conditions are true, the Philippians should follow through and make his joy full by being of one mind, love, and accord.

1. Consolation in Christ. The word "consolation" may mean either exhortation, encouragement, or comfort. It likely means "exhortation" here. This is the preference of the ASV and the RSV. This is favored by the fact that the subject is exhortation to unity. If they had received any exhortation from their connection with Christ, in the sense of Christ appealing to them through their experiences of having been with him, then as a result of their union with him, let them make Paul's joy full by being of one mind. As Robertson puts it, "If one's own life in Christ does not stimulate the soul to the noblest effort, it is useless to go on with the appeal" (*Paul's Joy In Christ* 62).

2. Comfort of Love. The word for "comfort" could just as easily be translated "encouragement" or persuasion, but "comfort" is acceptable here. It is almost equivalent to the word "exhortation" in the previous statement, and some see no difference in the two terms. There is, however, the added suggestion of tenderness involved. Vincent thinks Paul means "if love has any persuasive power to move you to concord" (*Epistles to the Philippians and to Philemon* 54). The RSV uses the word "incentive." Paul could refer to his own love for them, or the love that Christ has for them. But the thought seems to be, if Paul's love had provided them any comfort or consolation in their sufferings, they should respond by heeding his appeal and be of one mind and accord.

3. Fellowship of the Spirit. Paul means by this that if the Philippians have any participation with the Spirit, they will be ready to listen to his plea for unity. It is not the fellowship which the Holy Spirit imparts, but the life and blessings which one shares with the Spirit as a result of his connection with him. They all had become part of the one body of Christ as a result of the Spirit directing them to the one baptism that brought them into Christ (1 Cor. 12:13; Rom. 6:3-4), and they all alike have access to the Father through the Spirit (Eph. 2:18).

4. If Any Bowels and Mercies. The word for "bowels" is a word which in ancient times referred to the heart, liver, lungs, and kidneys; parts of the human body that identified the seat of emotions or feelings. It is rendered "tender mercies" (ASV) and "affection" (RSV, NASB, NKJV). Paul uses it here to describe the feelings of love and tenderness. The word for "mercies" refers to compassion or sympathy. Taken together the two words represent compassion of the heart. If the Philippians had any compassion in the heart for one another, or even for Paul in his condition and in his aims; if they had any affectionate sympathy toward each other, or toward Paul, they would hear Paul's plea.

To sum up: By mentioning these four things Paul is saying to the Philippians, "If then your experiences in Christ appeal to you with any force, heed my call to be of one mind, and in this way fulfill my joy." They did in fact possess the things named, and because of these possessions Paul expected them to respond favorably by heeding his call for oneness in relation to one another.

Chapter 5

Essential Qualities for Unity

It is important to understand how the body of Christ is one, what is called for in Paul's appeals for oneness, God's perfect plan for maintaining unity, and the basis upon which the call for unity rests. This is the ground we have covered thus far in our study. Another aspect of this subject that is so vital in making it possible for brethren to dwell together in unity is that each person in a local church possesses the kind of qualities necessary for peace and harmony to continue to prevail among them. Paul introduces these kinds of qualities in both Philippians 2 and Ephesians 4 where he calls for unity among brethren. They are actually prerequisites to the kind of unity he urges brethren to maintain. Some of the things Paul requires are things to be avoided, others are things to be put on.

The Harmony Desired

In Philippians 2 Paul begins his appeal for unity by saying, "that ye be of the same mind, having the same love, being of one accord, of one mind" (Phil. 2:2). These things would "complete my joy," he says. They introduce the kind of unity Paul wants to see realized among them. But they may also be viewed as qualities that are essential for unity to exist. It will prove beneficial if we will consider them in this way. They all point to the "one thing" of verse 3, which is "lowliness of mind" (ASV), or humble-mindedness.

These four things appear to answer for the four bases for unity that Paul has just named in verse 1 — things we previously called "grounds" for his appeal for unity (see under the heading, "Common Experiences As Christians" in Chapter 4)

1. The Same Mind. The first base in verse 1 makes reference to our relation to Christ. The first essential quality for unity that is named in verse 2 draws on this relation each of us has to Christ. Out of this same relation that each has to Christ let each have the same mind. When Paul says "be of the same mind," the word for "mind" has been taken in different ways. Some apply the word to the intellectual processes only, others broadening its meaning to include how one feels. Although the word means "to think," as Bruce points out, it is not used to mean this only, "or even primarily in the intellectual sense. It equally involves one's emotions, attitudes and will" (*Philippians* 67).

The context would favor this use of the word in this passage. Paul is calling for the Philippians to be the same in their inward attitude of mind or disposition of will. Robertson says, "Only where minds are in tune do two minds think as one. Then one will say, 'I was just thinking,' and both say the same thing at once." (64). How this quality is linked with "one mind" in this same list will be more clear as we proceed.

2. Having the Same Love. This quality grows out of the second base for unity from v. 1. The second ground of his appeal is love, either that of Paul for the Philippians, or the love of Christ for them. That love should have the power to stir their hearts to have the *same love* themselves. He is not speaking of the object of their love, as though they must all love the same things, but its feeling. Moule captures the sense when he says, "feeling the same love, 'the same' on all sides" (*Philippian Studies* 91).

3. Being of One Accord. These words answer to "fellowship of the Spirit" of v. 1. The word "accord" brings out the thought of heart to heart relationships, unity of thought and affection, or what Moule calls "soul and soul together" (91). It is almost identical to "with one soul" from Philippians 1:27 where Paul calls on the Philippians to "stand fast in one spirit, with one soul, striving for the faith of the gospel." It describes "harmony of feeling," as the terms are rendered by Weymouth.

4. Of One Mind. "One mind" corresponds to the realized love summed up in "tender mercies and compassion" (ASV) of verse 1. The words "one mind" are almost identical to the terms used in the first clause of verse 2. So why does he repeat the point in almost identical terms? Because this is the central thought running through the list of things he is naming here. In the first one he called on them to be like-minded, which means to mind the same thing. In this last quality he repeats the same thought: mind the one thing. But he hasn't yet told the reader what that one thing is that they must keep minding. It will be explained in detail in verses 3 and 4. Lenski points out that these four things belong in pairs, with the first two forming one pair and the last two forming another pair. The second and third are just more precise definitions of the one idea of minding the same or one thing.

Attitudes To Be Avoided

Before specifically identifying the "one thing" the Philippians must keep their mind on, Paul identifies some things that must be avoided. The things he lists will make it impossible for one to keep minding the one essential thing.

1. Quarrelsomeness or Selfish Ambition. When Christians are "of one accord, of one mind," there is no room for quarreling. So, Paul says, "nothing by way of rivalry," as he begins v. 3. There is no verb in the statement, so one must be supplied. The participle used in v. 2 conveys the sense, "*doing* nothing by way of rivalry," or one might use the word "thinking or minding" from the previous phrase; thus, "*contemplate* nothing by way of rivalry."

Some think that the word used here is the word for "strife" (*eris*) and conveys the meaning of rivalry, a party-spirit. Such an attitude is guaranteed to destroy unity. Whenever a party spirit prevails, it suggests that there is a faction in the church that wants to promote its aims and ambitions as opposed to another group. This was the condition that prevailed in the church at Corinth when Paul wrote 1 Corinthians. Paul had also used this word to describe the situation in Rome (Phil. 1:17, rendered "faction" [ASV]), the place from which he was writing this letter to the Philippians. He hoped to see this tragedy avoided in the church at Philippi.

Others think Paul is using another word here; a word that means "selfish ambition" (*erithian*), not the usual word for strife. But, of course, strife is always the result whenever selfishness is present in the congregation. Both words appear in the list of the works of the flesh in Galatians 5:21, and are also in Paul's list in 2 Corinthians 12:20. Any time there is a competitive, selfish spirit present among brethren division will ensue. We must never forget that rivalry which results from selfishness are both works of the flesh. Such attitudes are always behind petty squabbles and fights in the church or out of it.

2. Conceit. The word Paul uses next is rendered "vainglory" in the KJV and other versions. The NASB renders it "empty conceit." This also is given as a work of the flesh in Galatians 5:26. Other words used by Paul to describe this attitude are the terms "high minded" (Rom. 3:12, 16) and "puffed up" (1 Cor. 4:6, 14, 18, 19; 5:2; 8:1; 13:14; Col. 2:18). The connection between selfish ambition, strife and conceit should be noted. Unity cannot prevail where ambitious men aim to triumph over others because they "think more highly of themselves than they ought to think" (Rom. 12:3).

Conceit means an empty glory. Someone has represented it to be like a balloon. The larger it stretches on the outside, the bigger the emptiness on the inside. Robertson quotes Moody here: "Strife is knocking another down — vainglory is setting oneself up" (66). Oswald J. Sanders reminds us that . . .

> nothing is more distasteful to God than self-conceit. This first and funda-
> mental sin in essence aims at enthroning self at the expense of God. . . .
> Pride is a sin of whose presence its victim is least conscious. . . . If we are
> honest, when we measure ourselves by the life of our Lord who humbled
> himself even to death on a cross, we cannot but be overwhelmed with the
> tardiness and shabbiness, and even the vileness, of our hearts (*Spiritual
> Leadership* 142).

The Antidote: Humble-Mindedness

In verse 3 the adversative "but" sets the stage for introducing the one quality that Paul has had in mind since the outset as the antidote for negative qualities that would hinder and even destroy unity. The "one thing" these brethren must keep minding is lowliness — "but in lowliness of mind," Paul says. This identifies the one thing he is discussing and the one thing that Christians must keep their mind on, humble-mindedness. Contrary to the way of thinking in Jesus' day, he set humility as a virtue before his own disciples. It was not to be thought of as a weakness to be avoided. Humility in Jesus' teaching is a way of strength, and it is a mark of true greatness (Matt. 20:20-28; Luke 22:24-27). Not only did he teach this great lesson on humility many times, but he led the way himself and practiced humility (John 13:2-17) as he went about doing good (Acts 10:38). Beginning with verse 5 below Paul gives Jesus as the great example of humility that should be followed by all.

1. The Requirements of Humility. What does humility require? For the sake of unity among brethren it requires putting the things of others ahead of one's own things. The way Paul words it is, "each counting other better than himself; not looking each of you to his own things, but each of you also to the things of others" (vv. 3b-4, ASV). Some words in this statement should be carefully noted.

First, Paul does not say one should not take into account his own things, but that he should "also" take into account the things of others. We have to consider our own things, but it is wrong to do that and fail to consider the same for others. In fact, Paul says we should put the other person's things above our own.

Second, this applies to everyone. Notice the word "each" in the statement. Paul uses this word three times in this brief statement: "*each* counting other better . . . not looking *each* of you . . . but *each* of you also . . . ." Each and every member of the congregation has this responsibility imposed upon him. Any person (each and everyone alike) motivated by strife, selfish ambition, conceit, or vainglory is self-centered, and this is a sin. There is no room for love when these damnable attitudes exist. Love makes everyone a servant, not only of God but of other members of the family of God. It is not the Christian attitude for one to look only to his own things. As Robertson says, "There is no love in the rule of might, in ruthless overriding of the rights of others. Might does not make right in the state or in the individual" (67).

Third, take a look at the word "things." Other versions render this word "interests," and this helps bring out the thought Paul is getting at in this statement. The "things" Paul has in mind are the feelings and needs of each person, both of ourselves and of others. Each person has such feelings and needs, and they are not to be ignored.

2. Our Estimate of Others. But why must each member count the other person as "better than [himself]"? It is not because it is easy, but because it is the right thing to do. Jesus was the first to point us in this direction, and his reason for doing so is not just because it is right, but because to put one's own feelings and needs behind those of others is the mark of true greatness. And how can we do what is required in putting others ahead of ourselves unless we have a high view of them? Our judgment of others must begin by our seeing them as at least our equals, even if we possess greater gifts than they do. We do this by recognizing that all that we are and all that we possess by way of abilities and gifts is due to God (1 Cor. 4:7). This makes each of us equal before God.

But when it comes to "needs" we are required to put the other person's needs above our own. That is, we must get ourselves out of the way, or rid ourselves of selfishness, and meet our brother's needs. Paul teaches this same thing in Romans 12:10, when he says, "In love of the brethren be tenderly affectioned one toward another; in honor preferring one another" (ASV). What does this mean? It means to be happy to help honor another, not jealously seeking honor for oneself. Robertson calls this "the deliberate estimate and preference of others, not a momentary impulse of politeness" (67).

3. Helpfulness. What really matters most is how much a brother or sister in a local church really cares about unity. One who cares about getting along with others will not approach a situation with the thought, "What is in this for me? What will I get out of it?" Instead he will ask, "What are the needs of others?" "What will benefit their growth?" "What can I do to help them?"

This attitude toward "self" runs counter to what Paul is telling us in these verses. But it cannot be denied that putting self in this exalted position in relation to others is the central problem in our culture today, and this hurtful attitude too often carries over into church life. Paul Vitz in his book *Psychology of Religion*, explains the problem in the following way:

> It should be obvious — though it has apparently not been so to many — that the relentless and single-minded search for and glorification of the self is at direct cross-purposes with the Christians injunction to lose the self. Certainly Jesus Christ neither lived nor advocated a life that would qualify by today's standards as "self-actualized." For the Christian, self is the problem, not the potential paradise. Understanding this problem involves an awareness of sin, especially the sin of pride. Correcting this condition requires the practice of such unself-actualized states as contrition and penitence, humility, obedience, and trust in God (quoted by David Jeremiah in *Turning Toward Joy* 68-69).

Other Qualities That Matter
Paul begins his list of essential qualities for unity in Ephesians 4:2 with "lowliness," a quality we have just studied from Philippians 2:2-4. He adds three more that are so important for Christians to adopt if unity is to be maintained.

1. Meekness. Some may find it surprising just how close in meaning this word is to the word "lowliness" which is given right before it. These two qualities often appear together in Scripture. The word for "meekness" means submissiveness to God in whatever circumstances come upon us. It is often equated with spinelessness, but such weakness never enters into the meaning of the word. One misses the true meaning of this word when he thinks it suggests timidity, amiability, or mildness of disposition. Instead it is a very strong word.

The opposite of a haughty and self-assertive spirit, meekness implies forces and strength held in check. The term was once used of the training of horses and suggests energy controlled. As applied to man it represents forces of character held firmly in hand. As directed toward God it describes a "temper of spirit in which we accept his dealings with us as good, and therefore without disputing or resisting" (Trench, *Synonyms of the New Testament* 152).

Meekness, then, is submissiveness to God. It is a submissiveness that entails an acceptance of God's will for one's life without complaint. How, then, does it relate to gentleness? A gentle spirit is essential to such uncomplaining submissiveness, so that meekness, while it is more than gentleness, at least rests upon this important quality.

Jesus was meek and gentle (2 Cor. 10:1) but he sometimes was made angry when he saw the hardness of man's heart (Mark 3:5). He was unyielding when a matter of principle was involved. This is illustrated in the driving of the money-changers out of the court of the temple (John 2:13-17). His love for truth and righteousness would not permit him to allow such outrageous conduct to go unchecked. One who is meek will defend the gospel (Phil. 1:17) and contend earnestly for the faith (Jude 3). Moses was "very meek" (Num. 12:3), but he also was very strong. His life was well-ordered and fully under God's control. He firmly stood for what was right and rejected all that was opposed to the truth of God (see Exod. 32:15-28).

2. Longsuffering. This word means "patience, steadfastness, endurance, forbearance" (AG 489). It has often been observed that the best way to describe the meaning of longsuffering is to reverse the order of the words. It means to suffer long. One who has the ability to suffer long has a quiet spirit even when mistreated. He is able to patiently endure wrong. This same word is rendered "patience" in Hebrews 6:12 and James 5:10.

One who is longsuffering is not easily provoked. He is calm in spirit even when wrong is directed toward him. Any urges to strike back are kept well under control. James says that Christians should "be swift to hear, slow to speak, slow to wrath" (Jas. 1:19). If God is "merciful and gracious, longsuffering and abundant in goodness and truth" (Exod. 34:6; see also Rom. 2:4; 1 Pet. 3:20 and 2 Pet. 3:9) toward men, surely he expects men to be the same toward each other.

3. Forbearing One Another in Love. To "bear with" a brother suggests making allowances for him in certain ways. It is best connected with the word "longsuffering" as it is here and other places in the New Testament. We must be willing to suffer with, or bear with, our brother, for a long time. It does not mean to overlook his faults or shortcomings. The Bible nowhere indicates that we are to overlook sin in our own lives or the lives of others. Forbearance though is especially required when a brother attempts to make a comeback from some sin that has overtaken him. This is the situation of the brother at Galatians 6:2, where Paul tells Christians to "bear ye one another's burdens, and so fulfil the law of Christ." This brother needs understanding and acceptance, not ridicule and rejection.

Forbearance must be characterized by love. Love helps one stay close enough to a brother who is in this kind of situation to really help him. But it also will lead him to keep enough distance to allow his brother to make his own choices. For the sake of unity in the local church, good will among the members must prevail. Forbearance must be practiced among the members. Since forbearance is patience demonstrated, it is these kinds of opportunities that give brethren a chance to show their love one toward another.

Chapter 6

"To the Law and to the Testimony"

Does the freedom found in Christ give us liberty to be less concerned, or perhaps even indifferent, about what is taught by those who profess to be true teachers of the word of God today?

Isaiah's call for Israel to go "to the law and to the testimony!" for their guidance and not to the dead (Isa. 8:20) is simply an expression of what had been the practice all along in Israel, and what should be our practice as well. Homer Hailey, who lived to the ripe old age of 97, and who sadly is being buried on the very day of this writing, made the following comments on this passage in his *Commentary on Isaiah*:

> Let the people return to God! If they would be instructed, then let them hear Jehovah the loving God: *To the law and to the testimony!* This should be the watchword of the faithful. Here, not among the dead, is where men shall find the truth and direction for the living; here they shall find light even in the hours of national calamity. *If they speak not according to his word.* There will be no dawning light, but only stygian darkness and despair, void of all hope, for those who reject God's truth. What a tragedy, when it could have been otherwise! This principle has not changed; it is operative now as then (98).

In order to show that this is the general teaching of both the Old and New Testaments, we will now look at some of the passages that have to do with this subject.

Other Warnings From the Old Testament
1. Specific Prohibition: Deuteronomy 4:2.
No Addition or Subtraction. Moses specifically forbade anyone to add to or take away from the word of God: "Ye shall not add unto the word

which I command you, neither shall ye diminish ought from it, that ye may keep the commandments of the Lord your God which I command you" (Deut. 4:2). This charge is repeated in Deuteronomy 12:32. Proverbs 30:6 forbids *adding* anything to the Lord's words, when it says, "Add thou not unto his words lest he reprove thee, and thou be found a liar." The words from Moses refer specifically to the law that Moses was about to give to the people. It could not be supplemented, nor could it be reduced. There could be further revelations made available to the people, as indeed there would be from the prophets and others at a later period. Even Moses himself spoke of another like himself who would arise (Deut. 18:15-18) whom the people must hear. Peter applies these words to Jesus Christ in Acts 3:22-23.

Covenant and Commandments. The term "commandments" in Deuteronomy 4:2 is synonymous with the "statutes and judgments" ("decrees and laws," NIV) of verses 1, 5, and 8. These are the basic laws set forth in the "covenant" given on Mt. Sinai. The disallowance of anything being added or taken away from the covenant reflects the unilateral arrangement where the sovereign and he alone sets the terms of the covenant. Since God is the originator of the covenant, only he is capable of determining its content and extent. Yet, the covenant is also a bilateral arrangement wherein both parties (God and the people) agree to keep their respective parts of the covenant (see Exod. 20:7-9 and 24:3ff.). Each party expresses his commitments by pledging his love.

God is faithful in his love for his people and keeps "covenant and mercy with them that love him and keep his commandments" (Deut. 7:9). For those who do not love him and keep his commandments he will "destroy them: he will not be slack to him that hateth him, he will repay him to his face" (v. 10). God pledges to keep his covenant of love with them only if they are faithful to keep these laws and commandments (vv. 12-16). For this reason, he says, they must "keep the commandments, and the statutes, and the judgments, which I command thee this day, to do them" (v. 11). This shows that these statutes and judgments sometimes go beyond the Ten Commandments.

The "Book of the Covenant." Of the over three hundred times in the Old Testament where the word "covenant" is found, twenty-eight of them appear in the book of Deuteronomy. When used of the covenant between God and Israel, it sometimes has a restricted use, as in Deuteronomy 4:13, to mean the Ten Commandments. These "ten words" or commandments (used also in 10:4 and Exod. 34:28) are the heart of the larger covenant, what is called the "book of the covenant" recorded in Exodus 20:1-23:33. These statutes and laws which made up the "book of the covenant" were first spoken by Moses to the people, and the people agreed to keep them all (Exod. 24:3). Then Moses wrote them down, offered sacrifices, read the "book of the covenant" to the people, and sprinkled blood both on the altar and the people (Exod. 24:4-7). Again they said, "All that the Lord hath said will we do, and be obedient" (Exod. 24:7).

As the covenant is now being *renewed* with Israel (this is the subject or content of the book of Deuteronomy), it is clear that the laws beyond the "ten words" (commandments) of Deuteronomy 4:13 are also described as "statutes and judgments" (Deut. 4:14). These were taught by Moses and were to be kept by Israel when they took possession of the land. The statutes and commandments under consideration were about to be given in Moses' discourse (Deut. 4:40). The discourse begins in Deuteronomy 5:1. The Ten Commandments are elaborated upon in chapter 5, and other instructions follow beginning in chapter 6, and continuing throughout the rest of the book. Note that all these "stipulations, decrees and laws" (Deut. 4:45, NIV) are called "the law" in Deuteronomy 4:44. Thus the terms "covenant" and "the law" are used interchangeably in these passages.

What About Attitude? Interestingly, the prohibition in Deuteronomy 4:2 and 12:32 has nothing to say about attitude. Moses does not say, "Ye shall not be covetous, or puffed up, or worldly minded, and allow such sinful dispositions to lead you to add unto the word which I command you . . . ," for to do this will make you a false teacher! No, he simply warns against adding to or taking away from the word of God spoken by Moses. Whether or not such attitudes are present is not the point. Man is not given the liberty to add to or take away from the word of God as long as he does so in sincerity, or as long as some kind of sinful disposition does not lead him to break God's law in this way. Because such matters are not mentioned is no encouragement to receive one as a faithful teacher who violates the prohibition out of ignorance, or who does so sincerely without the intention of going beyond it or taking away from it. The warning is given in a straightforward fashion without making such allowances for failure to live up to the requirement for one reason or another. Neither is there any encouragement for one to make such allowances for someone else.

This is not to be taken to mean that the prohibition applies to a failure in judgment or understanding that would have nothing to do with one's practice. There may be any number of things one might not fully understand when it comes to his study of God's word. All would likely agree that to add to or take away from God's word has to do with practice, not merely faulty understanding on a matter of indifference.

2. The Problem of False Prophecy in Israel.

The Term "False Prophet." There does not appear to have been an exact definition of the term "false prophet" in the Old Testament. We learn what a false prophet is by how false prophets are described at different places, even though the term "false prophet" does not appear in the Old Testament. The Septuagint (Greek translation of the Old Testament, abbreviated LXX) used the Greek word for "false prophet" "to describe the prophets who lied [Jer. 6:13], denied the words of the true prophets [Jer. 17:29 = LXX 34:9; Jer. 28:1 = LXX 35:1], tried to kill the true prophets [Jer. 26:7 = 33:7], and deceived the people with their dreams [Jer. 29:8 = LXX 36:8]" (*ISBE* 3: 985).

The Meaning of False Prophecy. What then was false prophecy, and who was a false prophet? False prophecy was a message that was deceitful, a lie, or a falsehood. Jeremiah, though sometimes mentioning the bad motives prompting the false prophets in his day, uses these kinds of terms quite frequently to describe a false prophet. What makes him a false prophet is not his bad motives or his greed, but his false message: he deals "deceitfully" or "falsely" with the people, or he speaks "lies" (8:10; 14:14; 23:25, 32; 27:10, 14 16; 28:15; 29:9, 21). One example of this is those who prophesied peace when there was no peace. They are represented as prophets who misled God's people through "lies" or by speaking falsely to them (8:11; 23:17; with 28:2, 11; Ezek. 13:10; Mic. 3:5). Again, a false prophet was one who related visions that came from the prophet's own heart (Jer. 14:14; 23:16; Ezek. 13:2f; 22:28). Any message derived from Baal was a false message and made one a false prophet (Jer. 2:8; 23:13).

The mission of the prophet was to call upon God's people to return to the old paths (Jer. 6:14). It must be obvious from such examples cited above that in Israel the test of a prophet had more to do with the origin and content of his message than with his attitude. Whether one was deceived, covetous, dishonest, or ignorant was not the test. The true prophet himself sometimes identified such dispositions of heart or mind as being present, but he never called upon God's people to make such judgments about a prophet. How would it be possible for the average person to have such knowledge of a prophet?

Homer Hailey, in his *Commentary on the Minor Prophets*, makes some important observations on false prophets which are worthy of note.

The false prophets fall into two general classes, mercenary and political; some prophesied for money, others from political favor (see Mic. 3:5, 11). Oftentimes the false prophets were nationalistic — that is, they defended the national practices and rulers through ignorance; but whether false through ignorance or self-will, they and their messages were no less severely denounced by the true prophets. Albert C. Knudson has well said: "An ignorant conscientiousness may be quite as dangerous to a community as deliberate wickedness." When opposed by false prophets, the true prophets rise to their greatest height of zeal and fearlessness (18).

In commenting on Hosea 4:5, he says, "Both the people and the false prophets would stumble, and the mother — the nation — would be destroyed. The expression 'false prophet' is not found in the Old Testament; however, the prophets who spoke against the true prophets were utterly 'false' and were condemned by the true prophets" (148). On the words "their lies have caused them to err" of Amos 2:4, Hailey says, "These were their false religious teachings and their false concept of Jehovah which had led them into idolatry and which would now bring them to destruction" (96).

3. Examples of Violation. Under the law man was to keep whatever God commanded, and he was not allowed to add to God's law or take away from it, as we have seen already (Deut. 4:2; 12:32). In Deuteronomy 12:8, Moses said, "Ye shall not do after all the things that we do here this day, every man whatever is right in his own eyes." Man has never had the liberty to do whatever he wanted in worship and service to God. Human opinion has never been an acceptable basis for worship and service in attempting to carry out God's will. The people of Israel thought that having a king like the other nations around them would be best for them. They never thought that by having such a king they would be going against God's will. But God said to Samuel, "They have not rejected thee, but they have rejected me, that I should not reign over them" (1 Sam. 8:7).

The Case of Saul. Saul thought it was better that he should make an offering to the Lord than to have his army scattered (1 Sam. 13:8-12), but his offering was rejected by the Lord. Samuel said to him, "Thou has done foolishly: Thou has not kept the commandment of the Lord thy God, which he commanded thee: for now would the Lord have established thy kingdom upon Israel forever. But now thy kingdom shall not continue: the Lord hath sought him a man after his own heart, and the Lord hath commanded him to be captain over his people, because thou hast not kept that which the Lord commanded thee" (1 Sam. 13:13-14).

After being commanded to utterly destroy all the cattle of the Amalekites (1 Sam. 15:3), Saul became guilty of the same sin when he brought back the fat cattle to offer in sacrifice to God in Gilgal. No doubt he thought he was carrying out the Lord's commandment. But he was asked, "Wherefore then didst thou not obey the voice of the Lord, but didst fly upon the spoil, and didst evil in the sight of the Lord?" (1 Sam. 15:19). Saul defended himself by saying, "Yea, I have obeyed the voice of the Lord" (1 Sam. 15:20), but Samuel told him, "thou has rejected the word of the Lord, and the Lord hath rejected thee from being king over Israel" (1 Sam. 15:26).

Two Sons of Aaron. Nadab and Abihu were the two oldest sons of Aaron (Exod. 6:23) who, along with their brothers, Eleazar and Ithamar, were appointed to the priesthood (Lev. 8:30) just prior to the sin of Nadab and Abihu described in the early verses of Leviticus 10. We do not know exactly what the "strange fire" (Lev. 10:1) was which they offered up to the Lord. Was it that their incense was not lighted from the altar (Lev. 16:12)? Was their offering made at the wrong time of day (Exod. 30:7-8)? Whatever it was about the offering that made it unacceptable to the Lord, the last part of Leviticus 10:1 shows the reason why God rejected it. The divine record says it was an offering "which he commanded them not." Even though the words "strange fire" are somewhat imprecise, the added words, "which he commanded them not," point to the conclusion that they mean "unauthorized" by God. Nadab and Abihu had no word from the Lord permitting them to make the offering they brought before him.

This is a remarkable example of two men who failed to respect the "silence of God" and were condemned for it. Obviously God had given *specific* guidelines regarding the incense offering and the priests were not given the liberty to disregard them by adding to or taking away from them. A specific requirement limits action (that is, only what is specified with regard to kind of action is authorized), and no one is permitted to alter such instruction by either adding to it or taking away from it. In some way, either by adding something — such as another time, or getting coals from another place — or by leaving something out — perhaps failing to light the incense from the altar, Nadab and Abihu disregarded what God had specifically commanded. They did not respect God's *silence* when he had *specified exactly what he wanted to be done* in making the incense offering.

The judgment of God against Nadab and Abihu for their disobedience was immediate and severe. Leviticus 10:2 shows how displeased God is when man disregards his instructions: "And there went out fire from the Lord, and devoured them, and they died before the Lord." This fire of judgment "consumed them." God is holy and his people must regard him as holy: "I will be sanctified in them that come near me, and before all the people I will be glorified" (v. 3). What better way is there for man to honor God than to honor his authority as expressed in his word? God will not have it any other way, and this statement shows that these men had failed to glorify God when they failed to keep his word *exactly* as he had commanded.

New Testament Warnings

The question may be asked, "Is the New Testament as strict on the subject of obedience as the Old Testament?" Is doing things exactly right necessary today? Some would say that since we are not under law but under grace (Rom. 6:14), then strict obedience is not required today as it was under the former covenant. The subject of "law" and our relation to it today is the subject of another chapter. Here our only concern is whether or not the same kind of strictness, when it comes to obedience to God, is expected today as it was in the former dispensation. If we find that it is, then we would expect that there would be a pattern made known to us so that we can know when we are and when we are not adhering to that pattern. In the absence of such a pattern, how could strict obedience be required? We are now to see if the kind of strict obedience required under the Old Testament law is also required today.

1. Specific Prohibition: Revelation 22:18-19.

No Addition Or Subtraction. In the New Testament we find specific prohibitions about adding to and taking away from the word of God just as we find in the Old Testament. At the close of the New Testament we find this warning: "And I testify unto every man that heareth the words of the prophecy of this book, If any man shall add unto them, God will add unto him the plagues which are written in this book: and if any man shall take away from the words of the book of this prophecy, God shall take away his part from the tree of life, and out of the holy city, which are written in this book" (Rev. 22:18-19).

The warning is expressed in the same language as that found in Deuteronomy 4:2; 12:32; and Proverbs 30:5f. What is added here is the punishment that will ensue for the one who violates the injunction. Homer Hailey makes application of these verses in this way: "God's spiritual and moral truth must be neither altered nor perverted; it must be faithfully handed down from one generation to another. The principle applies to all the Word of God, but here Jesus is speaking particularly of this book, the Revelation" (*Revelation* 433). He goes on to say, "The words of the prophecy are the thoughts, principles, judgments, and messages of this book. The Lord is not speaking of an honest error in judgment and interpretation, even though this is serious. Rather he condemns the presumptuous and all who manifest a careless or flippant attitude toward the Word. As Lenski intimates, this makes writing about the book a serious and sublime matter to be pursued with the deepest of reverence for God and His truth" (433).

Refuse Not Him That Speaks From Heaven. One must never be careless in how he handles the word of God. When God speaks through his Son (Heb. 1:1-2), he expects man to hear, as well as to adhere to, what he has said. To take Christ's word lightly or to disregard it, to reject it, turn away from it, or to presumptuously go beyond it, or to leave something out, is to commit an egregious error. The Hebrew writer admonishes, "See that ye refuse not him that speaketh. For if they escaped not who refused him that spake on earth, much more shall not we escape, if we turn away from him that speaketh from heaven" (Heb. 12:25-26).

The one who speaks from heaven is Christ. To refuse to hear him is to "turn away from him," the words brought up later in this same passage. Paul gives an example of those in Asia who *turned away* (same word) from him: "This thou knowest, that all they which are in Asia be turned away from me: of whom are Phygellus and Hermogenes." This word also appears in Titus 1:14: "Not giving heed to Jewish fables, and commandments of men, that *turn from* the truth." 2 Timothy 4:4 is no doubt the most familiar: "And they shall *turn away* their ears from the truth, and shall be turned unto fables." No ulterior motive is assigned to any of these who are described as either having turned away, are turning away, or will turn away from the truth.

Thinking of Men Above What is Written. Paul was greatly concerned about how some of the Corinthians were puffed up over men. The first four chapters of his first letter were given to a discussion of this problem. Some were following one man, some another, so that each group was claiming to belong to a particular man, such as Paul, Apollos, or Cephas. Paul strongly condemned this practice (1 Cor. 1:10-13). It was basically a problem of glorying in men which Paul rejected as being contrary to the true wisdom of God. "Therefore," he says to them, "let no man glory in men" (1 Cor. 3:21). But such a charge is not given in isolation. In the preceding verses he shows that the problem of parties in the church at Corinth was founded upon a basic misunderstanding. They did not understand the meaning of true wisdom, nor did they have any true conception of its origin. "Let no man deceive himself. If any man among you seemeth to be wise in this world, let him become a fool, that he may be wise. For the wisdom of this world is foolishness with God. For it is written, he taketh the wise in their own craftiness. And again, The Lord knoweth the thoughts of the wise, that they are vain" (1 Cor. 3:18-19).

This provides the background for Paul's charge in 1 Corinthians 4:6: "And these things, brethren, I have in a figure transferred to myself and to Apollos for your sakes; that ye might learn in us not to think of men above that which is written, that no one of you be puffed up for one against another." By using himself and Apollos as examples Paul wanted to teach the Corinthians "not to think of men above that which is written." Presumably "that which is written" is the Old Testament Scriptures. Already in the first three chapters he has quoted from the Old Testament to make this point about how it is wrong to glory in men. This has come through especially in those verses that have addressed the subject of the futility of worldly wisdom and glorying in men: "I will destroy the wisdom of the wise, and will bring to nothing the understanding of the prudent" (1:19); "He that glorieth, let him glory in the Lord" (1:31); "He taketh the wise in their own craftiness" (3:19); "The Lord knoweth the thoughts of the wise, that they are vain" (3:20). Were not the Corinthians divided over men because they trusted in human wisdom? Then such Scriptures apply to them, and they must learn not to exalt themselves above God's written standard.

Those of us who live under the New Covenant, and who have come to understand that our authority in religious matters is derived from the New Testament Scriptures, may find it puzzling that Paul uses the Old Testament as he does here and elsewhere to make his point. He does this same thing later in 1 Corinthians 10:11, after he has given a number of examples of apostasy during the Old Testament period: "Now all these things happened unto them for examples: and they are written for our admonition, upon whom the ends of the world are come." He had already said in v. 6, "Now these were our examples, to the intent that we should not lust after evil things, as they also lusted."

From these kinds of uses of the Old Testament we are reminded that there are many things in these Scriptures that will provide Christians much benefit today. Paul illustrates this same truth in Romans 15:4, when he says, "For whatsoever things were written aforetime were written for our learning, that we through patience and comfort of the scriptures might have hope." There is much by way of principle from these Scriptures that can lead us in the right way. Examples, such as the warning examples cited here in 1 Corinthians 10:1-11, and examples of encouragement like the examples of faith found in Hebrews 11, have much to say to us today. From the Old Testament Scriptures we can learn patience, comfort, and hope.

Man is not to exalt men above "that which is written." Man is not the standard by which to measure things. Some may measure themselves by themselves, or they may measure themselves by others who have no true word from God (see 2 Cor. 10:12), but this is not the true standard of measurement. The written word of God is the standard (Matt. 4:4, 7, 10; John 12:48; 1 Cor. 4:6). To exalt men above God's ordained standard is to place them above the very thing by which man himself is to be tested and finally judged (John 12:48). To put one's trust in man, and thereby glory in men by lifting them above God's written standard, is to exalt human wisdom above divine wisdom.

What was written by the inspired writers of the New Testament was also viewed by the authors as being authoritative. Paul clearly understood that his writings were binding. He said to the Corinthians, "The things that I write unto you are the commandment of the Lord" (1 Cor. 14:37). He implies by the fact that he teaches the same things in all the churches that the things he teaches are binding upon all alike. His own words are, "Wherefore I beseech you, be ye followers of me. For this cause have I sent unto you Timotheus, who is my beloved son, and faithful in the Lord, who shall bring you into remembrance of my ways which be in Christ, as I teach every where in every church" (1 Cor. 4:16-17).

Going Beyond the Teaching of Christ. Though not stated in the form of a specific prohibition, 2 John 9, like 1 Corinthians 4:6, addresses the subject of keeping our practice within certain prescribed limits. John says, "Whosoever transgresseth and abideth not in the doctrine of Christ, hath not God. He that abideth in the doctrine of Christ, he hath both the Father and the Son." Literally, the first two words with the definite article say, "anyone who runs ahead," or "everyone going forward." But it is not merely going ahead that is meant, since progress and growth are commendable. The words are to be understood in connection with the remaining part of the statement, "and not remaining in the teaching of Christ." The one who moves ahead to the point of exceeding Christ's teaching is the one who does not have God.

The "doctrine of Christ" may be taken as either a subjective (teaching received *from* Christ), or objective (teaching *about* Christ") genitive. But it is most likely that John means the teaching that came forth *from* Christ, not the teaching about Christ. Though this has been a disputed subject, Brooke states the case well for what has become the view of the majority of commentators, when he says, "There is nothing in the context or the usage of the N. T. to suggest that *tou christou* [we have transliterated the two Greek words for "of Christ" here — *ww*] should be regarded as an objective genitive, the writer meaning by the phrase 'the apostolic teaching about Christ.' Such an interpretation would seem to be the outcome of preconceived notions of what the author ought to have meant rather than of what his words indicate" (*Johannine Epistles* 177).

John's writings favor this use of these terms. Jesus spoke of "my doctrine" which he said came from God (John 7:16-17). At other times we see others refer to "his doctrine" (John 18:19), an obvious reference to those things taught by Christ. Those who heard Jesus "were astonished at his doctrine" (Matt. 7:28). Luke reports that when Jesus was teaching in Capernaum "they were astonished at his doctrine: for his word was with power" (Luke 4:32). In Acts we read of "the apostles' doctrine," or body of truth being taught by the apostles (Acts 2:42). And in the book of Revelation there also are references to "the doctrine of Balaam" (Rev. 2:14) and "the doctrine of the Nicolaitans" (Rev. 2:15).

2. Human Traditions.

Among the Jews. According to Jesus, the Jews transgressed the commandment of God by their tradition (Matt. 15:3). McGarvey concluded that, from this statement of Jesus, "he charges that they, by their tradition, transgressed the commandment of God, and that the tradition itself was sinful" (*Matthew and Mark* 134). In Mark's account he said, "You reject the commandment of God, that you may hold your tradition" (7:9). They were, according to him, "making the word of God of no effect through your tradition which you have handed down" (Mark 7:13).

The true test of tradition is its origin. Those things received by revelation from God (Eph. 3:5) and handed down to others also are called "tradition" in Scripture. Paul instructs the Thessalonians to "hold the traditions which ye have been taught, whether by word, or our epistle" (2 Thess. 2:15). Later in 3:6 he tells them "to withdraw yourselves from every brother that walketh disorderly, and not after the tradition which ye received of us." The tradition they had received was whatever instruction they had received from Paul, including what was given to them in the epistle now sent to them. He charges them in 3:14, "And if any man obey not our word by this epistle, note that man, and have no company with him, that he may be ashamed."

Tradition *of men*, however, is tradition of another kind. In Matthew 15 and Mark 7 Jesus is discussing "the tradition of the elders" (Matt. 15:2; Mark 7:3, 5). Addressing the scribes and Pharisees he called these traditions "your tradition" (Matt. 15:3, 6) and "your own tradition" (Mark 7:9) because they had received these traditions from the elders *to hold as their own* (Mark 7:4). The elders among the Jews were the civil and religious leaders of Jerusalem and the nation. What originated with them is identified by Jesus as "the tradition of men" (Mark 7:8) and "the commandments of men" (Matt. 15:9; Mark 7:7). They were "of men" because they originated with man and were not from God. With Jesus the true test of anything religious was always, is it from men or is it from God (see Matt. 21:23-27)?

A clear distinction is made in Jesus' statements between that which comes from the word of God, on the one hand, and that which originates in the mind of man, on the other. The latter is called "the commandment of man." This is the "tradition" that is to be rejected. McGarvey makes the following observation on Matthew 15:9, "But in vain they do worship me, teaching for doctrines the commandments of men":

> So far, therefore, as a man's worship of God is a result of human authority, it springs from an improper source, and is vain. Every human addition to the commandments of God, so far as it induces any worship at all, induces vain worship, and there is probably not one such addition which does not, to a greater or less degree, make some commandment void. Thus the tradition of infant baptism, to the extent that it is adopted, makes of no effect the commandment concerning the baptism of believers, by baptizing persons in their infancy; and if it should become universally prevalent, by the baptism of all persons in their infancy it would bring to an end forever the only baptism of God (135).

> False teachers are not to be appeased as the disciples had attempted to do by criticizing Jesus for offending them by his sayings (Matt. 15:12). Jesus "had proved that by their tradition they were nullifying the word of God; he had charged them with hypocrisy; he had declared that all their worship based on the authority of tradition was vain worship; and he had swept away the entire fabric of their traditionary law of uncleanness by declaring that a man is not defiled by that which goes into his mouth. He had not only defended himself, but he had turned their own weapons with irresistible effect against them, and it is not surprising that they were offended" (McGarvey 136)

Of such teachers, Jesus goes on to say, "Every plant which my heavenly Father hath not planted, shall be rooted up. Let them alone: they be blind leaders of the blind. And if the blind lead the blind, both shall fall into the ditch" (Matt. 15:13-14). These teachers were "blind leaders" because of the errors they espoused. Were there corrupt motives that led them into such practices? Yes, Jesus clearly shows they stood opposed to the truth from corrupt motives. They were guilty of the sin of hypocrisy (Matt. 15:7). But they were not blind guides because they were hypocritical. They could have been sincere and yet have been blind guides. To see how this is true apply this point to those who would *follow* these blind teachers. There is no indication that Jesus thought that all those who might be in danger of following these teachers would be insincere, yet he describes them also as being "blind." They would be misled, but not insincere. The same is true of the teacher himself. A teacher who teaches false doctrine may have the purest of motives; he may simply be misled.

Yet, in spite of what appears to be an obvious truth, as a general rule, one may wonder if it is not true that those who bring in additions or substitutions into the service of the church, or who change in some way the truth of God into a lie, are prompted by some improper desire. And for all we know, all such changes of God's truth may be due to such impure motives. In commenting on Matthew 15:7 McGarvey remarks, "All similar substitutions of human expedients in the place of God's appointments are prompted by some improper desire, and are therefore liable to the same charge" (134). All may not be as obviously hypocritical as were these false teachers. But when one introduces unauthorized practices into the worship and service of the church, or he teaches something not taught in the word of God, are we to decide simply on the basis of motives whether or not he is a false teacher, when we cannot be sure about motive? Or is it his teaching and practice that must be the basis of our judgment?

The Colossian Threat. Paul gives a warning in Colossians 2:8 to "beware lest any man spoil you through philosophy and vain deceit, after the tradition of men, after the rudiments of the world, and not after Christ." The teachers who were troubling those in Colosse and would lead them away from Christ had developed an elaborate system of worship of angels (vv. 8, 18) and ascetic practices (vv. 16, 21-23) that were contrary to Christ himself. Paul calls such matters "philosophy and vain deceit," "the tradition of men," and "the rudiments of the world." They are "not after Christ." Those brethren were not to allow such things to be imposed upon them because they could not adopt such practices and continue to hold on to Christ as head (2:19). He warns ("beware," v. 8) them not to allow these false teachers to "spoil" them by these false practices. This word means "to carry off as booty or as a captive" (AG 784). They were in danger of losing their freedom in Christ by becoming entangled in these unauthorized practices that were being imposed upon them by these teachers. They must not submit to their man-made rules and regulations.

These teachers are described as practicing "will worship" (Col. 2:23). They worshiped angels (2:18) and had introduced into their ascetic practices all kinds of "ordinances" which they attempted to impose on others (2:20). Paul is basically warning these brethren against the practices of these teachers. He is condemning their unauthorized practices; not because they were prompted by ulterior motives, but because what they were doing originated with men, not with God. Sure, they were proud and puffed up ("vainly puffed up by his fleshly mind," 2:18), but this wrong attitude came *as a result of the heavenly visions which they thought they had experienced.* The question we need to answer, then, is this: What is Paul warning the Colossians about? The answer is simple: He is warning his brethren about *the kinds of religious experiences these teachers were claiming for themselves, and the kind of ascetic practices they would bind upon them.* He was not warning them about their puffed up attitude. What they were claiming was "after the commandments and doctrines of men" and "not after Christ" (2:8, 22). I have elsewhere made the following observations on the phrase "vainly puffed up by his fleshly mind":

> This third phrase describes the empty high-mindedness of these teachers. Just as some in Corinth became **puffed up** over supposed knowledge (1 Cor. 8:1), these false teachers in Colosse who were claiming special mystical experiences for themselves, and a superior knowledge gained through these experiences, had become inflated with conceit. What these teachers judged to be genuine spiritual insight, Paul castigates as being groundless because it rests upon their own **fleshly mind** (a mind governed and controlled by the flesh). Their mystical experiences had no real existence. Their entire service belonged to the "flesh." Instead of such experiences, which they claimed gave them deeper knowledge of spiritual things, originating with God, they actually had their origin in their own physical minds. These people had a materialistic or sensual outlook. Not only was this reflected in their attitude toward visions, but it was even more apparent in their attitude toward abstinence from such things as food and drink and festivals which they thought would prepare them (by resulting in a higher sanctity) for these experiences (*Philippians-Colossians* 218-19).

An important question one ought to consider is, would this teacher be the kind of teacher who should be accepted if he had not been "puffed up in the vanity of his mind"? One may assume that he would not be doing what he was doing and claiming what he was claiming had it not been for his feeling of superiority. But is this a safe assumption? Isn't this putting it in the wrong order? Isn't this person high minded because of what he believed and practiced, instead of believing and practicing what he did because of his attitude? The way Paul words it, it appears that he was puffed up *as a result of, or because* he thought he had knowledge others did not have, and he thought his superior knowledge came *as a result of* experiences he believed he had received through visions. His feeling of superiority did not give rise to his belief and teaching and practice; his belief, teaching and practice were the cause of his feeling of superiority. So, what made him a false teacher? A wrong *attitude*, what he *believed*, what he *taught*, or what he *practiced*? The answer probably lies in the answer to the question, what is Paul warning them about here?

Just what would enable the Colossians to determine whether or not these men were men they could accept and follow? This case is like many others we find in the New Testament. Paul is warning these brethren to be on guard against what is being *claimed* and what is being *done* by these men. He does not directly call them teachers, nor does he specifically identify them as *false* teachers. The word "false" is not found in the passage. In fact, the word "teacher" is not even used. But did Paul have to call them *false teachers* before we can know that this is what they were? Can we not tell by the kinds of things he says they believed, professed, and practiced, and by the warnings he gave in his description of them? What gives rise to false teachers is teaching that originates with men, or things they profess to have experienced that are not according to the truth. When men *teach* false doctrine (doctrine that originates with men), or when they profess to have had certain mystical experiences that are not according to the truth, they are false *teachers*.

Keep in mind that, at the outset of his warning, Paul spoke of "philosophy and vain deceit," and "the tradition of men," and "the rudiments of the world" (Col. 2:8). All of this had to do with what was being *practiced and taught* by these men. It was the body of teaching and the professed mystical experiences that were being advanced by these teachers that Paul felt they should be warned about at this place in the book. He does not say beware of men who have fleshly minds, but beware of men who would "spoil you through vain philosophy . . . ," etc. Their wrong attitude did not make them false teachers. They were false teachers because of what they professed and practiced, and, one would assume (though not specifically stated in the text), what was also being taught verbally by them.

Part Two:
Free In Christ —
A Response

Chapter 7

Free In Christ — "The Liberty by Which Christ Has Made Us Free"

There are passages of Scripture in the New Testament that speak of our "liberty" or "freedom" as Christians. No Christian would want to have his freedom in Christ taken away. And, when this subject is properly understood, none should fear that those who oppose the most liberal interpretation of this subject are about to rob Christians of their freedom in Christ. The issue that divides Christians on the subject of liberty is, what is to be made of the passages of Scripture that address this subject? Just what does freedom mean in the Bible? Freed from what, and freed to what?

Freedom From What?

Paul admonishes the Galatians, "Stand fast therefore in the liberty by which Christ has made us free" (Gal. 5:1). What is this freedom that Christ has given us? Sometimes it means freedom *as deliverance*. Christians have been delivered from the guilt and power of sin (Rom. 6:18). They are freed from an accusing conscience (Heb. 10:22) and from the wrath of God (Rom. 5:1; 1 Thess. 1:10). They have even been delivered from the power of Satan (2 Tim 2:26; Heb. 2:14). But none of this appears to be Paul's point in Galatians 5:1.

A careful reading of the book of Galatians shows that Paul is speaking of freedom *from the law of Moses*. In the first four chapters he has been dealing with the problem that the law poses. Through Christ man has been delivered from the curse which the law brings upon those who attempt to be justified by it (Gal. 3:10-13).

From what Paul says in Galatians 5:13 we conclude that he also is concerned about the problem of sin. "For you, brethren," Paul says, "have been called to liberty; only do not use liberty as an opportunity for the flesh, but through love serve one another." His first warning was, be sure to continue in the freedom Christ has given you (5:1). They were not to return to the law which would bring them into bondage again. The reason he gave was they had been freed from the law by Jesus Christ. Here in Galatians 5:13 he reminds them of that same freedom. But their new freedom from the law does not give them license to sin. It is easy for one to misunderstand freedom, and we shall see plenty of evidence for that as we proceed.

Our "Rights" and Liberty in Christ

As Christians we all have "rights." But is this the "freedom" Paul discusses in his letters? Consider the word "rights" for just a moment. The word in the New Testament that conveys this idea is the word *exousia*. This word means "authority, power" (*exousia*), and it "signifies a divinely given authority and freedom to act" (N. J. Opperwall, *International Standard Bible Encyclopedia* [Revised] 4:192). This word is used in connection with "freedom to act" in such places as Romans 9:21 and 1 Corinthians 9:12, 15, 18. In the first passage, Paul asks, "Does not the potter have *power* (*exousia*) over the clay, from the same lump to make one vessel for honor and another for dishonor?" It speaks of God's "power," or God's *right* in that sense, to make of one as he chooses. In 1 Corinthians 9 Paul is discussing his "right" (*exousia*) to receive support, or be paid wages, for his work in preaching the gospel. His authority as an apostle gave him a valid claim to be supported by the Corinthians, even though he freely renounced this "right" in order to be more effective in this particular circumstance.

There are also those passages of Scripture that speak of our "liberty" or "freedom" (*eleutheria*, a different word from *exousia*) as we have just noted in Galatians 5:1, 13. What is to be made of such passages? Are they speaking of our "freedom to act," as the word *exousia* does, or do they have something else in mind? Just what does freedom mean? Freed from what, and freed to what? As we have seen from Galatians 5:1, the subject is not "freedom to act."

Actually, one's "right" to do something, or his freedom to act, falls within the scope of divine authority; it "signifies a divinely given authority." Apart from this we would not have the "freedom to act." This means that our freedom in this sense is never to be thought of as being totally independent of God or God's *law*. This is why James can speak of "the perfect law of liberty" as he does in James 1:25 (this verse is considered below). Whether the "liberty" of this verse means deliverance, such as deliverance from sin and the law, or the freedom to act, which is not the usual meaning of this word, it is here directly connected to "law." Paul also had a high view of God's law for this age, as we are about to see.

When advocating the "freedom" of the Christian, some, in deprecating "law," would leave no room for *law* and *liberty* in the same phrase as we find them brought together in James 1:25. For many these are contradictory terms. But how could this be? If there were a contradiction James would not use them together as he does in this passage. In fact, one could well ask, how can there be liberty, in either of the two meanings of that word, where there is no law?

Meaning and Purpose of Law

What is law, and what purpose does it serve? The subject may be viewed from two sides.

1. Law Restrains and Reveals Sin. Where there is no restraint, there is the worse kind of slavery. Is this not the problem with the drunkard or the dope addict? Without restraint he subjects himself to the most hopeless and abject kind of slavery. When Paul says in Galatians 3:19 that the law was "added because of transgressions," this is the side of law he is describing. In relation to sin, the law was given for two purposes: (1) to restrain sin, and (2) to reveal and make sin known.

Paul elsewhere shows that the law served both of these purposes. First, *it restrained sin through its punishments*. Paul shows this in 1 Timothy 1:9-10: "Knowing this, that the law is not made for a righteous man, but for the lawless and disobedient, for the ungodly and for sinners, for unholy and profane, for murderers of fathers and murderers of mothers, for manslayers, for whoremongers, for them that defile themselves with mankind, for menstealers, for liars, for perjured persons, and if there be any other thing that is contrary to sound doctrine."

The law also served the purpose of *revealing and making known sin* so man might know what sin is. Paul says, "for by the law is a knowledge of sin" (Rom. 3:20). The law itself is not sin; yet, "I had not known sin," he says, "but by the law: for I had not known lust, except the law had said, 'Thou shalt not covet'" (Rom. 7:7). It was only by the law that man could see the "exceeding sinfulness of sin," or how bad sin really is (Rom. 7:13).

2. Law Provides Guidance. The other side of law is the *guidance it provides for man*. Man needs guidance for his life, a standard by which to walk in a dark world. He is not capable of providing such a standard for himself; he cannot direct his own steps (Jer. 10:23). So God made his law available for man so man would have the direction he needs. Jesus lived and died under the old law, and he acknowledged the written word of God to be a guide for man (Matt. 4:4). It was by his appeals to this written word of God that Jesus was able to overcome each temptation put before him (Matt. 4:4, 7, 10).

"Law" in the New Testament
1. The Law of God. In Romans 7:22 Paul says, "I delight in the law of God in the inward man." Here God's law (the law that finds its origin in him) is put in contrast with another law or rule which Paul found to be at work in his life. This "other law" is described in verses 21, 23, and 25. This "law in my members" which Paul describes refers to the tendency or rule in him to be influenced by the appetites and passions belonging to the flesh, which when yielded to produces sin. The "law" that is so described refers to the authority or rule of sin in him. In contrast to this law is "the law of God" in which Paul finds delight in his inner self or nature. In his spirit, or in his inner person, Paul joyfully agrees with the law of God.

The carnal mind, Paul shows in Romans 8:7, is not subject to "the law of God." Such a mind cannot receive and cannot obey the instructions coming from the law of God. Such a mind does not have the power to be subject to, or obey, the instructions that come to him from God's law. One does not have to have this kind of mind, but as long as one chooses to be dominated by the flesh (allows his mind to think of fleshly things), he cannot submit to the instructions of God's law.

2. The Law of Faith. Another way in which the word "law" is used in the New Testament is in connection with the word "faith" and in contrast with "works" of merit. In Romans 3:27 Paul asks, "Where is the boasting then? It is excluded. By what law? Of works? Nay: but by the law of faith." In the context the subject is salvation made possible through the blood of Jesus Christ. Salvation on these grounds leaves no place for boasting. Boasting is allowed only when one is justified on the merits of one's works. "Through what law," Paul asks, is boasting excluded? Is it excluded through "works," that is, through the law of works? Certainly not, he says. A "law of works" would provide grounds for boasting if one could be justified on this basis, or through such a system.

By "law" Paul means a principle, rule, or system. Boasting would not be excluded if one were justified through a system of works, but as he goes on to say, it *is* excluded through the rule or system of faith. If one were to keep God's law perfectly, which is what he must do in order to be justified by law, or a system, of "works" (see Gal. 3:10-13), then he would have grounds for boasting. But there is never reason for boasting through a system of faith. After one sins and forgiveness is needed, there can never be any grounds for boasting. It then becomes a matter of grace through faith. Since all have sinned, according to verse 23, salvation cannot be on the basis of "works," so Paul says, "therefore we conclude that a man is justified by faith without the deeds of the law" (v. 28).

This is not to say, that under such a system of faith, obedience to God's law is being set aside, or that under "faith" such obedience to God's law is no longer important or necessary. But it does say that one does not keep God's law without infraction (v. 23), and that since this is the case, a mere law system (what Paul calls a "law of works") can never acquit because there is no provision in such a system to cover sins. Once one becomes a lawbreaker no "works of law" can ever acquit and bring justification before God. It then takes propitiation, the kind Paul has described in the previous verses of this chapter (vv. 23-26), to obtain justification.

3. The Law of Christ. Paul also shows that we are "under (the) law of Christ" (1 Cor. 9:21). What does this mean? In this passage of Scripture, Paul is describing his own situation in relation to the law of Moses. He has just said (in vv. 20-21a) that in his work as an apostle he approached those who were "under the law" (i.e., the Jews, who were under the law of Moses) as being "under the law." He did the same for those who were "without law" (i.e., the Gentiles, who were not under the law of Moses). He treated them as people who were "without law." He is contrasting his different ways of working among the Jews and Gentiles.

After making this point about becoming all things to all men, Paul then shows that at the time he was writing this letter he was not under the law of Moses — "though not being myself under the law." This part of verse 20 is not found in the KJV, but the earliest manuscripts clearly favor its inclusion in the text. The NKJV points this out when it adds the footnote, "NU-Text adds *though not being myself under the law.*" This means that the earliest manuscripts include the phrase. Other English versions like the NASB and the NIV include it.

The phrase shows that Paul was no longer under the law of Moses, but this does not mean that he was without law, because, as he goes on to say, he was "under (the) law of Christ." This clearly shows that the law of Moses and the law of Christ are not the same, and that one is under only one law at a time. We are under the law of Christ today. The old law has been removed and replaced by the law of Christ.

4. The Law of Liberty. What is meant by "law of liberty" in James 1:25? James means *a law which gives liberty* to those who bring themselves under its authority. Indeed, only those who live in accordance with God's word are truly free. Manton points out that "duty is the greatest liberty, and sin the greatest bondage" (164, quoted by Vaughan, *James* 40).

One of the functions of law, you will remember, is to provide direction and guidance. Law is a standard by which life is regulated. Why else would one *look so intently into* (this is the meaning of the word "look" in this verse) this perfect law if he did not expect to find the guidance he needs for his life?

But in this context, what is meant by the term "law"? It is best understood in light of what was said of the "implanted word" which is able to save our souls in verse 21. It is the "word" of verse 23 which one must obey and not merely hear. What part of law does one obey? Only the part that gives him instructions or examples to follow, or commands to implement. Whatever this "implanted word" is that one must receive, and whatever the "word" is that must be obeyed, *it contains those things that one must "do."* This passage states that one must be a "doer" of the "word." In other words, God's "implanted word" of verse 21 and his "word" of verse 23 is the same as "the perfect law of liberty" of verse 25. One is not dealing fairly with the word of God when he makes the law of God one thing and the teachings he is to receive and examples he is to follow, as well as the commands he must obey, something else. Commands are a part of the law of Christ and, as has always been the case, God's commands must be obeyed.

The next word in this phrase is the word "liberty." We have seen Paul use this word to describe freedom from the law of Moses in Galatians 5:1 and 5:13. At other places it is the freedom made possible by God's law; a freedom from the bondage of sin and death.

5. The Law of the Spirit of Life. A well known example of God's law in this sense is what Paul says in Romans 8:2: "For the law of the Spirit of life in Christ Jesus has made me free from the law of sin and death."

What made Paul free? He says it was "the law of the Spirit of life." Notice how he uses the word "law" here. Law, as we have seen, sometimes means a principle of action, or system; it may also mean a rule or standard of conduct. Here "law" is a rule of conduct for Christians. This law is described as the law of "the Spirit of life"; that is, the law communicated by the Holy Spirit (see 1 Cor. 2:10-13).

The Spirit, who revealed and made known the word of God, is the Spirit "of life." These added words are important. The source of the new life we have in Christ is the Spirit, but it is through his "law," that revealed by the Spirit, or the gospel of our salvation, that this new *life* is given. The gospel is God's power unto salvation (Rom. 1:16). At one's initial obedience to the gospel he is "made . . . free from the law of sin and death," Paul adds. This "law of sin and death" is the law that works in our members, described in some detail in Romans 7. He describes this change that had been brought about in his brethren at Rome in Romans 6:16-18.

This same kind of freedom is also attributed to Jesus Christ. Jesus said, "So if the Son sets you free, you will be free indeed" (John 8:36). In Romans 8:2 Paul describes this freedom as being due to one's union with Christ: "For the law of the Spirit of life *in Christ Jesus* hath made me free from the law of sin and death."

Thus far we have seen that the "liberty" of the gospel frees from the law of Moses, but that it also frees from sin. Another kind of freedom the gospel brings is freedom from the *power* of sin. The first part of Romans 6:14 says, "for sin shall not have dominion over you." The reason why sin no longer has dominion over the Christian is given in the last part of the same verse: "for ye are not under the law, but under grace" (see the next chapter for our discussion of this subject).

This does not mean that we are not under any law at all, but that we are no longer under a mere law system which can result only in condemnation. As Hamilton states, "There is the assurance that the condemnation that comes to those who have only law will not be the eventual outcome because grace takes care of what nothing could atone simply under a system of law. If one has only law, and no grace, then the rule, control, or lordship of sin prevails in condemnation. Once one violates law, sin is the result. Obedience to law can never remove sin; only the blood of Christ can on the condition of an obedient faith" (*The Book of Romans* 395).

In James 1:25 James shows how one is blessed or benefitted by looking intently into God's word. The person who *lives* in this freedom will be blessed by God, not the person who only *learns* about it. "Within the boundaries of the law of God man is free, for there he lives in the environment God designed for him. When he crosses the boundary, he becomes a slave to sin. As long as he keeps the law, he is free" (Kistemaker, *James and I-II John* 62).

6. The Law of Love. In Romans 13:10 Paul says "love is the fulfilling of the law." There is no article in the Greek text with the word "law," even though one is supplied in the KJV giving the rendering "the law." One might suppose that Paul has the law of Moses in mind since he quotes from it in the preceding verse, but this is not conclusive. He likely is speaking of law in general in verse 10; thus, "love is the fulfilling of law." The "law of love" is the principle of love that fulfills law. Love, in other words, is the principle that should govern our relation with others.

Law requires that we do no harm to our neighbor. Love enables us to bring to completion this requirement placed upon us by law. In this way love is a "fulfilling of law." It is the principle that brings out the best in us in our relation to our neighbor. Hamilton makes this important observation: "One should not interpret this passage to mean that love is all embracing of the law of God, and that nothing else is necessary. One needs to keep the statement in context. He is not talking about every rule or law of God, but rather, he is speaking of the principle of love that should govern one in his relation to others" (730).

Chapter 8

Not Under Law But Under Grace

The liberty described in the New Testament and outlined in the previous chapter is far from what many who have been writing on this subject in recent years would have us believe. Most of these writers are advocates of a freedom of a different kind. They contend that the New Testament teaching on this subject gives them and others the "right" to believe and teach whatever they want to believe and teach. They also believe that this freedom demands that each Christian be willing to give all other Christians the "right" to believe and teach whatever they wish to believe and teach. Is this the "freedom" we read about in the New Testament?

The verse of Scripture often quoted in an attempt to bring us to this conclusion is, "for ye are not under the law, but under grace" (Rom. 6:14). John 1:17, "For the law was given through Moses; grace and truth came through Jesus Christ," is also sometimes used for this purpose. From such statements we are supposed to conclude: therefore we are not under law today; or, if we are under law, it is not a law where strict obedience matters. Under the gospel exact obedience to God is not required. This is the dispensation of grace. This approach usually runs along the following lines of argument.

Letter vs. Spirit

Romans 7:6 is also used to show that what has taken the place of the old law system is a new relationship with Jesus Christ: "But now we are delivered from the law, that being dead wherein we were held; that we should serve in newness of spirit, and not in the oldness of the letter." This relationship is entered into by the new birth through faith. But instead of being a legal relationship, we are told, it is a spiritual relationship.

What is Paul telling us in this passage? A careful reading will show us that Paul is contrasting the former life of the Jews under the law of Moses with their present life in Christ. "In the flesh" (v. 5) describes the time they were under the law. This is shown by how verse 6 begins: "But now we are delivered from the law." For Paul to use the word "flesh" to describe the Jews under the law is a good way to represent them since they were members of the covenant by virtue of the fact that they were connected to Abraham by the flesh. Circumcision in the flesh was a sign of their membership in the covenant.

Some versions render the word "spirit" with a capital "S," but there does not appear to be a reference to the Holy Spirit in this passage. The "new life of the Spirit" should be "new life of spirit" (small "s") as the KJV renders the terms. Paul is describing the life these Christians now had; a new life they had possessed since they were brought into Christ — the new life of the spirit into which they were raised at their baptism (6:4).

This new "relationship," according to this line of argument, is supposed to do away with an emphasis on "keeping commandments," or practicing strict or exact obedience, in order to receive God's approval. The contrast with "the oldness of the letter" is thought to establish this point. But does it? The context suggests that these words simply mean the old law. It is true, however, that our service has been brought to a higher level, and there will be plenty of evidence for this conclusion as we proceed. In this dispensation of grace there is a greater emphasis on the spiritual aspects of our worship and service.

Paul points this out in Philippians 3:3, "For we are the circumcision, which worship God in the spirit, and rejoice in Christ Jesus, and have no confidence in the flesh." Our service is different from that rendered under the law. We are not in "a legal relationship," if by this one means that we are not bound to a legal system where forgiveness of sins through the blood of Christ is not available and that there is no power under a mere law system that is sufficient to enable us to live successfully before God. But this is not what those who make this argument mean. They mean that the new law (as they would define it, of course) does not require exact obedience.

But our study already has shown otherwise. As we have seen, we are "under (the) law of Christ" (1 Cor. 9:21). See Chapter 7, "Free In Christ . . . ," 59. While the New Testament claims that the system of law has given way to a system of grace, it still affirms that only those who "do the will of the Father" will be accepted by God (Matt. 7:21-23). How could Jesus make such a statement if giving attention to details, or practicing exact obedience, no longer matters? It is one thing for us to say that man will be saved on the basis of law-keeping (perfectly keeping God's law, Gal. 3:10-13), and another to say that he will be saved on the condition of his obedience to God. The very purpose of gospel preaching is the obedience of faith (Rom. 1:5; 16:25-26).

One will not be saved on the basis of perfect law-keeping, but if he is saved he will be saved on the condition that he has obeyed the gospel of Christ (Rom. 6:17-19; 1 Pet. 4:17; 2 Thess. 1:7-9), and on the condition that he has been faithful in his service to God as a Christian (Matt. 7:21-23; 25:23; 1 Cor. 15:58; Col. 1:23; Jas. 1:25-27). God expects one to obey him even in details, and to be found *faithful* as a steward in this way (1 Cor. 4:1-5; 1 Pet. 4:10).

Oldness of Letter Vs. Newness of Spirit

Another line of argument on this subject is that our relationship to God is a covenant relationship, not a relationship based on a written code of law. Some use the statement, "for the letter killeth, but the spirit giveth life" (2 Cor. 3:6), to make this point. The false assumption in this argument is that, under the New Covenant, one cannot have a relationship based on both covenant and law, or that there is some kind of radical difference between God's New *Covenant* and his New Testament *law* today. In this case, as in many others, we have a wrong conclusion derived from a faulty interpretation of a passage of Scripture.

Again the word "spirit" should read "spirit" with a small "s" as the KJV renders it, although some versions say "Spirit." Hughes is clear on this point, when he says, "the contrast is still (as in verse 3) between what is external and what is internal; and the interpretation which we have offered is confirmed by the Apostle's use of similar terminology in Romans 2:28f., where he writes: 'He is not a Jew who is one *outwardly*; neither is that circumcision which is *outward* in the flesh: but he is a Jew who is one *inwardly*; and circumcision is that of the heart, *in the spirit, not in the letter*'" (101).

Under the New Covenant, God's work is basically that of making one new from within; this is his primary aim. Inward renewal, or making one into a new person by changing his heart, is accomplished by the gospel in a way that was not possible in and through the old law. The gospel, or New Covenant, is more adapted to this kind of work than was the law.

Even though Paul states as a matter of fact that Christians "serve in newness of spirit, not in oldness of the letter" (Rom. 7:6), there is still need for improvement once one has become a Christian. As a matter of fact, because Christians have new spirits (they have "newness of life," Rom.

6:4) from the time of their conversion (we are called "new creatures" in Christ, 2 Cor. 5:17), *as long as they keep faith in Jesus Christ,* they continue to improve in their service to God. Though Christians already are God's workmanship (Eph. 2:10), they are yet admonished to put off the old man (Col. 3:9) and put on the new man (Col. 3:10). They also are called on to be renewed in the spirit of their minds and to put on the new man which was created according to God in true righteousness and holiness (Eph. 4:21-24).

Because Christians have new spirits they now have a positive attitude toward God's law. This newness, as Cottrell points out (commenting on "newness of life" in Rom. 6:4), "results in a major change in our motivation for obedience: from 'have to' to 'want to,' from 'got to' to 'get to.' We now obey as willing slaves who have voluntarily attached ourselves as life-slaves to God because of our grateful love to him (Deut. 15:16-17)" (Cottrell *The College Press NIV Commentary: Romans* I:429).

Paul is not contrasting the external and internal aspects of a command in his use of the terms "the letter" and "the spirit." Some have argued this from this passage, and they have made it mean that in this age God is only concerned with man carrying out the *internal meaning* of a command. If this is what is meant, then to carry out the external meaning would be deadly since the passage says that the letter "killeth." Would anyone say that the command to be baptized (Acts 2:38), which is an outward act, is deadly? Or that the command to sing (Eph. 5:19) or eat the Lord's supper (Matt. 26:26-30), which are also external acts, are deadly?

In the very next verse Paul shows that what killed was that which was "written and engraven in stones," or the decalogue. In verse 9 this is called "the ministration of death" which was also written in stones (cf. vv. 3 and 7). This again was the Ten Commandments written on tables of stone at the time Moses' face shined (cf. vv. 7 and 13 with Exod. 34:27-35). The Old Covenant, which was not meant to be permanent (v. 7, "which glory was to be done away"), passed away, or has been abolished (vv. 11, 13). The New Covenant abides (v. 8 with vv. 6 and 11). So in 2 Corinthians 3 Paul is *not* contrasting the internal and external aspects of a command, but the Old Covenant with the New Covenant.

Covenant Relationship vs. Code of Law

What is meant by the statement, "our relationship to God is a covenant relationship, not a relationship based on a written code of law"? If all that were meant is that we are no longer under a legal system that requires perfect obedience, we would agree, for that is true. Where a system of grace is provided, perfect obedience is not required because forgiveness through the blood of Christ is now available. But those who make these kinds of statements usually have something quite different in mind. This becomes clear when such writers go on to say that the only kind of law we live under today is law as a "principle of action." What they mean by this and the application they usually make of it is to be taken up in the next section.

Are we in a relationship with God "based on a written code of law"? The position we are reviewing says, no, we are not under such a "code of law." But what is meant by the terms "code of law" in such statements? A law that contains commandments? A written or external law? If so, then we must strongly reject such a conclusion. *We are under a written law; even a written law that has commandments.* Yet, we also are in a new kind of spiritual relationship with God, as we have just explained. Hebrews 8:10, "I will put my laws into their mind, and write them in their hearts," does not mean that we are not under a written law today.

If by the statement "we are not under a written code of law today" one means that Christians are not under a written law that includes commandments from God, then this statement is not true. While we are not under a legal system where the only way of salvation is sinless perfection, we are under law of some kind (1 Cor. 9:21; James 1:25), *and that law is a written law.* Did not Paul tell the Corinthians, "the things that I *write* unto you are the *commandments* of the Lord" (1 Cor. 14:37)? Furthermore, if we are not under law, then there would be no such thing as sin, since sin is a transgression of God's law (1 John 3:4; Rom. 4:15). But what else could God's law be today, but those things that have been *written* by such men as Paul? To the Ephesians he said, "How that by revelation he made known unto me the mystery; (as I *wrote* afore in a few words, Whereby, when you *read*, ye may understand my knowledge in the mystery of Christ) Which in other ages was not made known unto the sons of men, as it is now revealed unto his holy apostles and prophets by the Spirit" (Eph. 3:3-5).

I have emphasized the words "wrote" and "read" in this quotation because it emphasizes the fact that even in the Christian dispensation what these men of God received by revelation would not have been conveyed to the Ephesians (nor to us, for that matter), unless it had been *written* down and passed on to them (and to us) and *read* by them (and by us). Apart from this *written* revelation we would not have God's law for us today, and without his *written* law (since this is the only law God has conveyed to us) there would be no sin, because sin is a transgression of law. And, allow me to ask for the sake of emphasis: Are we not also under law *that has commands*, commands that *must* be obeyed, and obeyed *exactly* as they are revealed?

On this subject, what do these words from Peter tell us:

> Wherefore, beloved, seeing that ye look for such things (such things as, the heavens being on fire and dissolved, and looking for new heavens and a new earth — *ww*), be diligent that ye may be found of him in peace, without spot, and blameless. And account that the longsuffering of our Lord is salvation; even as our beloved brother Paul also according to the wisdom given unto him hath written unto you; as also in all his epistles, speaking in them of these things; in which are some things hard to be understood, which the unlearned and unstable wrest, as they do the other scriptures, unto their own destruction. Ye therefore, beloved, seeing ye know these things before, beware lest ye also, being led away with the error of the wicked, fall from your own steadfastness. But grow in grace, and in the knowledge of our Lord and Saviour Jesus Christ. To him be glory both now and forever. Amen (2 Pet. 3:14-18).

If the law we are under today is only a "principle of action," the principle of love, and not a law that is written down, how are we to account for the "error" Peter is warning these brethren against? Was the "error" that threatened these brethren that they might fail to love as they ought; fail to "love" either God or their fellow man? The careful reader will note that Peter does not say anything, not even one word, about love anywhere in this warning. The danger was not failure to love, as though the only law they were under was the "principle of love," but failure to heed *teaching* that they had received from Paul on the very subject Peter is here *writing* to them about in his own *letters*. Paul had also *written* on this same subject in all of his *epistles*. We are indeed under a *written* law today — written law that requires *strict* obedience!

System of Law Vs. System of Faith

What made the law of Moses a "legal system"? It was not that God demanded that Israel keep *all* of it. Nor was it because it was a "code of laws." The law of Moses was a legal system because *apart from Christ* the only way one could be justified under it was to *actually keep* all of its laws. If one were to ask, what is the difference between the two systems, a system of law, like the law of Moses, and the law of faith, like we have in the New Testament, what would the answer be? Simply put, *the answer is Christ and his sacrifice.* Under the gospel, keeping God's law perfectly is not required *because one can find forgiveness in and through the blood of Christ.* This provision for sins was not offered to man *while he lived under the old law and under the terms of that law.* If man were to be justified by law while he was under such a system, he had to keep it all. In other words, once a person under that law became a lawbreaker there was no way provided *in the law itself, and on the basis of what was provided in that law,* whereby he could be forgiven. This is what made the law a legal system.

Though God still deals with man through "law," it is not a *law system* like that just described. Since it is not law itself that makes a system a legal system, there is no contradiction between law and grace. This is not the meaning of the statement, "grace and truth came by Jesus Christ" (John 1:17). Paul affirms that we are "saved by grace through faith" (Eph. 2:8), and that, "after faith has come, we are no longer under a tutor" (Gal. 3:25), which is the law. The law had served a good purpose in bringing man to Christ that he might be saved through him, but it had served its purpose and was therefore set aside once "faith," or the system of faith, had come. This faith, or system of faith, has taken the place of the system of law known as the law of Moses.

In the present age we have come to what is called "faith" — what we may describe as a system of faith as contrasted with the former system of law. It nonetheless is a system that involves law. This is verified by the fact that Paul says that he was "under (the) *law* of Christ" (1 Cor. 9:21), and James speaks of "a perfect *law* of liberty" (Jas. 1:25). See Chapter 7, *Free In Christ* for a discussion of these verses.

A few verses before Paul's statement that since faith has come we are no longer under the law (Gal. 3:25), he had discussed how man had been brought under a curse by the law. His statement is important because he describes for us how it was that the law became a curse for those who were under it:

> For as many as are of the works of the law are under the curse; for it is written, *"Cursed is everyone who does not continue in all things which are written in the book of the law, to do them."* But that no one is justified by the law in the sight of God is evident, for *"the just shall live by faith."* Yet the law is not of faith, but *"the man who does them shall live by them."* Christ has redeemed us from the curse of the law, having become a curse for us (for it is written, *"Cursed is everyone who hangs on a tree,"* Gal. 3:10-13, NKJV).

These verses give a perfect contrast between the two systems involved, the system of law and the system of faith. These are systems wherein men seek justification before God. Those who "are of the works of the law" seek justification on the basis of perfect obedience. But this system is doomed to failure. The reason one cannot be saved on this basis is that no one keeps the law perfectly. Once one has failed, or he has sinned against God, the law he has violated condemns him. Paul quotes from the Old Testament to show that the law itself pronounced all to be under its curse as a result of their failure to keep it.

The other system is that of faith, "for the just shall live by faith." This is a quotation from Habakkuk 2:4. As used in this passage, it is describing how one is accepted as righteous before God. The word "faith," as used here, means trust, confidence, plus conviction. It is placing one's trust in Jesus Christ (John 8:28), believing in the power of God, in the conviction that God has raised him from the dead (Col. 2:12). It represents man as being just before God as a result of taking God at his word and habitually doing what God says.

The law system, Paul says, "is not of faith." How could it be when it does not envision justification on the basis of forgiveness through faith? To follow a law system, or attempt to be justified on the basis of perfect obedience, is to assume that one is not a law-breaker, for once one breaks the law then the only way to be justified is through forgiveness, and this is to be saved by grace through faith. This involves admitting that one is a sinner and in need of God's grace, and then seeking his favor through faith in Jesus Christ. Paul explains in verse 13 how Christ did for man what the law had not done: "Christ hath redeemed us from the curse of the law, being made a curse for us."

The only thing a law system can do is condemn, or pronounce as guilty, the one who breaks the law under that system. It holds him under this curse without the hope of being redeemed from its condemnation. But through the system of faith, Jesus became a curse for us, he took our place, he suffered in our stead, and in this way redeemed us from the curse of condemnation brought upon us by our sin (Rom. 3:23-26; 2 Cor. 5:21; Gal. 3:10-13; 1 Pet. 2:20-22). With Paul we cry out, "I thank God through Jesus Christ our Lord" (Rom. 7:25), and "thanks be unto God for his unspeakable gift" (2 Cor. 9:15)!

Chapter 9

What Is the Law of Christ?

The Meaning of "Law"

On the question, "What is the law of Christ?" the definition of the term "law" becomes significant. If one begins with the assumption that the term always means a "principle of action" when used in connection with Christ's law, then "the law of love" would be the most appropriate answer to the question. But this is not the only meaning of this term as it is used in the New Testament to describe the law of Christ. We have shown already in the previous chapter that the word "law" in the phrase "perfect law of liberty" in James 1:25 is used interchangeably with the "word of truth" and the "engrafted word," or the gospel of our salvation, in James 1:18 and 1:21 respectively. This "law of liberty," which is the law of Christ, is not merely the law of love.

When one is begotten "with the word of truth" (Jas. 1:18), and he continues to "receive with meekness the engrafted word, which is able to save your souls" (Jas. 1:21), whatever terms he is *obeying* to make this possible are terms that are part of "the perfect law of liberty" mentioned in James 1:25. Notice what is said of the "law" James is describing in this verse. This "law":

- *begets* ("begat he us with the word of truth," v. 18),
- is *heard* ("swift to hear," v. 19; also v. 23),
- is *received* ("receive with meekness the engrafted word," v. 21),
- is *obeyed* ("be ye doers of the word," v. 22; also v. 25, a "doer of the work"),
- and is *intently studied* ("looketh into the perfect law of liberty," v. 25).

Doesn't sound like a mere "principle of action," or the law of love, does it? Clearly this is a *law* which serves as an *objective standard outside of one's self*. It contains commands, teachings, examples, principles, etc. that may be studied, received and obeyed. It is made up of truths that have been either spoken or written down so that one may listen to them — or read them — and study them carefully, and he may receive them immediately so that he may pattern his life according to them.

Paul calls upon his brethren in Ephesus to "walk circumspectly" (Eph. 5:15). Interestingly, the word used here is the same word used by Paul to describe his own conduct under the law. The word signifies an "accurate" and a "strict" walking. In Acts 22:3 Paul says he was brought up in Jerusalem "at the feet of Gamaliel, and taught according to the *perfect manner* of the law of the fathers. . . ." The word rendered "perfect manner" in this verse is the same word rendered "circumspectly" in Ephesians 5:15. Isn't it strange that, if God has not given Christians a law that must be strictly obeyed, Paul would use the exact word in both places — a word that means "precisely," "strictly," and a word used by Paul to describe his own manner of life under the law of Moses. Sounds like Paul is requiring of Christians that they first *exercise great care* in learning their duty and then that they do the *exact* will of God.

To be under the teaching of Christ and his apostles is to be under the law of God and the law of Christ. As Christians we are always within the compass of God's law for instruction and for subjection. Paul describes himself as one who is "not without law to God, but under the law to Christ" (1 Cor. 9:21). A literal rendering of this expression is, "not being without (the) law of God but under (the) law of Christ." There is no justifiable reason for making the "law" in this passage mean only a "principle of action," or the law of love.

This term does not have this meaning when Paul contrasts those who are "under law" (v. 20) with those who are "without law" (v. 21a) in the same context. It is clear that he is contrasting Jews with Gentiles, the former being under law (the law of Moses) and the latter being without law (the law of Moses). Does he mean that the Jews were under the law of love (law as a "principle of action") and the Gentiles were not under this law as a "principle of action"? Clearly he is not using the term "law" in this way. When he says he (now as a Christian) is not under the law (v. 20, "not being myself under law"), he means the old law. But when he adds, "not being without (the) law of God but under (the) law of Christ," does he mean, not under the old law but under a "principle of action," the law of love? The context does not favor this conclusion.

Christ the Lawgiver
Christ's law is within the scope of God's authority, so to be under the

law of Christ is to be under the law of God (1 Cor. 9:21, "being not without law to God, but under [the] law of Christ"). Christ is God's spokesman today, he is God's lawgiver as announced by Moses (Deut. 18:15-18). This promise from Moses points out that God would speak to his people through this prophet like unto Moses. Here are God's own words to Moses: "I will raise up a Prophet from among their brethren, like unto thee, and will put my words in his mouth; and he shall speak unto them all that I shall command him" (v. 18). All would be required to "hearken" unto this prophet like unto Moses (v. 15). To those who would not heed God's words revealed through this prophet, God said, "I will require it of him" (v. 19).

Peter applies these words to Christ in Acts 3:20-23: "And shall send Jesus which before was preached unto you: whom the heaven must receive until the times of restitution of all things, which God hath spoken by the mouth of all his holy prophets since the world began. For Moses truly said unto the fathers, A prophet shall the Lord your God raise up unto you of your brethren, like unto me; him shall ye hear in all things whatsoever he shall say unto you. And it shall come to pass, that every soul, which will not hear that prophet, shall be destroyed from among the people."

"Him shall ye hear in all things"! Why? Because he is God's prophet, God's spokesman, the new lawgiver. The "law" to be revealed through this new lawgiver consisted of the "all things" spoken by him. Moses had his law, and now Christ has his law. Just as Moses was God's spokesman or lawgiver in the former time, Christ is God's spokesman and lawgiver today. "God, who at sundry times and in divers manners spake in time past unto the fathers by the prophets, hath in these last days spoken unto us by his Son . . ." (Heb. 1:1-2a). In contrast to Moses, the great lawgiver, and Elijah, representing the Old Testament prophets, God announced from heaven, "This is my beloved Son, in whom I am well pleased; hear ye him" (Matt. 17:5).

New Testament Use of "the Law"
Christ has mediated God's new law to man. It is only in this sense that he may be considered as lawgiver, since this is a role assigned to God alone in James 4:12. But Christ's law is not merely a "principle of action," the law of love; nor is it a mere "code of law." Even "the law" of the Old Testament period was not always thought of as a mere "code of law" by those who refer to it in the New Testament. Jesus sometimes referred to "the law" when he had something other that the legal code of that law in mind. "The law" included not only Moses' "code" writings, but other kinds of writings as well. Take the writings thought to have been written by Moses, such as the book of Genesis, as an example. They are sometimes referred

to by New Testament writers as a part of "the law" (Gal. 4:21-22, 23-31; possibly also 1 Cor. 14:34 [Gen. 3:16?]).

This is also true of other parts of the Old Testament. "The law" that "came by Moses" that is put in contrast with "grace and truth" that "came by Jesus Christ" in John 1:17 is probably a reference to the Pentateuch, or the first five books of the Old Testament. The Psalms also were at times referred to and quoted in the New Testament and identified as "the law" (John 10:34-36; Rom. 3:10-12, 13, 14 with v. 19). The same is true of the Prophets (1 Cor. 14:21). If the Psalms and Prophets are thought of as part of "the law," the symbolism of the book of Revelation should pose no problem. There is some symbolic language in the books of the Prophets, not unlike what one finds in the book of Revelation. Since these books contained this kind of language and yet they were judged to be acceptable as a part of "the law" by New Testament writers, we should have no trouble accepting a book like Revelation as belonging to the law of Christ.

It appears that by Jesus' time, and likely at even a much earlier period, the Jews had come to see the entire Old Testament in this way. Some think that Jesus refers to the entire Old Testament Scriptures under the terms used in Luke 24:25-27. He first spoke of all that the prophets had said concerning the necessity of his death and the glory that would follow (vv. 25-26). Following this, Luke says, "Then beginning with Moses and with all the prophets, he explained to them the things concerning Himself in all the Scriptures" (v. 27, NASB). This indicates that there were parts of Scripture beyond what was found in the writings of Moses and the prophets. A little later, in discussing this same subject, Jesus spoke of "the Law of Moses and the Prophets and the Psalms" (Luke 24:44, NASB). Sometimes the terms "the law and the prophets" refer to the whole Old Testament writings (Luke 16:16).

How Jesus Used "the Law"

In arguing that the principle of love is all there is to Christ's law, one brother who rejects the idea that the entire New Testament is Christ's law, asked the following questions: "Then, is the account of the birth and temptation of Jesus the law of Christ? What of the love chapter, the resurrection chapter, and Revelation? Are these all parts of the law of Christ?" (*Free In Christ* 27). This man's own answers to these questions are given in this statement from him: "The law of Christ is not a book, a listing, or a code of laws. Where is a catalog of laws? The Jews enumerated 613 laws in their legal code. How many laws has Christ given us? Since we are to keep the law of Christ, surely someone has counted and listed those laws so we will have a check-list! Where is such a list?" (27).

The question on whether such events as the birth and temptation of Christ, the love and resurrection chapters, and the book of Revelation, could be considered as part of the "law" of Christ, can be answered affirmatively in the same way that one would answer the question, "Is the birth of Moses a part of the *law* of Moses." The answer would be, "yes," since the Pentateuch is most likely referred to as "the law" in John 1:17. In fact, the whole Old Testament is called "the law and the prophets" in Luke 16:16.

Historical events such as Christ's temptation and resurrection from the dead recorded in the New Testament by different writers would be historical incidents in the same way that Old Testament writers include certain historical incidents about various individuals, and of Israel as a nation, in their writings. The latter events were considered to be a part the Old Testament which is called "law" by New Testament writers. We will see beginning in the next paragraph that when Jesus used "what is written" to respond to the temptations put before him, he found no problem in citing events from the historical books of the Old Testament — books like Deuteronomy which was a part of the Pentateuch, and a part of what New Testament writers considered to be "the law."

The Temptation Story
Jesus lived under "the law" (Gal. 4:4), and as a Jew he kept the law and taught others to keep it. But he did not merely look to the "law codes" of the Old Testament for guidance. There was much in "the law," or the Old Testament Scriptures, which he looked to for guidance. This is well illustrated in the temptation account recorded in the gospels (Matt. 4:1-11; Luke 4:3-12). Here we find Jesus relying upon what was "written," but notice how he appealed to different kinds of Scripture from "the law" in his responses to the different temptations put before him. We will give emphasis to the first temptation because it teaches some important truths about how examples were considered to be a part of "the law."

1. The First Temptation. First, Jesus quotes Deuteronomy 8:3, "It is written, Man shall not live by bread alone, but by every word that proceedeth out of the mouth of God" (Matt. 4:4). The quotation is from "the law," since we have seen that this is how New Testament writers sometimes refer to this part of the Old Testament. But even though the quotation is from a part of Scripture that was written by Moses, and a part of "the law," we may well ask, was this a "code" law? And the answer clearly is, no. In its Old Testament setting it is a mere statement of intention. It shows what God had intended for Israel to learn from their wilderness experiences when he withheld manna from them: "And he humbled thee, and suffered thee to hunger, and fed thee with manna, which thou knewest not, neither did thy fathers know; *that he might make thee know* that man doth not live by bread alone, but by every word that proceedeth out of the mouth of the Lord doth man live" (Deut. 8:3, emphasis mine — *ww*).

Moses calls upon Israel to *remember* this experience and the lesson God had planned they would learn from it. He actually offers it as an *example* from their past history, which if they would remember it, they would be helped to do "all the commandments" which he was that day commanding them to "observe and do" (Deut. 8:1). The importance of remembering such events is brought out in verse 2, "And thou shalt remember all the way which the Lord thy God led thee these forty years in the wilderness, to humble thee, and to prove thee. . . ."

Let no one say, then, that *example* cannot be a part of law. Jesus used this example, and the lesson God had planned to teach Israel in dealing with them during their forty years of wandering in the wilderness, to help him resist the first temptation. McGarvey says, in fact, that "Jesus finds in this a precedent for himself. He, too, had been led by God into a wilderness where there was no bread, and he was now suffering from consequent hunger. The duty of Israel is now his duty, for his circumstances are like theirs" (*Matthew* 41).

This is a significant point to note, especially when we consider how some insist (as we noted earlier) that *examples* do not belong to "law." Yet, Jesus gets from "the law" under which he lived an *example* which he himself follows. It is an example that was used to help Israel learn dependence upon God by respecting his word as the source of their spiritual nourishment. Such examples from the Old Testament law are also helpful to Christians. They are used by Paul to warn Christians to be careful in their walk, lest they also fall away as many of the people of God did in the former times (1 Cor. 10:6, 11).

Other New Testament writers do the same thing. Some examples they give are examples of encouragement (Heb. 11), and others are examples of warning (Heb. 3:12-4:13; 2 Pet. 2:4-10). From the book of Genesis, which was a part of "the law," Paul cites Abraham as an example of one who was justified by faith (Rom. 4), and James uses him as an example of one who was justified by works (Jas. 2:21). Jesus refers to some from the patriarchal period as examples of warning to encourage us always to be ready for his coming (Matt. 24:36-41). Peter also cites the destruction of the world in the days of Noah and the destruction of the cities of Sodom and Gomorrah (2 Pet. 2:5-6).

Question: *If examples were a part of what was considered to be "law" in the Old Testament, how would it be inconsistent or out of place for those who are under the law of Christ to take* **examples from his law** *as a pattern for them today?*

2. The Second and Third Temptations. Second, in the second and third temptations Jesus appeals to direct commands from Deuteronomy 6:16 (Matt. 4:7) and Deuteronomy 6:13 (Matt. 4:10). They are found in what our Lord and New Testament writers call "law," yet these commands are not taken from the part of the Old Testament where such commands would be considered a part of a "code of law." Most of the book of Deuteronomy is a record of a sermon delivered by Moses to Israel shortly before his death. He has much to say about their past experiences during their forty years of wanderings in the wilderness, but often he is pointing back to their failures and the lessons they should have learned from these experiences. He covers such matters in an attempt to prepare them to be faithful to the Lord once they have entered the promised land.

We find that *commands* were a part of God's "law" before "faith" (the system of faith) came, and they are a part of Christ's "law" since "faith" (the system of faith) has come. The fact that in the Old Testament they were found in sermons, or interspersed into historical incidents, or even in historical documents such as the books of Numbers or Deuteronomy, does not in any way diminish or take away from their authoritativeness. A command is a command, and it doesn't matter whether it comes from a "code of laws," such as the laws revealed on Mt. Siani, or in some other way. In fact, we might well ask here, what makes commands or instructions handed down from God a "code of law"?

Should the three stipulations laid down by the apostles for the Gentiles in Acts 15:20 and sent out to the churches in the form of a letter (Acts 15:22-29) be classified in this way? It is a "list" of things. Is this what makes something a "code of law"? There are rules or guidelines that must be followed. Does this make them a "code of law"? These stipulations were to be received by the various churches and enforced upon the Gentiles when receiving them into the churches. Was this establishing a "legal system" in the church? How is one establishing a "legal system" when he uses examples and commands as a pattern for his life when this is the very method Jesus himself used? Was Jesus a legalist just because he found examples and commands from the "law" he was under to use as a guide as he responded to the tempter?

What about *implication* or *necessary inference*? Does Jesus ever employ this method of establishing a point of truth from "the law"? As a matter of fact he does. His appeal to Scripture in each of the assaults put forth by Satan "implied" certain conclusions that he had reached and which should be understood by the tempter. The arguments which he made in response to the Pharisees' objection to his disciples plucking grain on the Sabbath day also include this method of argument (Matt.12:1-9). Is it not "necessarily inferred" that, since they accepted David even though he *had* violated the law, they should also accept the disciples who *had not* violated the law of the Sabbath?

Another example of this kind is found in Jesus' response to the Sadducees' objection to a resurrection from the dead in Matthew 22:23-33. Their position, he said, denied both Scripture and the power of God (v. 29). "But as touching the resurrection of the dead," he asks, "have ye not read that which was spoken unto you by God, saying, I am the God of Abraham, and the God of Isaac, and the God of Jacob? God is not the God of the dead, but of the living" (vv. 31-32). What Jesus expected them *to conclude* from his statement was that there will be a resurrection from the dead. Though it is not certain exactly how Jesus expected them to draw this conclusion, it is clear that this is the conclusion they came to, for the text says, "when the multitude heard this, they were astonished at his doctrine" (v. 33). The Pharisees also "heard that he had put the Sadducees to silence" (v. 34), meaning that Jesus had been successful in his argument against them. Yet it was an argument from "implication."

What was the "implication," or what was "necessarily inferred" in his statement? God's use of the present tense — "I *am*," not "I was the God of Abraham," etc. — and Jesus' added statement, "God is not the God of the dead, but of the living," merely showed that these three patriarchs had survived death; they were yet alive (their spirits had lived on) after death. But from this the Sadducees *inferred necessarily* that there will be a resurrection from the dead.

McGarvey suggests that the reason they accepted Jesus' argument as sufficient to establish a resurrection from the dead was due to their understanding of the relationship that exists between the body and the spirit: "for human spirits, having been originally created for the exercise of their powers through the organs of a body must, unless their original nature be changed, which is an inadmissable supposition because unsupported by evidence, be dependent for their highest enjoyment on the possession of a body. This being so, the continued existence of spirits after the death of the body creates a demand for a resurrection of the body, and the Sadducees were philosophical enough to see this" (*Matthew* 192).

In light of Jesus' use of examples and commands, and necessary infer-ences from "the law," why would we not expect to find something similar to this when we come to the teaching of Christ for his disciples, and the practice of the church when we come to Acts and the epistles? Christ's life (Acts 1:1-3), including his example (John 13:13-15; Phil. 2:5f; 1 Pet. 2:21-23) and teaching (Acts 1:1, "all that Jesus began to do and teach"), as well as the example (Phil. 3:17; 4:9) and teaching (1 Cor. 4:17; 14:37; Phil. 4:9) of his apostles and prophets (Matt. 17:6-8; Eph. 2:20; 3:3-5; with John 14:26 ; 16:13; 1 Cor. 2:6-13) are also a part of Christ's law.

No Appearance of a "Code of Law"

It is no valid objection to say, "But the New Testament does not have the appearance of a 'code of law.'" Neither does most of the Old Testament. Yet those parts that were not written as "a code of law" were still called "law," and Jesus used examples, direct commands, and implications from these parts of the Old Testament law as his own pattern, or to teach others on certain subjects. Those who don't like to hear people quote Bible for their practices need to take another look at Jesus in the hour of temptation. He quoted Scripture to Satan to show him that the course he was suggest-ing in each of the temptations placed before him would not be the proper thing for him to do.

We need to remember that there are "lists" of certain sins appearing here and there in the New Testament (Rom. 1:28-32; 1 Cor. 6:9-11; Gal. 5:19-21). There are also "lists" of things to be put off and things to be put on as Christians (Eph. 4:22-32; Col. 3:8-14; 2 Pet. 1:5-11). To say that there is no one "codified" list means that the New Testament is not "law" overlooks the fact that one does not have to have this before he has law. This has been demonstrated from the way Jesus and New Testament writers used the term "law" in speaking of the Old Testament.

There are also places in the New Testament where a whole series of direct commands are given, one right after the other. Jesus gives such a list in Luke 6:27-38. In showing what love does, he includes things like love your enemies, bless them that curse you, give to those who ask of you, be merciful and judge not, and be liberal in giving.

In giving regulations for gatherings where spiritual gifts were being ex-ercised, Paul commanded the Corinthians, "Let all things be done unto edifying. If any man speak in an unknown tongue, let it be by two, or at the most by three, and that by course; and let one interpret. But if there be no interpreter, let him keep silence in the church; and let him speak to himself, and to God. Let the prophets speak two or three, and let the other judge"

(14:26b-29). More instructions are added in the verses that follow. Toward the close of this section Paul claims authority for what he writes, when he says, "the things I write unto you are the commandments of the Lord" (v. 37).

Is this series of commandments a "code of law"? For sure, they were to be obeyed. Why else would they be given? Are these commands merely "love directives," or are they something else? Did the church at Corinth have to follow these commands *exactly as written*, or were they "free" to treat them as they chose? If they had to follow them exactly, would this make them "lawful regulations"? If lawful regulations, would this not make them law?

Those who write against taking the New Testament as a "code of law" today are opposing taking *any* direct command in the New Testament as binding *just because it is commanded*, and yet these commands were given by those who had authority to bind and loose (Matt. 16:19; 18:18). None, so far as I know, would make the same application to the initial terms of obedience in becoming Christians. Is the command to repent and be baptized for the remission of sins in Acts 2:38, for example, binding just because an inspired apostle said it, or are there other factors that must be taken into consideration before one would accept it as binding — such as whether or not we look at it as a command of law, or as a love directive? The same question may be raised about any command found in the New Testament.

Under the Law of Christ

Paul has much more in mind in 1 Corinthians 9:21 when he says he is under the law of Christ than Christ's teaching on love. He is acknowledging Christ's lordship, but he also is describing Christ's role as lawgiver. He knew that all men must appear before Christ as judge and give account of their lives before him (Acts 17:30-31; Rom. 2:16; 14:10-12; 2 Cor. 5:10). This would not be the case if he were not the lawgiver.

God will judge the world in righteousness, but it will be "by that man whom he hath ordained; whereof he hath given assurance unto all men, in that he hath raised him from the dead" (Acts 17:31). Peter affirmed at the house of Cornelius that not only had Jesus commanded them "to preach unto the people," but that they also were "to testify that it is he which was ordained of God to be the Judge of quick and dead" (Acts 10:42). Jesus also pointed out concerning himself as the Son of man that not only had the Father given him to have life in himself, but he "hath given him authority to execute judgment also, because he is the Son of man" (John 5:26-27).

But what is to be the basis or standard for his judgment? Is it not the "law" made known by the lawgiver as described in James 4:11? The law by which man will be judged is the law laid down by the one who shall do the judging. For man this side of Calvary this is Jesus Christ. Jesus himself says it will be his own word that will judge us in the last day: "He that rejecteth me, and receiveth not my words, hath one that judgeth him: the word that I have spoken the same shall judge him in the last day" (John 12:48).

The specific law within God's law (Jas. 4:11does not say "the law"; James is not speaking to Jews, but Christians) that condemns slander (James 4:11) is not all that one violates when he slanders someone. Such a law is only one part of the law of God — the one James is dealing with here. James, however, is showing that when one commits such a sin he is in transgression against *the authority of law in general*, and therefore against God. To slander or run down a brother is to run down law. This shows that to break law by going against some specific requirement, or some specific prohibition contained in it, is to lift oneself above the lawgiver himself.

Carson summarizes the Christian's responsibility under Christ's law as it is described in 1 Corinthians 9:21 in this way: "Whatever Christ demands of him as a new-covenant believer, a Christian, binds him; he cannot step outside those constraints. There is a rigid limit to his flexibility as he seeks to win the lost from different cultural and religious groups; he must not do anything that is forbidden to the Christian, and he must do everything mandated of the Christian. He is not free from God's law; he is under Christ's law" (*The Cross and Christian Ministry* 119-120).

Will a Christian give account of himself as one who lives under, and is subject to, the law of Christ? Several passages of Scripture clearly speak of a final judgment that will include Christians (Rom. 14:10-13; 2 Cor. 5:10; Jas. 4:11-12). As pointed out already, James 4:11-12 shows that we are to be judged by the law of the one who does the judging. The thoughts, words, and deeds of each person will be remembered (except those which God has chosen not to remember through forgiveness, Heb. 8:12), so that each will be judged according to his or her works (2 Cor. 5:10; Rev. 20:12). Since sin is a transgression of law (1 John 3:4), and without law there is no transgression (Rom. 4:15), and since the judgment will be for what we have done "both good and bad" (2 Cor. 5:10), by what other standard but "law" could one be judged for what is "bad," or sinful?

Chapter 10

The Principle of Love and the Law of Christ

Are we under only a principle of action, that of love; love which God in his grace "infuses" into our hearts (Rom. 5:5) and thereby enables us to fulfill the law (Rom. 13:8f)? Some would say, yes, and they would say further that this law of love frees us, whereas a legal code enslaves. Galatians 5:1 and 5:13f are cited as proof of this conclusion. Hebrews 8:10, "I will put my laws into their mind, and write them in their heart," is also used to make this point.

Man has always been under the law of love, both under the First Covenant (Deut. 30:20) and the Second Covenant (Matt. 22:36f.; Rom. 13:8f). One reason for this is that God has always been love (1 John 4:8; 4:16). The New Testament, however, provides a fuller revelation of God as love, and it gives a more detailed picture of what it means for man to practice love toward God and his fellow man.

Jesus describes the law of love as embracing love to God and love to man when he points to the two greatest commandments of the law (Matt. 22:36-39). After citing these commandments, he says, "On these two commandments hang all the law and the prophets" (Matt. 22:40). J.W. McGarvey explained how these two commandments relate to each other in this way: "There is a tacit comparison of these two commandments to the hook in the wall on which are hung all the books of the law and the prophets. As the hook supports all, so to keep these two commandments is to do all that is required by the Scriptures. He who loves God as required will keep all of God's commandments, and he who loves his neighbor will fulfill every obligation to his neighbor" (*Matthew* 193).

Man becomes a lawbreaker because he fails to love as he ought. If he loved as he is commanded, he would not break God's law as he does. Love is the foundation on which all of the other commands of God are based. One cannot love and neglect the other commandments because they are all based upon love to God and love to his neighbor. Yet, it is also true, that when one loves God and man as he ought, man is careful to observe the other commandments. In a sense the other commandments are simply applications to concrete situations of these two laws.

Exactly how love relates to law, and how one comes to have this love, are subjects of great interest to all Bible students. They are also subjects about which good people have differed. Some would say that how law relates to love, and how man comes to have love, are the basic differences between the two systems of law and grace. Some would use this very point to suggest that it is only through love that one is set free. When one comes to serve God out of love, then and only then, the argument goes, does he have the freedom promised to him in the New Testament and made available to him through Jesus Christ.

Much of what is said here can be accepted by most brethren whatever their understanding of the subject of "law" in the New Testament may be. All will likely agree that love has been the key to success under both dispensations, that of Moses and that of Christ. But how one comes to love, how love comes to an individual, what is the basic difference in the two systems with respect to love, and how love relates to the law of Christ, are all important aspects of this subject. The way the argument is sometimes developed, and the application made of the argument, is troublesome to many who have worked with this subject. We will now take up the basic elements of the argument and discuss them one by one.

Love "Infused" Into Our Hearts?
Love, it is claimed, is received by a process of "infusion." It is sometimes maintained that God puts love into one's heart *directly* by the Holy Spirit. Romans 5:5 is the passage most often used as proof of this point: "And hope maketh not ashamed; because the love of God is shed abroad in our hearts by the Holy Ghost which is given unto you."

1. Whose Love? First, we should consider, whose love is being described in this passage? Clearly it is God's love for man, not man's love for God and his neighbor.

2. The Context. Second, how does Paul use this statement in its context? Again, the answer is not hard to find. He has been describing some of the blessings that come to those who are the children of God. These include peace with God through Jesus Christ, rejoicing in glory yet to come, and steadfastness of character through tribulations (vv. 1-4). Steadfastness gives one hope which makes one confident with what God has in store for him as a Christian. This hope will not be disappointing (v. 5a). The basic reason given is that God has revealed his love to the Christian through the Holy Spirit which he has given to him. Paul points out in verse 5 that the reason one's hope will not disappoint him is that God has given him the Holy Spirit who has shed abroad God's love into his heart. Such knowledge of God's love for him is essential to his well being as a Christian. This gift of the Spirit is given as a pledge from God (2 Cor. 1:21-22; 2 Cor. 5:5; cf. Eph. 1:13, "sealed with the Holy Spirit of promise").

3. God's Love Demonstrated. In view of this stated purpose of verse 5, it should be obvious that the verse is not meant to tell man *how he receives love* for God and his neighbor, *but how God has shown his love for him.* Neither does this verse say that God's love is "infused" into man's heart. The word for "shed abroad" (KJV) does not mean "infused." It means "poured out." The statement reminds one of Joel's promise that in the last days God would "pour out" his Spirit upon all flesh (Joel 2:28f). This outpouring of the Spirit began on Pentecost (Acts 2:17). Hamilton suggests that "the metaphorical sense indicates that there is an abundant and free giving of the love of God through the giving of the Holy Spirit" (307). This gift is a manifestation of God's love that is put into one's heart. It describes the abundant and free giving of the Holy Spirit to Christians; a figurative pouring out, if you will, of love by God through this gift of the Spirit to man.

John says "we love him, because he first loved us" (1 John 4:19). God's love for us was first, and his love serves as a motive for us to respond in love for him. But there is no suggestion in the verse, or any other verse, for that matter, that such love is directly "infused" into man's heart by the Holy Spirit. It merely describes the demonstration of God's love for us in the giving of the Spirit to man, a gift that moves Christians upon receiving such a gift to love him in return. Romans 5:5 illustrates only one way in which God has manifested his love for us, i.e., in giving us the Spirit.

4. Spirit Received into Heart. The gift of the Spirit, the expression of God's love for us as Christians, is received into our hearts. The word "heart" refers to man's inner self, the conscious inner life of the person. Thus it means the soul or mind as the fountain and seat of the thoughts, passions, desires, appetites, affections, purposes, and endeavors. When describing this love that God has for us as being shed abroad in our hearts by the Spirit most commentators focus entirely upon a subjective experience of some kind. Even some brethren who interpret this word to mean that God's love is "infused" into our hearts have in mind a direct imparting of God's love independently of the word of God. Even though love for God and man is the foundation of all true obedience to God, and love helps lift our service to God to a higher level, there is no evidence in Scripture that God directly "infuses" this love into our hearts.

Love As the Fulfilment of Law

The argument is made that love fulfills God's requirements (Rom. 13:8f) and thereby frees us, whereas a legal code enslaves. One brother in making this argument on love being a fulfillment of law asks these questions: What greater and more comprehensive law — principle of action — could we want? How would a listing of authoritative demands help a person show love? These questions are intended to show how love brings to pass, or accomplishes, what law cannot do; it frees us to carry out God's commands. Matthew 22:37f is brought in to show that the law and the prophets were attempting all along to help us love God and one another, and that God has shown us how to express that love through commands, exhortations, teachings, principles, and examples.

Though I find myself in basic agreement with what is said here, it does raise some questions on the subject of commands that should be considered. It is the reason that is given for these things that is not readily acceptable. Take the question, how do such things as commands, exhortations, teachings, etc. relate to love? Is it wrong to think of commands, exhortations, and teachings which come from God as *lawful requirements*? What is the difference in seeing them as lawful requirements and seeing them as *directives to love*?

Some, as no doubt our readers will know by now, are maintaining that commands, examples, principles, etc. are given only as the directives of love, or for the purpose of inciting man's response to grace, and not as "lawful requirements." Lawful requirements, according to this view, only lead to arguments and divisions. Surely all must agree that love must be the central motive for all our actions. None would question that the command to love is the foundation of all other commands. Without love we are nothing (1 Cor. 13:2). So there is not a point of difference on this aspect of the subject.

But this is not the issue that divides us. The problem, and the main point of difference on this subject, is *making love the only command*. Those who *argue* (note this word, please) that "lawful requirements" only lead to arguments and divisions assume, as one can see, that lawful requirements and love do not belong together. This is simply not the case. One wonders how the problem of arguments and divisions among God's people would be solved by reducing all commands, examples and principles to one law by saying that Christ's law is love and his only laws (plural) are to love God and one's neighbor? *Has not this very conclusion, or interpretation* (we could even say, *argument!*), *over this command produced more arguments and divisions?*

When one considers all the applications that have been made, and all the conclusions that have been drawn, as a result of this interpretation of the law of love, isn't it true that these applications and conclusions that have grown out of this hermeneutical method have themselves given rise to more arguments and divisions among brethren? Instead of solving the problem of divisions, it has just given one more reason to perpetuate them.

Another serious problem introduced by this interpretation of the law of love is that *it is meant to minimize the role of commands, examples, and principles found in Scripture, and in the end it annuls the authority of these ways of establishing exactly what God's will is from the word of God.* This means that by following this path, supposition, opinion, and the traditions of men have become just as authoritative as clearly stated commands, examples, and principles found in God's word.

Jesus and the Sabbath Law

Those who adopt this way of handling the word of God believe that the law of love gives them the "right" to exalt love *above* God's law and to act on their own feelings on what would be appropriate at a given moment. Some think Jesus' rejection of the Pharisees' interpretation of the Sabbath law is an example in point. They affirm that what Jesus teaches in response to the Pharisees on this subject shows that he denied "the arbitrary nature of law, declaring that there is something greater than law," that is, love or mercy.

The arguments advanced from Jesus on this subject usually run parallel with those made by the advocates of situation ethics. By employing the situation ethics argument in exalting love above law in given situations some of these brethren have been found trying to justify even lying and murder, including suicide and abortion. This approach to the interpretation of Scripture will lead one to set aside clear declarations of God's word on any number of things.

At this point in our study of this subject a very important question arises: Does Jesus deny "the arbitrary nature of law" by exalting love above law? Those who would affirm that commands in the New Testament are "directives of love" and not "lawful requirements" contend that this is what Jesus did when he condemned the Pharisees for their objection to his disciples plucking grain on the Sabbath (Matt. 12:1ff.). It is somewhat strange, however, that these advocates would use an *example* from the life and teachings of Jesus to make their point. Keep in mind that *these are those who affirm that no example in Scripture is a binding example in itself.* In other words, they affirm that there is no authoritative quality in an example *per se*. Yet, one should not forget that they are relying upon *this example* as *their authority* to make the point that love is greater than law.

No need to say that this example is only being used as an illustration of the *command* to love, and that the authority is in the command and not in the example itself. For if that is the case, where is the command that lies behind this example *that establishes this point?* The *command* to love *says nothing about love being greater than law*. If we are taught that in the New Testament, it is taught somewhere else, not in the command to love. So where is it? The fact is, these brethren are drawing this conclusion from this *example* of Jesus. They are using it to teach that there is *something greater than law*, which is love. Which, by the way, in their way of thinking comes out to mean: if something is done in love, one may even *change what the law says*, because love is greater than law.

If one feels compelled to reject this conclusion, then that only puts us back where we started. If the point that is being made does not mean that man, as long as what he does is done in love, is free to change the details of a command, a teaching, an example, or a principle in the word of God, then the commands, examples, etc. must be "lawful requirements" and no change is permitted. Yet, this is what is being rejected by the very argument being made. This is precisely how these advocates of "love above law" are using the *example* of Jesus and the Pharisees in Matthew 12:1ff.

The idea that in this example Jesus is teaching that love may override law, or permit one to set law aside in order to do the loving thing, is preposterous. It is totally against all reason. Why would not one concede that if this is not the point being made, then there is no problem in calling commands, examples, etc. "lawful requirements."

The issue between Jesus and the Pharisees over the Sabbath law was not one that had to do with which was greater, law or love. This is nowhere brought up in the exchange. Jesus does teach that he is Lord of the Sabbath (Matt. 12:8), and in this way he asserts his *authority* over the Sabbath law. He also teaches that the *service* rendered *to him* by his disciples was greater than the temple (Matt. 12:6). On this latter point, McGarvey observes, "It was their duty to serve him which was greater than the temple; that is, greater than the obligation of the temple service on the priests. If, then, the priests were justifiable, much more the disciples" (*Matthew* 104).

Jesus had justified the action of the priests in rendering certain acts of service in the temple on the Sabbath, thus showing that the Sabbath law permitted some work on the Sabbath day. It is noteworthy that in this example Jesus does not justify the conduct of his disciples' act of plucking and eating grain on the Sabbath on the basis of "the law of love." Mercy shown toward the disciples in this matter would have been more acceptable to God than sacrifice, but we must not overlook the fact that Jesus says that in condemning the disciples for their action they "condemned the guiltless" (v. 7). In other words, *they were not violating the Sabbath law* when they plucked the grain and ate some of it. If some work is permitted on the Sabbath day, as Jesus clearly shows that it was, then to do some work on that day *was within the scope of that law*, not above it or outside of it.

The main fault Jesus found with the Pharisees was their hypocrisy and the inconsistency he saw in their teaching and practice. *He does not in any way teach that some violation of God's law is permissible and justifiable on the basis of the examples he cites.* We do learn from the examples he uses that man is charged with the task of coming to understand the meaning of a command of God, and that he is to be held responsible for consistently applying his word in particular situations. The example of David in vv. 3-4 is *not* used *to teach that some violation of God's law is permissible*, and, that when this happens, the violator will be held blameless if it has been broken out of necessity. J.W. McGarvey was acquainted with this particular interpretation, and his insightful response to this position which we offer below is worthy of study:

> Jesus expressly admits that what David did was unlawful; and some have supposed that he here intends to justify it on the ground of necessity, and then to argue that his disciples, though guilty of violating the law of the Sabbath, are justifiable on the same ground. There is no doubt that on this ground David excused himself for eating the show-bread, and that the Pharisees did the same for him. But it cannot be that he who refused to turn stones into bread when tortured by the forty days' fast, and who said, "Whosoever shall break one of these least commandments, and teach men so, shall be called the least in the kingdom of heaven," would approve such a violation of law as David was guilty of. Neither can it be that he allowed his own disciples while under the law to break the Sabbath. If Christians may violate law when its observance would involve hardship or suffering, then there is an end of suffering in the name of Christ, and an end ever of self-denial. But it is clear that by the Pharisees

David's act was thought excusable; otherwise they would have retorted on Jesus thus: Out of your own mouth we condemn you: you class your act with David's; but David sinned, and so do you. Now the real argument of Jesus is this: David, when hungry, ate the show-bread, which it was confessedly unlawful for him to eat, yet you justify him: my disciples pluck grain and eat it on the Sabbath, an act which the law does not forbid, and yet you condemn them (*Matthew* 104).

Commands As Directives of Love

According to Webster a "directive" is "a general instruction or order issued by a central office, military unit, etc." By the very definition of this term the point being made is that the commands, direct statements, examples, etc. found in the New Testament are not to be taken as issuing *specific, binding* instruction that must be *exactly* followed. Would this not place *all* commands under the category of *general* commands?

What purpose would one have for treating all of the commands in the New Testament in this way? The only reason I know is it leaves one "free" to reject the specifics of a command, example, or direct statement as long as he respects the principle that is implied in the command. We will take up the subject of "principle" in commands in the next chapter.

Applies to All Alike?

But would this be true universally? Would this treatment of commands apply to alien sinners and Christians alike? Does it mean, in other words, that one may ignore the meaning of words — that is, he is not required to determine the *exact* meaning — in commands directed to alien sinners?

Take the command to *baptize* as an example. Even though the lexicons tell us that the root word for "baptize" in Matthew 28:19 means to "dip, plunge, or immerse," since the only command man is under is that of love (according to this argument), and love is greater than law, are we then "free" to change the command to immerse an individual in water to mean sprinkle or pour water on that person and call it baptism?

Peter commanded those on Pentecost to "repent and be baptized" (Acts 2:38). Is this command a general command, a "directive of love," or is it a legal requirement? Stated another way, is this a command that *must* be obeyed, and obeyed *only as the terms used in the command require*? If it must be taken as a specific command because it is a command given to alien sinners, then no change is allowed, and this would mean it is a "lawful requirement." If one insists that commands such as these are *must* commands, we would then have *some* lawful requirements in the New Testament, would we not? And if we have some lawful requirements in the New Testament, wouldn't this mean that all those (in this case, alien sinners) who *must* obey these lawful requirements are legalists?

This must be the case, according to the argument, since (we are told) this is how legalists are made. The whole argument was developed in the first place out of an attempt to do away with "legalism" by removing "lawful requirements" from the New Testament. The heart of the argument is that legalists are those who turn commands into lawful requirements.

There are only two possibilities. Commands directed to alien sinners are either directives of love, or they are lawful requirements. If they are lawful requirements they must be treated as such and obeyed strictly, or exactly as they are given. If they are directives of love then they are not binding in details. Which horn of this dilemma will the advocates of the view that commands are only directives of love take? That (1) commands to alien sinners are *directives of love*, thus saying that even these commands are not meant to be obeyed in their details, and thereby freeing them from legalism, or that (2) these commands are *lawful requirements*, thus saying that alien sinners are legalists — those who treat commands as lawful requirements, or as commands that must be obeyed in their details — according to the definition of legalism we are given by these brethren.

Peter adds "for the remission of sins" to the command in Acts 2:38, thus stating the *purpose* of repentance and baptism. Is this a "necessary requirement"? Aren't people *bound* to repent and be baptized just because Peter commanded it, and aren't they *bound* to be baptized for the purpose stated in the command? Peter had been given authority to bind and loose (Matt. 16:19), as had the other apostles (Matt. 18:18). What does the word "bind" mean? Doesn't it mean that they had *authority* to give "requirements" — *lawful* requirements, if you will — that must be submitted to?

And what about the Christian? If we turn from the alien sinner, who is addressed in this passage (Acts 2:38), to the Christian, how does this man who has now been saved from his sins fare? If he has formerly been under legal requirements (the commands to believe, repent of his sins, confess faith in Christ, and be baptized for the remission of sins), is he now freed from legal requirements and placed under directives of love? If so, wouldn't this mean that he formerly was under binding authority, but now he is not?

In case the reader is beginning to think we are carrying this point too far, let me illustrate what I mean by a case in point. There is a clear contradiction here on the part of those who are advocating the kind of freedom we are describing. Cecil Hook, in his book *Free In Christ*, says, "Baptism is a necessary part of our obedience" (84). On the next page he gives more detail on how baptism relates to the other "conditions" of salvation:

> Baptism is symbolic of the whole change of the sinner into a new crea-ture in Christ. It becomes as a metonymy a literary device where the part is used to represent the whole. Belief is for the remission of sins. Confes-sion is for the remission of sins. Repentance is for the remission of sins. Baptism is for the remission of sins. All of these combine in the whole process toward obtaining forgiveness. When a person is baptized, it must mean that all of these other conditions have been accomplished. When baptism is said to save us, a part of the conversion process is used to represent the whole with baptism being the finalizing act (85).

Wouldn't the word "necessary" in the first statement mean that the com-mand to be baptized is a "lawful requirement" or a "legal specification"? Since baptism and the other things connected with baptism are all "for the remission of sins" wouldn't this also place each of these "conditions," as they are called, in the category of "lawful requirements" or "legal specifi-cations," as our brother has defined these words in relation to law?

The place of purpose and principle in commands is the subject of our next chapter.

Chapter 11

Purpose and Principle in Commands

We come now to consider the place of details in commands. Do they matter? Some would say that it is *purpose* that matters, *not the specifics of the command*. To emphasize the specifics, we are told, is to make God's commands arbitrary. This is the reason some prefer to speak of "directives" rather than commands. With directives, they say, we only need to determine first if there is any significance to the command.

Unnecessary Commands?

The Bible often teaches in principles. We do not find a whole series of specific commands on every page of our New Testament. The New Testament is not a "code of law" in this way. Christians are to grow to the point where they will be able to use the principles they find in Scripture to help them make wise decisions in all the different situations they face in their lives. They have to learn to make intelligent choices where no specific instruction is given. Such decisions should of course be made out of love for God and one's fellow man.

Love can be increased, and such growth or increase in love enables one to become even better equipped to make the best choices in life. Paul prayed for the Philippians "that your love may abound yet more and more in knowledge and in all judgment" (Phil. 1:9). The word "abound" indicates the possibility, as well as the need for, *growth* in love. For love to grow in "knowledge" and "judgment" means that the kind of love that God wants from his children is an *intelligent* love. The love God accepts is not blind. As this love increases in knowledge and judgment it is better prepared to do what intelligent love is meant to accomplish. This is stated in the next verse: "That ye may approve things that are excellent; that ye may be sincere and without offense till the day of Christ" (Phil. 1:10).

Intelligent love is able to distinguish between things that are good and things that are best for us. A thing may be good and acceptable, but even though it is good it may not be best. We need to be able to recognize the best from among the good and pursue what is the best course for us.

When it comes to commands, however, it is hard to imagine that some brethren are advocating that God has put man in the position of judge and given him the "right" *to pass judgment upon HIS commands* — "to judge which ones are demands upon us" is the way one brother worded it. If this brother is right, this is exactly what God has done. He has made men *judges* of his commands. Has he forgotten that James says that we are *doers* of the law, not judges of it (Jas. 4:11)? There are, of course, cases where we have some choices when it comes to commands, but not in the way some are claiming. It is true, for example, that in the New Testament we find commands directed to different people, such as those given to alien sinners, to Christians in general, to elders, to evangelists, to the young, to those who are older, to husbands, to wives, to masters, to slaves, etc., and we must take such differences into account when studying the Scripture.

It is easy to see that all commands do not apply to everybody. Every person must make this kind of judgment by asking himself, "Is this a command that is directed to me?" But if it is a *command*, and *it is directed to ME*, what "right" do I have to sit in judgment upon it and decide if it is a *necessary* command? God has not given us *optional* commands. If it is a command directed to me, I am bound to give heed to it and to obey it, even in its details. If this is not true, then each one of us is free to develop his own standard by which to decide whether or not a particular command places a demand upon him. In this way, each man becomes a law unto himself, "doing that which is right in his own eyes" (Judg. 21:25).

Where, for example, did the rule which says, "It is the principle that should rule our conduct rather than the command," originate? We all understand that we must use sound rules of hermeneutics in interpreting Scripture, but they must be *sound* rules, and they must in no way discredit the command or lead one to "refuse . . . him that speaketh" from heaven (Heb. 12:25). Surely *no* rule is a valid rule that places *in man* the authority to pass judgment upon *God's* commands *to determine whether or not they are required commands*. Whoever heard of a *command* being optional?

I may sometimes have difficulty deciding if a particular command is directed to me, or if it belongs to a particular culture, and/or to a particular time that would not involve me today. But I have no doubt that it is a *necessary* command to whomever it applied when it was given by God, and that it is a *necessary* command for me if it has permanent value (not limited to a particular time and/or people). That is the very nature of God's commands.

What if no principle can be determined in a command? Does one then have the "right" simply to cast it aside? One brother said, "God's laws are not arbitrary expressions of authority," and then he added, "we should not perform just to obey commands, but also for the value to be received from what was commanded." We would agree that we need to see the principle in a command when we can, but that may not always be possible.

On the question of whether or not God's laws are arbitrary it is sometimes conceded that commands that expedite a principle may contain some element of arbitrary choice on God's part, but that if it is a "command" promoting no principle then *it is not really a command.* Think about that statement for a moment. What a bold claim! to say the least. Translated, wouldn't that mean, "A 'command' promoting no principle (*that I can see*) is not really a command." The fact that one may not be able to discern a purpose or discover a principle in a command does not mean that no such purpose or principle exists. Isn't this enough to show that this rule makes man's *opinion* the rule? Who is man to decide that a command of God is not a command?

Positive Divine Law
Benjamin Franklin, a pioneer preacher of the last half of the nineteenth century, preached a sermon titled, "Positive Divine Law" (*Gospel Sermons* II:195-217). I have always considered this sermon to be among the best of his sermons that have been put into print. It is an excellent treatment of the subject of commands. He contends that all commands of God fall into two general classes: those based upon the nature of God himself, and those which are right solely because God commanded them. Franklin distinguished between these two kinds of commands by calling them moral and positive law. Moral laws are things admitted to be right in themselves, not right because any special authority requires them. They are required because they are right, and their observance does not require any special test of faith.

Positive law, however, is of a higher order, and involves a higher test of respect for divine authority than moral law. The reason is that there is no apparent connection between the thing commanded and the object sought. Such a command or requirement is right, simply and solely, because God commanded it. When this is the case, the proper observance of the thing required is always an act of faith. This is how faith is tested. Of positive divine law, he says, "It has the force to make that right which is not right in itself, and is the highest test of respect for divine authority known to man." He further explains:

> It is also the greatest trial of faith ever applied to man. It is intended to penetrate down into the heart, and try the heart, the piety, the devotion to God. The very acts that some men have irreverently styled, "mere outward acts," "mere external performances," are the Lord's tests of the state of the heart, intended to penetrate deep down into the inmost depths of the soul, try the heart, the piety, the devotions to God. They try the faith. The man that will obey the commandment, when he cannot see that the thing commanded can do any good, or, it may be, that he can see pretty clearly that it cannot do any good in itself, does it solely through respect to divine authority; does it solely to please God; does it solely because God commands it. This has no reference to popularity, pleasing men, or to the will of man, but it is purely in reference to the will of God. This is of faith; it is piety, devotion to God. It rises above mere morality, philosophy, or the pleasure of man, into the pure region of faith, confidence in the wisdom of God, and in submission to the supreme authority—yields to it reverently when no other reason can be seen for it only that the divine will requires it. The man in his heart says, "It must be done, because the absolute authority requires it."

> There are three degrees in this before it can reach the highest test, the greatest trial of faith. 1. To obey when we can not see that the thing commanded can do any good in itself. 2. To obey when we can see pretty clearly that the thing commanded can not do any good in itself. 3. To obey when we can see that the thing commanded is clearly wrong in itself. It tries the state of heart, the faith, the devotion to Him who commanded, to obey a command when we can not see that the thing commanded can do any good in itself. The test is greater, and the trial more severe, when we can see clearly that the thing commanded can not do any good in itself. The test is greatest, and the trial of faith most severe, when we can see that the thing commanded is clearly wrong in itself, but only made right by the arbitrary force of the absolute authority. This will all appear presently.

The reader surely noticed Franklin's respectful references to "the absolute authority," and "the arbitrary force of the absolute authority" in his description of God's severest test of man's faith through positive divine law. Such language presents quite a contrast to what we are reading from many modern preachers like Cecil Hook who use such terms as "arbitrary commands," "legal requirements," "legal specifications," "lawful requirements," "the command approach," "exemplified details," and "legal justification" as they decry the role of positive divine law today. Hook's universal statement that "God's laws are not arbitrary expressions of authority," omits all room for such a thing as positive divine law.

1. Deliverance of the Firstborn in Egypt. The first example of positive divine law cited by Franklin is Exodus 12:1-13 where a lamb was required to be slain, and the blood sprinkled on the door-posts of the houses. The Israelites were promised deliverance of their firstborn when the blood was found on the door-posts. Franklin applies this example in the following way:

> No man could see any philosophical connection between the thing commanded to be done and the end had in view. What an opening there was here for a modern doctor, who talks of essentials, and non-essentials, outward ceremonies, external rites, etc., to have puzzled Moses. How many pert questions he could have propounded! He could have inquired of Moses, "do you think there is any saving efficacy in the blood of a lamb to save the life of the first-born?" Why apply the blood to the door-post? Could not the Lord see which houses the Israelites were in without the blood on the door-post? Why must it be a blood without blemish? Could not the Lord save the first-born in Israel without this *outward ceremony?*"

2. Uzzah and the Ark of the Covenant. The case of Uzzah is also used to illustrate this point. According to the law of Moses only a Levite was permitted to touch the ark of the covenant. The penalty for violation of this law was death. Franklin's remarks on this story are as follows:

> No man could see that it was any harm, in itself, for any man to touch the ark any more than for a Levite to do it. Merely touching it would surely not injure it. No man could see why it should not be touched, in anything, *only* that the Lord forbade it, and declared that he who did it should die. Here again is a test of respect for divine authority, a trial of faith. It cannot be seen to be wrong to touch the ark, in itself. Why may none but a priest touch it? No man can tell why, only that the Lord says *he shall not.* The commandment of God forbids it. This is enough for the man of faith. Faith requires this to be observed; unbelief inquires, "What harm is it to touch it?" Will not the "spirit of obedience" do, without the *outward act?* To touch the ark is a mere *external performance*, and has nothing to do with the heart? If a man is sincere, will he not be accepted of the Lord without doing the precise thing commanded? See 2 Samuel vi:7; 1 Chronicles xii.ll, and see how it turned out. What does the result show? A man, who appears to have been friendly to the ark, as it was borne along on the new cart, saw it shaking, and in danger of falling, and, though not a priest, put his hand against the ark to keep it from falling, and the moment he touched it he fell dead! What a warning in reference to *good*

intentions, in doing what God forbids! It availed nothing that he was friendly to the ark; that he was honest; that he meant it all well; that he aimed to save the ark from falling! He was taking charge of the ark, caring for it, but not minding the commandment of the Lord. His *good intentions*, in *doing what God forbid*, led him to ruin and made him an example to warn all others to let their *good intentions* lead them to do what the Lord has commanded. He followed his own wisdom, not the wisdom of God.

3. Adam and Eve in the Garden. The law forbidding Adam and Eve to eat of the tree of knowledge of good and evil in the midst of the garden was a positive divine law (Gen. 2:16-17). "No man can see any reason for refraining from eating it, in the fruit itself, no matter whether an apple or some other fruit; nor in anything connected with it, except that the Lord said: 'Thou shalt not eat it.' The reason, and the only reason, for refusing to eat was that the supreme authority *forbid it*. It is not human reason, nor human wisdom, nor philosophy, nor science, that forbids it, but the *absolute authority*. Here comes a test. Will man obey when he can see no reason for doing so, only *to please God*? His appetite is against obedience. The trial is now to be made; the matter is to be tested. There is but one thing in favor of obedience — that is, the *positive divine commandment*. Will that prevail, or will it be set aside?"

4. Abraham Offering Isaac. In his next example (Gen. 22:1ff.), Franklin suggests that even a harder question is this:

What would you do if you should come to a positive commandment that would come in direct collision with moral law? Do you say such a thing can never occur? But such a thing did occur. The question is not whether it occurred, or can occur, but what would you do in a case of that kind? Do you say that you would obey the moral law, and let the positive go? But you say, "Where did a case of that kind occur?" It occurred when God commanded Abraham to offer Isaac. It was wrong to kill, and worse to kill a child, and worse to kill an *only child*. . . .

. . . What does he do in the premises? What an opening was here for talk about *essentials* and *non-essentials*! for talk about "the spirit of obedience," without obedience itself! What a plausible speech might have been made, excusing himself from doing what was commanded! He might have argued that to execute this commandment will frustrate the promise of God, that in his seed all nations shall be blessed. Then, it is contrary to the moral law. It is wrong to kill. Not only so, but the sentiments of filial affection, which God has emplanted in his own breast, forbids that this thing shall be done; and even the common sentiments of humanity forbid it. Did Abraham institute any such reasoning? Not a word of it! No such unbelieving talk falls from his lips. God has spoken! The Jehovah has commanded! There is but one way of it. That which has been commanded must be done.

Oh, you of little faith, look at this man and you have before you an example of faith; not that caviling, carping and evasive thing that some style faith, that will not obey God; but the living, active and glorious faith that moves right on as the Lord commands.

5. Naaman Dipping in the Jordan. The example of Naaman dipping in the waters of Jordan (2 Kings. 5:1-10) also sets forth the principle involved in Franklin's discourse. He was required to dip himself seven times in these waters in order to be cured of his leprosy. "Never did any commandment have the appearance of a non-essential more than this. No man could see how dipping in Jordan could heal leprosy, nor why he must *dip seven times*. He was not to be healed when he dipped once, nor twice, but *seven times*. When the Lord requires certain steps to be taken to obtain an object, the object, or end, is never obtained till the last step is taken, or the last item in the programme is performed."

6. Israel and the Fiery Serpents. In Numbers 21 we read where Moses raised up a brazen serpent in response to God's command. The people had sinned by murmuring against God, and God had sent fiery serpents among them, and much people of Israel died. This was the Lord's remedy in response to their cry for mercy. "Make thee a fiery serpent, and set it upon a pole: and it shall come to pass, that every one that is bitten, when he looketh upon it, shall live." Moses made the serpent of brass and set it upon a pole in their midst, so any man who had been bitten, "when he beheld the serpent of brass, he lived."

Franklin asks,

What think you of this for an "outward performance," an "external rite"? etc. What think you many preachers in our day would have said of this pole and serpent? They would want to know whether there was virtue in the pole, in the brass, in looking, etc., etc., and whether they could not be saved *some other way*. Could not God save a man without looking? What good could it do to look at the brazen serpent? The wisdom of God was in this appointment. He intended that all men should know that there was nothing in the pole, the serpent, or looking, in itself, to save them. He intended that all men should see that it was not what *they did* that saved them, but that *God saved them*. Yet he did not please to save them without the pole, the serpent and the looking. He required them to submit to this appointment, as a test of their faith, a trial of their loyalty, in an act of submission that had *nothing in it but submission to him*. When they sub-mitted, he demonstrated his approval by healing them.

Suppose Moses had prepared a liniment, and it would have healed every bitten Israelite, what would have been the result? Would it have given God the glory? Not at all!! They would not have looked beyond the lini-ment, and nothing would have been heard of but the *liniment*, the *lini-ment* — the grand *panacea!* But no man thought the serpent healed any one, but that God healed them, and they gave the glory to God.

7. The Army of Joshua and the Walls of Jericho. Finally, in Joshua 6 we find Joshua and his army in siege of Jericho. The task was a difficult one. After many attempts they had been unable to take the city. "They had tried their battering rams," Franklin says, "and all the other engines they had for breaking down strong walls, and had utterly failed." Whether or not this is the case, we do know that the Lord gave Joshua a plan by which he would give the city into their hands. Franklin continues by saying that the Lord

> commanded him to march the army round the city once every day, for seven days, and on the seventh day to march round seven times; then to blow the trumpet and tell the men to shout. What a set of "outward per-formances" there was in this! What an amount of "external ceremony!" What an array of non-essentials! . . . Modern chaplains, many of them, would have argued that marching round the walls was not essential; that blowing trumpets could avail nothing, and the shout of men could not break down the formidable walls of Jericho.

> But Joshua was a man of faith. He did not expect the marching round the walls to throw them down, nor the blowing of the trumpet, nor the shout of the men; but he believed the Lord could throw down the walls and give them the victory; and what they had to do was to *obey him*. All men can see that what they were commanded to do could not, in itself, accomplish the object, or have any tendency to do it. God could have thrown down the walls without their doing anything, just as well as with it, so far as we can see. Why, then, did he command the marching round, the blowing of the trumpet, and the shout of the men? Because *so it pleased him to do*. They had no reason for doing what he commanded, only that it *was com-manded*. They could not see that it could do any good. On the first day they marched round once. In the evening there stood the wall, apparently as invulnerable as ever! On the second day they went round again — no sign of the wall giving way. Thus they continued to go round day after day, till they had gone round seven times. There stood the wall, as formi-dable as ever. On the seventh day they started and completed the seven rounds. Not a break in the wall yet! All they had done did not appear to do

any good. This was trying faith! Two items in the programme are lacking, and they certainly appear as much like non-essentials as anything the Lord ever commanded. Yet, if they are left off, all that has been done will be lost. No matter if they have marched round many times, and done it all right, if they stop now they will not receive the promised benefit.

The command is given to blow the trumpet. The trumpet is blown; but the wall moves not. Only one item remains in all the items commanded, and that was for the men to shout. All eyes are turned on the wall, not believing that the shouts would bring it down, but that *God would bring it down*. The men shouted; the wall fell, and Jericho was made an easy prey. No man gave the glory to the marching round the wall, to the blast of the trumpet, or the shout of the men; for all knew that these did not overthrow these strong walls — but the glory was given to the God of Israel, who is mighty in battle, and whose strong arm gave them the victory.

8. Water Baptism. After these examples of positive divine law had been carefully studied, application is then made to the baptism of Mark 16:16. Part of Franklin's comments on this subject are as follows:

Why, then, must man *believe* and be *immersed?* Man may see why he must believe, as the belief changes the heart, and prepares him in heart for pardon. But then, the belief cannot take away the sin, any more than the immersion. But who can see why any man should be immersed? No man can see that it can do any man good, in a religious, or a spiritual sense, to immerse him. What, then, is there to impel a man to be immersed? Nothing in rationalism. He can see nothing in it, in itself, to lead him to be immersed. Indeed, he can see pretty clearly that there is nothing in it, in itself, for soul or body; that, in itself, it can have no tendency to produce or bring what the sinner is seeking — the salvation of his soul, or the remission of sins. Yet there stand the words of the Great Teacher: "He that believeth, and is immersed, shall be saved." There is the promise, the other side of baptism — "Shall be saved." Does the sinner desire what is promised? If he does, there lies before him the commandment, "Be baptized." Why must the sinner be immersed? Not because he can see any virtue in water, immersing a man in water, or in all of it together; but because the supreme and the absolute authority has appointed it as the initiatory rite of the new institution; has ordained that men and women be "immersed into the name of the Father, and of the Son, and of the Holy Spirit;" that they shall "believe and be immersed," in order to come to the promise, "shall be saved;" that they shall "repent and be immersed, every one of them, in the name of Jesus Christ, for the remission of sins"; that "so many of us as have been immersed into Jesus Christ have put on Christ"; that all shall be "immersed into *one* body"; that, "except a man be born of water and of the Spirit, he can not enter into the kingdom of God."

. . . Baptism is the test of his belief on Christ — the trial of his loyalty to the King. Here, at the entrance of the kingdom, the question comes before him of *obedience* in a matter of the most trying nature — *obedience* to a commandment, where he can see no reason for the *obedience*, only that *the King requires it*. If he stops at this first formal act required of him, and refuses to *obey*, what may we expect of him at any subsequent time? If the very appointment intended to test his loyalty, try his faith, and develop the spirit of obedience in him, shall be set aside by him, what ground have we for expecting obedience of him in the future?

In this view of it, any one can see the wisdom of God in placing such an appointment as immersion at the entrance into the new covenant. In the first place, he cannot see that the thing commanded, in itself, can do any good to the soul or body. In the second place, he can see pretty clearly that the thing commanded can not, in itself, do any good, in any philosophical way, to soul or body. In the third place, it appears as if it might do the body injury. Then, it is humiliating to the last degree. Still further, as any one can see, the Lord could save a sinner without it as well as with it. Why, then, must it be done? The wisdom and goodness of the Supreme Majesty of heaven and earth require it. The absolute authority commands it. Shall this authority control? or shall poor mortal man decide that it is not essential?

These considerations have brought us to the place where we need to give some attention to the question of amoral actions and things and positive divine law. This is the subject of the next two chapters.

Chapter 12

Amoral Matters and Positive Divine Law (1): The Argument and Its Consequences

Jesus Christ is "the same yesterday, and today, and forever" (Heb. 13:8). His authority as God's spokesman is clearly established in Scripture (John 5:26-27; Heb. 1:1-2; 12:25). The Father himself announced at the time of his transfiguration, "This is my beloved Son, in whom I am well pleased; hear ye him" (Matt. 17:5). Following his resurrection and just prior to his ascension, Jesus claimed all authority had been given to him, both in heaven and on earth (Matt. 28:18). We are not to "refuse him that speaketh" (Heb. 12:25a), that is, "Jesus the mediator of the new covenant" (v. 24), who is "him that speaketh from heaven" (v. 25b).

The Argument Stated
We have no argument with the statement that as a rule actions and things are amoral, and that they have no inherent moral value. However, this is not the real issue. The question is, does God *today*, under the law of Christ, and through positive divine law, *sometimes* make that right which is not right in itself, or take what is amoral (neither right nor wrong in itself) and put it into his service?

Cecil Hook, in his book *Free In Christ*, never makes mention of positive divine law. Most of his discussion centers upon the subject of man's liberty in amoral things; at least in those things he considers to be amoral, whether or not they actually belong to that class. Basically, he affirms that actions and things are amoral, and that they are made sinful only by man himself. He maintains that *in the realm of the amoral the only thing that can make an action or a thing sinful is man's attitude toward it*. They can be made wrong, according to him, only by a wrong motive on man's part.

No Arbitrary Laws Are Named

Most of what is said in this chapter of his book is commendable, and, no doubt, will be acceptable to brethren generally. One is made to wonder, however, why Hook does not spend more time discussing actions and things that God *has* brought into his service *by arbitrary authority*, if indeed he believes that some things have been placed in the service of the church by such authority. Do such actions and things exist under the law of Christ today?

We would assume that Hook believes in some such matters, but you will not find them discussed in his book. His book is devoted to discussing the actions and things he believes must be thrown out, or, accepted as belonging in the realm of our individual liberties. Somehow he never gets around to telling which things *must* stay in God's service because they are absolutes and man does not have a right to exclude them or change them in any way. This raises a very serious question about whether he actually believes in any such positive divine laws from God today that are binding just because God has said that man is to put them into his service.

There is probably good reason why this brother, and all others pursuing the same course he has mapped out for himself, avoid bringing such matters into their discussions. Once one commits to arbitrary authority being expressed in *some commands* he then faces the problem of determining which commands are arbitrary and which are not. When one crosses this threshold and begins to make such decisions, he then runs the risk of becoming guilty of doing the same thing he is charging against others: he must now make a list of all such arbitrary commands. And when he begins to do this he becomes guilty of legalism, the very thing he has come to decry in almost everything he now writes! Besides, we are made to wonder, what about moral law? Is it okay to be legalistic about *moral* law? Why apply this rule only to amoral things? What is the difference about being legalistic about murder, theft, lasciviousness, social drinking, and gambling, and in being legalistic about amoral things or actions?

But on amoral things, we pose this question: Is there a place in this system of Bible interpretation for any law other than moral law? So far as we can see, Cecil Hook has only two categories, moral and amoral. And the amoral, according to him, is made wrong only by a wrong attitude or motive (we still wonder why this rule, if it were true, would not apply to moral law as well). Consider these words from page 49 of his book:

> Our purity or defilement is not determined by what we see, hear, taste, or touch, but by our motive for seeing, hearing, tasting, and touching. Jesus

explained that man is defiled by his thoughts rather than by what he eats (Matt. 15:1-20). Defilement is not in certain actions and things, but in improper use of and attitude toward those actions and things. Actions and things, generally speaking, are amoral. They have no inherent moral value.

What we are asking is this: Where in this statement (or anywhere in his book for that matter) does he make room for positive divine law; law which *makes right* religiously that which is not right in itself; an action or thing made right religiously *solely by the arbitrary force of the absolute authority* of God?

From his discussion of the subject of Christian liberties in chapter 7 of his book (which, for the most part, is an excellent treatment of the subject) one wonders if he doesn't put everything — with the exception of things immoral in themselves (though one wonders why Hook makes a distinction about things he labels "immoral"; is legalism acceptable in the immoral area?) — under amoral actions or things. This would place every thing *done* (all of our *actions*) in religion, and every *thing* used in the worship and service of the church, under the category of the "amoral." This means that all of the actions and things that are used in the worship and work in the church belong to the realm of "indifferent" matters, or matters which involve choice on man's part.

Think for a moment where the author of this book has attempted to bring his readers up to this point. First, the specifics in commands have been set aside as having no relevance for us today; only the principle and purpose of commands are thought to matter. Next, all that is left that should concern a person under covenant with God is how he treats amoral actions and things, and on this subject man himself has complete control. Attitude is the only thing that determines right and wrong in this area.

The Logical End of This Argument
At one place in his discussion of amoral actions and things, we are provided with a list of things which Hook believes belong to this class. In his discussion of the Judaizers' attempt to bind circumcision on the early church, he says the following:

> If they could bind circumcision, others can bring us into bondage to their scruples in demanding that our liberties be limited in studying in classes, using individual cups for communion, helping the fatherless, cooperating in evangelism, building up a large congregation, having food in fellowship in the building, and what else might be your local scruple. Although the abuse of any amoral exercise — and these are all amoral — can lead to sin, we are not condemned by a sensible exercise of them (56).

What else could one put into this list? An organ is an amoral thing, isn't it? Isn't the water the eunuch saw when he said, "Behold, here is water, what doth hinder me to be baptized?" (Acts 8:36, ASV), an amoral thing? What about the action of immersion in water? Isn't immersion an amoral action? Aren't the bread and the fruit of the vine in the Lord's Supper amoral things? And what about the number of elders as overseers in a local church? A number is an amoral thing. May one elder serve over a local church? If so, may that one elder oversee more than one church? May one elder oversee all local churches throughout the world? A number is amoral, so why does it matter how many churches one elder oversees? Isn't gender amoral? So why does it matter whether a man or a woman is appointed as an elder? What about the virgin birth of Christ, his sonship, resurrection, ascension, reign from heaven, and his return? These are all "amoral" things. Can one have an idol? An idol is a amoral "thing," so why not, Mr. Hook?

Such questions point out just where this approach to Bible interpretation leads us, and one wonders if those who are making the argument don't mind. Are they really willing to follow the argument to its logical conclusion and accept just anything as long is it is "amoral"? Will they accept just anything in the worship, terms of admission, organization of the church, etc. in the name of Christian "liberty"?

The Point Illustrated From Hook's Book
Let me now illustrate the point. The following list of actions or things from the book, *Free In Christ*, that are either judged by its author to be permissible, or at least actions and things that ought to be tolerated in others, should be informative to the thoughtful reader:

— Christians may partake of the Lord's Supper on any day of the week (21, 47-48).

— "the Lord's day" of Revelation 1:10 is not the first day of the week, nor is the first day of the week a special day of worship (47-48).

— the "burial" of Romans 6:3-4 and Colossians 2:12 takes place in the tomb with Jesus, not in water; the action in baptism symbolizes this burial. Therefore, we should be less dogmatic in opposing dipping the head, pouring, or sprinkling for baptism (46).

— suicide, abortion, and euthanasia are discussed in the context of "something greater than law," and yet the author says, "we are not defending euthanasia or attempted suicide"! But he writes in such a way as to make it appear that he is defending them. He is discussing "making responsible decisions." He concludes by asking, "Can we go too far astray when we in all circumstances make decisions on the 'weightier matters of the law'? Some may decry this as situation ethics or brand it with some other prejudicial disparagement, but Jesus took the Sabbath law as a test case to teach this lesson" (37-40).

— an unmarried man may serve as an elder in the church (43)

— the silence of women in the churches is not binding today (45)

— the collection of 1 Corinthians 16:2 was not to be taken in the assembly of the church (47)

— gospel (the death, burial, and resurrection of Christ, plus the Sonship of Jesus, his atonement and glorification, as well as his promise to raise the dead, are gospel) and doctrine (all teaching beyond the gospel) are not the same, and there should be no disruption of fellowship over any matters of doctrine (60-64)

— instrumental music is classed with kitchens in the church buildings, which the author believes to be a matter of indifference, and with "any such scruple, opinion, or conviction" (69)

— would accept someone as a brother "while he is still serving in the Christian Church or Assembly of God" (72-73)

— sectarian groups such as the Christian Church and Assembly of God are "a part of the whole church but not in fellowship with the whole. They are sectarian divisions." "The individuals in the two groups are in the same body of Christ. They should rejoice that they are in fellowship in Christ. They have differing scruples, but neither should judge or disdain the other any longer. They are in one body but two congregations. . ." (82)

— the adjective "false" describes the man rather than his teaching"; thus, the *false teacher* is "a teacher or prophet with a character defect of evil motivation" (73)

— one does not need to know the purpose of baptism in order for him to be baptized into the one body of Christ (85-88)

— "the five items of worship concept" is laid aside as having significance. It is replaced with the concept of the offering of one's whole self, or one's whole life, as a worship/service. "When one's life is dedicated to God, whatever he does is a worship/service." In this way "going to worship" is made light of, and limiting our worship to five items is dismissed as being without scriptural warrant. "The value is not in keeping details of a ritual precisely, but in what we think and express" (89-95).

— on church identity: "Now let's think of the essential nature of a church. It has only one elder. Is it still a church? It binds the holy kiss. Is it a church now? It changes its name. Has it ceased to be a church? It is filled with jealousy and strife. Has that destroyed its identity? It burns votive candles. Has that changed its essential nature? It accepts tongue speaking and belief in miraculous healing. Is it still a church? Many other deviations of belief and practice might change its quality as a church but they would not destroy the essential nature of a church" (116)

— on church organization: "Where is an exclusive pattern set forth and enjoined?" (131). "One congregation may have no elders, or only one elder. Another might appoint deacons to serve it while having no elders, even as they chose special servants in Jerusalem in earlier times. Still another might be overseen by an evangelist. Then, there may be churches following the traditional pattern with a highly organized program. Some churches may work independently while others may choose to share in certain efforts. None of the alternatives offered here are (sic) set forth as an exclusive pattern, but they are a suggestion of great flexibility of groups of disciples" (132-133).

— on church autonomy: "The earthly operation of the church is democratic even though in its spiritual form it is a kingdom with Christ as King." "If the will of the majority is not served, then self-government is lost to minority rule. If elders assume power to bind decisions on a church, that is episcopal rule and lordship" (137)

— on selection by majority vote: "In order for elders to represent the autonomous group, the whole group must be given opportunity to vote for or against their appointment. Yes, vote!" "A man who will not agree to majority vote approval is jealous of his position and has the spirit of lordship" (138)

— on rule by boards: "The elders are to be pastors of the flock rather than a board of directors administering from a meeting room. Let the elders be involved chiefly in the spiritual care of the members. Business of the congregation can be carried on by selected servants, done with the general approval of the church" (139)

We have already dealt with commands in a former chapter. We must now take a close look at this second major area of concern in the book, *Free In Christ*.

How Apply the Rule?

Does this rule apply only to those who are already in covenant with God? At times one is left with the feeling that the discussion is taking into account only covenant people, or those who have been made free in Christ.

But at other times one is made to wonder if what is being said is not also being applied to those who are not yet Christians. Note the following statement where the new relationship one enters into by the new birth is being discussed:

> . . . This new relationship is accomplished through the new birth (John 3:3f), by which we are all sons of God through faith (Gal. 3:26f), and in which our life becomes hidden with Christ in God (Col. 3:3). It is not a legal relationship, but a spiritual one.
>
> We enter into a covenant relationship. God made a covenant with Abraham and sealed it by circumcision (Gen. 17:9f). Later the law was given to guide the covenant people (Deut. 4:4f). The law was not the covenant of promise, nor did it make them covenant people.
>
> The new covenant is sealed in us by the Holy Spirit (Eph. 1:13f). This is done when we receive the Spirit at the time of our obedience to the gospel; the other teachings are given to guide those in covenant relationship (*Free In Christ* 24-25) .

What does "obedience to the gospel" entail? This is the time at which one enters into covenant with God, which covenant is sealed by the Holy Spirit which is given to us, according to the above statement. And "the other teachings are given to guide those in covenant relationship." But what of the teachings that one obeys in coming into this relationship? Since they are not covenant teachings, what are they? Are they "lawful regulations"? Are they "requirements" that one must obey to come into this covenant relationship?

Perhaps the answer is given in the following statement: "How can law be written on our hearts if we are not under law? (a reference is made to 2 Cor. 3:6 and Heb. 8:7-8 which was used in the preceding paragraph to point out that we are not under a "written code" today — *ww*) To say that we are not under law is not to say that we are not under the lordship of Christ and the sovereignty of God. *Law* has a range of meanings. Law may be a legal system which demands perfect obedience. Law also can be a principle of action. We are justified through the principle of grace through faith (Eph. 2:8f; Rom. 3:27f; 8:1f). That grace activates our love" (*Free In Christ* 25).

The last part of this statement appears to apply justification through the principle of grace through faith to one's initial obedience to Christ (conversion), yet it is in a context where *law* as a "principle of action" is being discussed. Does this mean that this principle is being applied to one's entrance into covenant with God? If so, perhaps someone will show us how this "principle of action," which is said to be love, "activated" *love* in the hearts of those who heard Peter's sermon in Acts 2.

The 3,000 who were converted at that time were "obedient to the gospel" on that day. They were indeed saved by "grace through faith." They were "pricked in their hearts" by what they heard, and this conviction led them to obey the gospel to the saving of their souls (v. 41). But nothing is said in the sermon about love. Neither was the word "grace" used by Peter, nor the word "faith." Some grand truths were preached about Christ, but not one of those who were saved on that day knew one thing about how commands must be obeyed out of love. Nor is there any indication anywhere in the divine record that a single one of them was responding to God's love for them as they repented of their sins and were baptized for the remission of sins as they were *commanded* (v. 38). All they had learned was that Jesus was the Christ who now was in heaven ruling from the right hand of God, and they were guilty of crucifying him. It was their conviction that he was the Christ, and their sense of guilt for having put him to death, that caused them to cry out, "What must we do?" They were obeying simply because they were *commanded* to repent and be baptized for the remission of sins. May we charge them with legalism because they were not thinking in terms of responding out of love for God?

What was the nature of the commands these people were obeying? Consider the "act" of baptizing, or baptism (immersion in water) as a "thing"? Where does this "act" and "thing" belong? Since this action and thing are not *in themselves* a religious act or thing, and they are amoral (neither right nor wrong *per se*), has God taken this action and thing and made them right religiously *by his absolute authority*? If God gives significance to an act or thing like the meaning he has given to baptism, has he not done so by his *absolute and arbitrary* authority?

What if man does not give the same significance to baptism? What if, for example, he changes the *action* required in the command (from immersion to sprinkling), or what if he changes the *purpose* which God gives to it (from *in order to receive* the remission of sins to *because of* the remission of sins)? If man changes the action or the purpose of baptism from those which God has given it, but his motives are good, does his good motives make his action and purpose right?

Or, what about commands directed to the Christian. On the Lord's supper we have a command, "Do this in remembrance of me." This brother says, "This is no arbitrary command. It has a purpose." This is the same as to say that because it has purpose it cannot be an arbitrary command. *But who made this rule?* The fact of the matter is, the *purpose* that Jesus assigned to *this act* of eating unleavened bread and fruit of the vine is itself arbitrary. Eating bread and drinking fruit of the vine have no significance in themselves except to satisfy one's hunger, or perhaps even for one's own pleasure. But notice that when Jesus said "in remembrance of me" *he assigned significance to the eating and drinking of these elements*, and he did so *absolutely and arbitrarily*. The same may be said for the elements themselves. May we use other elements? Why bread, and why fruit of the vine? Why not some other elements? Answer: because Jesus "took bread" (Matt. 26:26) and commanded them, "take, eat" (v. 26). He then "took the cup" (v. 27), the fruit of the vine (v. 29), and commanded them, "drink ye all of it" (v. 27). There is no other reason for using these elements. This is what gives them significance.

What about the *act* specified in the command? Why not just *pour* the fruit of the vine *over* the bread instead of eating the bread and drinking the fruit of the vine as long as we do this "in remembrance" of Jesus' death? In other words, are the commands to *eat* and *drink* the Lord's Supper (the *acts* involved) *must* commands? Aren't *these acts* required, and aren't these acts *the only acts permitted* just because Jesus commanded them, and *for the reason* he gave for eating and drinking them? Are we "free" to perform some other act or acts to serve the same purpose? The only reason *these acts* have significance is because Jesus gave them significance, and he did so by a *command* — and he did so arbitrarily by an *arbitrary* command!

Though some are saying that only the purpose of a command matters, our contention is that as long as Jesus or his apostles have *specifically commanded* an action or a thing, *that alone* gives it enough significance for man to limit his practice to *exactly* what they have commanded him to do. To say otherwise is to say that man is wiser than God! "O the depth of the riches both of the wisdom and knowledge of God! How unsearchable are his judgments, and his ways past finding out! For who hath known the mind of the Lord? Or who hath been his counsellor? Or who hath first given to him, and it shall be recompensed unto him again? For of him, and through him, and to him, are all things: to whom be glory for ever. Amen" (Rom. 11:33-36).

This passage shows that man is not in a position to instruct God. What man is there who knows more than God? None would *say* of course that he knows more than God, but from what we are reading in some places it would appear that some must *think* that they know more than God knows about a lot of things. For man to presume, for example, that he is "free" to make light of the details of commands given *by God* has an air of superiority about it. Is this a doctor of the law speaking? What else but arrogance would lead man to think that because he can't see the significance of a specific action or thing in a given command, he has the right to disregard it? That is the wisdom of man speaking, not the wisdom of God. No such idea ever came from the mind of God.

Are we *required* to do what God has commanded or not? Even when we do not understand why he has commanded it? A passage most have known from their youth tells why we must obey God's commands even when we do not understand them: "For my thoughts are not your thoughts, neither are your ways my ways, saith the Lord. For as the heavens are higher than the earth, so are my ways higher than your ways, and my thoughts than your thoughts" (Isa. 55:8-9). Given this fact, why would God give man the "right" to change something specified by him in a command just because he can't see the purpose or significance of it?

Is it not true that one's understanding of a given command will improve as he grows and matures in the faith? The reason for a given command, or the purpose God has in requiring it, may forever be hidden from us, or it may become clearer with growth on our part. Is man responsible at the point of understanding but not responsible when he fails to see the reason for a command? Is he responsible to obey at one point but not at another?

We may not understand why God has commanded something, and on the surface something he has commanded may even appear to be foolish to us. But does the fact that man (in his arrogance? — what else would it be?) thinks something done by God, or something commanded by him, is "foolish," gives him the right to ignore it or change it? As every reader knows, this is what some thought of the cross. And what was God's answer? "For it is written, I will destroy the wisdom of the wise, and will bring to naught the understanding of the prudent. Where is the wise? Where is the scribe? Where is the disputer of his world? Hath not God made foolish the wisdom of this world? For after that in the wisdom of God the world by wisdom knew not God, it pleased God by the foolishness of preaching to save them that believe. . . . Because the foolishness of God is wiser than men; and the weakness of God is stronger than men" (1 Cor. 1:19-21, 25).

Chapter 13

Amoral Matters and Positive Divine Law (2): The Specifics of the Argument

By now all who are reading this book understand that the reason for the statement that principle and purpose are the only things that matter in commands (the subject studied in Chapter 11), and the reason for saying in the quote given from Cecil Hook at the last of the preceding chapter that only attitude matters in amoral actions and things, is to discredit *arbitrary* authority. None should doubt that the argument on amoral actions and things not being sinful in themselves is but another way of trying to accomplish the same end. It is an attempt to discredit arbitrary authority, or positive divine law.

But we must now take up the specifics of the argument that is being made on this subject.

Vain Worship Through Human Traditions
The first passage cited to prove that only wrong motives make amoral things wrong is Matthew 15:1-20. The subject being discussed in this passage is human traditions. The first question brought before Jesus has to do with uncommanded religious washings. The scribes and Pharisees ask him, "Why do thy disciples transgress the tradition of the elders? For they wash not their hands when they eat bread?" (Matt. 15:1-2).

The washing in this case was not as a means of cleanliness, but as a ceremonial or religious act. The practice was an *addition* to the commanded washings of the law; it was an uncommanded and traditional perversion of the legal washings or Levitical purifications, as prescribed in Leviticus 12-15. The washings from this part of Leviticus were restricted to certain states of body *representing* the defilement of sin, but by oral tradition they had been extended without meaning to familiar acts of life. This was true in this particular case which is now brought before Jesus. Mark 7:3-4 shows that this practice had been extended to include other washings of the body on other occasions, even the washing of ordinary house furnishings such as cups, pots, brazen vessels, and tables.

As Jesus often did in his confrontations with the Pharisees, he responded to their question with a question: "Why do ye also transgress the commandment of God by your tradition?" (v. 3). In his question he shows that, if his disciples are guilty of a crime by not washing their hands, as they charge, they (the Pharisees) are guilty of a worse one. McGarvey accurately points out that Jesus admitted their charge against his disciples, but then he defends them "by attacking tradition itself; not this particular tradition, but all tradition. He charges that they, by their tradition, transgressed the commandment of God, and that the tradition itself was therefore sinful" (*Matthew* 134). By the example which he brings up, Jesus shows them how they actually circumvented the command of God to honor father and mother by imposing the tradition of "corban" upon it (vv. 4-6; Mark 7:11 inserts "corban").

This leads Jesus to his conclusion on this matter. He first charges them with hypocrisy and says Isaiah prophesied concerning them when he said, "This people honoreth me with their lips; but their heart is far from me" (vv. 7-8). What they were doing by invoking the "it is a gift" ("corban" in Mark) tradition (v. 5) to avoid taking care of their parents was actually a *false pretense* of doing for God's honor what was really done to gratify their own covetousness. Jesus then quotes from Isaiah 29:13 what we have in verse 8 to make his point. They offered him only lip service, service that did not truly come from the heart. He applies these words to the accusers. To these words he adds, "But in vain they do worship me, teaching for doctrines the commandments of men" (v. 9).

This last verse is not to be taken by itself. It must be understood in connection with the preceding verse. For, as Alexander points out, if taken by itself it "might seem to mean that they served God merely in obedience to human authority, and then would imply no censure on the persons thus commanding, but only on the motives of those by whom they were obeyed" (*Matthew* 411). But in Jesus' application of the passage from Isaiah to the hypocrites of his day (v. 8), he has reference particularly to the religious teachers as corrupting the law by their unauthorized additions.

At verse 10 Jesus turns to the multitude and addresses the people around him with the words of verse 11: "Not that which goeth into the mouth defileth a man; but that which cometh out of the mouth, this defileth a man." What is Jesus' point? Does he mean that amoral things are made wrong only by wrong motives? That is how the passage is being used by those who contend that the details of commands do not matter and that amoral things are only made wrong by wrong attitudes. Again, is this Jesus' point in this statement? Then too, what about the *additions* of their own traditions to what Moses had commanded. Why is this subject passed over by those who are using this passage to support their argument?

Keep in mind the subject that was discussed in verses 1-9. Jesus had successfully exposed the folly of uncommanded religious washings, and how wrong the religious leaders were in setting aside moral obligations by such human traditions; that is, setting them aside by their own man-made laws. One could not find a more fitting description of what is being done by Cecil Hook and those who think like him than what we find here. They, as the liberals of our day, are the modern Pharisees who reduce obligations to obey law! They make their own laws, or human requirements (traditions), for this very purpose. Notice how what Jesus says here describes the liberals of his day (and of our time as well), not the conservatives, as the liberals often charge. The real modern Pharisees are liberals like Hook who say we are free from responsibility to keep commandments (of worship, etc.), just like the Pharisees of Jesus' day argued that they were free from the commandment to support their parents.

Jesus now turns to the most prevalent of all merely ritual distinctions, that of clean and unclean meats. Not only was this the favorite of all such distinctions made in the law, but it also had come to be the chief means by which social separation between Jews and Gentiles was maintained. This in fact was the very purpose of the food laws enumerated in Leviticus 11 and Deuteronomy 16 (see Lev. 20:24-26). The law on this subject was meant to separate the chosen race from every other by restrictions on their food which should render it impossible for them to live together. By these laws it would virtually be impossible for the Jews to interchange the ordinary courtesies of life without a constant violation of their religious duty.

What was the effect of such laws upon the Jews? There was both a good and an evil effect which resulted from this practice. The good effect was that the laws had accomplished what God had intended in securing the kind of separation he wanted for his people. *The evil effect was the problem Jesus is dealing with in this passage of Scripture.* Through the centuries there had developed a constant disposition on the part of the religious teachers among the Jews to "make a positive and temporary regulation for a perpetual invariable law, and to regard the forbidden meats as having an intrinsic efficacy to defile, not only ceremonially but morally" (Alexander *Matthew* 412). They had, in other words, forsaken the original intent of the law; they had carried it far beyond what God meant by it.

Some imply by the way they use Jesus' statement in Matthew 15:11, 20 that he meant to call in question the authority or obligation of the precept regarding the eating of meats as specified in the law, when he is only challenging the ground and purpose of that law *as usually understood by the people and taught by their religious leaders.* Such laws were not meant to be permanent, and they were designed only for the purpose of keeping God's people separate from the Gentiles, and to symbolize the differences between heathenish corruptions and the holiness that ought to have characterized his own chosen people. But, as Alexander points out,

> . . . by gradual departure from this clearly revealed purpose of the legal prohibitions now in question, they had come to look upon the unclean meats as *per se* morally defiling, and by necessary consequence, upon the strict use of the clean meats as intrinsically purifying, or at least meritorious in the sight of God. This is the error here refuted or condemned, and not obedience to the dietetic laws of Moses while the system was still binding, upon which these words of Christ have neither a remote nor an immediate bearing, as some eminent interpreters imagine, and as many of his hearers no doubt thought at that time, notwithstanding the admonitory warning against inattention and misapprehension, which we learn from Mark [7, 16] though not from Matthew, that he uttered upon this as on so many other similar occasions (413).

Jesus did not say that as long as they maintained the original purpose of the commands regarding the eating of certain meats, or if they would but return to the original purpose God had in mind when enacting such laws, *the details of the commands regarding them would not matter.* Far from it. He simply shows, first, that they had left the original purpose of these commands, and, second, that they were adding commands of their own to the original ones given by God. Some of the commands they were adding actually were added to enable them to circumvent God's law on other matters. In this way, by adding their human traditions, they were making God's word void.

So what is the meaning of, "Not that which goeth into the mouth defileth a man; but that which cometh out of the mouth, this defileth a man"? Whatever these words mean, we can be assured that they are not meant to *deny* that whoever eats forbidden food is ceremonially defiled. That would be to deny what the Old Testament Scriptures clearly affirmed. Jesus would never have *denied* that the person who transgressed this part of God's law incurred guilt (at least legally or ceremonially) by his action. It was the ground and purpose of such restrictions as they were generally understood by the people and taught by the religious leaders that he challenged with this statement.

It was not the food in itself that defiled a man, because there is nothing *intrinsically* defiling with meat, nor in the eating of meat. Meat always had been clean *in itself*. This was so from the beginning, or from the time of creation (Gen. 1:20-25, 29-31; 9:2-3; Rom. 14:14; 1 Cor. 10:30; 1 Tim. 4:3-4). There was, however, a *legal* uncleanness brought upon a man when he ate meat that later was forbidden *by a direct command from God*. And this was true *regardless of the man's attitude*. It simply was not true, and Jesus did not say as much in this passage of Scripture, that as long as one maintained a good attitude (his heart was right), he could give little attention to the details of the commands concerning cleanliness as prescribed in the law.

God *arbitrarily commanded* that certain meats were to be eaten while other meats specified by him were not allowed. Even though no meat was unclean in itself, God took that which was clean and pronounced it unclean, and any person who ate meat that had been pronounced unclean by God became *ceremonially* or *legally* unclean as a result. Over the centuries many Jews had come to see such meat as unclean *in itself*, and *they were giving a significance to such external matters as eating and not eating meat that God himself had not given to it*. Jesus is correcting this false idea about meats as he deals with the question about his disciples not washing their hands for ceremonial purposes before eating. In overturning the superficial, unscriptural tradition of hand washing, Mark adds a note that Jesus by his statements "declared all foods clean" (7:19, NASB).

What does Jesus mean by "defile" in Matthew 15:11, 18, and 20? Broadus gives the following explanation:

> The word rendered "defileth" is literally, *makes common*. Some kinds of food were especially set apart, as alone proper for God's chosen people, and were thus in a certain sense sacred, all other things being "common" (Acts 10:14); for an Israelite to partake of these forbidden things would destroy his exclusiveness, make him common. Hence, "to make common" came to mean to defile, pollute (*Matthew* 336).

The Pharisees had difficulty understanding the statement of Jesus in verse 11 (v. 12), and so did the disciples (vv. 15-17). Broadus goes on to explain how Jesus' statement actually corrects a long-standing misapprehension of the Jews on this subject:

> Ceremonially, various things did defile by entering the mouth, but this
> was only designed to *represent* the idea of *moral* pollution, while the
> great mass of the Jews, however scrupulous about the representative pu-
> rity, were careless of the inward purity. Our Lord, therefore, by this say-
> ing directs attention to the internal and real impurity (336-337).

Many of the Jews at that time were serving God with the lips, but not
from the heart. Jesus pointed this out in verse 8 of Matthew 15. This was
just before he made this statement about evil things coming from within a
person. But no Jew thoroughly grounded in the law should have been surprised at Jesus' teaching. He was not teaching something new. He was
simply reinforcing truths that God's word had already taught. Their own
law told them that "God sees not as man sees, for man looks at the outward
appearance, but the Lord looks at the heart" (1 Sam. 16:7, NASB). Circumcision was looked upon by the Jews with great reverence, but before Israel
entered the land promised to Abraham, God declared through Moses, "And
now, Israel, what doth the Lord thy God require of thee, but to fear the
Lord thy God, to walk in all his ways, and to love him, and to serve the
Lord thy God with all thy heart and with all thy soul, to keep the commandments of the Lord, and his statutes, which I command thee this day for thy
good" (Deut. 10:12-13). Three verses later, Israel was told, "Circumcise
therefore the foreskin of your heart, and be no more stiff-necked" (v. 16).

No religious ceremony or activity required in the Old Testament pleased
God unless it came from a contrite, pure, and loving heart. This is made
abundantly clear in many passages in the Old Testament text itself (Josh.
24:23; 1 Kings 8:23; 2 Chron. 11:16; Isa. 51:7; 57:15).

But the Jews had come to put too much confidence in the externals.
There was so much ritualism involved in their service, much of it enacted
by God himself. There were many ceremonies and restrictions involving
so many different things: the many exercises that had to be performed in
the sacrificial system of the priests, certain animals unclean for any Jew to
eat, foods that had to be carefully prepared before they could be eaten, etc.
Many things were forbidden even to be touched; and certain diseases, such
as leprosy, and some physical conditions, such as menstruation, were considered ceremonially defiling. Under the Old Covenant, being involved in
or having contact with a ceremonially unclean thing rendered a person
unfit to participate in certain worship ceremonies or certain social activities. MacArthur points out that such things "illustrated in a practical way
the spiritual defilement of sin, as circumcision illustrated the need for a
heart to have the sin 'cut away'" (*N.T. Commentary: Matthew 8-15*:459).
McGarvey distinguishes between these practices and what Jesus describes

(Matt. 15:19-20) as the difference between the type and antitype. He says that the "Pharisees, confounding the type with the antitype, thought that the *soul* was defiled by that which caused only legal uncleanness. Jesus corrects this mistake, and in giving the true significance of the type, gives the true conception of uncleanness under the Christian dispensation" (*Matthew* 137).

Nothing Unclean In Itself

In the book, *Free In Christ*, the same line of argument we have been considering in the above section is continued by citing a statement from Paul in Romans 14 and Titus 1:

> Is not this the point Paul would enforce upon us? "I know, and am per-suaded in the Lord Jesus, that nothing is unclean in itself; but it is unclean for anyone who thinks it unclean . . . for the kingdom of God does not mean food and drink but righteousness and peace and joy in the Holy Spirit" (Rom. 14:14-17). Our purity of thought or defilement of purpose determines whether a thing is moral or immoral. Sin is not in things, but in people — in the heart. This is what Paul expressed when he wrote, "To the pure all things are pure, but to the corrupt and unbelieving nothing is pure; their very minds and consciences are corrupted" (Titus 1:5). Shakespeare only expressed this truth when he said, "Nothing is good or bad, but thinking makes it so" (49).

Yet, when it was wrong to eat certain kinds of meat under the law, and a man broke one of those laws by eating some unclean meat, was his act in eating such forbidden meat an *immoral* act whereby a man became im-moral as a result of breaking that law? Such meat was *legally unclean*, as was the one who ate it, but one did not become *morally* unclean by eating such meat. Jesus shows that one becomes morally unclean from within, not by eating meat which only makes one legally or ceremonially unclean. This is the point made in Matthew 15:11, 18-20.

This is the point we have been making on the difference between moral law and positive divine law. No meat was ever unclean *per se*. But many of the religious teachers had come to view certain meats as unclean in them-selves, and that is why both Jesus in the passage considered in the previous section, and Paul in Romans 14, make the point they do about meats. They are correcting a misunderstanding. But in doing this neither of them teaches that when the law was in effect such divine commands governing them did not matter. Neither Jesus nor Paul is discrediting the commands of God as some are attempting to do today by their use of these statements from them.

Once the law had ended all men were to view all meats as clean. This was but to see them as they were originally before God made some meats unclean by arbitrary command. Under the law of Moses God had temporarily, and in an arbitrary way, made it wrong to eat certain meats. Such meats were wrong during that period because God had made them wrong by positive divine law. In the same way, as illustrated in chapter 11, he has made some things right that are not right in themselves.

The wording from Paul that "there is nothing unclean of itself" makes it evident that the Mosaic prohibitions regarding certain kinds of meats (the subject under discussion in Romans 14) had no foundation in the nature of the meats themselves. At the time he was writing this letter, not all had this knowledge. Those who had this knowledge are called the "strong," and those who did not have this knowledge are called the "weak." In such matters of liberty each person must live according to his own knowledge of the subject. They become unclean only when one judges them to be unclean.

What does Paul mean by "of itself" when he says, "I know . . . that there is nothing unclean of itself"? He means "when the food is the only medium for our considering it" (Lenski, *Romans* 834). But what about when there is a direct command of God requiring a certain practice with regard to meat? Wouldn't a divine precept, a positive divine law, on whether or not certain meat is to be eaten change our responsibility with regard to it? Would we still have the same liberty which Paul grants here on the eating of meats if there were still certain regulations concerning the eating of meat? What about the eating of blood? We have not been loosed from that law. Is this a matter of liberty even though God has not loosed the law concerning it? Is one "immoral" if he eats blood? Paul is not saying that we are free from the details of commands that apply to us today, nor is he saying that only principle and purpose matter in commands that we are under in this age.

The real question to be answered is this: Is Paul's statement, "I know, and am persuaded by the Lord Jesus, that there is nothing unclean of itself," a universal statement that would apply to everything? This appears to be the way it is being used by Cecil Hook in his book, *Free In Christ*. Isn't this the point of the statement that "our purity of thought or defilement of purpose determines whether a thing is moral or immoral"? He only considers things moral, immoral, and amoral. He never speaks of things religious, or of positive divine laws. But he certainly applies this rule to commands, and he seems to make application to *all things* (not just amoral actions and things) when he quotes Shakespeare's statement that "nothing is good or bad, but thinking makes it so." Doesn't this mean everything without exception, including positive divine law?

It would appear that if this brother believes in positive divine law, he would apply this statement to positive law as well as to what he calls amoral matters. Yet, neither Jesus nor Paul in the passages being used to support this theory means that the sole determining factor of right and wrong in *religious* matters is "purity of thought or defilement of purpose." That was not true regarding unclean meats during the time such laws were in effect, nor has it ever been true of any other positive divine law. Such universal statements like this are subject to being misunderstood and misapplied.

Would this rule, for example, apply to baptism or the Lord's supper? This point was considered in the previous section when we studied Jesus' statement in Matthew 15:11, 17-20.

Others who have written on this subject have given the same kind of warning that we are giving here. Hendriksen, for example, says: "This does not mean that sin is wholly a matter of subjective opinion or of conscience. No, there are many things that are definitely forbidden. No mere opinion on man's part, or even the silence of conscience, can make right what God has declared to be wrong. But it does mean that even a human activity — in the present case eating meat a person considers to be unclean — is wrong for those who consider it to be wrong" (*Romans* II: 462). Arnold issues a similar warning on the limited role of conscience: "Men are not always doing right when they act according to their consciences, for conscience is not the *ultimate* standard of right, since it may be only partially enlightened. But men are always guilty when they act *contrary* to their consciences, when they do what they do not believe to be right. Paul was conscientious in persecuting Christians before his conversion (Acts 26:9), but this did not make his conduct right as he himself came fully to understand afterward (1 Cor. 15:9). There was nothing morally defiling in eating meat that had once been forbidden to the Jews, *but . . .* they would defile the conscience of him who should eat them, believing them to be still forbidden" (*Romans* 287).

To the Pure All Things Are Pure

To say that "our purity of thought or defilement of purpose determines whether a thing is moral or immoral," that "sin is not in things, but in people — in the heart," and that "nothing is good or bad, but thinking makes it so," and mean that *no action or thing can be wrong unless the motive is wrong* is to misapply these passages. It denies the existence of positive divine law, or, to say the least, it denies the authority of such law that comes from God. But what does Paul mean when he says, "unto the pure all things are pure: but unto them that are defiled and unbelieving is nothing pure; but even their mind and conscience is defiled" (Tit. 1:15)?

A statement such as this must be understood in light of the context where it appears, just as the other passages we have considered have to be taken. Here Paul is dealing with a certain class of false teachers who were a serious threat to the people in Crete where Titus was doing the work of an evangelist. The verse quoted is a concluding point that Paul wants to make and also provides a summary of what he has said in the preceding verses concerning these teachers. What he says is a proverbial sounding statement concerning "the pure." This word alone lets us know that a significant element of the false teaching concerned Jewish ceremonial practices which no doubt were being taught as necessary in living the Christian life. In addition to the use of the word "pure" in this verse, there is also a direct reference to "the circumcision" in v. 10 which confirms the point we made about the word "pure," i.e., it shows that the false teaching concerned Jewish ceremonial practices.

No doubt these teachers were claiming that certain dietary regulations made them "pure." Because of how they were using this term, Paul uses the same word to identify Christians in contrast to unbelievers. Christians are the "pure" even without the regulations the Jews were attempting to impose upon them. The unbelievers are the "defiled," or the unclean. On this basis, it would seem logical to conclude with Lea and Griffin that "to those who are pure, all things are pure in the sense that ceremonial cleanliness is totally unnecessary and of no value" (*1, 2 Timothy, Titus* 292). Since this passage is treating the same subject as the two passages we have already taken up in the preceding discussion, our comments on those passages of Scripture should be sufficient.

We will, nevertheless, share with the readers the following added comment of Lea and Griffin on this subject: "This basic truth reflects Jesus' teaching in Mark 7:1-23, and it was impressed upon Peter in Acts 10:9-15; 11:1-18. Such dietary rules are only the commands of men and therefore do not please God. Obviously Paul was *not* suggesting that the pure cannot sin or be tainted with moral failure and sinful behavior." We might add, nor was he suggesting that the only thing that determines right and wrong is the motive of the individual

The Kingdom Not Meat and Drink
And finally: Yes, it is true, "the kingdom of God is not meat and drink; but righteousness, and peace, and joy in the Holy Spirit" (Rom. 14:17). But does this mean that the only thing that matters in a command is motive? If so, then the only thing that matters in *eating* the bread and *drinking* the fruit of the vine in the Lord's supper is our motive. But are "eating" the bread and "drinking" the fruit of the vine (the actions involved in the Lord's

supper) *necessary* parts of our worship and service in the kingdom? Again, as we have said before, we must keep what Paul says in context. Paul has shown that one must take into account his brother's need even when practicing a matter of liberty. Yet, in the context of what Paul is discussing (eating meats that some regarded as unclean), and the kinds of things of which he says the kingdom of God does consist (righteousness, and peace, and joy in the Holy Spirit), it is true, as Whiteside says, that

> . . . the kingdom does not consist in distinctions about meats and drinks; but no man could conclude that freedom from the law in which such distinctions were made gives him the right to eat and drink as he pleases regardless of consequences. Righteousness has to do primarily with our treatment of others; it is doing right by others. You do not treat your fellow-Christian right, if in the exercise of your supposed freedom you lead him to do wrong. And peace in this connection refers to peace among members of the church. In a church where all members treat one another right, and are at peace among themselves, there is joy in the Holy Spirit. And the one who promotes such conditions in the church is well-pleasing to God, and is approved by all right thinking people (*Paul's Letter to the Saints at Rome* 273).

This is a far cry from saying that only motive matters in commands, or that only motive determines whether or not a thing is right or wrong. What Paul says falls far short of saying that the only thing that is important in commands is principle and purpose.

Chapter 14

The "Lawyer-Like" Approach (1): The Interpretation of Scripture

Some find it troublesome that many brethren have taken what they call a "lawyer-like approach" to the interpretation of Scripture through the years. They sometimes speak of this as "the legal approach." One brother who has been critical of this "self-defined" approach to studying the Scriptures spoke of legalism in this way: "Legalism misses the general concept and emphasizes the details as arbitrary, escalating them to life-and-death issues. It results in endless controversy and hair-splitting issues. It is a built-in system for dividing people" (Hook, *Free In Christ* 43).

It is certainly a mistake to "miss the general concept" of a passage of Scripture. But what if one gives due attention to the general concept of a passage and at the same time respects the details found in it? Is he still to be condemned as a legalist? Jesus condemned the scribes and Pharisees for paying tithe of mint and anise and cummin, and omitting the weightier matters of the law, such as judgment, mercy, and faith. But he did not say they should have left the less important things undone. He said, "these ought ye to have done (the "weightier matters" — *ww*) and not to leave the other undone" (Matt. 23:23).

Which was more important, being scrupulous in paying their tithes or being fair in their treatment of others? Maybe those who would criticize us in this way are being unfair to us. Do you suppose they are the ones who are guilty of the sin of the Pharisees? The Pharisees, you will remember, had failed (by omission) in judgment, mercy, and faith, *especially in reference to Jesus.* To see how they mistreated Jesus may help others see how they are mistreating those who are more conservative in their interpretation of Scripture.

In his comments on the Pharisees' mistreatment of Jesus, McGarvey points out that "they pronounced unjust judgments against him; they were unmerciful toward him in reference to the faults which they pretended to find in him; and they had no faith either in his word or the words of the prophets which were written of him" (*Matthew* 199). We do not ask that others have faith in our words in the same way the Pharisees should have had faith in Jesus' words. We only ask for a fair and impartial hearing.

Please notice that nowhere in his condemnation of the Pharisees does Jesus say it is unimportant to be particular about small matters. In fact, he says *that the Pharisees should NOT have left the smaller things undone.* He had reference of course to their tithe of mint, anise, and cummin.

The Lawyers In New Testament Times
The lawyers in Jesus' time were lawyers in relation to the law of Moses. *They were the same as the scribes in Jesus' day.* The term "lawyer" was applied to them because of their expertise in the Mosaic law. Since this law was the sole legislative word from God to Israel, in both civil and religious matters, it was their duty to interpret and teach exactly what was taught in the Scriptures of their day; that is, the Old Testament Scriptures.

1. The Religious Function of the Scribes. The religious function of the scribe seems to have developed during and after the exile. In Babylon the priestly cast became specialists in, and guardians of, the Mosaic law. Ezra, we are told, "was skilled in the law of Moses" and "had set his heart to study the law, and to do it, and to teach his statutes and ordinances in Israel" (Ezra 7:6, 10). In this respect Ezra "is the prototype of scribes of New Testament times, who were professional interpreters and teachers of the Old Testament" (Metzger, *The New Testament, Its Background, Growth and Content* 47).

Most scribes in Jesus' day belonged to the party of the Pharisees, but such expressions as "the scribes of the Pharisees" (Mark 2:16) and "some of the scribes of the Pharisees' party" (Acts 23:9) imply that some of them had other affiliations. Some likely belonged to the party of the Sadducees. The fact that we often find reference to "the scribes and Pharisees" shows the prominent status of the scribes as professional members of the Pharisaic party. They were not, however, paid professionals. Their work of teaching and transmitting the law was gratuitous. They had to depend upon other means of obtaining a livelihood.

The professional employment of the scribes was basically threefold. They were concerned with (1) the more careful theoretical development of the law itself; (2) the teaching of the law to their pupils; (3) and the practical administration of the law in pronouncing legal decisions. It is in the first and third of these categories that we find the best examples of infractions upon the proper role they occupied as professional teachers of the law. Jesus found no fault with the fact that they were concerned with detail in the interpretation of the law. The problems he saw with the lawyers, or the scribes, were to be found elsewhere.

Because the law attempted to regulate all areas of one's life, the teachers of the law were naturally forced to decide not only theological questions, but legal ones as well. They found themselves trying to provide answers to such questions as: Just how far could one go in labor before he violated the command that no work was to be done on the Sabbath day? What was the proper method of formulating a marriage contract or effecting a divorce? How was one to certify the purchase of a field or a house?

2. The Training of the Scribes. The two main problems with the scribes were that they had a heart condition that needed to be corrected, and they had also come to depend too much upon what had been taught by the rabbis (teachers) who had gone before them. This method of interpretation had developed over a long period of time. The training of the scribes helps one understand how they came to this practice. Anyone who wished to become a scribe, or a learned teacher of the law, had to undergo a long and thorough course of study. Lohse describes this process in the following way:

> A group of pupils would gather around a famous teacher. Then, when a pupil applied for acceptance into the school of the teacher, the teacher would examine him and decide whether to accept or reject him. If accepted the pupil entered into a lifetime association with the teacher. He accompanied him on his journeys, listened to how he approached and solved problems, and questioned the teacher in order to glean his knowledge. The teacher delivered his teaching while seated (cf. Matt. 5:1); the pupil sat at his feet (cf. Acts 22:3) and had to assimilate the abundance of material that had been handed down in order to become familiar enough with the wealth of tradition to be able to apply it. The course of study consisted in large measure of remembering and repeating what was set forth. Within the framework of the teaching conversation the pupil questioned the teacher, then by means of counter-questioning by the teacher he was instilled with the proper method of meditation and reflection. In response to a first question (cf., e.g., Luke 10:25), the teacher suggests: "What do you read, what do you find in the Scripture?" (Luke 10:26). When the pupil brings forward what he knows that he can cite from Scripture (Luke 10:27), the teacher answers that he has spoken correctly (Luke 10:28). By means of further inquiry by the pupil, then, a detailed exposi-

tion by the teacher is evoked. The discussion is finally resolved by the presentation of a question which furnishes the pupil with the insight to recognize the inescapable conclusion (Luke 10:37). Jesus, in his instructional discourse, also converses with his disciples or with other men who come to him in various forms of questioning. But Jesus' relationship to the disciples differed, from the very outset, from that of a scholar to his pupils because the disciples did not apply for admission to a circle of pupils, but were called by Jesus to follow him and were taught, in contrast to the scribes, with unprecedented authority (cf. Mark 1:22 par.; Matt. 7:29, *et passim*).

When the pupil had completed his course of study, he was declared a scholar by his teacher, who laid his hands upon him and ordained him. Thereby, he was incorporated into the chain of tradition which was traceable to Moses and was given the authority to answer questions and discuss the Law independently, as a teacher. As a master he was addressed with the title of respect "rabbi" (Matt. 23:7-8), and might now wear the long robe of the scholar (Mark 12:38 par.). In the synagogue the place of honor on the cathedra of Moses belonged to him (Mark 12:39 par.). People greeted him with respect (Mark 12:38 par.) and were ready to follow his word. . . . (*The New Testament Environment* 117-118).

3. The Contrast Between Jesus and the Scribes. The contrast between Jesus' method of teaching and that of the scribes is striking. In connection with the point made by Matthew that he "taught as one having authority, and not as the scribes" (Matt. 7:29), as pointed out in the above quote, Jesus also often used the word "verily" in his speeches, and in this way he distinguished himself from other teachers among the Jews. This word means *amen* and implies a finality and authority of his message quite unparalleled elsewhere. Metzger, in the statement below, emphasizes the importance of this practice and how it underscores the closing statement of the Sermon on the Mount:

The entire range of Jewish literature knows of no example of a scribe or rabbinical teacher prefacing his remarks with the expression, "Verily (*amen*), I say to you. . . ." This solemn formula, however, appears thirty times in Mark, six times in Luke, and twenty times in John (who usually doubles the word, "Verily, verily . . ."). The sayings which are thus prefixed are of varied individual content, but most of them have to do with Jesus' own person, either as Messiah or as demanding faith in his messiahship in spite of outward appearances and mistaken views. The point of the *amen* before such sayings is to show that their truth is guaranteed because Jesus himself, in his *amen*, acknowledges them to be his own sayings, thus making them valid. The whole implication is that through this characteristic mode of speech Jesus affirms his unique authority, presenting himself as one who speaks in the name and with the sanction of God himself. The reader is not surprised, therefore, to be told at the close of Jesus' Sermon on the Mount that "the crowds were astonished at his teaching, for he taught them as one who had authority, and not as their scribes" (156).

4. The Scribes and Tradition. We have said already that there were two main problems with the lawyers, or the scribes of Jesus' day. They needed a heart transplant (a new heart), and they relied on human tradition as their authority as they attempted to apply the Old Testament Scriptures to everyday life. The best example we have of both of these problems is found in Mark's account of Jesus' encounter with the scribes and Pharisees in Mark 7:1-23 and its parallel in Matthew 15:1-20 (see Chapter 13, "Amoral Matters and Positive Divine Law (2): The Specifics of the Argument," for a more thorough treatment of this passage). Several things are brought out that will add to one's understanding of the scribes and Pharisees, but in these passages there are two sins charged against them that we should briefly note.

Tradition Equal With the Word of God. First, Jesus charges them with putting human tradition on an equal with the word of God. They actually had such a high estimate of tradition that they would "leave God's commandment, and hold fast the tradition of men" (v. 7). Were the interpretations of the recognized legal experts of Jesus' day (the scribes of yesteryear) as important as the written word of God? The lawyers of that time thought so! Let those of our own day who decry the specifics of a command — and who would hold on only to the principle revealed in it that they might practice their own human traditions (which, in fact, is what Jesus calls "the doctrines and commandments of men") — weep in shame for doing the same thing as the lawyers of that day.

Jesus was strong in his denunciation of the scribes and Pharisees for this practice. Would he not do the same today? How are the religious practices of our own day that are *based solely upon human tradition* any different? Does the fact that they are promoted under the guise of religion make them different? How could it, when this was also true of the traditions of the scribes and Pharisees. Or, ponder this question: Why would Jesus condemn them if only the principle of a command matters? The issue then was, where is the authority for such practices? And the issue is the same today. Does not the warning of 2 Timothy 4:3, 4 address this subject: "For the time will come when they will not endure sound doctrine, but, having itching ears, will heap to themselves teachers after their own lusts; and will turn away their ears from the truth, and turn aside to fables." Those today who are advocating only the "principle" of commands matters and not the specifics found in a command, would be hard pressed to find *anyone* who has *ever* fallen prey to such a practice as foretold by Paul in this passage!

We must not lose sight of the fact that the Pharisees were the liberals of their day. They wrote laws that God had not revealed *in order to free men from the responsibility of keeping the laws he had revealed.* This is the very lesson Jesus is teaching in Matthew 15:1-9 when he illustrates his point by citing the rule of "corban." This was a man-made rule, an invention of men, meant to free them from certain responsibilities God had clearly imposed upon them. This rule of "corban" had become their tradition, and by this rule, and other such rules (traditions), they had set aside the law of God and made it void. Can anyone find a more perfect example of a *modern day Pharisee* than the modern day liberals like Cecil Hook? What else is his "principle above specifics in commands" rule but his way of writing a law God has not revealed (we might call it *his modern day "corban" rule*) to take the place of the laws (commands) God has revealed?

Guilty of Hypocrisy. Second, Jesus charges the scribes and Pharisees with being guilty of the sin of hypocrisy. He taught his disciples that what the teachers of the law taught that came from the written law itself was to be respected and adhered to. This must be the meaning of his statement, "whatsoever they bid you observe, that observe and do," in Matthew 23:3. He could not in these words be referring to the traditions of the elders which were being taught by them, for the traditions which they had adopted were repudiated by him. He goes on to caution, "but do not ye after their works: for they say, and do not." What were the "heavy burdens" put on others by the scribes (v. 4)? Again, they would not be the things required of them in the law, but the human traditions which Jesus had strongly repudiated. Many of these traditions they did not observe themselves. This was illustrated by the "corban" rule which Jesus used to make this point in Matthew 15:4-6 and Mark 7:10-13. Jesus goes on to show that even the things which they did were done to be seen of men (Matt. 23:5f.).

Hypocrisy is rooted in self-righteous pride. It is more than being inconsistent, for all men are inconsistent to some degree, and yet Jesus does not call all men hypocrites. The sin of self-righteous pride is illustrated best in Scripture in the story of the Pharisee and the Publican (Luke 18:9-14). The parable was spoken to those who "trusted in themselves that they were righteous, and despised others" (v. 9). This shows that one's heart is important. God looks at the heart (1 Sam. 16:7), and he looks to see that our worship and service come from an honest and good heart (see also Luke 8:15; Rom. 6:17-18; Eph. 6:5-8, etc.).

Does one always know when he is guilty of the sin of hypocrisy? No, probably not. Bales outrightly rejects such a conclusion when he says that "hypocrisy . . . does not mean that the individual is always conscious of the fact that he is play-acting at religion, or that he is using the pretense of being good to cover an evil heart. The person may have play-acted in religion so long that he thinks that he is truly religious. He may have deceived others so long, that it has become habitual with him and he has deceived himself. Men may rationalize so long and so shrewdly that they may finally hide their real motives from themselves. The Pharisees had evidently done this . . . (Matt. 23:16, 24; Lk. 12:56; 13:15; John 16:1-2)" (*Woe Unto You?* 12).

Remember, too, that Jesus is charging the scribes and Pharisees with *two* sins: (1) hypocrisy, and (2) adding human traditions to the written word of God. He is not saying that the only thing that is wrong with them is bad motive, or an evil heart.

5. The Ridiculous Applications of the Scribes. Some of the interpretations of the scribes bordered on the absurd. In their efforts to help others avoid violating a divine commandment they sometimes went far beyond what most today would consider reasonable. Metzger illustrates this point with the following examples:

> Thus, in order to obey the commandment forbidding work on the Sabbath day (Exod. 20:8-11), one needed to know what activities constituted work and what did not. Obviously, for example, threshing grain and lifting burdens of the sabbath were work and were therefore prohibited. But many, many other activities might also fall into the same category, and these needed to be determined in order to avoid violating the divine commandment. In the course of centuries it was decided that one might be allowed to walk through a grain field on the sabbath when the grain was ankle-high, but not if it were knee-high; for then one's legs would strike the ripened seeds of the grain, and, by such action, one would thresh some of the grain. Again, a poultice might be placed on a boil on the sabbath in order to prevent it from becoming worse, but not in order to promote its healing. If a cotton wadding which was worn in one's ear happened to fall out on the sabbath, it might not be replaced, for this was judged to constitute lifting a burden. Even certain actions, not unlawful in themselves, were forbidden on the sabbath lest they should become the occasion of actions deemed to be labor. Thus, a woman was forbidden to look in a mirror on the sabbath lest perchance she see a grey hair and be tempted to pluck it out, which would involve "working" (48-49).

Metzger goes on to point out that "even the most trivial problems were debated by scribes with great earnestness. It was agreed, for example, that if one threw an object into the air and caught it with the same hand he had violated the sabbath commandment, but there was some doubt about one's guilt if the object were thrown into the air with one hand and caught with the other hand" (49). What did and what did not violate the divine law was determined by the interpretations of the scribes and accepted by the Pharisees. It was these kinds of ridiculous interpretations or legal pronouncements that constituted "the traditions of the elders" (Matt. 15:2; Mark 7:3, 5).

Lost in the Interpretative Maze?

Those who have not fallen prey to the "grace-fellowship" syndrome that has captivated the thinking of many in our time are charged with having become "lost in the interpretative maze" of the "lawyer-like" interpretation of Scripture of Jesus' day. But surely from the examples we have just cited representing the way the scribes handled Scripture (for example, setting it aside when it did not harmonize with their traditions) does not describe those against whom the charge is made in our day. This method of interpretation more aptly fits the hermeneutic which says that the specifics of a command do not matter! This treatment of Scripture allows one to cast aside a specific in a command in order to make room for the traditions of men, or the doctrines and commandments of men, that our "liberal" brethren want to bring into the church today.

So, exactly what do such critics have in mind when they charge conservative brethren with practicing a "lawyer-like" interpretation of Scripture?

1. Sitting in Judgment of All Others. For one thing, like the lawyers of Jesus' day, we are told, they (meaning those who advocate strict obedience) have "put on their robes and sit in judgment of all others," pronouncing all who have "made a wrong turn" to eternal punishment. According to these critics (who, by the way, *sit in judgment* of *us*), lawyer-like people are needed only because such people have "conceived of a system of law half revealed and half concealed in biography, historical accounts, treatises, personal letters and prophecy" (*Free In Christ* 41).

We have already discussed the subject of whether or not we are under a system of law today (see Chapters 6 through 9). In Chapter 9 we saw that the law of Christ includes "biography, historical accounts, treatises, personal letters, and prophecy" in the same way that the Old Testament "law" included all of these different kinds of material. Christ's law, however, is not a "system of law" if one means by these terms that all of the commands of Christ are given at one place in the New Testament as a codified list of laws. The terms "system of law" as applied to the Old Testament describe that law as a "system of works" wherein one is required to keep all that the law requires before he can be saved under it (Gal. 3:10-13).Those who sought a "works righteousness" were condemned for this reason, but they were not condemned for attempting to be faithful to God by keeping his law.

"Walking Circumspectly," Yet Dependent Upon Christ. When Cecil Hook charges his conservative brethren with "legalism," he redefines the term and gives it a meaning his conservative brethren do not accept. I know of no brother who thinks his justification is "dependent upon keeping the details of a legal code." Yet this is how Hook describes one whom he *judges* to be a legalist. Why would he define this term as he does except for the purpose of using it in a *pejorative* way? In this way he has become *our* judge! Every brother I know is fully aware that he cannot be saved by his own good works, or by mere law-keeping. Under the law of Christ we are saved on the basis of faith in the blood of Christ (Rom. 3:23-26), but that does not free us from giving careful attention to details when it comes to obeying God. Like Paul who commands Christians to "walk circumspectly," or in a strict manner before God (Eph. 5:15), even though we do our best to be true to him in every way (even every detail!), we yet have no confidence in the flesh, or in our own accomplishments; our confidence is in him who died for us (Phil. 3:1-9).

We must repeat, we are still under law in relation to Christ. This is what Paul calls "the law of Christ" (1 Cor. 9:21). To become a Christian we had to obey Christ, which involved our meeting certain conditions laid down by Christ the lawgiver (John 8:24; Luke 13:3, 5; Mark 16:16; Acts 2:38). Then to be faithful to him as Christians we have to continue to obey him and be true to him (Matt. 7:21-23; Luke 6:46; 1 Cor. 15:58; 1 Pet. 4:10 with 1 Cor. 4:2).

Does this mean keeping the details of God's law? Yes, but that is not legalism. It simply means that love for God requires that we give him our best, that we keep his commandments (John 14:15). Jesus did not say keep my commandment (singular), but "keep my commandments" (plural). He did not say keep my "two" commandments, to love God and neighbor. He said, "keep my commandments." He did not say keep *some* of my commandments, nor did he say, keep those commandments *in which you can discern a principle* of some kind. He did not say *disregard the details* in my commandments, just seek out the principle, and if you can find a principle in a commandment of mine, keep that and don't bother with the rest. He said, "If you love me, keep my commandments."

One Lawgiver and Judge. "There is one lawgiver and judge, who is able to save and destroy" (Jas. 4:12), so I have never had the desire to attempt to legislate for God or to "sit in judgment of all others" by pronouncing them to eternal punishment when I think they have "made a wrong turn." I am not legislating for God when I give attention to, and am careful to obey, the details of a command. The one who is legislating for God is the man who is saying, find the principle in the command, and don't bother about the details. Where has God said that?

Anyone who is so presumptuous as to add to God's commands, or who takes away from them, is putting himself into the place of a legislator. By his very act of omission or addition to God's commands he is saying that he knows more than God. And by this same act of omission or addition to the commands of God one is saying either (1) that he needs *less* than what God has said in a command (the act of omission), which means he has greater confidence *in himself* to decide what he does *not* need than he has in God to tell him what he does need; or (2) that he needs *more* than God has revealed to him in a given command (the act of addition), which says he has more confidence *in himself* to decide what he *does* need than he has in God to tell him what he does not need. What is said here of commands would also apply to other ways God has in letting man know what he expects of him, i. e., to approved apostolic examples and necessary implications.

Man Must Make Some Judgments. Even though no man is the final judge of another, and should not try to be, that does not mean that man is free from making judgments. Far from it. The very ones who pronounce all who give attention to the specifics of commands with being "lawyer-like" in their approach to the interpretation of Scripture, and say that they are "legalistic," have become "judges," and think of themselves as "the spiritually elite" — these very ones have themselves made a judgment concerning us! They have become judges of those whom they condemn for acting as judges! Let them charge us with "seeking legal specifications," or with preferring the "command approach," if they choose, but in doing so they become guilty of the very crime they charge against others.

The Bible requires that we all make certain choices and judgments regarding both things and persons. "Buy the truth and sell it not" (Prov. 23:23) and "I hate every false way" (Ps. 119:104) mean that there is a difference between God's way and man's way. One is true, the other is false. Man must decide. He must make the judgment as to what belongs to God's truth and what does not; what originates with God and what comes from man. When a person decides certain things belong to "truth" — that they are right because they are according to God's truth — he must necessarily think that whatever else is done by others is not according to that truth and is therefore wrong, and that those who do these things are wrong. If one did not think this, then he could do what others do, and he would call it "truth," because he would be convinced that those things are the truth of God on the subject involved.

Try the Spirits. John admonishes, "Beloved, believe not every spirit, but try the spirits whether they are of God: because many false prophets are gone out into the world" (1 John 4:1). How can one do that without becoming a judge? He has to decide between the spirits, or between what is preached by the different ones who have gone forth to preach. Is what one preaches from God, or is it from men (see Matt. 21:23-27)? In view of the admonition, let the hearer beware. He must judge between the spirits. How is man to do that? In the same way the Bereans judged Paul's preaching. They searched the Scriptures to see whether or not the things he was preaching were so (Acts 17:11).

Prove All Things. Paul urged the Thessalonians, "Prove all things; hold fast that which is good" (1 Thess. 5:21). Why is there a need to prove "all" things to be able to hold on to the good if only the principle of a command is important? To say that all things must be put to the test of truth does not sound like the Bible only speaks to us in general terms. In fact, when the Bible does speak to us in principle, or in general terms, our knowledge must continue to increase to the point that we can even distinguish between the good, or know what is best for us in things permissible (Phil. 1:9-10). But whether the Bible speaks to us at a given place in specific terms or in principle only, it yet remains that in the former case one must decide what is true as over against what is false, and in the latter case he must decide what is best for him in the things that are good.

Fairness Required. We must strive to be fair in our judgments, which means that we must "judge righteous judgments" (John 7:23); and we must consistently practice impartiality (Jas. 2:1-13), for as James says, "for he shall have judgment without mercy, that hath showed no mercy; and mercy rejoiceth against judgment" (Jas. 2:13). These two areas are the places where the scribes and Pharisees failed in the judgments they made of others. The scribes worked to place heavy loads on others which they themselves were not willing to bear (Matt. 23:4). These "heavy burdens" were the traditions of the elders, or the doctrines and commandments of men. Jesus said to the Pharisees, "for with what judgment ye judge, ye shall be judged: and with what measure ye mete, it shall be measured to you again" (Matt. 7:2). They needed to get the plank out of their own eye before they attempted to get the speck of sawdust out of their brother's eye (Matt. 7:3-5). "Blessed are the merciful; for they shall obtain mercy" (Matt. 5:7). All such sayings are not intended to condemn all judging, but to put important guidelines upon it, as well as to keep it within certain limits.

2. Preach the Word — Some Will Not Endure Sound Doctrine. The work of the gospel preacher is to "preach the word: be instant in season, out of season; reprove, rebuke, exhort with all longsuffering and doctrine" (2 Tim. 4:2). Some however will not endure "sound doctrine" when it is preached (v. 3). If Paul is merely concerned about "principle" being preached why would he use words like "sound doctrine" to express that idea, and why would he warn that men will often turn a deaf ear to this sound doctrine if all Timothy will be preaching is the principle of love? For men to turn away "their ears from the truth, and . . . be turned unto fables" is more than to turn from one set of principles to another set of principles. Paul says men turn away from the truth unto "fables." These "fables" or myths were *genealogical narratives* described as "myths and genealogies" in 1 Timothy 1:4. Hendriksen points out that Paul here refers to

> man-made supplements to the law of God (see verse 7), mere myths or fables (2 Tim. 4:4), old wives' tales (1 Tim. 4:7) that were definitely Jewish in character (Titus 1:14). Measured by the standard of *truth*, what these errorists taught deserved the name *myths*. As to *material contents* these myths concern *genealogical narratives* that were largely fictitious.

> We feel at once that here we have been introduced into the realm of typically *Jewish* lore. It is a known fact that from early times the rabbis would "spin their yarns" — and *endless* yarns they were! — on the basis of what they considered some "hint" supplied by the Old Testament. They would take a name from a list of pedigrees (for example, From Genesis, I Chronicles, Ezra. Nehemiah), and expand it into a nice story. Such interminable embroideries on the inspired record were part of the regular bill of fare in the synagogue, and were subsequently deposited in written form in that portion of *The Talmud* which is known as *Haggadah*.

> *The Book of Jubilees* (also called *The Little Genesis*) offers another striking example of what Paul hand in mind. It is a kind of *haggadic* commentary on the canonical Genesis; that is, it is an exposition interspersed with an abundant supply of illustrative anecdotes. The book was probably written toward the close of the second or at the beginning of the first century B.C. It covers the entire era from the creation until the entrance into Canaan. This long stretch is divided into fifty jubilee-periods of forty-nine (7 X 7) years each. In fact, the entire chronology is based on the number 7, and heavenly authority is claimed for this arrangement. Thus not only does the week have 7 days, the month 4 X 7 days, but even the year has 52 X 7 = 364 days, the year-week has 7 years, and the jubilee has 7 X 7 = 49 years. The separate events regarding the patriarchs, etc., are

pin-pointed in accordance with this scheme. The sacred narrative of our canonical book of Genesis is embellished, at times almost beyond recognition. Thus, we now learn that the sabbath was observed already by the arch-angels, that the angels also practiced circumcision, that Jacob never tricked anybody, etc.

In every age there are people who love to indulge in such strange mixtures of truth and error. They even treat these adulterations as being the all-important thing. They carry on lengthy debates about dates and definitions. Instead of brushing aside all such syncretistic rubbish, they discover fine distinctions and engage in hairsplitting disputes. They pile myth upon myth, fable upon fable, and *the end* is never in sight. Thus the law of God is made void by human tradition (cf. Matt. 15:6), and the picture drawn in the sacred original becomes grossly distorted (*I-II Timothy and Titus* 58-59).

3. The Pattern of Sound Words. In the first chapter Paul admonished Timothy to "hold fast the form of sound words" which he had received of Paul (1 Tim. 1:13). The word "form" shows that Paul's own teaching provided Timothy a "model," a "pattern," to follow. We could call it a blueprint, a term which those who argue that the New Testament is not a constitution are hard pressed to explain. Of course, the fact that the Scriptures are described as furnishing us a source from which we are to determine "every good work" ought to be enough to convince any that they are a constitution or blueprint.

This body of truth that Paul refers to in 1 Timothy 1:13 consists of the "words" Timothy had heard from Paul. Timothy was required to *hold to* this *pattern*, never to depart from it in his preaching. No one can remain "sound" or healthy in relation to the truth of God when he leaves the truth, the *pattern* of sound words. The idea so often advocated today that a man has a right to his own beliefs as long as he is honest and sincere in holding them is a lie. Such a view is outrightly contradicted by these kinds of statements from Paul found throughout the letters of 1-2 Timothy and Titus (see 1 Tim. 1:10; 6:3; 2 Tim. 4:3; Tit. 1:9, 13; 2:1, 2, 8).

These "words" of truth are sometimes used by God to bring out important principles that must be respected, received, and implemented, but oftentimes God uses "words" to take one beyond the mere principle of a subject to the specifics of it. The word "fable" or "myth" is used here to identify the content of the false teaching. To ignore such words, or to turn away from "the truth" conveyed by such words used by God himself, just because one wants them to say something else, is clear proof that one does not love God, and that he does not love the truth that has been revealed by

God. To be properly received and communicated the words used by God to convey his truth and to issue warnings about teaching that is contrary to the truth, one must "hold" or cling to these words in "faith and love" (2 Tim. 1:13). This describes the true spirit in which Timothy and all other faithful teachers of the word of God are to cling to the truth and pass it on to others.

If Timothy had been a preacher like those of our time who are promoting unity in spite of major differences that pertain to the truth of the gospel, he would have seen little danger in the "myths" being espoused in his day. In the spirit of brotherly love he would have urged all others to receive these men as "brethren." Those who were espousing such myths would also have contended that these teachers should be received by their brethren in the name of "liberty," or because of the freedom we have in Christ. We are about to see in the next section that there were "liberals" among the scribes or lawyers in Jesus' day just as there were conservatives.

When conservatives are charged with taking a "lawyer-like" approach to the interpretation of Scripture, they must read further before they can know which method of interpretation the writer is alleging against them. In the first century the Pharisees, who were greatly influenced by the scribes or lawyers of their day, were divided into two schools of thought. These different schools of thought reflect the liberal and conservative approaches to the interpretation of the law. The two methods of interpretation are well illustrated in the two leading teachers of the day.

Hillel and Shammai
Hillel (c. 60 B.C.-c. A.D. 20) gained a prominence among the rabbis of the first century due to his excellence in the elucidation of legal rules from the Scripture. He had a great zeal for Torah study (Torah = the law), and he became a model for later students. He had come to Jerusalem to study biblical exegesis, where he was trained by Shemaiah and Abtalion, two of the early great expositors of the law. Hillel was either the father or grandfather of the Gamaliel we read about in Acts 5:33-40. He is described by Luke as "a doctor of the law, had in reputation among all the people." Paul received training "according to the perfect manner of the law of the fathers" from this great teacher (Acts 22:3). Hillel is usually thought of as belonging to the most liberal interpreters of the law, favoring a freer interpretation of the biblical text.

Shammai (c. 50 B.C.-c. A.D. 30) was more conservative in his interpretations of the text of Scripture. These two different methods of interpretation are well illustrated on the subject of divorce. It is likely that the rivalry between these two schools is reflected in the questions put before Jesus on this subject as recorded in Matthew 19:1ff. In his answer to their question Jesus evidently sided with Shammai against Hillel. The question was, on what grounds might divorce be allowed according to the law? The question likely had the statement from Deuteronomy 24:1 in mind. According to this passage of Scripture, Moses allowed a man to write his wife a bill of divorcement if he "found some uncleanness in her." Hillel interpreted this passage liberally, saying that a man might divorce his wife for the most trivial of reasons, including even that of putting too much seasoning in his food! Shammai, on the other hand, interpreted this passage from Moses strictly, permitting divorce only on the grounds of unchastity.

The technical terms used of rabbis when issuing authoritative decisions were "binding" and "loosing," the same terms used by Jesus when speaking of the apostles' power to bind and loose in Matthew 16:19 and 18:18. To bind was to declare an action unlawful, and to loose was to declare it lawful. We see this authority exercised by the scribes on the subject of gathering wood in the two differing points of view held by Hillel and Shammai. The liberal interpretation of this law vs. the conservative method of interpretation is again made clear: "Concerning gathering wood on a feast day, the school of Shammai binds (that is, forbids) it — the school of Hillel looses (that is, permits) it."

Some think that in the decades prior to the catastrophe of A.D. 70 the more conservative attitude of the Shammaites tended to prevail among the Pharisees generally, but that from the following reconstruction onward it was the gentler viewpoint of the Hillelites that won out. This means that during this period the division within the Pharisees came to an end.

Learning from the Pharisees
Whether one was of the liberal or conservative schools of thought among the Pharisees, the problems generally were the same, because both groups tended to major in minors (Matt. 23:23). The Pharisees were right in longing for a righteous Israel and the hope of the coming Messianic kingdom. But, as so often is the case, their attempt to be faithful to the law in every area of their life led them into extremes. Bringing their lives into subjection to the law in all of these areas was a noble and worthy aim. This was no doubt what motivated them. Yet, the excesses were not to be excused. The hypocrisy (whether known or not) on the part of some, and the addition of the traditions of the elders to the law — traditions which they had received from the scribes — were not justified. One's concern for righteousness should not be allowed to drive him to such extremes. Too often those who are properly motivated to live righteously become convinced that they have attained the righteousness they seek. This was

true of the Pharisees. Yet, unknowingly they rejected their only hope of righteousness.

Such vices and virtues of Pharisaism are a good reminder to all of us that no matter where we are in our Christian lives, the Pharisees have much to say to us today. Their desire for righteousness should be regarded by all — both liberals and conservatives alike — as attractive and biblical. But their love for praise and pomp, and their devotion to the traditions of the elders which they received directly from the scribes, should be a warning to all of those who profess to be Christians. We say this not just to the liberal minded among us, as some might think, but to the conservatives as well.

Those who are liberal in their interpretation of Scripture may charge their conservative brethren with legalism, but if legalism was the sin of the Pharisees, what was it that made them guilty of this sin? Not only is it sinful to trust in one's self as though he is "right" 100% of the time, or right in all of his beliefs and practices with no possibility of being wrong, but it is also sinful to presume upon God and take liberties where God has given none, or to add to the word of God like the Pharisees did in bringing in their human traditions and thereby making their worship vain. One does not have the "right" to throw out all pattern authority and change the laws of God into liberties.

The liberal interpreter tends to loose where God has not loosed; but he also tends to bind where God has not bound. The Pharisees exemplified both tendencies. Someone may say, "But isn't it the conservative interpreter that is more likely to bind where God has not bound"? He may of course do that, but not necessarily so. The tendency to make laws is a liberal act, as we have seen from our study of Matthew 15:1-9.

Isn't it possible for one to be a "Biblical literalist" without inventing laws for God? A person may interpret Scripture strictly without trusting in himself. A true conservative simply trusts in God to reveal to him what he should do and how it should be done. He believes the Bible is the word of God and that whatever he does must be authorized by God from Scripture. He acts on the premise that he is not permitted to take from the word of God or add to it. Shammai was a biblical literalist; he had the mindset of a true conservative. He was what some would call a "strict constructionist." He interpreted Scripture strictly, as Paul did, and Paul also taught Christians to walk in the same way, i.e., "strictly" ("circumspectly," in Eph. 5:15).

There were others in the first century from among the Pharisees who belonged to this class. On one occasion when Jesus' life was threatened by

Herod "there came certain of the Pharisees, saying unto him, Get thee out, and depart hence: for Herod will kill thee" (Luke 13:31). These reflect a more noble element in Palestinian Pharisaism. Joseph of Arimathaea, "an honourable counsellor, which also waited for the kingdom of God," who came to make request of Pilate for Jesus' body (Mark 15:43-46), and Nicodemus, who came to Jesus by night (John 3:1; 19:39), were also of this class of Pharisees. Some think that the chief Pharisee who had Jesus for dinner belongs in this class as well (Luke 14:1).

If one could be a Pharisee and not be a legalist (one who trusts in himself and his own righteousness for his salvation), like those we have just noted, could not one who is a Christian be such a person and yet not be a legalist? Such a person believes in interpreting Scripture strictly, but he does not believe in law-keeping as a way of salvation. Nor does he trust in his own performance in keeping the law of God. He knows he is saved by the blood of Christ, and that, even if he were able to do all it is his duty to do (which he is not, of course), he is yet an unprofitable servant (Luke 17:10).

Any person who has been in the Lord's church for a number of years surely knows that there are no doubt some among the conservative interpreters of the Bible who need to come to have a better understanding of this subject. Although J. D. Thomas has in years past defended some things that many of us strongly oppose, the following observation made by him in his book, *Harmonizing Hermeneutics*, on the subject of "the legalistic mindset" is worthy of consideration:

> All of us in the Restoration Movement still have some legalistic tendencies in our outlook because the movement from earliest times has emphasized an obedience to commands, and we preached this to our religious neighbors. As a group, we admittedly have spent much thought, comparatively, on first principles and not enough on second, or later, principles. Our total understanding has remained, for many of us, at an elementary level, and we have thus not yet risen above an obedience mindset in service to Christian duty.

> Many of our people feel a crucial obligation to worship weekly, but only on Sunday morning. Obedience is consciously and deliberately held to a minimum. Probably no congregation among us enjoys as many in attendance on Sunday night as Sunday morning. We are willing to obey minimally (to save our souls from hell), but not to do any more than the legal contract calls for. We want to get credit for punching the time-clock each Sunday, but we really do not care about the overall success of the Lord's cause. Our hearts do not ache for the lost. This attitude is not motivated by love for the Lord and our neighbors — our hearts are not really into

putting God first in our lives. We should love God (and our fellow-man) with all our hearts!

The denominational world has little respect for us because it believes that we preach only:

> The right church;
> The necessity of baptism;
> Vocal music only;
> Christianity is just a new-model law (no grace);
> What the Holy Spirit *doesn't* do.

This wrong conception, which is even promoted by some enemies of the church, certainly is not true of all of us, but in general, many do not realize that we preach Christ crucified as the central theme of our message, nor does it recognize that we have any deep consciousness of our being "one with the Lord as one spirit" (1 Cor. 6:17) — that each of us is "married to Christ" and enjoys a strong spiritual union.

As a people, we have not yet really comprehended God's grace. We still believe that we save ourselves. For us to realize fully that we have a Savior and that we are saved because of Him is difficult (82-83).

For people who depend on their own perfect rule-keeping in hopes of being saved, we encourage them to lean on Jesus. He can save us, but we cannot achieve perfection ourselves. This is the essence of Christianity. God sent Him down to save us because we cannot save ourselves. This is why He had to die for us — there was no other way. Jesus had to die.

Too many of us believe that one unforgiven trivial sin will send us to hell, even if we have otherwise spent a lifetime of faithfulness. We want our last breath to be a prayer of forgiveness so that we will not die with even the least bit of guilt still staining our souls. We pray, "Lord, save us, if we have been found faithful," when the truth is no one of us is going to be faithful in the sense of keeping all the commands perfectly. Such an attitude reflects pure legalism; it is based upon a human merit concept of law-keeping as the basis or ground of salvation rather than upon faith in the sin-offering of an atoning Christ who died to become our Savior.

We cannot preach the true Gospel to the world unless we understand it ourselves, and practice it in our lives (84).

Lessons from the Lawyers

Not all Pharisees were lawyers, or scribes, nor were all scribes members of the sect of the Pharisees. It is likely that the first several verses of Matthew 23 (through v. 22), and then verses 29-36, are directed at the scribes, and then verses 23-28 are leveled against the Pharisees, even though the char-acteristic address, "scribes and Pharisees," is used all the way through the first section. Even though Jesus uses this same address in verse 25, he immediately uses the singular (v. 26) "thou blind Pharisee" as he continues. In Luke's par-allel account the two groups are addressed separately. The scribes are addressed in Luke 11:46-52; 20:46-47, and the Pharisees in Luke 11:39-42, 44.

The charges leveled against the scribes were: (1) imposing very strict religious laws (the traditions, as pointed out earlier) on others, while avoiding them themselves; (2) building "tombs of the prophets" while ready to con-demn to death men sent by God; (3) keeping their learning secret and so cutting off the people's access to the kingdom of God, while making no use themselves of their own knowledge; (4) inordinate pride in dress, in saluta-tion, and in order of seating, particularly with regard to the synagogues.

The charges against the Pharisees were: (1) hypocrisy in carrying out the laws on purity, while remaining impure inwardly; (2) hypocrisy in pay-ing tithes on certain vegetables not required by the law, while neglecting the religious and moral obligations contained in it (see Jeremias, *Jerusa-lem in the Time of Jesus* 235-236 on these points). What we learn from this, according to Jeremias, is that the reproaches against the Pharisees "have absolutely nothing to do with a theological education; they are leveled at men who lead their lives according to the demands of the religious laws of Pharisaic scribes," whereas the reproaches against the lawyers or scribes "have a general bearing on their scribal education and its resulting privi-leges in social life."

So what may we learn from the scribes? We should learn to be more careful in doing what God has said. This is the only way to be sure not to leave undone the weightier matters of God's law. Had the scribes been more careful in doing God's will they would not have put the traditions of men above his law. It is no mark of spirituality to be indifferent to "command-ments" that come from God, perhaps due to some kind of aversion one might have to "law" in relation to Christ. Paul told the Corinthians that the things he was writing to them "are the commandments of the Lord" (1 Cor. 14:37).

There is also a warning to be found here against selfish pride. On this subject, Bales issues this warning: "We must exercise great care less we become proud that we are not Pharisees (or scribes — *ww*); and lest we try to prove it by freeing ourselves from all rules and principles of God. If we do this we are endeavoring to justify ourselves; for we are relying not upon what God has said, and upon His mercy, but upon our own inclinations and opinions" (*Woe Unto You* 131).

Chapter 15

The "Lawyer-Like" Approach (2): Alleged Inconsistencies

The Bible is not written just for the astute. It is written for the average man. At the end of a certain discourse Jesus gave in the temple, Mark says, "And the common people ("large crowd," NASB) heard him gladly" (Mark 12:37). This was said of average folk who made up the crowd nearby in contrast to the scribes about whom Jesus had been speaking (Mark 12:35). The crowd was enjoying what Jesus was saying about the scribes, even though they were not very receptive of him either. They liked what they heard but did not want to do what he taught.

Jesus goes on to give a strong rebuke of the scribes in verses 38-40. He says the kinds of things we have already learned about them: they loved to wear their long white robes of authority, to be greeted with titles of distinction (rabbi, father, master), and to sit in special seats in the synagogues and places of honor in the market places. They also took advantage of widows when they offered them a place to stay, and prayed long prayers just to be heard and seen of men. In the next section, Jesus describes a widow who loved God so much that she cast into the treasury all that she had. He wanted to show his disciples, in contrast to the scribes who would "devour widows' houses," how widows really should be treated.

But the strong denunciation presented here is not meant to represent every scribe as being this kind of person. Is not the scribe of whom Jesus said, "Thou art not far from the kingdom of God" (Mark 12:34), a scribe of a different sort? He had a clear understanding of what were the two greatest commandments of the law, and this clear perception of the teaching of the law is what led Jesus to compliment him in the way he did on this occasion (Mark. 12:32-34). This should be a reminder that we ought to be careful not to judge by stereotype.

There were a few good scribes in Jesus' day, and there were some good Pharisees, as we saw in the closing part of the last chapter. No doubt there were many of the kind Jesus rebukes, but there were at least a few who were better. These loved God supremely, loved their fellow man, and they loved the law of God. They were also honest and sincere, and there may have been some who, like Zacharias and Elizabeth, were "righteous before God, walking in all the commandments and ordinances of the Lord blameless" (Luke 1:5-6). Paul, though a highly trained man, also was this kind of person, even though he was a Pharisee (Phil. 3:1ff.). He came later to see how miserably he had failed to be righteous before God *on the basis of the law*, but at least he should be credited with being the kind of person he truly was while he was under the law and living as a Pharisee.

Supposed Examples of the Legal Approach

The true test of what is called "the legal approach" to Bible interpretation is not whether one is educated or uneducated. One may be a lawyer and "handle aright the word of God." On the other side, one may be uneducated and "twist the scripture to his own destruction." All false teachers are not of the elite class, nor do they all come from among the common folk. If legalism is "hair-splitting," or "emphasizing details as arbitrary," while overlooking the general concept of a passage, as alleged, the only way to determine whether or not one is guilty of such a charge is to examine the cases brought against him.

1. The Qualifications of Elders. In referring to the two lists of qualifications of elders in 1 Timothy 3:1-7 and Titus 1:5-9, one brother said Paul "is not giving a checklist of legal details" (*Free in Christ* 43). To throw the word "legal" into the mix, he means to identify any who would take these lists of qualifications in any kind of serious way as being guilty of legalism. To this brother's way of thinking, for anyone to insist that these qualifications are to be understood in an absolute way is absurd. As long as a congregation selects "men of spiritual maturity, reputation, and ability to teach and minister to the welfare of the congregation," it meets the demands of the qualifications. To insist on taking the qualifications one by one and applying them to see if one qualifies to be appointed to serve as an elder is not called for, according to this brother. H.E. Phillips effectively answers a similar position in his book, *Scriptural Elders and Deacons*, a number of years ago. He was addressing the view that "all qualifications are flexible and not absolute." What he said will answer Cecil Hook's argument as we have just described it:

> The detestable effort in this idea is to weaken the standard of God to the extent that the range from side to side is so broad that almost any sort of

person may be initiated into the eldership. The final end, with respect to other Bible matters, will not be accepted by its supporters. Are the qualifications for a Christian so flexible that one may believe what he wants to believe, repent after his own notion, confess about anything pertaining to religion, and be baptized in any form and for any purpose that pleases him? The answer comes back an unquestionable No! But if the qualifications of elders are so pliable, why are not the other requirements of God equally flexible? Why not allow the plan of salvation to be curved or reformed for different men in different situations if this be true of the eldership?

After one becomes allied with this proposition there are some other questions that must challenge his attention, and they certainly demand an answer. Just how flexible are the qualifications for the eldership? How far will they stretch? and how far can one shrink them? Who is permitted to do the stretching? It is perfectly consistent with the rules of Bible study to allow every man the same liberty granted to any one. If, then, one be permitted to stretch a point here and there, all others may stretch where they want to. Now who will be in authority to say when the stretching has reached its limits and in what points a man can stretch? But if there is no man who can rightly limit the flexibility of these qualities, what is to hinder someone from stretching them completely out of existence? These are pertinent questions to the issue and, to the honest, must be fairly answered. But when he undertakes them in the light of Bible truth, the whole structure of this theory falls because there is not one single scriptural stone in its foundation. The whole attitude is contrary to inspiration. The truth of the matter is that there is nothing in all the Bible that pertains to qualifications for any work of God that is so flexible as to allow man to bend to suit his own purpose (79-80).

Does the fact that brethren have differed through the years on the meaning of "the husband of one wife," or "having faithful children," prove that these qualifications do not count? That they really don't matter? One would think so from the way Hook treats these subjects. With him, though, the only way to have it right is to accept *his* interpretation of these qualifications — or should we say, with brother Phillips, be willing to "stretch" them as far as he is willing to stretch them; that is, in brother Hook's case, "out of existence"! I will not go into the meaning of these qualifications. Anyone who is interested enough to do so may read with great profit brother Phillips' book on these subjects.

There have been good men on both sides of the question of whether unmarried men may be appointed as elders. The same is true on whether he must have more than one child to be qualified, and whether his children must be Christians. But all have not been willing to "stretch" these qualifications out of existence, as this brother does. We would ask this brother, are all those who differ with him the cause of the "endless controversy" that arises over such matters? Does the controversy arise over "emphasizing details as arbitrary," or does it come from the efforts of those who would make these qualifications meaningless? No doubt, all would be well, and all controversy would cease, if all those who see details as being important when interpreting the Bible would let those of brother Hook's persuasion decide just how far to stretch the word of God.

But H.E. Phillips' point is a valid one: "If, then, one be permitted to stretch a point here and there, all others may stretch where they want to. Now who will be in authority to say when the stretching has reached its limits and in what points a man can stretch. But if there is no man who can rightly limit the flexibility of these qualities, what is to hinder someone from stretching them completely out of existence?" This man will undoubtedly say that he has not gone that far. Maybe not on all of them. Just some of them! But what about the next man? If he stretches further, who is to decide that it's too far?

The implication is that all who give attention to the details of these qualifications view them as a "checklist of legal details," thus making them guilty of legalism. Evidently without knowing it, this brother uses a man guilty of this very crime when he later quotes with approval a statement from Alexander Campbell on the subject of gospel and doctrine (59). He would like for everyone to believe that Campbell is of the same mind with him on the matters he is writing about. No doubt he was on some things, but not on all. Campbell, in fact, believed that elders must be married men! "It is essential, in my opinion," Campbell says, "that a bishop be a married man. Indeed, the Holy Spirit by Paul has decreed that he should be the husband of one wife" (*Campbell-Purcell Debate* [255], quoted by Phillips [105]).

Was Campbell guilty of legalism here? According to Hook's argument throughout his book, he must have been. Campbell takes the qualifications of elders to be a list of specific qualities ("lawful specifications," if you will). He believed they were a list of things that must be true of the man who is to be appointed as an elder in the local church.

To say that because a man had two teenage children "who lived under his parental training and authority since their first breaths, that would not mean that he knew how to oversee a congregation of many adults" (44) is a true statement if this is all we know about a man and the children who have lived under his supervision for this period of time. But when he "ruleth well his own house, having his children in subjection with all gravity" (ASV), what does *God* say about it? By way of a question, He says this: "but if a man knoweth not how to rule his own house, how shall he take care of the church of God?" [v. 5, ASV] (1 Tim. 3:5). Not only does that mean he is *not* qualified to serve as an elder in the church if his children are "disobedient and rebellious," it also means that he *is* qualified to do the work named if his children are in subjection to him. If the latter is not true, why is the qualification given? "The whole point is to gain experience in leading in the way of the Lord, and to prove that ability to the church" (Phillips *Scriptural Elders and Deacons* 154).

This is not, however, the only qualification. But in God's wisdom this qualification, plus the others which he gives, makes such a man one who is qualified to take on the work of overseeing a congregation. No one else qualifies for this position. I think I can see why God thought that this quali- fication is important, whether the term "children" means one child or more; but if I can't see why God thinks so, I would have no right to question him on it. I see human wisdom running all the way through Cecil Hook's dis- cussion on the qualifications of elders. Like the lawyers of Jesus' day, he is willing to make the word of God void by his own inferences and conclu- sions!

This point is clearly illustrated in Hook's claim that he can make a better case for a man who is a successful business man than he can for one who has two teenagers who have been under his parental training and authority since their births. Here are his words: "We could make a better case for his need of being successful in business. A man's household evidently included his servants. That was his business operation. Managing his business/house- hold well would show his ability to deal with people effectively" (44).

Where is the justification in this context for defining the word "house" in verse 5 to include household servants? What if one of the "household servants" were guilty of riot or unruly, would this disqualify the man? When Paul says "children" in verse 4 he has by this term placed a limit on how he is using the terms "his own house" in the same verse. The statement in verse 5 is then added to clarify the point he has just made in the preceding verse. As a matter of fact, Paul says the same thing in verse 5 that he has said in verse 4, only this time he states it in the form of a question.

Whether this brother likes it or not, Paul says that for a man to be incom- petent in the rearing of his *children* shows that he is not prepared to fill the office of an elder in the church. Lenski says it well, when he says, "This is elementary logic, concluding from the less to the greater: one who does not

know how to superintend . . . 'his own house,' how will he handle the
great responsibility of caring for 'God's church'" (*St. Paul's Epistles
to the Colossians, to the Thessalonians, to Timothy, to Titus, and to
Philemon* 587). The meaning of the word "house" in this verse has
already been identified as "his own house," or his "children" in the preceding verse.

Since it is contended that "house" includes household servants, we repeat the question asked a few lines back: Would the man who is appointed
an elder in the church become disqualified if one of his "household servants" became guilty of riot, or became unruly? Or, what about this one:
Would Hook be willing to stretch these qualifications far enough to include *women* as elders in the church? The passage says "if any *man* desires
the office of a bishop," but according to Hook's line of argument, why
should that matter? What do you suppose Cecil Hook believes about that?
Is he legalistic about an elder being a *man*? Following his line of reasoning, would it not follow that for one to insist that only men may be appointed to serve as elders makes the list of qualifications "a checklist of
legal details," and thus would make him guilty of legalism?

2. Custom and the Silence of Women. This last question brings us to
another alleged case of the "lawyer-like" approach to the interpretation of
Scripture. It pertains to the place of women in the church. Our "interpretative weakness" here is supposed to be "our lack of consistency in applying
the same rules and principles to similar cases" (*Free In Christ* 45). We are
charged with inconsistency when we say that the instruction given in 1
Corinthians 11 forbidding women to remove their veils during the worship
assembly is based on custom, and is therefore not binding today, but we
then treat the instruction on the silence of women in 1 Corinthians 14 in a
different way. Is there an inconsistency here? Such a charge is but to over-
simplify the issues involved in these two subjects, to say the least. An *alleged* inconsistency does not establish an inconsistency.

There is not just one possibility when it comes to interpreting 1
Corinthians 14:34-35. It is a well known fact that brethren have taken different positions on the meaning of this passage, and some of them do not
require that Paul is dealing with custom in these verses as he is in 1
Corinthians 11:2-16. But I have also seen some brethren argue that both
passages are dealing with spiritual gifts, and that both are dealing with the
custom of the veil. Yet, for them, this does not mean that in societies today
where such customs do not prevail, women are free to teach over the man,
or usurp authority over him, in our public assemblies. Let's look briefly at
the different possibilities.

(1) One view is that both passages involve spiritual gifts and the veil.
Ken Green (*The South End Expounder* bulletin [March 23, 1970] Vol. 5,
No. 12: 1-4), taking essentially the same view as Bill Cavender in his book
on this subject, explains his understanding of these passages in the following way.

First, based on the meaning of the word "prophesying" in 1 Corinthians
11:4-5, it is thought that Paul is discussing the exercise of a spiritual gift.
This gift was used for "edification, exhortation and comfort" (1 Cor. 14:3).
It was to edify the church (vv. 4, 22). In 1 Corinthians 11:2-16 Paul is
dealing with prophetesses, women who possessed the gift of prophecy, like
those who are mentioned in Acts 2:16-21 and Acts 21:9.

Second, it is also argued that the situation in 1 Corinthians 14:34-35 is
the same as that in 1 Corinthians 11:2-16. In the context of both passages,
"praying" was also a spiritual gift, as one would learn from reading 1
Corinthians 14:13-19. To sing and pray "with the spirit" means to do these
things by divine inspiration, according to his view. In these verses these
things involve the use of the gift of tongues, or speaking in other languages.

Men, when speaking by divine inspiration, were speaking for God, and
to show respect for and subjection to God, they were not allowed to speak
with covered heads. Women, on the other hand, when speaking by divine
inspiration, were not to show disrespect for men, their head. To demon-
strate that she was not assuming an unlawful authority over the man, the
woman was not permitted to remove the covering from her head. Her head
covering was "a sign of authority" (1 Cor. 11:10), a symbol to show subjection to man.

Those who hold this view do not believe that either of these passages
establishes a practice that is meant for all women for all time for the following reasons: (1) *We do not pray and prophesy by the Spirit in our day.*
Such spiritual gifts ceased, or passed away, once God's will had been fully
made known, or "that which is perfect" had come (1 Cor. 13:8-13). (2) *A
head covering does not symbolize subjection in our land and days.* What
remains is that women demonstrate their subjection through the culti-
vation of a meek and quiet spirit (1 Tim. 2:11-12; 1 Pet. 3:1-6; Tit. 2:1-
8; Eph. 5:22-33). It is pointed out how it is inconsistent for some to
argue that women must wear the veil *in our assemblies* today in order to
show her subjection to man, but then go on and argue that it is not necessary that these same women when praying or prophesying *in the home*
wear them. (3) *If this was bound for all time, it was the first and the only
local custom which was bound universally by God.* Other things like the

kiss for salutation, and the washing of feet as an act of hospitality, were not bound for all time.

Even if one does not agree with this interpretation of 1 Corinthians 14:34-35, at least, the view is consistent and harmonizes well with the interpretation that the veil of 1 Corinthians 11:2-16 is describing a custom that no longer prevails in most parts of the world.

(2) Another possibility: one passage involves a custom, the other does not, but neither applies to us today. Some believe that the instructions regarding the veil in 1 Corinthians 11:2-16 involve a custom of the time in which Paul was writing, and it is for this reason that it does not apply to us today. Yet, while 1 Corinthians 14:34-35 does not involve the practice of the wearing of the veil, the instructions of this passage do not pertain to us today any more than the instructions concerning the veil in the other passage applies today, but for a different reason. There are those, for example, who believe that one should not overlook the context where the instructions are given to the women of 1 Corinthians 14:34-35. These instructions appear in a setting that involves instructions on the use of certain spiritual gifts (in particular, those possessed by the prophets of vv. 29-33), and the women involved in these two verses are the *wives* of the prophets of the preceding verses, not women in general. The central point has to do with maintaining order in the assembly where such spiritual gifts were being exercised. This is suggested in verse 40. Other men (v. 30) were to take their turn when another was speaking, and the wives of the prophets who were speaking (vv. 34-35) were to remain silent and ask any questions they may have of their husbands when they are at home.

James P. Needhem has offered this view of 1 Corinthians 14:34-35. He also believes that Paul's instruction concerning the veil in 1 Corinthians 11:2-16 is dealing with a custom, and he does not see the veil as a matter of Paul's concern in the present passage. He is answering the question as to whether or not a woman may ask a question in the public assembly, and, in particular, he is concerned with whether or not 1 Corinthians 14:34-35 would prohibit such a question being asked, and, if not, how this would harmonize with 1 Timothy 2:11-12. Here is how he answered this question:

> There is other corroborating evidence that 1 Corinthians 14:34, 35, applied to a special meeting unlike any we can have today. For instance, Paul said, If the women would "learn anything, let them ask their husbands at home." One thing is abundantly clear from this statement: ALL WOMEN ADDRESSED HAD HUSBANDS! Otherwise, this verse makes no sense at all. If husband doesn't mean HUSBAND what would Paul

have said had he meant husband? Those who want to apply 1 Corinthians 14:34, 35 today often say that if a woman doesn't have a husband, she can ask her father, brother, uncle, elders, or the preacher! That is quite a strange interpretation. If this would be satisfactory, it would have been very simple for Paul to have said it. The fact is, he didn't!

What we need to understand is that 1 Tim. 2:11, 12 is the general passage which regulates the behavior of women today. It says, *"let the women learn in silence (quietness ASV) with all subjection. But I suffer not a woman to teach, nor to usurp authority over the man, but to be in silence (quietness ASV).*

Two things are forbidden in this passage: (1) A woman's teaching OVER a man, (2) A woman's usurping authority over a man. To teach over a man simply means that she would be in charge of a class where men were present. The teacher is in authority; women are forbidden to be in authority over man in the church. To usurp authority over a man is to take it by force. A woman can do this in a class situation where she dominates the class and more or less takes it away from the teacher. This is a violation of the scriptures. But, it is not wrong for a woman to ask a question in a mixed class as long as she does it in a humble manner and does not seek to dominate, or usurp the authority of the teacher. If the teacher grants permission for women to ask questions or make comments, then when they do so, they are not usurping his authority (*PSD Bulletin* [Feb. 5, 1979] 11:6: 2-4).

Whether or not one agrees with these interpretations of 1 Corinthians 14:34-35, they are consistent with the view that 1 Corinthians 11:2-16 is dealing with a custom. As long as one is consistent in how he treats these two passages, what rule of interpretation requires that one make the exact application of both of these passages of Scripture?

(3) Others contend there is no indication that the custom that is being discussed in chapter 11 (that of the veil) is also being discussed in chapter 14, and that 1 Corinthians 14:34-35 does apply to us today. For them, to say that "we quickly abandon that approach to interpretation" (by saying that Paul is dealing with a custom in 1 Cor. 11) when we come to 1 Corinthians 14:34-35, and then charge those who do so with inconsistency, would be a true charge only if one is required to interpret the latter passage in the same way that he has interpreted 1 Corinthians 11:2-16. But where is the evidence, they ask, that Paul is giving instructions regarding a custom in 1 Corinthians 14:34-35? Does not Paul's statement, "as also saith the law" in v. 34, have some bearing on whether or not the subject of Paul's discussion lies outside the realm of custom and belongs to the realm of law instead?

But we are told, "the only difference is that one relates to headdress and the other relates to the abuse of the privilege of teaching publically" (*Free In Christ* 45). But must both passages be dealing with a custom before one can be consistent in his interpretation of the passages? Of course not. Some contend that one of the central points that Paul is making on women being silent in the assemblies in this passage is for them to show subjection to their husbands *when their husbands are speaking in such assemblies.* Why must they be quiet and ask questions of their husbands at home? One reason was that "all things be done decently and in order." But is this the only point that is being made? Is Paul saying that women could exercise "the privilege of teaching publically" if they did so in a way that would honor the authority of their husbands over them? Hardly. Paul is doing more than correcting an abuse.

What is the significance of "let your women keep silence in the churches: for it is not permitted unto them to speak" (1 Cor. 14:34)? Notice, in the first place, that this idea of "keeping silence" in the assemblies is required not only of women, but also of tongue-speakers when there was no interpreter present to translate their message (1 Cor. 14:28). In this case to be "silent" could have meant not to address the assembly publicly. This is a common interpretation of this passage. When no interpreter was present the one who spoke in tongues was to "speak to himself, and to God." In other words, in such a case he was not permitted *to speak publicly in assembly.*

Notice also that the same was true of the prophet who received a revelation when another was speaking. In verse 30 Paul told him, "let the first hold his peace" (i. e., "keep silent," NKJV), or wait on the other who was speaking publicly until he had finished speaking. This also means that he was not permitted *to speak publicly in assembly,* or to address the assembly, when another was speaking.

So, those who interpret this passage of Scripture in this way, would ask: Why would it not follow that what is true of the tongue-speaker and of the prophet would also be true of women who are told to "keep silent in the churches" and that "it is not permitted unto them to speak"? In keeping with how the word "silent" has been used of others in this context, they would tell us, both of these statements would mean that women are not permitted to publicly address the assembly. With the woman, however, it is not a matter of custom, nor is it simply a matter of orderliness. It is a matter of "what saith the law" (v. 34). In each of the cases (concerning the tongue-speaker, the prophet, and women) to "be silent" and "not to speak" means not to address the assembly in a public manner.

One is not inconsistent just because he sees a custom involved in 1 Corinthians 11:2ff. and a matter of divine law in 1 Corinthians 14:34-35. It is contrary to fact to say that in the latter passage Paul is merely dealing with "the abuse of the privilege of teaching publicly." Paul was not dealing with a mere custom here.

3. The Holy Kiss and Baptism. Does immersion in water, or baptism, belong to the same class of things as that to which the holy kiss belongs? If so, then if we can change the holy kiss to a loving handshake, then why can't we change immersion in water to sprinkling or pouring? Are we inconsistent here, as charged? Again, it is clear that by introducing what he feels to be an inconsistency in our practice, Hook would hope to influence his brethren to make what most have before considered to be a thing that is permanent (baptism by immersion) to be a mere custom. To convince brethren that the practice of immersion is a mere custom would make room for a change in our practice regarding it and it would lead us to look with less disfavor toward those who practice sprinkling and pouring. This is what he had hoped to do concerning women teaching publicly, now he would do the same on the subject of baptism.

Again, as with the matter of women teachers, he offers no proof that immersion in water should be treated as a mere custom. When he states that we shake hands instead of kissing and then asks, "Can we do this consistently while refusing to allow an alteration of the method by which baptism is expressed?" he assumes the two things belong to the same class? Do they? It is Hook's responsibility to show that they do, not our responsibility to show that they do not. What does he offer? He does at least attempt to give some reason for being "less dogmatic" on this subject, which is more than he gave us on why women teachers should be used in our public assemblies today.

So what does he do? He attempts to discredit our practice of insisting that a *burial* in water is required by Paul's statement that we are "buried with him" in Romans 6:4 and Colossians 2:12. He does this first by stating that this does not mean that Christ is buried with us in the baptistery, but that we are buried with Christ. Then, we are told, "Jesus was buried, not in water, but in a rock-hewn tomb. In baptism, symbolically, one is transported back through time and space and buried with Christ where atonement was made. So the burial is in the tomb. The action of baptism symbolizes that. To millions of persons the ritual of dipping, pouring, or sprinkling of water symbolizes this action" (*Free In Christ* 46).

Before we come to address this point, let's look briefly at the word "baptize." What is the *action* involved in baptism? When Peter said that one is to "repent and *be baptized* for the remission of sins" (emphasis mine — *ww*), it appears that we are being asked to let this mean, "repent and have a little water sprinkled or poured on you for the remission of sins." But is this the *action* that is to be performed in the command to "be baptized"? The lexicons say the word "baptize" means to "to dip repeatedly, to immerge, *submerge*" (Thayer, *Greek English Lexicon of the New Testament* 94). Arndt and Gingrich define this term as meaning *"dip, immerse,* mid. *dip onself, wash" (Greek-English Lexicon of the New Testament* 131). To "be baptized" is a passive act, something one lets another do *with him*, to have oneself baptized, as in Matthew 3:13; Luke 3:7, 12; John 3:23b, *with water (hudati)* in Mark 1:8a; Luke 3:16a; Acts 1:5; 11:16a. On the water of baptism see also Acts 8:36 and 10:47.

Keep in mind that for one to *be baptized* is not to let someone do something *with water* upon the candidate. The act of being baptized is something done with the person being baptized, *not* something done with the water of baptism. If the word "be baptized" means to sprinkle or pour then it means to sprinkle or pour *the person* being baptized! Read it: " . . . and be baptized *every one of you*" (Acts 2:38). The action involved is an act of doing something *with* (not to) *the person* who is being baptized, and it is not something being done with the element of baptism, or with the water.

To pour or sprinkle water upon a person is one kind of act, and to immerse a person in water is another kind of act. In one act something is being done with water, and in the other act something is being done with the person who is being baptized in water. The subjects of baptism are not being baptized *with* water, but *they themselves* are being baptized *in* water. Only the act of immersion fits the act that is being performed when one lets another baptize *him*. When Philip "baptized" the eunuch "they both went down into the water, both Philip and the eunuch; and he baptized *him*" (Acts 8:38, emphasis mine — *ww*). Philip did something *with the eunuch*, not with the water. The text says: "and he baptized him." Since he baptized him, the eunuch, what did he do with him? If the word means "sprinkle" or "pour," did he sprinkle him? Not sprinkle something upon him, but did he sprinkle *him*? The answer should be obvious. Philip baptized (immersed) the eunuch in water; he did not baptize (sprinkle or pour) the water on the eunuch. The action is with the person, what one does with the person, not what one does with the water.

But, as we have been told already, according to the wisdom of Cecil Hook, the meaning of words, or the specifics of a command, are not to be insisted upon. They do not matter. But, in fact, they do matter. If they do not matter, then Cecil Hook cannot prove from Scripture that scriptural baptism is (1) immersion (2) of an adult — one capable of believing in Christ and repenting of sins — (3) in water, (4) for (in order to receive) (5) the remission of sins. Not one of these five things about baptism can be proved from Scripture without getting into the details of what is taught about baptism in the word of God. Much of what is involved in a study of this subject involves the meaning of words which one cannot discover without studying this subject in detail. And no one can demonstrate that only adults were baptized without using an argument based on a necessary conclusion, or that it is *necessarily* inferred that baptism was *only for adults*. And yet it is pretty clear that he rejects any argument for teaching some truth that one would attempt to bind on another on the basis of a necessary conclusion. So how would he prove from the Bible that the only scriptural candidate for water baptism is a responsible adult?

What would Hook do with the Quaker position that baptism is Spirit baptism and does not require water at all? How would he go about showing that water is the element required for baptism for the remission of sins? If he uses an *example* from the Bible, how would he know it is a *binding* example when there is *no specific command behind it* that requires water? If he uses an *implication*, how could he be sure it is a *necessary* implication? And if he uses either of these ways to show that water is the only acceptable element for the baptism of the great commission, it appears that he is getting into a lot of details to make his point. From Hook's own argument, this would get him into legalism. Guess we'll just have to turn Cecil Hook over to the Quakers!

Now to the point made about being baptized (buried) with Christ in his tomb instead of being buried in water. If we grant that the word "buried" in Romans 6:4 takes one back to the tomb so that one is buried with Christ there, would that raise any doubt as to whether or not baptism is a burial in water? What Hook overlooks here is the fact that Paul says that we "were *buried* with him *through baptism* into death" (Rom. 6:4). If he would give more attention to *exactly* what Paul says (that means paying attention to the details!) in this statement, he would not be guilty of mishandling the word of God as he does in this argument. Since the word "baptize" (*baptizō*) means to "dip, plunge, or immerse," then when Paul says we "were buried with him *through baptism*," he is saying that we were buried with Christ *through immersion*. That Paul uses both terms "buried" and "through baptism" is significant. Not only were they buried with Christ, but they were *buried* with him *through baptism*, or *by being immersed in water*!

Although we are told that the points that are made on this subject are "not to convince you of the validity of dipping the head, pouring, or sprinkling for baptism," the effect is the same. If we are made "less dogmatic against one who is convinced that these forms are acceptable expressions," which is Hook's stated objective in making these points about baptism, the consequence is the same. Should we also be less dogmatic in arguing for the element of water being required for baptism just because some do not believe water is required? And why not the same for baptism for the remission of sins, or faith coming before repentance as all Calvinists believe something different? To fail to strongly oppose such unscriptural practices or teaching is to become guilty of compromise in matters of principle, or matters of scriptural truth. How can one "contend earnestly for the faith" while being "less dogmatic" on a matter that is clearly taught in Scripture?

Hook says, though, that these people are "convinced that these forms are acceptable expressions." So? These same people are convinced that infants are born in sin, and that they are acceptable candidates for baptism. They are also convinced that those who are saved (infants and adults alike) are saved *before* baptism. Are we, on the basis of these people's conviction on these subjects, to be "less dogmatic" in opposing their false teachings just because they are convinced that they are right on them?

Don't you suppose that Hymenaeus and Philetus were convinced that the resurrection had already passed? No doubt they fully believed that their teaching on this subject was "acceptable." But did Paul allow their strong conviction to cause him to be "less dogmatic" in opposing them? Doesn't read like he did in 2 Timothy 2:16-18. This same point could be made on every departure from the truth, even on such things as "forbidding to marry, and commanding to abstain from meats" (1 Tim. 4:3), which Paul calls a departure from the faith (v. 1). Was Paul being too dogmatic against people who most likely were convinced that what they were teaching on these subjects was the truth?

4. The First Day of the Week As the Lord's Day. In charging "the churches of Christ" with "scholasticism," which is defined as "an effort to prove by the Bible what had already been accepted and practiced tradition-ally" *(Free In Christ* 46-47), the example cited which is thought to demon-strate our guilt of this sin is our acceptance of the "the Lord's day" (Rev. 1:10) as being the first day of the week. We are also charged with believing that the first day of the week was "a special day for assembly and devo-tion" for Christians in the first century. The line of argument used to dis-credit this belief and practice is as follows.

Although "it seems evident that the very early disciples began to use the first day of the week as a special day for assembly and devotion," and that "this was such an accepted practice that, at the end of the persecutions in the fourth century, Constantine declared Sunday to be a holiday (holy day) for the benefit of Christians," the practice is mere tradition, according to Cecil Hook. There is, according to his argument, no conclusive evidence that this was the practice of the Christians in the first century.

What is the historical evidence for the first day of the week being a day of worship for Christians in the first century? First, let's briefly consider extra-biblical sources right after the close of the first century. At a very early date sources outside the New Testament confirm that the Lord's day was the first day of the week and that this was the day on which Christians assembled for worship.

— The *Didache*, written in the late first or early second century, says, "having earlier confessed your sins so that your sacrifice may be pure, come together each Lord's day of the Lord, break bread, and give thanks" (14:1).

— Ignatius (c. A. D. 110), writes, "If therefore those who lived according to the old practices came to the new hope, no longer observing the Sabbath but living according to the Lord's day, in which also our life arose through him and his death (which some deny), through which mystery we received faith, and on account of which we suffer in order that we may be found disciples of Jesus Christ our only teacher, how shall we be able to live apart from him for whom even the prophets were looking as their teacher since they were his disciples in the spirit" (*Magnesians* 9).

— Barnabas, early second century, is credited with having written what is called "The Epistle of Barnabas," although it is an anonymous epistle. Here we read: "Moreover, God says to the Jews, 'Your new moons and Sabbaths I cannot endure.' You see how he says, 'The present sabbaths are not acceptable to me, but the Sabbath which I have made in which, when I have rested from all things, I will make the beginning of the eighth day which is the beginning of another world.' Wherefore, we [Christians] keep the eighth day for joy, on which also Jesus arose from the dead and when he appeared ascended into heaven" (15:8f.).

— Justin Martyr, the most important second century apologist, wrote: "We are always together with one another. And for all the things with which we are supplied we bless the Maker of all through his son Jesus Christ and through his Holy Spirit. And on the day called Sunday there is a gathering together in the same place of all who live in a city or a rural district. [There follows an account of a Christian worship service . . .] We all make our assembly on the day of the Sun, since it is the first day, on which God changed the darkness and matter and made the world, and Jesus Christ our Savior arose from the dead on the same day. For the crucified him on the day before Saturn's day, and on the day after (which is the day of the Sun) he appeared to his apostles and taught his disciples these things" (*Apology* I, 67:1-3, 7). Justin illustrates for us how it was customary for those of his day to speak of the eighth day when referring to the first day of the week: "The commandment of circumcision, requiring them always to circumcise the children on the eighth day, was a type of the true circumcision by which we are circumcised from error and evil through the resurrection from the dead on the first day of the week of Jesus Christ our Lord. For the first day of the week, although it is the first of all days, yet according to the number of the days in a cycle is called the eighth (while still remaining the first)" (*Dialogue with Trypho the Jew* 41:4).

After giving these and other quotations from this early period, Everett Ferguson makes the following observations (references to sources are omitted where dots appear):

The evidence for the early Christians' day of worship is clear and unmistakable. They did not observe the seventh day, the Sabbath, as the Jews, but they assembled on the first day of the week, the day of the resurrection of Christ. A rest day and a day for the worship assembly of the whole congregation were united in Judaism and in much modern Christian practice, but the two are distinct matters and were distinct in the early church. Christians kept no day as a rest day, neither Saturday nor Sunday, until the civil legislation of Constantine in the fourth century made Sunday a legal holiday for many occupations. An exception was furnished by certain Jewish Christians who continued to keep the law and so had Saturday as a rest day and Sunday as their day of Christian worship. . . .

The term Sunday, or "day of the Sun," was the pagan designation, and it appears in the writings of the Christian apologists who were addressing pagan audiences. . . . The phrase "first day of the week" (literally "first of the Sabbaths" — the first day between the Sabbaths) was a Jewish expression based on the practice of designating the days of the week by their number leading up to the sixth (the Preparation) and the seventh (the Sabbath). This was the common terminology of the New Testament and of early Christian writers from a Semitic background . . . . "Lord's day" and "eighth day" were distinctive Christian names and will be discussed further.

Lord's day is used by Christians with reference to Christ's resurrection, and the term is consciously distinguished from the Sabbath day . . . . The Sabbath is never referred to as *kuriakē*, "Lord's," or "lordly." It became common to omit the word "day" after *kuriakē*, leaving the adjective alone with the noun to be understood. (Revelation 1:10 reflects the earliest usage in giving the full phrase.) Thus in modern Greek the word for Sunday or the first day of the week is *kuriakē*. This usage was well established at an early date, for in Christian Latin the word for Sunday was *dominica*, the exact translation of the Greek, "Lord's." The word for Sunday in modern Romance languages is derived from this usage — *domenica* (Italian), *domingo* (Spanish), and *dimanche* (French).

Early Christian sources repeatedly connect the first day of the week with the resurrection. . . . It is clear that it was this decisive event in salvation history which made that day the "Lord's day." The resurrection of Christ and his meeting with his disciples on this day provided the basis for Christians to assemble on the first day of the week. At that time the risen Christ was preeminently present with his followers. This connection with the resurrection may have some relevance to the partaking of the Lord's supper at dawn. . . . (*Early Christians Speak* 70-71).

If one asks whether or not assemblies on the first day of the week are "clearly defined and stipulated in the Scriptures," the answer is "no, they are not," if by the question one is asking if there is a *direct command* in the Scriptures themselves for Christians to meet on that day. But if one means is there *sufficient evidence* in Scripture for one to safely conclude that this was the practice of the first century church, the answer to this question is, "yes." The fact that no statement in Scripture *directly* links the first day of the week gatherings with Christ's resurrection on the first day of the week does not prove that the gatherings of the disciples on that day were not based upon such a reason. It just says that we don't know *for certain* that this was *the reason*. But when Christians were giving this as a reason not more than fifteen years following the death of the apostle John on the Isle of Patmos in A.D. 95 or 96, there is good extra-biblical evidence that this was the reason why Christians met on the first day of the week to break bread. The Bible itself shows that Christians were to "lay by in store," and this was to be done "on the first day of the week," according to 1 Corinthians 16:1-2.

This shows that Christians already were in the practice of gathering together on the first day of the week, and that the churches had a common treasury into which such gifts were cast. To say that "that says nothing about an assembly" (*Free In Christ* 47), shows why we sometimes need to give more attention to the *details* of a statement in Scripture. McGarvey, in his commentary on 1 Corinthians, does this, and thereby avoids some of the mistakes that are commonly made in the translation, as well as the interpretation, of this passage:

The word *thesaurizoon*, translated "in store," means, literally "put into the treasury;" and the phrase *"par'heauton,"* translated "by him," may be taken as the neuter reflexive pronoun, and may be rendered with equal correctness "by itself." Macknight thus renders these two words, and this rendering is to be preferred. If each man had laid by in his own house, all these scattered collections would have had to be gathered after Paul's arrival, which was the very thing that he forbade. Again, had the collection been of such a private nature, it would have been gathered normally at the *end* instead of at the beginning of the week. But the first day of the week was evidently set apart for public worship (John 20:19-26; Acts 20:7; Rev. 1:10), and this offering was part of the service. It was put in the public treasury of the church, but kept by itself as a *separate fund*. The translation of the Revised Version is unfortunate, as it obscures the idea of the weekly service of the church. According to Paul's method of collecting, each rendered a weekly account of his stewardship, and gave more and felt it less than if he had attempted to donate it all at one time. Paul had promised to take such offerings (Gal. 2:10). As a Christian he tries to relieve that distress which, as a persecutor, he had aided to inflict (Acts 26:6-10). He wished each one, rich or poor, to contribute to the offering, and he wanted the whole matter disposed of and out of the way when he came, that he might turn his attention to more important matters (*Commentary on Thessalonians, Corinthians, Galatians and Romans* 161).

In his comments on Acts 20:6-7, not only does McGarvey discuss the subject of the Lord's day being the time when the disciples gathered to eat the Lord's supper, but he also describes the two different approaches that people take today in using Scripture to determine what the Lord's will is for his people. The careful reader should have no trouble seeing which avenue is being advocated by Cecil Hook in his book, *Free In Christ*, when he reads the following comments from McGarvey:

6. The delay of Paul at Philippi may be well accounted for by the strong affection which he bore toward the congregation there, and his present expectation that he would see their faces in the flesh no more (Comp. verse 25). (6) *And we, after the days of unleavened bread, sailed away from Philippi, and came to them in Troas in five days, where we remained seven days*. The "days of unleavened bread" here mentioned remind us that it had been nearly one year since the close of Paul's labors in Ephesus; for he was awaiting the approach of Pentecost when the mob was aroused by Demetrius. He probably left there between the Passover and Pentecost, and as the Passover had now returned again, the time he had spent in his tour through Macedonia and Achaia and back to Philippi must have occupied ten or eleven months.

The voyage from Philippi to Troas occupied, as here stated, five days, though, on a former occasion, they had sailed from Troas and reached

Philippi in two day's journey. The delay on this trip is suggestive of adverse winds.

The brethren who had preceded Paul and Luke to Troas had already spent there the five days occupied by the latter on the journey, and a portion of the seven days of unleavened bread which they spent in Philippi. The seven additional days now spent there by the whole company, making an aggregate of more than two weeks, gave sufficient time to accomplish much in a community where a door was already opened by the Lord.

7. The last period of seven days included and was terminated by the Lord's day. (7) *And on the first day of the week, when the disciples came together to break the loaf, Paul discoursed to them, about to depart on the next day, and continued his discourse till midnight.* This passage indicates both the day of the week in which the disciples broke the loaf, and the prime object of their meeting on that day. It shows that the loaf was broken on the first day of the week; and we have no apostolic precedent for breaking it on any other day.

The disciples came together on that day, even though Paul and Luke and Timothy, and all the brethren who had come from Greece, were present, not primarily to hear one or more of them discourse, but to "break the loaf." Such is the distinct statement of the historian. That such was an established custom in the Churches is implied in a rebuke administered by Paul to the Church at Corinth, in which he says: "When you come together into one place, it is not to eat the Lord's supper." Now, for this they would not have deserved censure, had it not been that to eat the Lord's supper was the proper object of their assemblage. These facts are sufficient to establish the conclusion that the main object of the Lord's day meetings was to break the loaf.

This conclusion will be of service to us in seeking to determine the frequency with which the loaf was broken. If the prime object of the Lord's day meeting was to celebrate the Lord's supper, then all the evidence we have of the custom of meeting every Lord's day is equally conclusive in reference to the weekly observance of the Lord's supper. But the former custom is universally admitted by Christians of the present day, and therefore there should be no dispute in reference to the latter.

It must, in candor, be admitted, that there is no express statement in the New Testament that the disciples broke the loaf every Lord's day; neither is it stated that they met every Lord's day. Yet the question, how often shall the congregation meet together to break the loaf, is one which can not be avoided, but must be settled practically in some way. The different religious parties have hitherto agreed upon a common principle of action, which is, that each may settle the question according to its own judgment

of what is most profitable and expedient This principle, if applied by
congregations instead of parties, is a safe one in reference to matters
upon which we have no means of knowing the divine will, or the apostolic custom. But when we can determine, with even a good degree of
probability, an apostolic custom, our own judgment should yield to it. So
all parties have reasoned in reference to the Lord's day. The intimations
contained in the New Testament, together with the universal custom known
to have existed in the Churches during the age succeeding that of the
apostles, has been decided by them all as sufficient to establish the divine
authority of the religious observance of the Lord's day; and yet they have
not consented to the weekly observance of the Lord's supper, the proof of
which is precisely the same.

As a practical issue between the advocates of weekly communion and
their opponents, the question really has reference to the comparative weight
of evidence in favor of this practice, and of monthly, quarterly, or yearly
communion. When it is thus presented, no one can long hesitate as to the
conclusion; for in favor of either of the intervals last mentioned there is
not the least evidence, either in the New Testament, or in the uninspired
history of the Churches. On the other hand, it is the universal testimony
of antiquity that the Churches of the second century broke the loaf every
Lord's day, and considered it a custom of apostolic appointment. Now it
can not be doubted that the apostolic Churches had some regular interval
at which to celebrate this institution, and seeing that all the evidence there
is in the case is in favor of a weekly celebration, there is no room for a
reasonable doubt that this was the interval which they adopted

It is very generally admitted, even among parties who do not observe the
practice themselves, that the apostolic Churches broke the loaf weekly;
but it is still made a question whether, in the absence of an express commandment, this example is binding upon us. This question is likely to be
determined differently by two different classes of men. Those who are
disposed to follow chiefly the guide of their own judgment, or of their
denominational customs, will feel little influenced by such a precedent.
But to those who are determined that the very slightest indication of the
divine will shall govern them, the question must present itself in this way:
"We are commanded to do this in memory of Jesus. We are not told, in
definite terms, how often it shall be done; but we find that the apostles
established the custom of meeting every Lord's day for this purpose. This
is an inspired precedent, and with it we must comply. We can come to no
other conclusion without assuming an ability to judge of this matter with
more wisdom than did the apostle."

We return to the meeting in Troas. The extreme length of Paul's discourse
on this occasion is in striking contrast with the brevity of his other speeches,
as reported by Luke. It is to be accounted for by the anxiety of the apostle,

in bidding them a final farewell, to leave the brethren as well guarded as possible against the temptations which awaited them (*A Commentary on Acts of Apostles* [original] 245-248).

In light of books like *Free in Christ* that have been written in recent years, McGarvey's statement that "when we can determine, with even a good degree of probability, an apostolic custom, our own judgment should yield to it," is no longer valid with many among us. But why would it not be? Why would Christians who love the Lord and the truth want to pursue an avenue of doubt and uncertainty in the name of "liberty"? Is not "a good degree of probability" about "an apostolic custom" (custom = a practice) much better than doubt and uncertainty?

To conclude that any or all of the other days of the week is "the Lord's day," as Cecil Hook does in his book *Free In Christ*, is to draw a conclusion based upon mere conjecture without any degree of proof. It is true that there is a sense in which we may say the other days of the week are days which belong to the Lord. With the psalmist of old, we would say of every day of the week, "This is the day the Lord has made; we will rejoice and be glad in it" (Ps. 118:24). But, of course, we would also say that the same may be said of all suppers, because everything, including our meals, ultimately find their source in the Lord. This is why Jesus teaches us to pray, "Give us this day our daily bread." Yet, we would never treat the term "the Lord's supper" as these brethren are treating the term "the Lord's day." If we did, we would say, "the term 'the Lord's supper' means any or all of the other suppers (common meals) that we eat because all suppers are the Lord's suppers or meals," since we believe our ordinary meals are provided by the Lord as well. This type of fallacious reasoning is due to an unwillingness to yield one's own judgment on the basis of "a good degree of probability" concerning "an apostolic custom." This is one of the major differences between Cecil Hook's approach to the interpretation of the Bible and the approach of the rest of us who are desirous of yielding to "a good degree of probability" on matters where absolute certainty cannot be had.

The "intimations contained in the New Testament, together with the universal custom known to have existed in the Churches during the age succeeding that of the apostles," offer no proof to Cecil Hook, or any others who want to have it another way. Their way allows them to have whatever they want, on whatever terms they want it, and on any subject they want. Then they expect all others to let them have it as they want it — even when "a good degree of probability" concerning "an apostolic custom" points in another direction.

It is affirmed that "there is no clear example of the Lord's Supper ever being eaten on the first day of the week" (*Free In Christ* 21). Hook's "proof" is, as usual (and we have by now come to expect this from him), an "if" situation. "If" they met according to Roman time, he says, "they met to eat it on Sunday night but did not partake until Monday morning because of Paul's long discourse." This would be true, as one can readily see, only if "break the bread" in verse 11 refers to eating the Lord's supper — which I am willing to concede because of the use of the definite article before the word "bread."

On the other hand, we are told that "if" the Jewish calendar was being followed, "they met to partake of it on our Saturday night." The point being, it doesn't really matter on what day of the week we eat the Lord's supper, as long as we accomplish the purpose of the communion. Then it is wrongly assumed that for us to take it in any other way is to try "to be righteous by keeping legal specifications."

What is the situation, then, if Roman time was being followed? Well, the day according to Roman time was from midnight to midnight, the same as our time. Represented by a time-line it would look like the following:

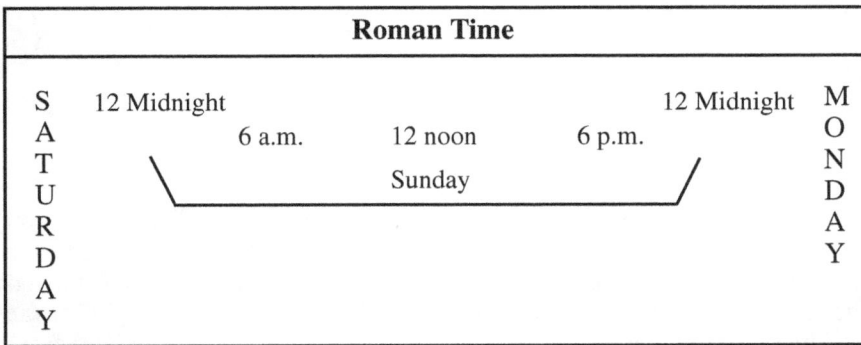

Roman Time
S A T U R D A Y   12 Midnight   12 Midnight   M O N D A Y
6 a.m.   12 noon   6 p.m.
Sunday

According to this calendar "the first day of the week" would be from midnight Saturday night until Sunday midnight. The time of meeting was at night (Acts 20:7-12), as indicated by the fact that Paul "prolonged his speech until midnight" (v. 7), and Luke makes a special point that there were "many lights in the upper chamber where we were gathered together" (v. 8). To say they were following Roman time (the day was from midnight to midnight) would place their meeting at night on the first day. Night on the first day would be from about 6 p.m. till 12 p.m. This would mean that they waited until the end of the first day (sometime within the last six hours of it, from sunset to midnight) to meet. This is not likely since Paul would place a great deal of importance upon the purpose of their gathering.

But why would one ever "assume" that these disciples were following Roman time, when to make such an assumption would place their eating the supper on Monday morning, a thing these disciples never *purposed* to do? The passage clearly says they came together "on the first day of the week to break bread." This is the stated purpose of their coming together on that day, the first day of the week. Was their purpose thwarted? I think not.

How would it be different if they were following the Jewish calendar? Would they have eaten the Lord's supper on a day other than the first day of the week, or on Saturday night, as Cecil Hook says? Absolutely not. Here is the way the first day of the week would look if they were following the Jewish calendar:

Jewish Time				
S	6 p.m.		6 p.m.	**M**
A				**O**
T	12 midnight	6 a.m.	12 noon	**N**
U		Sunday		**D**
R				**A**
D				**Y**
A				
Y				

The only way Hook can come to the conclusion that the disciples met on a day other than the first day of the week is for him to say they would have eaten it "on *our* Saturday night." Notice it, if you will: "If they followed the Jewish calendar, they met to partake of it on *our* Saturday night" (*Free In Christ* 21; emphasis mine). To say "*our* Saturday night" is to shift from Jewish time to Roman time in order to make the point that they met on Saturday night! But any careful reader can surely see that if they were following the Jewish method of counting time, it would have been the *first part* of the *first day* of the week *for them*, since they met at night, sometime before midnight. Remember, by noting the time-line above, the twenty-four hour day, according to the Jewish calendar, was from sunset to sunset (6 p.m. to 6 p.m.). After midnight, which marked the end of the first six hours of the first day, when the Lord's supper was served (Acts 20:11), was still the first day of the week following the Jewish calendar. To say it would have been Saturday night *for us* is to deliberately attempt to mislead because it introduces another method of determining time, the Roman calendar.

It is amazing how far some will go in their attempt to make a passage of Scripture appear to be saying something different from what our customary practice has been through the years. Cecil Hook does this many times over in his book. He bends over backward to make passages appear to say something they do not say at all, in order to try to convince his readers that his brethren have been wrong in their interpretation of these passages for the past one hundred years. Every passage is reinterpreted in light of his "new hermeneutic," which is actually not new at all. It is the old "liberal" way of handling Scripture. Nothing is authoritative except commands, he says, but even here, he is careful to emphasize, the *details* of commands *are not binding*. His hermeneutic throws out everything except the law of love, and it offers nothing more than "the new morality" principle applied to doctrinal matters. Shall we call his method of interpreting Scripture "situation doctrine"?

I am willing to concede that "there is nothing to identify 'the day' (Heb. 10:25) and 'the Lord's day' (Rev. 1:10) as the first day of the week" (47), as Hook states. The reference to "the day" in the former passage does not appear to refer to a day of assembly, but to a day of judgment. It should be obvious that the Hebrew writer does not mean, "do not forsake the assembling of yourselves together as you see the day of assembling drawing nigh." The "day" these brethren saw drawing nigh cannot be a particular day of assembling. Their "assembling" with Christians was to be whenever Christians were gathering together. No particular day of assembling is specified in Hebrews 10:25, and such assembling is not limited to the first day of the week assemblies.

To say, "we do not meet because it is the first day and we are required to do so, we meet to fulfil the purposes to be accomplished in assemblies" (48), assumes that the first day of the week has no special significance for worship, and that this day is no different from the other days of the week. But, as we have shown, the "intimations contained in the New Testament, together with the universal custom known to have existed in the Churches during the age succeeding that of the apostles," point to a different conclusion. And there is good reason that the early disciples and the churches during the age succeeding the apostles gave the significance they did to the first day of the week.

1. This was the day Christ rose from the dead (Mark 16:2-9).

2. It was on this day that Jesus met with his disciples after his resurrection (John 20:19, the first meeting, on the same day as the resurrection; then in v. 26, a second meeting, "after eight days," or the next first day of the week).

3. The church was established on the first day of the week (Matt. 16:18; Acts 2:1-47 with Acts 11:15, "the beginning"). Pentecost (Acts 2:1) always came on the first day of the week, fifty days after the seventh sabbath; the day "after the seventh sabbath" would always be the first day (Lev. 23:15f.; Deut. 16:9f.)

4. This day was "the beginning," according to Peter in Acts 11:15. The beginning of the church, and the beginning the gospel dispensation.

5. This was the day on which the terms of admittance into the kingdom of God were preached for the first time "in the name of Christ" (Luke 24:49; Acts 2:38).

Mosheim, the noted historian, points out that it was not on Saturday, nor on both Saturday and Sunday, but on Sunday, that the disciples met: "In vain some learned men labour to persuade us that in all the early churches *both* days, or the *first* and *last* days of the week, were held sacred. The churches of Bithynia, mentioned by *Pliny,* devoted but *one stated day* to their public worship, that was what we call *the Lord's Day*, or the *first day* of the week" (*Institutes of Ecclesiastical History, Ancient and Modern, in Four Books* [1847]: I, footnote #3, 85). On this same page he further states: "The Christians of this century assembled for the worship of God and for their advancement in piety, on the *first day of the week*, the day on which Christ reassumed his life; for that this day was set apart for religious worship by the apostles themselves, and that, after the example of the church in Jerusalem it was generally observed, we have unexceptional testimony." He grants that only in certain situations were some brethren "accustomed also to observe the *seventh day* of the week, as a sacred day." This was where those congregations "either lived intermingled with Jews, or were composed in great measure of Jews."

A question we might consider is this: Is there any indication in Acts 20:7 that this meeting on the first day of the week was a planned meeting, not one that simply happened as a result of an arbitrary decision on the part of the disciples at Troas? There is this bit of information. The term rendered "came together" (KJV) is rendered "we were gathered together" in the NASB and other translations. If this is the correct rendering, it shows that

Luke also was present in this gathering. Some have suggested that the passive voice form of the word suggests that this was an assembly that had been called together by "an extraneous directive — the most obvious inference being, by *divine authority*" (Wayne Jackson "The Weekly Observance of the Lord's Supper" *Christian Courier Web Edition* [Archives] 4). This conclusion is reached due to the way Arndt and Gingrich define the passive form, "*bring or call together, gather* a number of persons" (*Greek-English Lexicon* 790).

Our next two chapters on "A Study of New Testament Worship" will first (Chapter 16) give us an opportunity to cover some basic matters that are necessary for a sound foundation in the study of the subject, then (in Chapter 17) we will review some things being said about worship among brethren today.

Chapter 16

A Study of New Testament Worship (1)

God is the only true object of worship. This is affirmed by Jesus himself in one of his responses to Satan when he was being tempted by him: "Thou shalt worship the Lord thy God, and him only shalt thou serve" (Matt. 4:10). As the only true object of worship, God alone has the right to stipulate exactly what is to be offered to him in worship. The reason man is not to be rash in his words, according to the writer of Ecclesiastes, is, "God is in heaven, and thou upon earth" (Eccl. 5:2). The difference between God and man is that God is the Creator and man is the created. The creature does not instruct the Creator on how he is to worship him. To use Paul's words, "For who hath known the mind of the Lord? Or who hath been his counsellor? Or who hath first given to him, and it shall be recompensed unto him again? For of him, and through him, and to him, are all things: to him be glory forever. Amen" (Rom. 11:34-36).

Jesus makes these same two points about worship in his conversation with the Samaritan woman recorded in John 4:7-26. But he also says more on the subject, which we will now consider.

Jesus' Description of Divine Worship

The background for this discussion between Jesus and an unnamed Samaritan woman is rooted in the ancient animosity between the Jews and the Samaritans. The story of the beginning of the Samaritans is recorded in 2 Kings 17:24-41. The king of Assyria had resettled Samaria, which he had conquered, with peoples of five different ethnic origins. At a later period these peoples had learned something about the true God of Israel from a priest from the northern captivity. The result of this amalgam of peoples was a syncretistic worship (syncretism is the combination or reconciliation of differing beliefs in religion). The main point of contention between the Jews and the Samaritans in Jesus' day was due to the presence of this mongrelized people (i. e., people produced by the mixture or crossing of different races) and a mongrelized worship (different elements of worship from these different peoples having been brought together) in the land of Israel. Such differences between them became the natural focal point of the conversation between them. The climactic part of the conversation is found in verses 20-24.

1. The Place of Worship. Involved in the question concerning which worship, the Jewish or Samaritan, was valid, was the question regarding where the center of worship was to be located. Based on what is recorded in Deuteronomy 5:5-14; 12:5-26; 14:23-25; 15:20; 16:6-15; etc., for the Jews this would have been Jerusalem (John 4:20b). The Samaritans insisted upon Mt. Gerizim as the center of worship (v. 20a). Based upon the teaching of the law itself, they were wrong about that, but this is not the point of difference Jesus discusses, except to say this subject which they had debated for centuries, is about to become a non-issue.

In his response Jesus turns the conversation in a way that no Jew would ever have expected. He announces a new alternative. "Woman," he said, "believe me, the hour cometh, when ye shall neither in this mountain, nor yet at Jerusalem, worship the Father" (v. 21). In the future neither Jerusalem nor Mt. Gerizim is going to matter. The debate over the place of worship is about to cease. As a matter of fact, it becomes clear that the real problem had nothing to do with place; the issue concerning true worship was not much longer to be a question that had to do with *where*, but *of whom,* as Jesus goes on to show.

2. The Object of Worship. What was wrong with the Samaritan worship? The point that Jesus chooses to discuss has to do with the fundamental difference between the worship systems of the Jews and the Samaritans. The difference that would continue to be relevant was *not place*, even though they were wrong on this subject since place did matter under the law. What would matter would be the *object* of their worship. Both Jews and Samaritans saw themselves as worshiping the true God, the God of Abraham, Isaac, and Jacob. They also both revered the books of Moses as God's divine will for them, but the Samaritans rejected all the rest of the Old Testament. Jesus pointedly says to the woman, "Ye worship ye know not what; we know what we worship: for salvation is of the Jews" (v. 22).

What does Jesus mean when he says in contrast to the worship of the Samaritans, "we know what we worship"? By giving this contrast he turns the discussion to the *object* of worship and shows that the Samaritans had a misconception of the God they worshiped. They may have *thought* that they were worshiping the true God, but in reality they were not worshiping him at all. How can one's worship be true worship when one does not *know* the God whom he professes to worship?

Even after the Samaritan religion had been purified from the original mixture with idolatry, it remained a mutilated religion. It was based only upon the first five books of the Old Testament without the advantage of clearer revelations from the Prophets and other books of the Old Testament. "Such a religion," Plummer points out, "when contrasted with that of the Jews might well be called ignorance" (*The Cambridge Bible for Schools and Colleges: The Gospel According to John* 112). Or, as Carson words it, "The Samaritans stood outside the stream of God's revelation, so that what they worship cannot possibly be characterized by truth and knowledge" (*The Gospel According to John* 223).

"Salvation is of the Jews," first, because God had made the promises to Abraham and Isaac, and, second, because the expected salvation was to proceed from them through the Messiah who came from the Jewish nation. Yet, more than this is meant by this statement. As Carson puts it, "The idea is that, just as the Jews stand within the stream of God's saving revelation, so also can it be said that they are the vehicle of that revelation, the historical matrix out of which that revelation emerges" (223-224).

3. The Nature of Worship. The kind of worship that is offered to the one true God also matters with God. Wherever one chooses to worship — whether it is in Jerusalem, Samaria, or elsewhere — the worship that is offered must be according to the *desire* of the Father. He seeks "true worshipers" (John 4:23). Let no one assume that the true God that man worships is indifferent toward the kind of worship offered to him. The regulating principle of the worship directed to God is *HIS desire*. Commenting on the phrase, "for the Father seeketh such to worship him," Plummer says, "that worship should be 'in spirit and truth' is required by the fitness of things: moreover God himself desires to have it so, and works for this end" (113).

It is not man who regulates acceptable worship. When man begins to regulate worship, or to determine *within himself* what God will accept and what he will not accept, in that very act he abandons God. Only the Father regulates the true worship offered to him, and those who would worship him *must submit to HIS revealed desire.*

But what does the Father desire? He desires "true worshipers." "'True,' as opposed to what is spurious and 'unreal'" (Plummer 112). Our Father wants *genuine* worshipers. This shows that only God can determine the true *nature* of worship. And what is the true nature of worship, according to him? Jesus says true worshipers are to worship him "in spirit and truth" (v. 24). God is concerned with both the *quality* and the *content* of worship.

In accordance with his own nature ("God is spirit," Jesus says), God wants to be worshiped in "spirit." Mere outward forms will not do; the person's whole self, his inner being, must be involved. The forms of worship, or the outward aspects of our worship to God, matter, but not the forms alone. To worship God in mere forms is a distortion of worship. In order for worship to be true, spirit must relate to God as spirit. The whole man must engage in the worship of God.

"True worshipers" also worship God in "truth." This word has been understood in more than one way.

1. It means that worship must be in harmony with the truth of God. Hendriksen, for example, says that "truth" here means "doing this (worshiping — *ww*) in full harmony with the truth of God as revealed in his word. Such worship, therefore, will not only be spiritual instead of physical, inward instead of outward, but it will also be directed to the true God as set forth in Scripture and as displayed in the work of redemption" (*New Testament Commentary: John* I: 167).

Others think that the word "truth" as used by Jesus in this passage is not truth as opposed to error, although this is an important aspect of worship. Here, according to this view —

2. Jesus means truth as opposed to shadow. John Murray summarizes the meaning of "true" as used in the Gospel of John in the following way:

> We should bear in mind that "the true" in the usage of John is not so much the true in contrast with the false, or the real in contrast with the fictitious. It is the absolute as contrasted with the relative, the ultimate as contrasted with the derived, the eternal as contrasted with the temporal, the permanent as contrasted with the temporary, the complete in contrast with the partial, the substantial in contrast with the shadow. Early in the Gospel John advises us of this. "The law was given through Moses; grace and truth came through Jesus Christ." (John 1:17) It is to miss the thought entirely to suppose that truth here is contrasted with the false or the untrue. The law was not false or untrue. What John is contrasting here is the partial, incomplete character of the Mosaic dispensation with the completeness and fulness of the revelation of grace and truth in Jesus Christ. The Mosaic revelation was not destitute of grace or truth. But grace and

truth in full plentitude came by Jesus Christ. The ultimate reality of which Moses was the shadow . . . now appeared (*Principles of Conduct* 123-124).

Man has always been required to serve God "in spirit and truth" (see Josh. 24:14), but now all service rendered to him is to be "in truth" instead of "in shadow." Worship in the new era that Christ was about to introduce was to be consistent with the New Covenant. Man is no longer under the First or Old Covenant (Heb. 8:7, 13); God has "taken away the first, that he may establish the second" (Heb. 10:9). The First Covenant belonged to the way of shadows, but Christ was now in the process of introducing "the new and living way" (Heb. 10:22) in contrast to the way of shadows.

This shows that though there is an unchanged principle that runs through both covenants, now we are to conform to the New Covenant in its unique differences. Worship, for example, has always been grounded in God's nature, so that worship to him, even in this age, must still be *spiritual* in nature. Another way to say this is, the *quality* required in worship ever remains the same, yet, there may be differences in *content*. This latter aspect of our worship means that worship also has to do with God's *purpose*. In the former age his purpose was that worship would be in "shadows," but now in this time his purpose is that it be in "truth" as opposed to shadow. The books of Galatians, Colossians, and Hebrews elaborate upon this point.

This latter point reinforces the fact that the principle that God regulates his worship and has not left it to man's determination, is a New Testament principle. We also find that this was true of the Old Testament. Man is not now, nor has he ever been, free to worship God just as he pleases, nor is he free to worship him according to the Old Testament pattern. Man's worship must be as God directs, and it must be in harmony with his revealed will *as it has been made known for this age.*

Other Aspects of New Testament Worship
1. Vain Worship. What Jesus in an implicit way teaches about worship in John 4:23-24 finds explicit enunciation at other places in the gospels. This is true especially in what we find in Matthew 15:2-9 and Mark 7:7-9, 13. Though the emphasis in these passages is on the inviolable sanction of the commandment of God in opposition to the tradition of men, and the discussion is not restricted to worship *per se* (the particular subject under discussion was the subterfuge by which the fifth commandment was being made void), the specific case introduced was but an example, for Jesus says, "and many such like things ye do" (Mark 7:13).

Worship did come within the compass of Jesus' discussion in these passages, because it was the matter of worship that Jesus used to introduce his subject: "In vain do they worship me, teaching for doctrines the commandments of men" (Mark 7:7, with Matt. 15:9). Jesus' point of emphasis is the antithesis of human prescription (i. e., something ordered or prescribed by man) to the commandment of God: "Leaving the commandment of God ye hold fast the tradition of men . . . full well do ye reject the commandment of God, that ye may keep your tradition . . . making void the word of God by your tradition" (Mark 7:8, 9, 13).

The conclusion is apparent. First, *worship that is regulated by human prescription is vain.* It rejects the command of God and makes void his word. Second, *man must adhere to the commandment of God; we may not leave it or depart from it.* Man must be constantly under God's guidance and direction; he is subject to the prescription of God's word.

We should pay particular attention to the repeated references to the commandment of God by our Lord in these passages. This is of paramount importance. It emphasizes the regulative principle of the worship of God. It is a strong reminder that God regulates our worship by his commandments. Any tradition that is not based upon and derived from the word of God (which is the same as to say, upon divine authority) is of human origin and incurs the condemnation of the Lord's teaching on this subject.

Paul also speaks of "the tradition of men" (along with philosophy and vain deceit) in Colossians 2:8, and of "the doctrines and commandments of men" in Colossians 2:22. Some were teaching that every Christian must keep certain Jewish laws, such as certain holy days, new moons, and sabbath days (v. 16), even though such practices had been abolished by Christ's death on the cross (vv. 13-14). Some were also insisting upon the observance of certain dietary practices ("meat" and "drink," v. 16, or "ordinances," vv. 20-22). Such practices, including visionary experiences and the worship of angels (v. 18), would lead one away from Christ, the head (v. 19). Those who were caught up in these kinds of *practices* were being "beguiled" (v. 18) and defrauded "through philosophy and vain deceit, after the tradition of men, after the rudiments of the world, and not after Christ" (v. 8).

2. Will Worship. Paul describes the worship of those whom we have just described in the preceding paragraph as "will worship" (v. 23, KJV). The first part of the word used by Paul for "will worship" is a word that emphasizes the idea that something is derived at by specific decision. It suggests something being engaged in with the full approval of the will. The last part of the word (rendered "worship") pertains to that which men hold as sacred. Thus, with the use of this word Paul is describing that aspect of religion that is based on man's desire to offer worship according to his own inclinations without reference to what may have been revealed by God.

In keeping with the suggestions made in the above paragraph, the word Paul uses here has been translated in the following ways: "in will worship" (KJV, ASV), "in self-made religion" (NASB), "in promoting rigor of devotion" (RSV), "in promoting self-imposed rigor of devotion" (Amplified N.T.), "with their self-imposed efforts at worship" (Phillips), and "with their self-imposed devotions" (Williams). What is said about "self-made religion" in this passage would lead us to the conclusion that man has never been given the freedom to determine his own way of worshiping God. History confirms that when man is inclined to follow his inclination, it is not long before he is intentionally following his own dictates in the hope that God will be pleased with him. On this statement from Paul, J. W. Shepherd has well said:

> However plausible and specious such worship may appear, however much of show of wisdom it may exhibit, the Holy Spirit has written its folly and emptiness so plainly that none but the willfully blind can fail to see it. Loyalty to the divine government requires hearty obedience to divine law. Whatever God commands, therefore, we must do. To hesitate is to falter, is to forsake our allegiance. To set up any "commandment of men," and honor it as a command of God, is treason. God's will is expressed in his commandments. Every commandment, even the least, is an expression of his will, and an embodiment of his authority as the monarch of the universe. To obey his commandments, to do his will, is, therefore, the very essence of true piety. Everything else is mere will-worship (*Ephesians, Philippians and Colossians* 287).

3. Ignorant Worship. Paul told the Athenians that the one true God is the God "whom therefore ye ignorantly worship" (Acts 17:23). His purpose in his discourse was to make this God known to them. That there might be such a God unknown to them they readily admitted. The inscription "TO THE UNKNOWN GOD" was witness to the fact that they acknowledged such a God might very well exist.

When Paul said that they worshiped God "ignorantly" note that he does not speak of the God "whom" they worshiped, but "what" they worshiped. Polhill, after making this point, says, "They did not know God; they didn't worship *him* at all. Their worship object was a thing, a 'what,' and not a personal God at all" (*The American Commentary: Acts* 372). He goes on to point out that the strong emphasis in Paul's statement is "on ignorance, on not knowing. For Greeks, as for Stoics, ignorance was a cardinal sin. The greatest virtue was to discover truth through pursuing the divine reason within oneself. Not to live in accordance with reason, to live in ignorance, was the greatest folly imaginable. Paul accused them of precisely this ignorance, this sin. He would return to this theme in verse 30 with his call to repentance. The time had arrived when such ignorance of God was folly without excuse" (372).

The worship offered by these people "TO THE UNKNOWN GOD" had been in vain. How could it be otherwise when they had no knowledge of the one whom they were worshiping? Ignorant worship is not acceptable worship, or else Paul would have had no reason to inform the people here about the one true God. If it did not matter that they did not know God, wouldn't it have been better to leave them in their ignorance? It is evident that Paul saw that it was necessary to give them the knowledge they did not yet have about God. After they had the proper knowledge of him, he then called on them to repent, or turn away from their false worship and turn to God (v. 30).

Worship Authorized by God Today

So what is the worship authorized by God today? Some would tell us that worship is not specific acts (singing, praying, partaking of the Lord's supper, giving, and teaching the word of God) engaged in at specific times (such as the Lord's day) and a specified place (that is, in assembly), but that all that we do as Christians is worship. Does worship refer to specific acts done at a particular time and a particular place? Or does it include all that we do?

1. The Old Testament Background. When Abraham was preparing to offer Isaac upon an altar as he had been commanded by God, he was specifically told to go into the land of Moriah, and offer Isaac there for a burnt offering (Gen. 22:3). A specific place and a specific offering was required. If the whole of Abraham's life was worship to God, how can we explain his statement that he and Isaac would "go yonder, and we will *worship* (*shahah*) and come again to you" (Gen. 22:5)? Would not the things Abraham had done thus far in obeying God's command (all the work done in making preparation to offer Isaac) have been worship, if this view it true; and wouldn't this have included the travel involved as they went forward ("go yonder") to carry out the task God had placed upon Abraham? Yet, Abraham makes a difference between the two. He calls what he is about to do "worship," which means what he had done up to this point was not worship.

It is interesting that the language used here is foreign to what some will allow today. They will not accept such expressions as "going to worship." Yet, Abraham plainly says, "we will go yonder, and we will worship and come again to you" (Gen. 22:5). Could we not describe this as "going to worship"? The passage says they would "go . . . worship" and "come again to you." That's saying they would go to a certain *place* and worship and then they would come back again from that place to those whom they had left behind. That's *going to* and *coming from* worship!

Before continuing with Abraham, we will pause to briefly note that similar language is used in the New Testament. John 12:20 describes certain Greeks as "going up that they might worship at the feast." From this it is clear that one can "go to worship." Furthermore, would any deny that they were *serving* God on their way up to the feast? Yet, the trip itself was not worship or it would make the statement that they were going to the feast "that they might worship" meaningless. They also were going to a specific place (Jerusalem) and a specific event (the feast) "that they might worship," and this is contrary to the claim that all of the activities of our lives are worship when offered as service to God. The trip to the feast on the part of these Gentiles was offered in *service* to God, but it was not worship.

In a similar way, Luke tells us that the Ethiopian that we read about in Acts 8 "had come worshiping in Jerusalem, and was returning . . ." (vv. 27-28). The same points just made in the two previous cases are also true in this case. Here is a man who had gone to Jerusalem (a specific place) to worship (in specific ways), and he was returning home from that particular place and from engaging in those specific acts of worship.

Now back to Abraham. At an earlier time we find Abraham expressing worship to God in specific ways. He built altars (Gen. 12:8; 13:4, 18; 14:20), prayed (Gen. 18:22f), and offered tithes to the king of Salem (Gen. 14:17-24). Are we to suppose that such specific ways of expressing worship to God were all Abraham's idea? We might remember this question when we take up the matter of whether or not God can *demand* worship of us. How would Abraham have known how to express his worship to God unless God had provided such instruction in the form of specifics to him? Consider also Genesis 24:26-27.

Prior to the time of Abraham, Cain and Abel offered sacrifices to God (Gen. 4:1-15). God was not pleased with the offering of Cain, for the Bible says, "unto Cain and his offering he had not respect" (v. 5). But, as we well know, God "had respect unto Abel and to his offering" (v. 4). If God had not specified the particulars with regard to both the spirit and substance of such offerings, on what grounds could God accept one man's offering and reject the other? The acceptable ways of worship from Cain and Abel had been made known by God.

Some time later the divine record describes Enoch as "calling upon the name of the Lord" (Gen. 4:26). Immediately after the flood, Noah built an altar for burnt offerings (Gen. 8:20f). This is the first explicit mention of the altar. It was erected to Jehovah, and the offering was offered to him. "The Lord," the text says, "smelled a sweet savor," which means that God accepted the offering. Did such expressions of worship offered to God originate with God himself, or did they originate with man?

Soon after the Israelites left Egypt and the Mosaic period had begun, a clear "pattern" for worship begins to emerge. After the people were formed into a nation at Sinai, God began to deal with them as one people. In the Decalogue certain implications are laid out with respect to worship (Exod. 20:3-6). God is the only true object of worship (v. 3). Visible representations of anything in the heavens, or anything on the earth, or beneath the earth, for the express purpose of worshiping them is a sin (vv. 4-5). Emphasis now begins to be placed upon doing all that God has commanded without adding or taking away from his word (Deut. 4:2), and man does not have the liberty of doing what God has not commanded (Lev. 10:1-2; 2 Sam. 6:6-7). All those things that are commanded of the Lord "shall be in thine heart" (Deut. 6:6) and they were to be taught to the children by precept and example (Deut. 6:6-7).

All things pertaining to the tabernacle were to be built "according to the pattern" given by God himself through Moses (Exod. 25:9, 40). There was also a pattern for the building of the temple (1 Chron. 28:11-12). Daniel, at a later time, shows that it is God's right to command, when he says, "I praised and honored him that liveth forever, whose dominion is an everlasting dominion, and his kingdom is from generation to generation: And all the inhabitants of the earth are reputed as nothing: and he doeth according to his will in the army of heaven, and among the inhabitants of the earth: and none can stay his hand, or say unto him, What doest thou?" (Dan. 4:34-35). Without God speaking and revealing his will to man on the subject of worship, man would be "a law unto himself," and anything that he chooses would be acceptable worship. Where, then, would be the possibility for vain worship, will-worship, or ignorant worship which we read about in the New Testament?

For those who think that there are no specific guidelines for acceptable worship, the words spoken by Samuel to Saul, who evidently thought that

God would accept anything offered to him in worship as long as it was the best of the cattle being offered, should be noted: "Behold, to obey is better than sacrifice and to hearken than the fat of rams" (1 Sam. 15:22).

2. The New Testament Pattern. The word "pattern" as used in the passages just noted is a word derived from a term which means "to build." It signifies a model, a prototype, an exemplar. The implication is that it refers to something sensible, corporeal, or substantial, as distinguished from another word sometimes used in the Old Testament which means "a likeness," in the sense of representation, picture, or image. The main difference in the two terms is that the latter term does not carry the idea of a framed model of any kind. The two words are used together in 2 Kings 16:10: "And king Ahaz sent to Urijah the fashion (*demuth*) of the altar and the pattern (*tabnith*) of it according to all the workmanship thereof." The word for "pattern" signifies a model, while the word for "fashion" refers to some other representation, either verbal or pictorial. The NEB distinguishes these terms in the following way: "he [Ahaz] sent a sketch and a detailed plan to Urijah the priest."

The "pattern" in the Mount represented heavenly things, according to Hebrews 8:5: "Who serve unto the example and shadow of heavenly things." This shows that the things pertaining to the ministry of the priests in the tabernacle were but "types" or shadows of the real things that were then yet to come. The service in the sanctuary was not "the true tabernacle" (Heb. 8:1). As Lenski points out, "If Jesus were to join the Jewish high priests in such a sanctuary and under such a law pertaining to such a sanctuary, it would mean that he, too, never gets beyond 'sketch and shadow,' never rises to the 'true or real Tabernacle' (v. 2), to the completeness and finality (. . . , 7:11) without which he cannot actually save us (. . . , 7:25), without which even all the sketch and shadow promised as to the substance and reality cannot be attained" *(The Epistle to the Hebrews and Epistle of James* 256).

What significance does this have as it pertains to the Old Testament system, and how may we make application to the new system introduced by Christ? We should be reminded how God would not under the old economy, or in the time of types, allow any device of man to come in for representing any thing heavenly. That being the case, how much less would he do so now in the age of Christ. Whatever God himself has ordained he would have man to observe, and he would have none of what he has appointed to be omitted. Bish comes to the same conclusion in the following words:

In the New Testament also his compliance with the command is repeatedly adverted to and the order itself expressly quoted, Acts 7:44, Hebrews 8:5. What then was the reason of such minute particularity? Why must such and such thing only be made, and they too of such precise materials and shapes? Undoubtedly because the whole was intended to be a typical character shadowing and leading feature of the gospel dispensation. Now as none but God could know all things that were to be prefigured, so none but He could know how to adjust and designate them in the way best adapted to their end. Had Moses been left to contrive anything from his own ingenuity there might have wanted a correspondence between the type and the antitype. But when a model of anything was shown by God Himself, the whole must of necessity accord most perfectly with the mind and purpose of the divine Designer (*Notes Critical and Practical on the Book of Exodus* 119).

John Gill states that the passage "teaches us, that every thing in matters of worship ought to be according to the rule which God has given from which we should never swerve in the least" (*An Exposition of the New Testament* 215). God had purpose in the external requirements provided in the tabernacle worship. He sought to bring his people to Christ. To this end, all other modes of worship were false and spurious. Only God can give direction in such matters. Man does not have the liberty to invent beyond God's command. From what we have seen already in Jesus' statement in John 4:24, we know that in the new age which he introduced this same rule is enforced by Jesus himself, since he says that God seeks "true worshipers," for "those who worship him must worship in spirit and truth."

3. Corporate Worship in the New Testament. To my knowledge no one would deny that there were specific expressions of worship in the assemblies of the church in the first century. But for several years now some have been raising voices of concern about our "compartmentalizing religion" by using the terms "worship service" the way we sometimes do. They do not separate *religious* acts from acts of *service*. They reject the idea that there are "five acts of worship."

Some Examples. As an example of this view, note how one brother describes our life as a Christian:

When one's life is dedicated to God, whatever he does is worship/service. It is not a matter of 'Take time to be holy,' for he is holy. It is not a matter of "Lord, we come before Thee now," for we are in Him and His Spirit is in us constantly. Through our commitment as a disciple, we "continually offer up a sacrifice of praise to God, that is, the fruit of lips that acknowledge his name" [Heb. 13:5] (Hook *Free In Christ* 90).

His entire life, in other words, is

> . . . a whole-life offering in worship. This will include all the mundane,
> secular things that relate to life. Although he may be working at a job,
> mowing his lawn, vacationing with his family, or taking medicine, these
> are not earthly, materialistic goals. They are a part of the upkeep of the
> temple which is continually devoted to God in all of its purposes (91).

Others have expressed the same view by using the most often quoted
passage to justify it (Rom. 12:1). Note these examples:

> We are the temple of God. And worship never ceases. Our presentation
> of ourselves as "a living sacrifice" is not something we do once . . . and
> get it over with. Not at all! Our giving of ourselves in worship is a con-
> tinual offering. Day by day. In all we do (John J. Wright "Worship Will
> not Fit into a Pigeonhole," *Firm Foundation* 97 [Nov. 25, 1980]: 246).

> Is driving a truck or diapering a baby worship? Yes, if done with a view to
> pleasing the Lord. Paul wrote the Roman Christians, "Present your bod-
> ies a living sacrifice to God, which is your reasonable service" (Rom.
> 12:1). And the word he used for service is one that means worship as
> well. . . . Our everyday lives are supposed to be presented to God as
> reasonable (KJV) or spiritual (ASV) worship. . . . We are prone to think
> of worship as something that occurs in a meeting-house. But the worship
> of God includes far more than participation in the "five items" on the
> Lord's day. We are encouraged to present our bodies as living sacrifices
> twenty-four hours a day, not three or four hours a week. . . . A mother
> wiping her baby's runny nose is offering worship to God as surely as is
> the most eloquent preacher delivering the greatest sermon since the Mars
> Hill address. . . . (Don Bassett, "Our Daily Life As Worship," *Christian-
> ity Magazine* 3:1 [January, 1986]: 21).

Is All This Worship? There is a common thread running through all of
these statements. Anything done in the name of the Lord, to God's glory,
out of devotion to God, or for the good of the physical body as God's
temple, is worship. But is this a true definition of worship? Personally, I
agree with T. Pierce Brown, who wrote an article on "Worship" a few months
after the article by John J. Wright was published. Here is a sample of what
he said that puts the issue squarely before us:

> One may say in a general way that for a Christian, his whole life is a life
> of paying homage to God. I would agree with that in the same sense that
> I would agree that one's whole life would be a life of prayer. Or that one's
> whole life should be a life of service to his fellow man. But that does not
> mean that as one ties his shoes or brushes his teeth or goes to the bath-

room, those acts are acts of prayer or service to humanity, or *acts of worship* for the Christian.

One may worship *while* he cleans his teeth, takes a bath, stops at a traffic light, or performs other acts or duties, such as giving a cup of cold water to a little one, but that does not prove nor indicate that these are acts of worship. I may worship while someone rings a cowbell, or blows a train whistle, but that does not mean that I am authorized to use these things in worship.

The fact that the Jews worshiped in Jerusalem, the Samaritans in a mountain, and we worship *anywhere* in spirit and in truth, does not in any sense indicate that every act is an act of worship.

A housewife should be able to wash the dishes or sweep the floors in an awareness that she is fulfilling one of the functions God provided for her, and she can do it in such a way as to glorify him, but that does not necessarily make them acts of worship. A house husband may change his baby's diapers and give him a bottle in the awareness that he is fulfilling a proper function as a father (some men may not know that!) and he may do it in such a way as to glorify God, but that does not prove that changing a diaper is worship in any Biblical sense ("Worship," *Firm Foundation* 98 [April 21, 1981]: 246).

Much of the confusion on this subject is a result of misunderstanding the meaning of the word rendered "service" (KJV) in Romans 12:1. Some other translations have rendered this word (*latreia*) "worship" (RSV, NASB, NIV), adding to the confusion. In certain contexts this word may be rendered "worship" (i. e., Rom. 9:4), but the basic meaning of the word is "serve."

This service may be service rendered to God or to men. Vine says of *latreuō*, the verb form of this word, "primarily to work for hire (akin to *latris*, a hired servant), signifies (1) to worship, (2) to serve," and he then gives a long list of instances from the New Testament where it means "to serve God" (Matt. 4:10; Luke 1:74; 4:8; Acts 7:7; 24:14; 26:7; 27:23; Rom. 1:9; 2 Tim. 1:3; Heb. 9:14; 12:28; Rev. 7:15). From this list one might note especially how Paul uses the word of a *lifetime of service to God* when he says, "for there stood by me this night the angel of God, whose I am, and whom I *serve*" (Acts 27:23), and Hebrews 12:28, "wherefore we receiving a kingdom which cannot be moved, let us have grace, whereby we may *serve* God acceptably with reverence and godly fear."

The context of Romans 12:1 favors a similar use of the word. Paul is describing the *use* of one's body as a living sacrifice, which is a lifetime of *service* offered up to God (see below on "*present* your bodies" = "*use* your bodies"). Jesus used a word (*latreia*) akin to this term (*latreuō*) when he spoke of those who supposed they are doing "service to God" when they persecuted his disciples (John 16:2). On the former word (*latreia*) used by Paul in Romans 12:1, Vine says, "of the intelligent service of believers in presenting their bodies to God, a living sacrifice" (349).

It is no doubt true that the expression "five acts of worship," terms often used to describe the things done in our congregational worship, is subject to misunderstanding. Worship is basically an attitude of mind that is expressed *through* the *acts* of singing, praying, teaching, giving of our means, and eating the Lord's supper, and we should not think of these acts as worship *in themselves*. Yet, these acts are important because they are the ways in which God himself has ordained that we express our worship to him and edify one another. Man is not at liberty to invent other avenues through which to express worship to God in the assemblies of the church.

A Closer Look At Romans 12:1-2. The subject of these verses is not worship but yielding — the yielding of ourselves to the Lordship of Jesus Christ. The reader should be careful not to miss the close link between the beginning of this chapter and Paul's discussion in chapter 11. His reference to "the mercies of God" in verse 1 points back to his discussion of God's dealings with Jews and Gentiles in that chapter, and in verses 30-32 he makes specific reference to their justification by the *mercy* of God: "For as you [Gentiles] were once disobedient to God, yet have now obtained *mercy* through their [the Jews] disobedience, even so these [the Jews] also have now been disobedient, that through the *mercy* shown you [Gentiles] they [the Jews] also may obtain *mercy*. For God has committed them [the Jews] to disobedience, that He might have *mercy* on all" (Rom. 11:30-32, emphasis and words in brackets added).

As the Gentiles in the church at Rome came to chapter 12 they would fully understand how the justifying grace that had reached them was a special extension of God's mercies. This provided the Roman Christians with a powerful motivation for offering to God the living sacrifice of their bodies. The realization that they had been fully accepted before God on the basis of justification by faith due to God's immense mercy to the Gentile world provided them the most powerful motivation that could have been given them to yield themselves to the Lord Jesus Christ.

The language used by Paul in these verses is also similar to the terms he used in his discussion of the proper use of our bodies in chapter 6. The word for "present" in connection with the body is used no less than five times in Romans 6:13-19. Formerly they had *presented* their bodies to serve sin, now they must *present* them as slaves of righteousness for holiness. What does the word mean? It means that they formerly had *used* the members of their bodies for sin, so now they must *use* them for righteousness. Whereas they once had *given their bodies over* as actual instruments of sin, they must now *hand them over* as actual instruments of righteousness. In Romans 6:16 "present yourselves slaves to obey" in the first part of the verse is equal to "obey" in the second part of the verse. One is the slave of the one whom he *obeys*.

This same principle is stated by Jesus in John 8:34, "whoever commits sin is a slave of sin." To the extent that we *use* the physical members of our bodies for the purpose of sin, to that extent we are acting as bondslaves of sin. But Paul, in Romans 6:16, calls for a different kind of service. He calls on his readers to serve a new master, to *use* (= "present") the members of their bodies as bondslaves to "obedience."

The word "present" in Romans 12:1 is to be understood in the same way. Both passages refer to the same subject matter, that of how we are to live as Christians. Presenting our bodies as a sacrifice to God means *using* them *in obedience* to him. This is an on-going commitment to God that is expressed in on-going acts of obedience to God's will. It is when one is *actually obeying God* that he is *presenting* the sacrifice of which Paul speaks. This is what the Christian life is all about. It is a continuous *act* of *sacrifice* in which we use our bodies to carry out God's will.

The word "living" that is placed before the word "sacrifice" is really one of the three characteristics of this sacrifice. This sacrifice is "living," "holy" and "acceptable." Romans 6 also sheds some light on how Paul is using the word "living" in connection with this sacrifice. In that chapter Paul uses the word "to live" six times. The ones most helpful to us appear in verses 11 and 13. In both of these verses Paul describes how Christians are to consider themselves as "dead indeed to sin, but *alive to God*" (v. 11, emphasis added), and they are to "present (themselves) to God as *being alive from the dead*, and (their) members as instruments of righteousness to God" (v. 13, emphasis added). As one uses his body in *service* to God — that is, gives himself in sacrifice to God — he is presenting (using) his body as a vessel for the expression of the very life of Christ which is within him as a Christian (see v. 4, "newness of life"). This "sacrifice," or handing over (presenting, using) of his body in such service to God, is not only a "living" sacrifice, but it also is a sacrifice that is both "holy" and "acceptable to God."

But in what sense is the use of one's body in *service* to God to be thought of as a "sacrifice"? We are not to suppose that every time the word "sacrifice" is used it is somehow connected with worship. Similar language of sacrifice is used elsewhere when it is not worship but service that is meant. Such metaphorical use of this term, or similar terms, are often employed by Paul in his letters. One of the most notable uses of such a word appears in Philippians 2:17 and 2 Timothy 4:6 where he uses a term that means "poured out" (as a libation). Interestingly, in the former instance he uses this term with both the terms "sacrifice" and "service," even though he moves away from his metaphor in doing so.

On these two words David Williams suggests that "because the Greek nouns for 'sacrifice' and 'service' here share one article, they should be understood as expressing a single thought: 'the sacrificial [i. e., self-giving] service' that flowed from their faith in Christ" (*Paul's Metaphors: Their Context and Character* 248). Paul is not describing his death in Philippians 2:17, but his service. He describes his death in 2 Timothy 4:6, but not here, because as Williams points out, "the context suggests otherwise. For example, in the context Paul talks about 'running' and 'laboring' (v. 16). These are metaphors of ministry, not of death. He refers to his and the Philippians' joy at his being 'poured out,' and he expresses the hope of visiting Philippi before very much longer (v. 24). It all sounds too hopeful, too full of life, for Paul to be talking of death. This metaphor is actually Paul's picturesque way of describing the hardship of his life as an apostle. The Philippian Christians were making their own sacrificial offering of service to God, and Paul was adding 'the libation' of his service to theirs" (248-249).

To use these kinds of metaphorical terms to describe acts of service does not make the acts of service worship. It is simply a way of illustrating the sacrificial nature of the service that is rendered. The way in which God accepts such service is also sometimes described with the use of similar terms connected with the sacrificial system. He describes the gift sent to him by the Philippians through Epaphroditus as a gift that was "a fragrant smell, an acceptable sacrifice, pleasing to God" (Phil. 4:18). Again, the point is not that the gift is acceptable worship to God, but that God is pleased with their sacrificial act of service. For it to be an "acceptable sacrifice" means that their gift to Paul pleased God, as Paul himself explains by adding the words, "pleasing to God." Williams concludes that "the lesson here is that whatever is done for the servant is done no less for the Master. Their gift was as much to God as to Paul" (250).

Paul in verse 1 of Romans 12 calls this kind of service "your reasonable service." The word used for "reasonable" suggests something that is related to man's rational or reasoning abilities, so that the word "spiritual" as used in some translations (NASB, NIV) is not adequate to convey the meaning. It is related to the word "reckon" used by Paul in Romans 6:11, "Likewise, you also, *reckon* yourselves to be dead indeed to sin, but alive to God in Christ Jesus our Lord" (emphasis added). One could not carry out the command without employing the mental faculties. He must *consider* (which involves the use of his reasoning powers) himself dead to sin but very much alive in his new relationship to God.

On the meaning of the word "service" in this verse see our comments on 183-184.

In the next chapter we will continue this study of New Testament worship. The central theme will be, can God *demand* worship and it still be worship?

Chapter 17

A Study of New Testament Worship (2)

Service and Worship by Demand

Some have argued that for God to demand that service and worship be offered to him with restrictions imposed makes God an egocentric God. Cecil Hook, for example, contends that we make God a child abuser if he *requires* our gifts, or *demands* our praise, adoration, and devotion. He charges that "this is one of the cruelest aspects of legalism" (*Free in Christ* 97). We will first consider whether God has a right to make demands on our worship, then we will take up his charge that this makes God egocentric.

1. Does God Bind Things Today? The key words in the paragraph where the above statement is found are the words "bind," "require," "demand," and "arbitrary" (97). The language used indicates that Cecil Hook, and those who are of his persuasion, outrightly reject the idea that God would bind or demand anything of man in this age on the subject of worship. According to him and others like him, such restrictions make God egocentric! But such a view of God is opposed to the plain statements of Scripture. What does Jesus mean when he tells Peter, "And I will give you the keys of the kingdom of heaven, and whatever you *bind* on earth will be *bound* in heaven, and whatever you loose on earth will be loosed in heaven" (Matt. 16:19, emphasis added)?

Does this include worship? Has *anything* been *bound* when it comes to the worship that man offers to God? This kind of argument would lead one to the conclusion that man is absolutely free with reference to the kind of worship he offers to God. No limitations, no restrictions whatsoever, could be placed on him, because for God to place any restrictions at all on man would make him egocentric!

Was not Jesus here giving the apostles the *power to bind* certain things? But what things? Has anything been bound when it comes to worship? If so, what? We never get the answers to such questions from Cecil Hook. He only talks about liberties, not things that have been bound. Why would God give the apostles power to bind if for God to bind anything on man would make him egocentric, whether in worship or anywhere else? Does anyone seriously think that these brethren will answer such questions? Please answer, Mr. Hook: Is there not even *one thing* that has been *bound* on man *in worship*? If our brother were to name even one thing, wouldn't his rule apply that says such binding would make God egocentric?

Please keep in mind that according to our Lord's own statement in this passage, whatever the apostles bound would be *bound in heaven*, which means that not only would God approve of the binding on their part, but the binding was being done by God himself through his apostles. Things bound by the apostles would be the very things God planned for them to bind. Let no one be mistaken about it — *God does* BIND *certain things on man*, Cecil Hook to the contrary notwithstanding. As a matter of fact, God is the only one who has the power or the right to bind things on man. According to Jesus' statement to Peter (Matt. 16:19), and the same statement made later to all the apostles (Matt. 18:18), God delegated the power to bind and loose to his apostles.

It is difficult for reasonable minds to imagine how brethren who profess to love the Lord, and who are attempting to persuade others to love him more, would at the same time be trying to convince them that such words as "require," "demand," and "bind" cannot describe God's way of dealing with man today. But how could this be when Jesus himself speaks of God "binding" things on man? How can one make such claims while at the same time totally ignoring how the very words they reject are words used by the Lord himself to describe how God expects man to respond to him?

Is not this approach to Scripture the strongest sort of rebellion against the very authority of God? This way of thinking also suggests the attitude of the "me" generation that demands "liberty" — freedom from any rules of any sort. It was this spirit that led to situation ethics and now this same spirit has led some of our brethren to "situation doctrine"!

2. Is God Egocentric? Has Hook seriously thought through what he has said here? The first part of his statement concedes that this is how God dealt with man under the law of Moses (i.e., through specifics, or by re-quirements, demands, etc.). If this is the case, might we not ask, then was God "egocentric" under the law, Mr. Hook? If it is the "legal ritualistic specifics" that Hook is opposing for this age, and if it is true that he is opposing them on the grounds that such a system makes God egocentric, as his above statement charges, *then it must follow that, since such a system existed under the law of Moses, under that law God was egocentric!* Let the reader judge as to whether or not our brother is dealing fairly in presenting such an argument. It goes without saying that we have become used to these kinds of inconsistencies from him. But surely our readers have every right to expect better things of one who professes to be teaching *the truth* on such an important subject. This would surely be the case before one would give any merit to what he has to say. How can truth have these kinds of inconsistencies in it?

Would we be told by this brother that God did not operate that way under the law. Then please explain the words: "this concept was born of the legal ritualistic specifics of the Law of Moses." Were the "specifics of the Law of Moses" from God? If they were, as this statement suggests, what does this say of God under the Old Testament period? Did God deal with man on the basis of "specifics" under the Old Testament law and then cease to deal with him on these terms under the law of Christ? We will have more on this subject under the next section.

Assemblies and Vertical Services
We then read:

> This philosophy has turned our assemblies into vertical services in our efforts to obey God's commands to worship Him. We have turned what should be edification into a system of rituals. Our successful achievement is in dotting each *i* and crossing each *t* so as to perform the ritual "well-pleasing in thy sight." But pleasing God through proper performance of rituals is not the purpose of our meetings together. Yet we have defined, refined, alienated, and divided over the ritualistic details in such practices as teaching and communion (Hook *Free In Christ* 97-98).

Are we being told here that the only *purpose* of our assemblies is for edification? Evidently. Hook argues that we don't assemble to worship, but to edify one another. This is true, according to him, because all of life is worship. Again, we see the same kind of inconsistency. When discussing this subject, Hook says absolutely nothing about the *purpose* statement in Acts 20:7, "Now on the first day of the week, when the disciples came together *to break bread*. . . ." Unless he wants to claim that the Lord's supper is for edification purposes *only,* and that it has *no aspects of worship* in it *at all*, then the purpose statement of Acts 20:7 contradicts his claim that we do not assemble *to worship*. The way he states it is, "God has not instructed us to assemble for the purpose of vertical communication," and "we do not attend meetings that we may carry on a vertical communion" (98).

Much of what is said on this subject serves at least one good purpose: it reminds us that no service or worship is acceptable unless it is done in love. But as Hook is prone to do in almost all of the areas he discusses, he goes to an extreme in one direction in his attempt to avoid an extreme in another. Yet, in describing what he thinks we are to do in our assemblies, he includes "pray for one another" (98, last paragraph). Now, pray tell me, to whom is prayer directed? Is not prayer a "vertical communication"? He as much as concedes that it is when he says we are to pray *for* one another, not pray *to* one another.

When we remember all of the attempts this brother has made to discount "pattern authority," even contending that specifics are not binding, they are merely love directives, we would do well to ask this question: Just exactly *where* does this brother get his *instruction* on what we *are* to *do* in our assemblies? Is he using the New Testament as a "pattern" to come up with the "list" of things he says we are to do *in our assemblies?* He says, "In our gatherings we are to encourage one another, pray for one another, teach and admonish one another in song, teach one another, give to help one another, and proclaim the atonement to one another" (98).

Think about what this brother has done here. It is certain that he did not get all of the things in this list which he says are to be done "in our gatherings" from a "list" found somewhere in the New Testament, therefore, on the basis of his own argument made elsewhere in his book, how could he *bind* any of them on anyone? Throughout his book he objects to making "lists" of things that are to be done in our assemblies. To do this, he says, turns the New Testament into a book of law, which, according to him, it is not. Yet, he has just given us a list of things we are to do "in our gatherings"! When he gives us his "list" of things that are to be done, he is attempting to show that vertical acts of worship are not included. The legs of the lame are not equal!

On the matter of turning our assemblies into vertical services, does Cecil Hook think that the last item in his "list" — "proclaim the atonement to one another," is all that is done in eating the Lord's supper together? One would assume that by this statement he means the Lord's supper, but aren't we also "remembering" Jesus in our eating of the supper? That's what Jesus *commanded* — unless of course this is a mere "love directive" and not binding on us as a "legal requirement"!

How do we remember Jesus? Do we do this to one another, or is this a vertical act? Jesus is not saying that we are to remember him to one another, is he? Why is not this a vertical act done by all Christians and done in obedience to the Lord's command, "This do in remembrance of me"? By the way, Mr. Hook, was Jesus egocentric when he *commanded* his disciples to remember *him* in the eating of the Lord's supper?

We can also raise the same questions about prayer and singing. Is the only thing we do in prayer and song in our assemblies for the benefit of other brethren who are present? Since prayer is directed to God (Matt. 6:9), and Christians in the first century church prayed publicly in their gatherings (1 Cor. 14:14-17), it follows that they engaged in vertical activities in their public meetings. In fact, in 1 Corinthians 14:17-18 Paul shows that they engaged in *both kinds of activities* (vertical and horizontal) in their assemblies when one spoke in a language that was understood: "For indeed you give thanks well, but the other is not edified" (when there is no interpreter). In their prayers God was praised and man was edified, meaning that there was both vertical and horizontal communication.

What about singing in the assemblies? Was there nothing vertical about it? Of course there was something vertical in singing. In the same verse where we are told to "let the word of Christ dwell in you richly in all wisdom, teaching and admonishing one another in psalms and hymns and spiritual songs," Paul adds, "singing with grace in your hearts to the Lord" (Col. 3:16). What does it mean to sing with grace in the heart *to the Lord*? Whatever it means (and surely it at least means being grateful to him as we teach and admonish each other in song) it tells us that our gratefulness is to be directed *to the Lord*, and that is *vertical* — it is worship directed to the Lord.

From this and other verses of Scripture we can see that some of the very verses that would be used by Hook to show we *are* to encourage, and admonish and teach one another in our gatherings, *also speak of offering thanks or praise to God* while we teach and admonish. So why does he say, "in our gatherings we ARE to encourage . . . , pray . . . , teach" etc., yet, when it comes to what he calls "vertical" activities, he says that "in gatherings of disciples we MAY praise God, thank Him, and express reverential adoration" (98-99, emphasis mine — *ww*)? On what basis does he make the vertical activities optional but the others required when both are sometimes found in the same verses? This is what is called *selective* reading. As a matter of fact, his book is filled with selective reading.

At places Hook seems to be attempting to dot each *i* and cross each *t*, the very thing he charges against us! He gives us a list of things we *are* to do in our gatherings, but then he doesn't want to include the vertical things we would add to the list from the same verses. Evidently he is attempting to give us a scriptural basis for our gatherings. But in his attempt he becomes guilty of the very thing he charges others with doing. Using his own words which he uses against us here is how we could criticize him: "This philosophy has turned our assemblies into (horizontal) services in our efforts to obey God's commands to (edify one another). . . . Our successful achievement is in dotting each *i* and crossing each *t* (on things that pertain to edification) so as to perform the ritual 'well-pleasing in thy sight.'" Now that is simply saying of him as he emphasizes the place of edification in our gatherings the same thing he says of us when we emphasize the place of worship in our assemblies.

This brother's objection to vertical worship is unbelievable. His emphasis on this subject reveals his problem. He has replaced worship to God in assemblies by putting man (instead of God) in the center of our gatherings. In his system man has actually become the object of service and worship, since he uses these terms interchangeably.

Does Hook not know that his "list" of things he says Christians *are* to do in their gatherings is subject to the same criticism he makes of the list of things we offer? If the things in our list make our efforts an attempt at "pleasing God through proper performance of rituals," why do not the things in his list do the same? Is it not true that he is in fact defining, refining, alienating, and dividing brethren over what he calls "the ritualistic details" in his attempts to show that only things that pertain to edification belong in our assemblies, and that edification is the *only purpose* for such gatherings?

On what basis did Hook come to this conclusion? How does he determine that this is the purpose of assemblies without turning the New Testament into a "code of law"? If he can make a list of things Christians *are* to do in their gatherings and not be guilty of this charge, why do others become guilty of it just because they say some items of worship belong in the list?

We are just as much opposed to ritualism as is Cecil Hook. But insisting that God requires certain things in our worship, and contending that some things are not authorized by God in worship, does not make our worship ritualistic. If this is ritualism then Hook is guilty of the same sin he charges against us since he is insisting that only certain things belong in our assemblies, and other things do not.

Can Praise and Devotion Be Demanded?
This brother tells us that "because of their very nature praise, adoration,

and devotion cannot be demanded" (99). Oh? Then how explain Psalms 146-150, or Colossians 3:16 ("singing with grace in your hearts to the Lord"), where God's people are specifically commanded to offer praise and thanksgiving to God? If by "demanded" Hook means "commanded," then he is wrong. But commanded does not mean forced, except in the sense that something commanded is not optional; whatever is commanded must be done in the way God wants it done. We all agree that any command is to be carried out in love. Obedience that is accepted by God is obedience that is rendered in faith and love; "faith working by love" (Gal. 5:6). This is obedience that comes from the heart (Rom. 6:17-18).

Our brother probably will say that commands that call for praise and devotion are only "love directives," not commands that make demands upon people. But that is Cecil Hook 4:32 talking, not the Bible. A command is a command, and commands make demands upon people. 1 Corinthians 16:22 comes very close to doing what this brother says God could never do: "If anyone does not love the Lord Jesus Christ, let him be accursed. O Lord, come!" If God does not *demand* the affection which the phrase "love the Lord Jesus Christ" describes, how could Paul pronounce this curse upon those who do not love him?

Matthew 22:34-40 is a *commandment* — the greatest commandment — that man love God with all his heart, etc. This is the passage Hook relies upon the most, and yet his favorite passage on love does the very thing he affirms God never does — *demand* that we love him.

Hook asks if the statement, "you praise me and give me gifts, or I will consign you to eternal hell" (98) is the threat of a loving Father. We ask in turn if Paul's statement in the above passage (1 Cor. 16:22) correctly expresses the Father's will; is this the Father speaking to us through Paul? Threats are used to encourage obedience, but they are not used to bring out the full measure of one's response to God. This is why Hook's question, "Can threats bring forth praise?" is not the same question as, "Can praise be demanded?" The answer to the first question is, not directly. But threats may help a person begin to give some thought to his condition in relation to God, and eventually help bring him around to make some important changes in his life so that full devotion will be given to him. This begins to happen when one realizes he is not devoted to God as he ought to be.

The illustrations used are really an attempt to prove something that is not necessary. Hook thinks that the poor widow of Luke 21:1-4, Mary anointing Jesus with expensive nard (John 12:1-11), and the sinful woman of Luke 7:36-50 prove that threats cannot bring praise. This is not a point of great concern with us, but let's take a closer look at the illustrations to see what they do teach us.

In the first place, it is understood that God had not *demanded* the last penny of the poor widow, but that is not to say that God had not made certain demands of her. So what is to be made of Hook's point that, if God had made *this* demand (required her last penny), "we would see her appeasing a demanding God rather than offering an expression of devotion and love"? The statement is faulty because it assumes that God is not a demanding God, which is not the case. Nothing in the story suggests that she was acting totally on her own. To say that she was is mere assumption.

The fact that others were also casting *something* into the treasury shows that they were all acting out of demand. So far as we know the widow would have given nothing had God not demanded *something* of her. Hook does not know otherwise; he merely *assumes* that she acted apart from *any* demands. The law of tithing under the law of Moses placed demands on her. But she went beyond these demands. She gave beyond the requirements of the law. That is quite different from saying that she acted apart from any demands whatsoever that had been put upon her. The widow is commended for her liberality; she gave more than the others when her gift is viewed in proportion to what she had — she gave "all the livelihood that she had," while the others "gave out of their abundance." Hook's argument on this point, and the examples he cites in an attempt to establish it, are but another example of *his revulsion to divine authority*.

The other examples prove basically the same thing. Both Mary and the sinful woman were going beyond what was demanded. God does delight in such devotion, and there is no doubt that the higher motive will produce the higher and better service and devotion. But that is not to say that service, praise, and devotion rendered in response to commands, or out of a sense of demand from God, is not true service.

Every statement that Hook makes about God not needing to demand praise to add to his self-image, or feed an ego defect, or meet his selfish satisfaction, is on the verge of being sacrilegious. We all know that God is concerned with our edification, but not to the neglect of our worship of him, as Hook would have us believe. His statements along this line would make our Lord's statement in John 4:23 that God is *seeking* true worshipers to worship him completely false. For some reason Jesus did not see that, for God to be "seeking true worshipers," put God on an ego trip of some kind. But then Jesus wasn't trying to make everybody who worshiped God out of demand a legalist either. That's what Hook does, and in the process he makes Jesus and other New Testament writers out to be liars. Let the reader be the judge as to who is right.

Think about it for a moment. Would God be *seeking* true worshipers to worship anyone but himself? Jesus says God is the true object of worship, and he says that God *desires* that they worship him in truth. Is Jesus charging God with being egocentric? No, that's what Cecil Hook says is the case if God demands such worshipers. Let the reader judge whether it is Jesus or Cecil Hook who is right.

"Pie-Shaped Religion"?

1. A Puzzling Pattern? In his chapter titled "Pie-Shaped Religion," Hook ridicules the "five items of worship" concept by speaking sarcastically of them in the following way: "After all, anyone who 'searched the Scriptures' here and there could find pieces of this puzzling pattern to put together" (91). Yet the criticism he makes of the "five items of worship" concept equally applies to his own *man-centered concept* of the "items" he says are to be placed in assemblies. These are things he says we *are* to do when we are gathered together. We referred to this list earlier, but just as a reminder, we here provide the list again from page 98 of his book:

— encourage one another
— pray for one another
— teach and admonish one another in song
— teach one another
— give to help one another
— proclaim the atonement to one another

Again we ask: Where did Hook find these "items"? Did he find them all at one place in the New Testament, or did he "go here and there" to "find pieces of this puzzling pattern to put together" (to use the same words he uses against us in his criticism of "pattern authority")? Remember the old expression, "what's sauce for the goose is sauce for the gander"? If this saying ever applied to anyone, it applies to this brother.

2. Man-Centered vs. God-Centered Assemblies. The reader will note that in this list this brother emphasizes the "one another" concept. His wording shows that he believes that what we are to do in our gatherings is man-centered, not God-centered. Yet when one reads the verses he would use to show that the items of worship/service that he has chosen are to be done in assembly, he will find that some of these verses also include instruction on some God-centered items. This is particularly true of our prayers, singing, and partaking of the Lord's supper. In addition to praying *for* one another, we pray *to* God (Matt. 6:9) and *glorify him* in prayer (1 Cor. 14:17-18; 2 Cor. 9:13-15). In our singing we teach and admonish one another, but we also sing "with grace in (our) hearts to the Lord" (Col. 3:16). In the Lord's supper we proclaim the Lord's death (1 Cor. 11:26) to one another, but we also remember our Lord in the eating of the supper (Matt. 26:26f; 1 Cor. 11:24).

One may also be led to worship when teaching is received. Paul says the following concerning an unbeliever who comes into an assembly and hears a prophet speak words he can understand: "But if all prophesy, and an unbeliever or an uninformed person comes in, he is convinced by all, he is convicted by all. And thus the secrets of his heart are revealed; and so, falling down on his face, he will worship God and report that God is truly among you" (1 Cor. 14:24-25). This describes a worshipful act. Was what this man did in falling down on his face and worshiping God in assembly just a part of this man's "whole-life sacrifice," or was it an act in itself apart from and distinct from all the other activities of this man's life? Was what he did here in this assembly on the same level with all the other kinds of responses he made in relation to God, such as the brushing of his teeth, taking a bath, going fishing, and visiting the sick?

3. Only One Purpose in Our Gatherings? It is true that worship is worship, whether in assembly or out of assembly (98, last paragraph). But to say that in the man-centered activities in which we engage in our gatherings "we fulfill the purpose of meetings which is to sustain the whole-life offering" (98-99) assumes that there is only *one* purpose for our assemblies. Note the wording: "*the purpose* of meetings." It also assumes that the only purpose of our gatherings is *to build up one another*, to "sustain the whole-life offering," as Hook words it. But how can that statement be reconciled with Acts 20:7, "And upon the first day of the week, when the disciples came together *to break bread* . . ." (emphasis added)? Why did they come together for *that purpose* at that particular time, the first day of the week? Was it to "sustain the whole-life offering"? Not according to Acts 20:7. Other things were done in that assembly, because the verse goes on to say that "Paul preached unto them, ready to depart on the morrow." Yet, the fact remains, the verse does not say that the disciples had come together to hear Paul preach and be edified. Other passages show that we are to come together for these other purposes (Heb. 10:24-25), but that is not the purpose stated in Acts 20:7.

The statement, "that which edifies man fulfills God's purpose" (99), says that this is the only *purpose* God has *in our assemblies*. There are a couple of reasons why we know that this is not a true statement. First, the example we have just cited (Acts 20:7) shows there were gatherings in the first century when brethren came together *for the specific purpose* of doing something that should be acknowledged by all as being worship. Even if it were true that "discerning the Lord's body" (1 Cor. 11:29) means "to discern the oneness of the body," the church, and not Christ's own fleshly body which was broken for us, as Hook claims (20) in an attempt to bolster his "whole-life concept" as the only purpose of assemblies, it would not follow that our eating of the Lord's supper is man-centered rather than God-centered. To partake of the bread and drink of the fruit of the vine "in remembrance of me" (1 Cor. 11:24-25) shows these acts are God-centered. We do not do these things merely "to strengthen and express our faith in the atonement" (20). When we properly discern the Lord's body which was broken for us, and his blood that was shed on our behalf on the cross, we do derive some benefit for ourselves. But to discern his body and remember him in his death is to put our minds *on him*, and *what he has done for us*.

We might do well, just for the sake of emphasis, to remember a point we made earlier about our singing. There is a two-fold purpose in our singing. We are command to "let the word of Christ dwell in you richly in all wisdom; teaching and admonishing one another in psalms and hymns and spiritual songs" (Col. 3:16a). That this was being done in assemblies is brought out by the terms "one another." As we teach and admonish one another in the way specified, Paul adds that we are to do this "with grace in our hearts to the Lord" (Col. 3:16b). What does this mean? For one thing it means that something is to be going on "in our hearts" *while we are teaching and admonishing one another* in song. Secondly, Paul is precise in his statement of what it is that we are to be doing in our hearts as we sing words of admonition to each other. The passage says we are to sing with grace in our hearts "to the Lord." The grace in our hearts is directed to the Lord, not to man. Finally, Paul specifies what is to be in our hearts as we sing: *thankfulness* ("with *grace* in your hearts") to the Lord.

In the last two quotes we have given from Hook he says that praise, thankfulness, and reverential devotion *may* be offered to God in our assemblies, while things that are the "primary purpose of our fellowship gatherings" (that is, to edify one another, according to him) *must* be done. The latter things have to do with ways in which we benefit each other in our meetings. This brother actually believes that the things we do in our assemblies for each other's benefit are required, but the things we do in expressing our thankfulness to God are optional. He must believe in "pattern authority" or he would not speak of things that *must* be done in our gatherings! Has he become legalistic on us? Only when he wants to. Yet everything he rejects, he casts out on that very basis!

4. The Matter of "Specified Rituals." The abuses that one might find in our gatherings will never offset or diminish in any way the fact that the Christians in the first century came together for *both* edification and worship. All of the attempts used by Hook to scare some away from accepting this fact by talk about the Catholic mass, the Holy Eucharist, specified rituals, imparted grace, and the failure of some to communicate with other worshipers in our assemblies (98) will be to no avail. Such efforts can never circumvent the plain statements of Scripture.

If it is true that too many have inherited the concept "that when specified rituals are performed exactly as prescribed by law, grace is imparted into the heart of the worshiper" (98), then that is an *abuse* of what God has prescribed for worship in our gatherings. But such an abuse (that is, believing that grace is imparted directly when God's specific instructions for worship are being carried out) is no legitimate argument against specific acts being prescribed by God for worship.

There is a play here on the word "rituals." What is a ritual? We are not told how the word is being used, but we assume he means something commanded that is repeated as an act of worship done in assembly. As a matter of fact, the closest our English versions come to using such a word is in Numbers 9:3 where it means "statutes" (citation in the NKJV), and there it is used with the word ceremonies. We must conclude that Hook uses the word "rituals"to prejudice people against such specifics in worship because he does not like for anything to be "prescribed" as *acts* of worship, especially in our assemblies. But don't forget that he has himself given us a "list" of things that he says must be done in our gatherings. What is the difference in his list of things that are "prescribed," and things which he says must be done in assembly, and the rituals he is describing and condemning?

We would all agree that Luke did not have in mind grace imparted directly into the hearts of Zacharias and Elizabeth when he says they were "both righteous before God, walking in all the commandments and ordinances of the Lord blameless" (Luke 1:6), but we can be sure that walking in the commandments and ordinances of the Lord included some "rituals performed exactly as prescribed by law." The performance of such rituals did not in the least keep them from being righteous and blameless before God. In fact, it was just such a walk that led Luke to describe them as being righteous and blameless.

5. The Meaning of "Pie-Shaped Religion." What is religion that is "pie-shaped," according to Hook? Is it religion where nothing is offered specifically and directly to God? Not exactly. But he does not want to speak of such attitudes and actions of devotion as worship in distinction from service. For Hook "pie-shaped religion" is "segmented worship/service," or religion that has "set times with detailed rituals," offered as worship, which he rejects. For him, to say that God *requires* a first day of the week meeting in which we are to eat the Lord's supper, to lay by in store as prospered, to sing, and to pray, as acts of worship, is no better than what was required under the law, though he concedes that all the activity in the Jewish temple was not ritual.

Hook argues, for example, that "the whole of the temple operation was a continuous offering even as, in a ritualistic way, the showbread and candles were continuous, living sacrifices" (90). One wonders, doesn't he, just how such dead things as showbread and candles can be "living sacrifices"! Nevertheless, from this he concludes that religion that is *not* "pie- shaped" is religion that sees the whole life as a spiritual offering to God, so that there is no special significance given to specified acts as acts of worship. When making this point this brother comes to the following conclusion:

> Some actions and thoughts are directed specifically to God (we have ritualized these into *worship service*), some are directed to other people, and some are rendered toward self in the maintaining of the temple. When one's life is dedicated to God, whatever he does is worship/service. It is not a matter of "Take time to be holy," for he is holy. It is not a matter of "Lord we come before Thee now," for we are in Him and his Spirit is in us constantly. Through our commitment as a disciple, we "continually offer up a sacrifice of praise to God, that is, the fruit of lips that acknowledge his name" (Heb. 13:15) (90).

The first requirement for acceptable sacrifice on the part of the Christian is his identity with Christ. The Jews had to leave their Judaism behind and come "unto him (Christ) without the camp, bearing his reproach" (Heb. 13:13) before their worship and service offered up to God would be acceptable. Christ is the true basis of such offerings. It is "by him" (Heb. 13:15a, KJV) or "through him" (NASB), that all such offerings are made to God. This is the peculiar privilege of the Christian. We have one through whom we fulfill the duty of grateful worship and service, even Jesus Christ, our great high priest and sacrifice.

Christ occupies the central place in all of our sacrificial offerings, in both worship and service. In addition to the passage in Hebrews 13:15, this

is also made clear in many other New Testament passages. Peter emphasizes the place of Christ in such offerings when he writes, "you also, as
lively stones, are being built up a spiritual house, a holy priesthood, to
offer up spiritual sacrifices, acceptable to God *by Jesus Christ*" (1 Pet.
2:5). Two chapters later, he writes, "If any man speak, let him speak as the
oracles of God; if any man minister, let him do it as of the ability which
God giveth: that God in all things may be glorified *through Jesus Christ*, to
whom be praise and dominion for ever and ever. Amen" (1 Pet. 4:11). Paul
opens his letter to the Romans, saying, "First, I thank my God *through
Jesus Christ* for you all, because your faith is being spoken of throughout
the whole world" (Rom. 1:8). He closes this same letter saying, "to God
only wise, be glory *through Jesus Christ* for ever. Amen" (Rom. 16:27). In
a summary fashion, Paul says in Colossians 3:17, "And whatever ye do in
word or deed, do all *in the name of the Lord Jesus*, giving thanks to God
and the Father *by him*."

The writer of Hebrews describes three sacrifices: the sacrifice of the
animals under the law, the sacrifice of Christ, and our own sacrifice. Christ's
sacrifice is the basis of our sacrifice through him. There is a close analogy
made between the animals whose blood was brought into the sanctuary by
the high priest, and their bodies being burned "outside the camp" (Heb.
13:11), on the one hand, and the blood of Christ offered to atone for our
sins, and his suffering "without (outside) the gate" (Heb. 13:12), on the
other. Westcott suggests, "the relation in which the Christian stands to Christ
— the perfect sin-offering and the continuous support of the believer —
carries with it two consequences. Believers must claim fellowship with
Him both in his external humiliation and in his divine glory, both as the
victim consumed (v. 11) and as the Priest who has entered within the veil.
Hence follows the fulfillment of two duties, to go out to Christ (v 13, 14),
and to offer through Him the sacrifice of praise and well-doing (v. 15, 16)."

The reader may want to revisit our discussion of the words *sacrifice* and
service in the last chapter, especially where we gave particular attention to
how the term sacrifice is used oftentimes to describe our *service* to God
without meaning that such service is worship (see pp. 185-189). It is simply a matter of fact that when the word sacrifice is used in Scripture, one
does not know that worship is meant simply by the use of the word itself.
What is said in connection with the word is what helps one know when
worship is the subject under consideration. In Hebrews 13:15 to "offer up
a sacrifice of praise to God continually" is a phrase that describes worship.
The wording itself leaves little room for doubt that worship is meant. One
does not come to this conclusion just because the word "sacrifice" is used,
but because the author goes on to describe the nature of the sacrifice he has

in mind: "the fruit of our lips giving thanks to his name." This is not service. Service is an act of a different kind.

The Hebrew writer speaks of both of these kinds of acts in these verses (Heb. 13:15-16), but he speaks of them separately, and he does not confuse them by making them the same thing, as some are doing today. What we mean is, the writer does not make all sacrifice worship. A careful study of the places where the term sacrifice(s) is used will show that the word is not used in that way in the New Testament. It was noted earlier that the terms sacrifice and service are used with one article in Philippians 2:17, and that Williams correctly points out that in this place it means "the sacrificial (i.e., self-giving) service" of the Philippians (see p. 188 for his statement), not the worship of the Philippians. Sacrificial service in this case was service that cost these brethren something, i.e., the giving up of self. From this use of the term we can see that the word "sacrifice" does not always mean worship, and that it may describe service that is not worship.

So, then, let's take a moment to discuss the two uses of this word in Hebrews 13:15-16, one in connection with worship, and the other in connection with acts of service.

1. The Sacrifice of Praise. What is "the fruit of our lips" in Hebrews 13:15? It is the *vocal acknowledgment* of the thankfulness that is in our hearts, what is here said to be "a sacrifice of praise to God, that is, the fruit of lips that acknowledge his name" (NIV). Since we are told specifically that it is "a sacrifice of praise," that is, "the fruit of our lips," it cannot be what Hook suggests when he says it means the whole life offered up by a committed disciple.

To acknowledge Christ's name is to confess him by confessing who he is in himself; it is to avow with our lips that we believe in our hearts that he is the Christ, and our redeemer. Is this kind of praise limited to our public gatherings? Of course not. But neither is it our every act and deed, or what some call the whole-life-offering of a committed disciple. We offer to God what is called "a sacrifice of praise" with our lips both in assembly and out of assembly because we are always thankful for what Jesus is to us. In fact, making it vocal is the significant thing, and it is done especially in our assemblies, though not limited to them. Raymond Brown describes this act in the following way:

> If the sacrifice is made by our lips and not merely in our hearts, then it becomes vocal and public; other people are soon aware of it. Although the phrase obviously amplifies *the sacrifice of praise*, it does express

another aspect of Christian gratitude, and one which might have been specially relevant to the first readers of this letter. They are to use their lips, literally "to make confession" (*homologountōn*, the verbal term of the noun used in 4:15; 10:23). Possibly, as Manson suggests, they did not want to expose themselves to the kind of harassment which would inevitably come their way if they openly confessed their faith and acknowledged Christ's name. It is one thing to express one's indebtedness to God; it is quite another to allow other people to know how much he means to us. In a spiritually ignorant society, like our own, regular attendance at Christian worship presents the Christian with an opportunity to witness. As we too offer *the fruit of our lips*, people with no clear faith may become aware that we too *acknowledge his name* (*Christ Above All: The Message of Hebrews* 261).

This is a clear example of how an act of worship such as confessing the name of Christ in the offering of praise to God in the presence of others may bring great benefit to others. This means, as we have seen before, that the same act may serve both horizontal and vertical purposes — edify one another and worship God.

What of the word "continually" as it is used in Hebrews 13:15? Cecil Hook would have us believe that the word shows that as committed disciples we worship God in all our words and deeds. Thus, in his words, as we quoted from him at the beginning of this section, "When one's life is dedicated to God, whatever he does is worship/service. It is not a matter of 'Take time to be holy,' for he is holy. It is not a matter of 'Lord we come before Thee now,' for we are in Him and his Spirit is in us constantly."

This raises an important question. Is it true that there are no special times, both in our individual lives, and in our public gatherings, that we "take time to be holy" and "come before" God for special periods of worship? Jesus already was holy when he went out "a great while before day . . . and departed into a solitary place, and there prayed" (Mark 11:35). Was he "coming before God" in this act — even though he already was in God and God's Spirit was in him constantly? What was he doing in Matthew 26:39 when he went ahead of Peter, James, and John "and fell on his face, and prayed"? Was he not "taking time to be holy" in a way that was different from how he spent the greater part of his day on an hour to hour basis? How could any deny that he was at this moment drawing closer to God through prayer? This particular moment was to prove to be a very stressful time for him (see v. 38). He repeats this act two more times on this occasion (vv. 42, 44).

Would any deny that a Christian draws himself *closer* to God when he comes to God in prayer than he is when he makes a stop at the grocery store to pick up an item or two for his wife on his way home from work? When Peter and John were released by the rulers in Jerusalem and "went to their own company, and reported all that the chief priests and elders had said unto them," those who heard their words, "lifted up their voice to God with one accord" and prayed that he might "behold their threatenings: and grant unto thy servants, that with boldness they may speak thy word, by stretching forth thy hand to heal; and that signs and wonders may be done by the name of thy holy child Jesus" (Acts 4:23-30). They already were holy, and they already were in God's presence (near to him), but upon hearing these words from Peter and John they took time to draw even closer to him through prayer. With one voice they came before God with this request.

Consider these questions. Weren't these disciples (in Acts 4:23-30) simply doing what the Hebrew writer calls on all Christians to do, when he says, "Let us therefore come boldly unto the throne of grace, that we may obtain mercy, and find grace to help in time of need" (Heb. 4:16)? Doesn't this call to "come . . . unto the throne of grace" distinguish between the kind of things we do throughout the day in making a living, taking care of family needs, etc., and those times when we come before God in worship? If some should say that the brethren the Hebrew writer addresses in this letter had already come before the throne of grace (or, come near to God) in becoming Christians, and that all Christians are ever before this throne, who would deny it? How, then, can such people come to a place where they already are in their everyday lives? The answer is simple: They do this in worship, both as individuals, and as God's people collectively when they are gathered together for that purpose! This is how one can be holy, and yet sing, "Take Time to Be Holy," or be in God's presence and near to him, and still sing, "Lord We Come Before Thee Now." To Christians, the Hebrew writer later says, "Let us draw near with a true heart in full assurance of faith, having our hearts sprinkled from an evil conscience, and our bodies washed with pure water" (Heb. 10:22).

Some brethren seem to have overlooked the fact, however, that not everything that Scripture says is offered "to God" is worship. There are some things that are described in the New Testament under the metaphor of an offering, or a sacrifice, that obviously are not meant to be taken as worship to God. Take the description of Christ's offering-up of himself in Ephesians 5:2 as an example. There Paul says that Christ has "given himself for an offering and a sacrifice to God for a sweet smelling savour." Was Christ's death on the cross an act of worship on the part of Christ? Romans 8:32 says that God "spared not his own Son, but delivered him up for us all," a statement that appears to be the language of sacrifice. Was this offering of Christ an act of worship on God's part? To raise such questions is to answer them. No one would contend that because such metaphorical language is used of God and of Christ it means that Christ was worshiping when he gave himself on the cross, or that God worshiped when he delivered up his Son. If sacrificial language can be used of the Godhead without meaning worship, why can't we see that the same kind of language may at times be used of men without it meaning worship?

2. The Sacrifice of Good Deeds. Most of what needs to be said on this subject has already been covered in the preceding discussion. The same kind of figurative language is used to describe deeds of kindness, or what the Hebrew writer calls doing "good and to communicate" (Heb. 13:16), as that which was used to describe a certain kind of worship in the preceding verse (Heb. 13:15). The only question that should concern us here is, in what sense are such "deeds" to be thought of as "sacrifices"?

It will be noted that neither the word "worship" nor the word "service" is used in these verses. Only the word "sacrifice" is used, and, as we have seen already, the word "sacrifice" does not in itself mean worship. The words to "do good and communicate" are not words that support the idea of worship when used with the word sacrifice. The term "sacrifices" does suggest an "offering," but one may offer something to God without it involving an act of worship.

What, then, is a sacrifice? A sacrifice is anything offered to God, either as an act of worship, or as deeds done for our fellow-man. Sometimes such "deeds" done for the benefit of others involve cost to us, even more than we can afford, but that is not the basic idea in the word. That thought comes through sometimes, as in the case of the Philippians (Phil. 2:17), but this is not an essential part of a sacrifice. In describing the Philippians Paul speaks of "the sacrifice and service of your (their) faith." He uses the words sacrifice and service together to describe the sacrificial *service* they offered to God through their faith, not their worship to him.

In the next chapter we move on to a different subject, that of "Faith, Opinion and Romans 14."

Part Three:
Other Areas of
Concern Today

Chapter 18

Faith, Opinion and Romans 14

The discussion of our responsibilities to civil authorities (13:1-7), to our neighbor (13:8-10), and to the Lord Jesus Christ (13:11-14) in chapter 13 has set the stage for Paul now to take up in Romans chapter 14:1-15:13 a particular responsibility that Christians have *toward one another* in the local church. The heart of what Paul is attempting to accomplish in what he says in this section appears at the following places:

> Therefore let us pursue the things which make for peace and the things by which one may edify another (14:19).

> Let each of us please his neighbor for his good, leading to edification (15:2).

> Now may the God of patience and comfort grant you to be likeminded toward one another, according to Jesus Christ, that you may with one mind glorify the God and Father of our Lord Jesus Christ. Therefore receive one another, just as Christ also received us, to the glory of God (15:5-7).

The Persons Involved

1. Jews and Gentiles. That there were both Jews ("the circumcision") and Gentiles in the church at Rome is pointed out in 15:8ff. Yet, it does not necessarily follow that the problem of the weak and the strong in the church there fell along these lines. The subject of the eating of meats and observing days might make one think so at first, but further reflection would lead to a different conclusion. It is practically impossible to determine exactly who the two different groups were that gave rise to the problem.

But different possibilities have been suggested:

Ex-idolaters. This view says that Paul is *dealing with* such people whose over scrupulous conscience would not allow them to eat meat which, before being sold by the local butcher, had been used in sacrifice to an idol (the same problem addressed in 1 Corinthians 8). But even though there are many similarities in 1 Corinthians 8 and Romans 14, there is no reference in Romans 14 to meats offered to idols and no hint that the question of idolatry was involved in the dispute.

Ascetics. Though some say there were ascetics among the brethren in the church at Rome, there is not enough evidence to support this view. We might contrast the view with how Paul deals with the ascetics in Colossians 2:16ff. where he says those who were binding such ascetic practices and the observance of days were robbing the Christians of their reward. Paul makes no such claim in his discussion in Romans 14.

Legalists. Some have argued that those who were "weak in faith" were *legalists* like those Paul deals with in the book of Galatians. But if this is the case, why did Paul not deal with them in the same manner as he dealt with the Galatians? There he pronounced a solemn anathema upon them.

Jewish Christians. If the problem centers around Jewish Christians, it would be Christians who were yet committed to Jewish regulations regarding the eating of certain foods and the observance of certain days. The problem with this view is that Jewish Christians would only be bothered by meat prepared by pagan hands, and yet Paul is dealing with a group who left off the eating of all meat: "For one believes he may eat all things, but he who is weak eats only vegetables" (14:2).

It actually is not necessary that we be able to identify the two groups along any of these lines. The next two categories that are specifically named in this section are all that is needed.

2. Brethren. Paul is not discussing the Christian's relationship with outsiders. For the first several verses he uses the words "one" and "person" and "he who" when speaking of the different parties he has in mind, but when he comes to verse 10 he uses the word "brother." He does the same in verses 13, 15, and 21.

In Romans the person who is a "brother" is one who has been justified by faith in Jesus Christ (3:21-26). This is the person who has repented of his sins (Rom. 2:4; 6:1-2), confessed the faith that is in his heart with the mouth (10:9-10), and been baptized into Christ (6:3-4).

The "one another" relationship Paul is describing (vv. 13, 19) in this section of Romans is the relationship made possible by our being together in the local church. It is in the local church that we are to "pursue the things which make for peace and the things by which one may edify another" (v. 19).

3.Weak and Strong. There are two classes of brethren under consideration, the "weak" (14:1, 2; 15:1) and the "strong" (15:1). The "weak" brother is described by Paul as one who is "weak *in the faith*" (14:1). He does *not understand* that he is free to eat all meats. He does not, however, love the Lord less than the "strong" brother, nor is he indifferent toward his duties as a Christian. Nor does he have less faith (that is, a less degree of faith in his Lord) than his strong brother. He himself is strong in love and zeal for the Lord. He is simply weak on account of his misunderstanding regarding the faith of the gospel on the matter of eating meats. We will consider the meaning of "the faith" in more detail in the next section.

In contrast, there is the "strong" brother who is put over against the weak brother. This is the term Paul uses to identify him in 15:1. Strong, though, in what way? In the context of Paul's discussion, "strong" means strong *in the faith* of the gospel (i.e., in his *understanding* of the matter that pertains to the faith which is being discussed in this chapter) in contrast to the brother who is weak in the faith (i.e., *in his understanding* of the gospel on the subject of meats and days). Paul however does not repeat the words "in the faith" when he uses this term of the weak brother. The brother who is "strong" is strong "in the faith" in that *he can in full conviction or conscience* engage in that which the weak brother cannot.

But how can he do this? Because he has a correct understanding regarding eating meats and the observance of certain days. *He has a correct apprehension or understanding of* what the truth of the gospel is on the subject being discussed.

The Nature of the Problem
What is the meaning of "the faith" as that term is used by Paul in this chapter (14:1)? We have assumed the answer to this question already in the comments made about the two different classes of persons involved in this discussion. But in an attempt to accurately define the nature of the problem, we will now address the subject by attempting to answer the following questions.

1. Personal or Objective Faith? There are only two possible answers to this question: "the faith" means either (1) *the faith* in the objective sense, meaning the gospel, or it means (2) *faith* in a subjective sense, i.e., the personal faith or conviction of the individual.

Personal faith either springs from "the faith" (the gospel message) because the basic source of faith is the word of God (Rom. 10:17), or it comes from some other source, involving a misunderstanding of a particular matter. In the latter case, one's faith is just as strong as that of the other brother who has a correct understanding, but it is a faith not founded upon "the faith." The brother who does not yet fully understand a matter, as in the case of meats and days, may be described, as here, as one who is "weak in *the* faith." That is, he is weak (in understanding) on the particular subject under consideration. In my own judgment, this is how Paul sometimes uses the word "faith" in this chapter, and "the faith" in v. 1. One reason for this conclusion is that in v. 1 Paul uses the definite article "the" with the word "faith." But more importantly, in this passage it is clear that what Paul is dealing with is a problem of *misunderstanding* on the matter of food and the observance of days. At issue is, what is the *truth* on this subject? It is the (weak) brother's *failure to understand the truth on this subject* that makes him "weak in the faith." Again the issue is, what is the Lord's will on this matter?

2. What Does "Disputes Over Doubtful Things" (NKJV) Mean? For sure, whatever the problem was that was dividing these two classes of brethren from each other (we will consider the problem itself in just a moment), Paul uses a word that clearly identifies the *nature* of the difference between them. In 14:1 he describes the difference between the weak and the strong with the words "disputes over doubtful things" (NKJV). What does he mean by these terms? There are two words involved. The two words he uses are as follows, and they can mean:

(1) *diakriseis*, "passing judgment," and (2) *dialogismnōn*, "doubts, scruples," thus, "passing judgment over [the weak brother's] doubts or scruples."

Yet there is a second possibility. The words can also mean, respectively, (1) "quarrels" and (2) "opinions," thus, "quarrels over opinions."

The first word appears only two other places in the New Testament (1 Cor. 12:10 and Heb. 5:14) where it means "distinguishing, discerning," but the act of discernment can easily pass over into the meaning, "stand in judgment over," and discerning can also involve quarrels.

The second word either refers to (1) the process of reasoning, or its result: "thought," "opinion" (Matt. 15:19; Mark 7:21; Luke 2:35; 5:22; 9:47; Rom. 1:21; 1 Cor. 3:20; Jas. 2:4), or (2) "doubts," "disputes" (Luke. 9:46; 24:38; Phil. 2:14; 1 Tim. 2:8).

New Testament usage slightly favors the first alternative. Some, however, believe that the plural form of the word would tip the scale slightly in favor of the second meaning. But since Paul is discussing a matter that pertains to "the faith," and how one understands the subject of meats and days, *the first meaning is probably better here.*

If this is what Paul is saying, as we believe it is, then what he is telling the strong brother is this: do not accept the weak brother *for the purpose of entering into debates with him* over his way of thinking, or how he reasons about the matter under consideration.

3. Is the Difference Over a Matter of Sin? One may well ask, how can it be called a dispute or argument over a certain way of thinking if it is a matter that pertains to "the faith"? Or, worded more precisely: how can one be wrong *in his understanding* about a matter that has to do with "the faith" of the gospel and yet Paul call it a matter over which brethren should not be divided?

The importance of this question cannot be overestimated. It gets to the heart of one of the central differences that has developed among brethren on the nature of the problem being discussed in this passage of Scripture. Some maintain that Romans 14 teaches that even when we have differences over *doctrinal* matters we may continue to have fellowship with those brethren *whom we judge* to be wrong in their beliefs or practices. Others say, no, Romans 14 is not discussing doctrinal matters, but matters of *opinion.*

So, who is right? Actually, there is a sense in which both are right! Yet, we want to be careful to notice how these terms are used here. *Definitions of the terms used must be in keeping with the nature of the subject being discussed in Romans 14.*

Even if the subject of Romans 14 concerns a "doctrinal" matter, we should keep in mind that *Paul gives these brethren specific instruction as to what the truth is on this subject.* The very fact that Paul makes allowance for *different ways of thinking* about the subject under discussion, and at the same time calls it a matter that pertains to "the faith," should cause us to exercise caution in the application we make of it. The question, how can Paul call it something that pertains to "the faith" and at the same time allow (at least temporarily) different ways of thinking about it, should cause us to pause and carefully consider what this means for us today.

The very nature of the subject itself has an important bearing on this question. The subject being discussed pertains to foods and the observance of certain days. But Paul shows in this chapter that the eating of food and the observance of days that had created the problem among them *is no longer* a matter about which they should be concerned. He actually goes on to show that God himself had loosed the matter of food and days. This makes the situation Paul is facing in this chapter a unique situation, to say the least. Since the practice of eating only certain foods had been loosed by God, was now a *liberty*, and was not now to be imposed upon Christians, then it no longer mattered that one person now eats foods previously not allowed, or that he observes days that no longer are bound. Such things are *now* (at the time Paul was writing to these brethren) *a matter of indifference* with God. On meats, Paul later says, "For every creature of God is good, and nothing is to be refused if it is received with thanksgiving; for it is sanctified by the word of God and prayer" (1 Tim. 4:4-5).

More Questions to Consider

Perhaps someone says, "But the weak brother *thought* the strong brother was sinning by eating such meats and treating all days alike, and yet God tells this weak brother not to judge (condemn) him (14:2). Isn't this the same thing as our accepting one whom we *think* is engaging in a sinful practice?" In other words, in an effort to "pursue the things which make for peace and the things by which one may edify another" (14:19), aren't we placed under the responsibility of accepting a brother today, and having fellowship with him, even when *in our judgment* he is wrong in his understanding and practice that is a doctrinal matter?

In answer to this question it would be helpful if we begin with another question: Is the dispute with the brother over something that God himself has loosed? As we already have pointed out, this is the subject of Romans 14. Does anyone know of any other reason than this as to why God required the weak brother not to condemn the strong brother? Even more to the point for our present day purposes, *just who is the strong brother and who is the weak brother today?*

Some say that the *weak* brother is (1) one who *misunderstands* the truth on a subject, and (2) one who also *practices* what he thinks is right on that subject (though he is wrong in both his understanding and practice), and the *strong* brother is the one who is to accept him even though he is wrong on both counts. This, according to this interpretation, is what is taught in

Romans 14. But if this is the correct interpretation of this chapter, wouldn't the next logical question be, *wrong on what?* Wrong in both his understanding and practice on just anything? If one answers, no, and begins to back off some, the next question is, how does Romans 14 help him know where to draw the line on what *kind of things* one is to be tolerant about? My own conclusion is that there are no such guidelines in this chapter except on the *subject* Paul is discussing, and Paul himself says "that there is nothing unclean of itself," meaning that all meats are clean and a brother has the *right* to eat any and all meats.

This means that Paul gave the weak brother the *information* he needed to have a *correct understanding* of *this* subject. He knew however that some might still have scruples about eating all meats, so he instructed those who had such doubts to forego eating meats until they could do so in all good conscience. But he did not allow the weak brother to condemn the strong brother who could eat all meats.

But why would he not allow the weak brother to condemn the strong brother when he was *convinced* (though wrong in his conclusion) that his brother was sinning? Because the strong brother was *not* sinning when he ate meats or failed to observe certain days. Could Paul have been more clear about that? The only restriction Paul placed upon the strong brother was that he was not to eat meats when by doing so he "offended" his weak brother, or caused him to "stumble," which was to *cause him to sin* by eating meats without the approval of his conscience.

To enable us to think more carefully on whether Romans 14 is applicable to other situations, consider the following question: Does the brother who eats all meats (*the strong brother* whom the *weak* brother *thought* was sinning in eating such meats) and a person who commits fornication, practices idolatry, commits murder, and steals from others, and believes he is *right* in such practice, belong in the class of "strong brethren" because he can do these things without having any scruples about them? The answer is, of course, no, because the Bible specifically condemns all these practices. There does not appear to be any disagreement among brethren on these kinds of matters because such things are specifically condemned in the Scriptures. All agree that these kinds of things do not belong in Romans 14 no matter how much some may try to put them there. That there is some limitation on how Romans 14 may be used is not a matter of dispute among brethren.

But let's carry this point of agreement a step further. We want to go back to the first century to a city like that of Corinth where, let's say, we find a brother who had just come into the body of Christ who still *thinks* (this is his *understanding on this subject*) that the fornication he had been in the habit of committing in worship to a pagan god in a pagan temple is still okay. Would Paul's instruction in Romans 14 apply to him? Again we feel confident that all would agree that it would not. But why not? It would be interesting to see how those who are using this chapter to justify brethren accepting one another in spite of differences over things they judge to be unauthorized in Scripture would answer this question. Let me suggest that Romans 14 would not apply to such a case for the following reasons.

1. *Their standing.* Both classes of brethren in Romans 14 were specifically told the following:

- Do not "despise" the other, because "God has received him" (14:3).

- "Who are you to judge another's servant? To his own master he stands or falls. Indeed, he will be made to stand, for God is able to make him stand" (14:4).

2. *The reason.* Was it because the brother misunderstood, and God was willing to overlook it and accept him anyway, or because it was a subject that God now considered to be a matter of indifference, since meats and days don't matter any more? Clearly it was the latter.

3. *Question*: Would God make a brother stand, even though still young in the faith, who does not yet *understand* that fornication is a sin, and as a result of his misunderstanding still practiced it as an act of worship to a pagan god?

Keep in mind that the problem discussed in Romans 14 *is not dealing with a matter that is sinful.* If it were, would it not follow that a case over fornication as just described would then be parallel to it and the same instructions would also apply. This would also mean that God would accept such a brother in his misunderstanding and practice, even though the matter involved is a matter of sin.

Does he? Of course not. The reason that such a case is *not* parallel is that the subject under discussion in Romans 14 is clearly *a matter of indifference with God.* In addition to what he says in verses 3-4, Paul says: "I know and am convinced by the Lord Jesus that there is nothing unclean in itself; but to him who considers anything to be unclean, to him it is unclean" (14:14). Would Paul make such a statement about anything that is sinful? He makes the same point a few verses later: ". . . All things indeed are pure, but it is evil for the man who eats with offense" (14:20). He means the same thing when he says, "for the kingdom of God is not eating and drinking" (14:17). See our discussion of these verses in Chapter 12, "Amoral Matters and Positive Divine Law."

It is true that Paul does show in this chapter that one *may* sin *even in a thing that is a matter of indifference* with God, and he will do so, Paul says, if he should engage in such an act without faith (14:23). "Without faith" in this case is without conviction that he is right. Though the meats and the days being discussed in this chapter are nothing with God, should one eat such meats or observe such days without faith (i. e., without full confidence that his eating these meats and observing these days is right), the lack of such faith in the rightfulness of his act is a sin.

Two Opposing Views

What appears to be two opposing views on how to apply Romans 14 to present day differences among brethren are represented in the two following quotations.

STATEMENT #1: . . . Specifically, Paul teaches that those who retained conscientious scruples about various rituals of the law should understand that those issues were not matters bound by God. But the intent of the passage clearly encompasses more than that clarification. The subject of Romans 14 is the question of brotherly disagreements.

Neither can one argue that the passage simply proves that we can disagree about indifferent matters. Common sense tells me that without the need of revelation. (Of course, even if that interpretation were true, we would still be left with the burden of separating matters of "faith" from matters of "indifference.") The issue in Romans 14 is precisely the establishment of the right of brethren to differ in matters of "faith." It gives sanction to private conscience: "Hast thou faith? Have it to thyself before God" [verse 22] (David Edwin Harrell, "The Bounds of Christian Unity (3)," *Christianity Magazine*, April [1988] 102).

STATEMENT #2: Grubbs observes, "The right to hold [an opinion, CDH] is absolute; the right to practice it is relative. A man may use a correct opinion as to be damned; or he may so use an incorrect opinion as to be saved" (164). He also states, "We can not waive a duty; we can waive what we deem a privilege" (165). What God has bound, none of us can put in the realm of indifference such as food. Indifferent things, however, can in certain contexts become prohibited by the law of God. None of us has a right to set aside what Christ binds. That is not a matter of indifference. Baptism is a matter of immersion in water as an act of faith for the remission of sins. Sprinkling or pouring in lieu of immersion is not an indifferent matter. Brethren need to understand Paul's argument and not seek to make it apply to what it does not. . . . (Clinton D. Hamilton, *The Book of Romans* 768 [comments on Rom. 14:15]).

We must exercise care, as well as some caution, in our evaluation of the views expressed in these two statements. But, it must be admitted, for many of us there are some things in the first statement that give a great deal of concern. Surely the objection in the first statement that if Romans 14 is merely dealing with disputes over indifferent matters then "we would still be left with the burden of separating matters of 'faith' from matters of 'indifference'" is not a serious one.

For one thing, if the fact that Paul is discussing a matter of *faith* means that his instructions are to be applied to our differences in areas of faith today, would we not then face even a more difficult problem? Unless we are willing to put *everything* that is a matter of "faith" in the class of what is being discussed in this chapter, we would then be left with the burden of separating matters of "faith" from matters of "faith"! That would be even more difficult than attempting to separate matters of faith from matters of indifference.

If this is where Romans 14 leads us, one is made to wonder how one then places a *limit* upon what a brother may teach and practice that is of a doctrinal nature. If those who hold this view of Romans 14 *believe there are limits* upon what a brother may teach and practice, and a brother is not left free to believe and practice any and every thing imaginable, *how do they determine these limits*? How is it easier to make judgments between matters of faith than it is to make judgments between matters of faith and matters of indifference?

In the next place, the illustration given in the second quotation brings out the importance of this point. "Baptism is a matter of immersion in water as an act of faith for the remission of sins. Sprinkling or pouring in lieu of immersion is not an indifferent matter. Brethren need to understand Paul's argument and not seek to make it apply to what it does not." To all who hold the view that Romans 14 is showing brethren how to get along with each other when they differ over doctrinal matters, we would ask: Is sprinkling for baptism one of those matters about which brethren may differ? By "differ" we mean *teach* and *practice* different things concerning it. With brother Hamilton, those who hold that this chapter is discussing matters of indifference, would also with him insist that sprinkling in the place of immersion cannot be justified (allowed to be taught and practiced) on the basis of the teaching of Romans 14.

But how does one who holds that Romans 14 is discussing the right of brethren to differ in matters of "faith" going to reject such a teaching and practice? Does Romans 14 cover this subject? Does it allow a difference in *teaching* and *practice* on the matter of sprinkling for baptism? If not, why not? Since, as we are told, "the issue in Romans 14 is precisely the establishment of the right of brethren to differ in matters of 'faith,'" we must continue to ask the question, *are there limits* imposed upon what a brother may teach and practice or not? If there are, what are those limits, and *how is one to determine* what they are? How far, in other words, are those who are advocating this view of Romans 14 willing to carry this point?

What, for example, besides the subject of divorce and remarriage (which many seem to want to put here) may one place in Romans 14? Take the items we have gathered and listed from Cecil Hook's book (see our list on pp. 109-113) that he has been willing to sacrifice in order to bring about unity among professed Christians and let us know which of those things belong in this class. For Cecil Hook it is strictly a matter of motive. *What* one teaches is not at issue, but *what motivates* him to teach what he does. For him this is the only thing that makes one a false teacher. What say ye?

Does Paul Side With the Strong Brother?
On who was right in the controversy discussed in Romans 14, one brother said, "Paul tantalizes the legalist by not telling which side was right on the matter of eating foods and keeping days. Instead, he shames us, 'Who are you to pass judgment on the servant of another? It is before his own master that he stands or falls. And he will be upheld, for the Master is able to make him stand'" (Hook, *Free In Christ* 67). Yet, if verse 4, which is here quoted, means that Paul "did not tell which side was right" on this issue, how are we to explain verse 14, and other similar sayings such as 1 Timothy 4:4? The words "nothing unclean" in verse 14 is a reference to the class of things Paul is discussing, food and days. The statement of 1 Timothy 4:4 specifies "every creature of God" and calls them "good." In light of such statements how can one say that Paul did not tell "which side was right" on this subject?

If this is the correct understanding (that is, that in v. 14 Paul tells the weak brother that all foods are "clean"), someone may ask, then why would it be necessary for Paul to tell these same weak brethren to stop passing judgment (v. 4) on the strong over this subject? The answer to this question is provided in the last part of verse 14. If a brother yet considered certain foods to be unclean, they were unclean *for him*, and it would be a sin for him to eat such food. But since in God's sight such food was *not* unclean, then the weak brother who still had such scruples was not to condemn the strong brother for eating such food, and the strong brother on the other hand was not to condemn the weak brother for *not* eating such foods.

Hendriksen is right when he says concerning verse 14, "By expressing himself as he does the apostle accomplishes two things: (a) He encourages the strong by clearly showing that he takes their side; see v. 14a; (b) he helps the weak by reminding the strong that the weak are right in refusing to eat that which *they* (the weak) consider to be unclean (verse 14b)" (*Romans* II: 462).

Isn't the affirmation of verse 14a that "nothing is unclean of itself" the very conclusion the strong brother had come to, and also the basis upon which the strong was convinced he could "eat all things" (v. 2)? It was his *correct* understanding of the subject that gave him the *right* to act upon his convictions on this matter. Paul is simply stating in verse 14a what had been concluded by this brother. He knew that the strong acted properly in eating meats because this was the Lord's will on the matter. His words were, "I know, and am persuaded by the Lord Jesus Christ."

Murray suggests that the reason why Paul made this statement "that there is nothing unclean of itself" at this place (v. 14a), was because "otherwise the plea would lose its character as one based entirely upon consideration for the religious interests of the weak. If certain things were intrinsically evil, then the strong would be required to abstain from their use out of regard to their own religious interests" (*Romans* 189). This is the reason why Paul must make the point that in the case before him it was not "things" (food) *per se* that was at issue, because food is not intrinsically evil. If certain foods were wrong *in themselves* Paul would not be telling the strong to abstain from eating them if it caused their weak brother to stumble, but to abstain for their own sake. So again, with Murray, we find ourselves agreeing "that 'nothing is unclean of itself' is the justification of the belief entertained by the strong that he may eat all things (v. 2) and is the reason why abstinence on the part of some is due to weakness of faith" (188). This is, in fact, the point we made at the beginning of the previous paragraph.

On Romans 14 our brother also says, "Paul says that believers may disagree on meats and days and both be right for God welcomes and upholds both and makes both to stand (Rom. 14:1-4)" (*Free In Christ* 67). But as we have just shown, Paul sided with the strong brother on the subject of food and days. *Both* were *not* right in their understanding of this subject, in spite of our brother's claim to the contrary. The *weak* brother was *wrong* in his conclusion that certain foods could not be eaten and that certain days must still be observed. It is true that there are many things about which we may disagree, but that is not the issue. How a brother *holds* his differing opinions is the issue, and this is a matter that can and does divide us.

If the Strong Brother Was Right, How Does God Uphold Him?

If the issue between the weak and the strong as discussed in Romans 14 was now a matter of indifference with God (that is, one could either eat or not eat the food involved and observe or not observe certain days, with God's approval), then why, one may ask, would we be told that God will uphold the strong brother and make him stand, according to verse 4? Whatever the reason may be, it is not because this brother was wrong on the subject of food and days and God approves him anyway. This is what is assumed by Hook, and also argued by all others who use this chapter to justify different teachings and practices among brethren over doctrinal matters. The passage does *not* say that God makes *either* the weak brother or the strong brother right *even though he is wrong* in his teaching and practice. This appears to be the claim of Hook when he says both are "right for God welcomes and upholds both and makes both to stand" (emphasis added). Clearly he claims far more than what we find in verse 4.

In the first place, in this verse only one of the two men (either the weak or the strong brother) is represented as one whom God will hold up and make him stand. The use of the personal pronouns "he" and "him" in contrast to the "thou" tells us that something is said to one group about the other. The "thou" is told that "he shall be holden up, and God is able to make him stand." Is this not said *to* the weak brother *about* the strong brother?

At the beginning of verse 4 Paul reprimands the weak brother because of his censorious judgment of the brother who eats all foods and chooses not to observe certain special days. The one whom God enables to stand (second part of v. 4) is the strong brother who is being condemned by the weak brother. Paul is here telling the weak that they must avoid such judgments against the strong; they must not think that the brother who eats all food and does not observe special days is failing in his devotion to Christ. He is not.

The strong brother will stand firm for the simple reason that Christ's power will enable him to remain steadfast. Murray states the case well when he says, "The appeal to the power of Christ offers poignant reproof to the sin of censorious judgment. The suspicion which the latter involves is a reflection upon the sustaining power of Christ and overlooks the fact that conduct which meets with the Lord's approval cannot imperil the steadfastness of the person concerned" (177).

We will now move on to the subject of faith and opinions, and how brethren have treated this subject through the years.

Chapter 19

The Problem of Differing Opinions (1): An Historical Perspective (1800-1850)

To understand what the Restoration Movement was all about in its inception, it is necessary to give some consideration to the writings of the early restoration leaders. We have no desire to "restore the Restoration Movement," as some might think, but we do believe that when the aim of the movement is properly understood the restoration principle itself is a valid one. This principle is just as valid today as it was when efforts were first begun to implement it. Exactly what were the leaders of the Restoration Movement of the early 1800s trying to accomplish, and how did they hope to be successful in what they had set out to do? How did the problem of opinions impact their early efforts, and how did they propose to deal with them so they would not be hindered, or even worse, defeated, in their quest? These are some of the questions we wish to address in this and the following chapter.

No attempt will be made in these two chapters to evaluate the proposals offered by these brethren. Our personal observations on this subject will be given in the chapters that follow.

Unity and the Restoration Principle

1. Thomas Campbell. To discover the meaning of the Restoration principle we must begin with Thomas Campbell, the first from among the Restoration leaders to fully develop the idea of restoration. In his *Declaration and Address* published in 1809, he gives a thorough or detailed treatment of the Restoration principle. He had come to see the church upon earth as "essentially, intentionally, and constitutionally one" (*Declaration and Address* in *Pioneer Sermons and Addresses* 39). In light of this understanding of the nature of the church, when he looked at the divided state of the religious denominations he stated in the strongest of terms

> . . . that division among the Christians is a horrid evil, fraught with many evils. It is antichristian, as it destroys the visible unity of the body of Christ; as if he were divided against himself, excluding and excommunicating a part of himself. It is antiscriptural, as being strictly prohibited by his sovereign authority; a direct violation of his express command. It is antinatural, as it excites Christians to contemn, to hate, and oppose one another, who are bound by the highest and most endearing obligations to love each other as brethren, even as Christ has loved them. In a word it is productive of confusion and of every evil work (*Pioneer Sermons* 42).

But how may this unity among Christians be brought about? Campbell's answer to this question is a straightforward answer: "Nothing ought to be received into the faith or worship of the Church, or be made a term of communion among Christians, that is not as old as the New Testament" (*Pioneer Sermons* 40). But he went beyond this and insisted that not only must all accept the New Testament as the divine constitution for the church, but they must also *voluntarily abandon* any practice *not expressly authorized* in the New Testament. If this were to be done, he said, then all such divisions would disappear. What did he mean by "not expressly authorized"? In Proposition 3 (there were thirteen *propositions* in all, summarizing the contents of the *Declaration and Address* — found on pp. 39-43 of *Pioneer Sermons*), Campbell says that "nothing ought to be inculcated upon Christians as articles of faith; nor required of them as terms of communion, but what is expressly taught and enjoined upon them in the word of God. Nor ought anything to be admitted, as of divine obligation . . . but what is expressly enjoined by the authority of our Lord Jesus Christ and his apostles upon the New Testament Church; either in *express terms* or by *approved precedent*" (*Pioneer Sermons* 39; emphasis added).

By "express terms" in the closing part of this statement, Campbell meant direct commands, and by "approved precedent" he meant a New Testament example. This same point is made repeatedly throughout the document. He keeps repeating over and over that any practice must be *expressly authorized* in the New Testament, and in particular by *precept* and *precedent*. Notice the following statement from him:

> Let *us* do as we are expressly told *they* did, say as *they* said; that is, profess and practice as therein expressly enjoined by precept and precedent, in every possible instance, after *their* approved example; and in so doing we shall realize and exhibit all that unity and uniformity that the primitive Church possessed, or that the law of Christ requires (*Pioneer Sermons* 72).

Such statements from Thomas Campbell in the *Declaration and Address* show conclusively that his plea for unity was a plea for unity through *restoration*. Believing that the New Testament was a divine pattern for what God expected the church to be in any age, he said "the New Testament is as perfect a constitution for the worship, discipline, and government of the New Testament Church, and as perfect a rule for the particular duties of its members, as the Old Testament was for the worship, discipline, and government of the Old Testament Church, and the particular duties of its members" (*Pioneer Sermons* 40).

2. Alexander Campbell. The challenge of attempting to implement the plan proposed by Thomas Campbell for bringing about unity among all Christians was to become the major work of his son, Alexander. In 1825 Alexander Campbell began to write a long series of articles (twenty-five in all) in *The Christian Baptist*, which he published for seven years (1823-1830), on "A Restoration of the Ancient Order of Things." He began by emphasizing the fact that he was talking about *restoration*, not reformation. In Campbell's mind the latter is what sometimes needs to be done to human systems, but it is not for men to reform Christianity. How can one reform, he asked, that which was perfect in its beginning? There must be a "restoration," and more specifically, "a restoration of the ancient order of things," which became the title of his series of articles on this very subject. "Every attempt to reform Christianity," he said, "is like an attempt to create a new sun, or to change the revolutions of the heavenly bodies — unprofitable and vain" (see "A Restoration of the Ancient Order of Things" No. 1, *The Christian Baptist* II [1825]:135-36).

How was such a restoration to be accomplished? In keeping with the proposal of his father, Campbell insisted that we

> must bring the Christianity and the church of the present day up to the standard of the New Testament. This is in substance, though in other terms, what we contend for. To bring the societies of Christians *up* to the New Testament, is just to bring the disciples, individually and collectively, to walk in the faith, and in the commandments of the Lord and Saviour, as presented in that blessed volume; and this is to *restore* the ancient order of things" (136).

But before this could be accomplished certain things needed to be discarded. Campbell introduced this point in the following words:

> . . . When we have found ourselves out of the way we may seek for the ancient paths, but we are not at liberty to invent paths for our own feet. We should return unto the Lord.

But a *restoration of the ancient order of things*, it appears, is all that is contemplated by the wise disciples of the Lord, as it is agreed that this is all that is wanting to the perfection, happiness, and glory of the christian community. To contribute to this is our most ardent desire — our daily and diligent inquiry and pursuit. Now, in attempting to accomplish this, it must be observed, that it belongs to every individual and to every congregation of individuals to discard from their faith and their practice everything that is not found written in the New Testament of the Lord and Saviour, and to believe and practice whatever is there enjoined. This done, and every thing is done which ought to be done (Article No. 2:152-53).

What were those things that must be discarded?

First, *would be "creeds or compilations of doctrine in abstract terms," or "in other terms other than the terms adopted by the Holy Spirit in the New Testament."* All such, he said, are to be discarded (Article 2:153). His evidence for this claim was given in some detail in the second and third articles.

Second, *"there must be, and there shall be an abandonment of the new and corrupt nomenclature, and a restoration of the inspired one"* (Article 4:222). The terms that men use to describe God, and all other supernatural truths, such as those which speak of his Son and the Holy Spirit, instead of the terms that God himself uses in Scripture, are given as an example. Men, Campbell argues,

> select such terms as suit their apprehensions of revealed truth, and hence the terms they use are expressive only of their conceptions of divine things and must be as imperfect as their conceptions are. It is impossible for any man, unless by accident, to express accurately that which he apprehends imperfectly. From this source spring most of our *doctrinal* controversies — Men's opinions, expressed in their own terms, are often called Bible truths. In order then to a full restoration of the ancient order of things there must be "a pure speech" restored (222-23).

A long list of "those Babylonish terms and phrases which must be discarded from the Christian vocabulary" is taken from "the approved standards of the most popular establishments" and published on page 223 of this fourth article.

Beginning with the fifth article Campbell began his inquiry as to "what was the ancient order of worship in the Christian church." By "order" he did not mean "whether one action shall be always performed first, another always second, and another always third," but "that there are certain social acts of Christian worship, all of which are to be attended to in the Christian assembly, and each of which is essential to the perfection of the whole as every member of the human body is essential to the perfect man" (240). In this connection he insisted upon two things regarding worship: (1) *"Either there is a divinely authorized order of Christian worship in Christian assemblies, or there is not."* (2) *"Either this Christian worship in Christian assemblies is uniformly the same, or it is not."*

Campbell first took the last part of each of these statements and showed how absurd it would be to affirm them. The absurdity would be that there are no limitations whatever on worship: no disorder, nor error, no innovation, and no transgression, regarding the acts of worship. The conclusion would be that "where there is no order established there can be no disorder, for disorder is acting contrary to established order; where there is no standard there can be no error, for error is a departure or a wandering from a standard; where there is nothing fixed there can be no innovation, for to innovate is to introduce new things amongst those already fixed and established; and where there is no law there can be no transgression, for a transgression is a leaping over or a violating of legal restraints" (240).

Campbell approached the subject of uniformity in worship in the same way. If there is no uniformity "then it is different. These differences are either limited or unlimited. If they are unlimited, then it is uniformly different; and what is uniformly different has no order, standard, or rule, and thus we are led to the same absurdities which followed from supposing there was no divinely authorized order of Christian worship, for a worship uniformly different is a worship without order. But supposing that those differences are limited, those limitations must be defined or pointed out some where. But they are not. Now differences that are nowhere limited or pointed out are unlimited, and consequently may be carried *ad infinitum*, which is to say there is no order appointed, and thus we are again encompassed with the same absurdities" (242).

After establishing that "there is a divinely authorized order of Christian worship in Christian assemblies, and that this worship is uniformly the same," Campbell went on in subsequent articles to discuss the proper acts in public worship — weekly observance of the Lord's supper, singing, prayer, and teaching.

Later in the series of articles Campbell took up the matter of church organization. He believed the New Testament did not authorize any organization but the local church. All other forms of church organization, whether it be the Presbyterian presbyteries, Episcopal systems, or the Baptist associations, were without biblical support. He contended for the independence of the local churches, with a plurality of elders serving as overseers of each local group.

Opinions: A Subject of Concern from the Beginning

The question of how to hold differing opinions and pursue peace at the same time, admittedly, is a difficult subject. How can brethren receive one another while holding differing opinions without at the same time compromising "the faith"? All who have worked with this thorny problem have come away with the realization that there is no easy solution, for no solution has been discovered that all are willing to accept, much less consistently apply and abide by.

If all could agree on a definition of "opinion" so that all would know when they were dealing with an opinion and not a matter of faith, there would still be the problem of deciding on how to treat opinions so that all could "pursue the things which make for peace and the things by which one may edify another," as Romans 14:19 requires.

The preachers in the early days of the Restoration Movement understood this problem and did their best to deal with it.

1. Thomas Campbell. At the very beginning of this movement Thomas Campbell grappled with the problem of opinions in the *Declaration and Address*, written in 1809. The end which he proposed was:

> To restore unity, peace and purity to the whole church of God. This desirable rest, however, we utterly despair either to find ourselves, or to be able to recommend to our brethren, by continuing amid the diversity and rancor of party contentions, the veering uncertainty and clashings of human opinions, nor, indeed, can we reasonably expect to find it anywhere, but in Christ, and his simple word, which is the same yesterday, today and forever. Our desires, therefore, for our brethren and ourselves, would be that rejecting human opinions and the inventions of men as of any authority; or as having any place in the church of God, we might forever cease from further contentions about such things, returning to and holding fast by the original standard, taking the Divine word alone for our rule; the Holy Spirit for our teacher and guide, to lead us into all truth . . . that, by so doing, we may be at peace among ourselves, follow peace with all men, and holiness, without which no man shall see the Lord (*Pioneer Sermons* 16).

By "opinions and the inventions of men" Campbell means any conclusions other than what is to be found in the "original standard" or "the Divine word alone." Such opinions are the result of man's reasoning and are not to be bound. Only what is stated *explicitly* in Scripture is to be required as a basis for unity.

The same may be said of his charge to the preachers of the denominations. Only the "primary and authentic revelation" (what is *explicitly* stated) can be required. Anything else is but "assumed authority." Here are his words to these preachers:

> To you, therefore, it peculiarly belongs, as the professed and acknowledged leaders of the people, to go before them in this good work, to remove human opinions and inventions of men out of the way, by carefully separating this chaff, from the pure wheat of primary and authentic revelation, casting out that assumed authority, that enacting and decreeing power by which these things have been imposed and established (*Pioneer Sermons* 34).

> That in all their administrations they keep close by the observance of the Divine ordinances, after the example of the primitive church, exhibited in the New Testament without any additions whatsoever of human opinions or inventions of men (*Pioneer Sermons and Addresses* 43).

Thomas Campbell, however, did acknowledge a legitimate place for what he termed "human expediency," yet this was a subject of great concern to him:

> That if any circumstantials, indispensably necessary to the observance of Divine ordinances, be not found upon the pages of express revelation, such and such only, as are absolutely necessary for this purpose, should be adopted under the title of human expediency, without any pretense to a more sacred origin, so that any subsequent alteration of difference in the observance of these things might produce no contention nor division in the church (*Pioneer Sermons and Addresses* 43).

But, one might ask of Campbell, are *true* deductions "human," or are they of God because they are true deductions drawn from what God teaches in his word? Elsewhere in the *Declaration and Address* Campbell conceded that "inferences and deductions from Scripture premises, when fairly inferred, may be truly called the doctrine of God's holy word." Yet he said they are not "formally binding upon the consciences of Christians farther than they perceive the connection, and evidently see that they are so; . . . Therefore, no such deductions can be made terms of communion . . ." (*Pioneer Sermons* 40). This raises the question, how can a thing be human and at the same time the doctrine of God's holy word?

2. Alexander Campbell. Alexander Campbell, the son of Thomas Campbell, also frequently wrote on the subject of opinions in the church. In fact, Alexander Campbell went so far as to say that we ought to confine ourselves to the very terms used in the Scripture to express the things to be believed and done, and in this way the opinions which separate Christians would be removed as barriers to unity among them:

> To disparage these terms, by adopting others in preference, is presumptuous and insolent on the part of man. . . . From this source spring most of our doctrinal controversies — Men's opinions expressed in their own terms, are often called Bible truths. In order then to a full restoration of the ancient order of things, a pure speech must be restored ("A Restoration of the Ancient Order of Things, NO IV," *The Christian Baptist* II [1825]:222, 223).

As a case in point, to make application to differing opinions on the Godhead, Campbell said the following:

> Now, suppose that all these would abandon every word and sentence not found in the Bible on the subject, and without explanation, limitation, or enlargement, quote with equal pleasure and readiness, and apply on every suitable occasion, every word and sentence found in the volume, to the Father, to the Son, and to the Holy Spirit; how long would divisions on this subject exist? *It would be impossible to perpetuate them on this plan. . . .* And as to any injury a private opinion may do the possessor, it could on this principle do none to society ("A Restoration of the Ancient Order of Things, NO. XVII. Purity of Speech," *The Christian Baptist* IV [1827]:154)

We will return to Campbell's writings on opinions shortly, after taking a brief look at a statement from John Smith.

3. "Racoon" John Smith. When attempts began to be made to bring the Barton W. Stone and Alexander Campbell movements together, at a meeting in Lexington, Kentucky in 1832,"Racoon" John Smith presented the teaching of the New Testament for unity. He emphasized unity through restoration, as we saw was true of both Thomas and Alexander Campbell, but like them, he also had much to say about opinions as a great barrier to the unity he proposed. In part, he said the following:

> God has but one people on the earth. He has given to them but one Book, and therein exhorts and commands them to be one family. A union such as we plead for — a union of God's people on that one Book — must, then, be practicable.

> Every Christian desires to stand complete in the whole will of God. The prayer of the Savior, and the whole tenor of his teaching, clearly show that it is God's will that his children should be united. To the Christian, then, such a union must be desirable.

But an amalgamation of sects is not such a union as Christ prayed for and God enjoins. To agree to be one upon any system of human inventions would be contrary to his will, and could never be a blessing to the church or the world; therefore, the only union practicable or desirable must be based on the word of God as the only rule of faith and practice.

I have the more cheerfully resolved on this course, because the gospel is a system of facts, commands, and promises, and no deduction or inference from them, however logical or true, forms any part of the gospel of Jesus Christ. No heaven is promised to those who hold them, and no hell is threatened to those who deny them. They do not constitute, singly or together, any item of the ancient and apostolic gospel. While there is but one faith, there may be ten thousand opinions; and, hence, if Christians are ever to be one, they must be one in faith, and not in opinion. When certain subjects arise, even in conversation or social discussion, about which there is a contrariety of opinion and sensitiveness of feeling, speak of them in the words of the Scripture, and no offense will be given and no pride of doctrine will be encouraged. We may even come, in the end, by thus speaking the same things, to think the same things.

For several years past I have stood pledged to meet the religious world, or any part of it, on the ancient gospel and order of things as presented in the words of the Book. This is the foundation on which Christians once stood, and on it they can, and ought to, stand again. From this I cannot depart to meet any man, or set of men, in the wide world. While, for the sake of peace and Christian union, I have long since waived the public maintenance of any speculation I may hold, yet *not one gospel fact, commandment, or promise will I surrender for the world!* (*The Life of Elder John Smith* 452-54).

That John Smith was of one mind with the reformers of his day is obvious. He had a desire for the restoration of the ancient order, and he also had the same basic understanding of the difference between faith and opinion as that expressed by Thomas Campbell in the *Declaration and Address*. His statements about "deductions," "inferences," and "opinions" show that he had come to the same conclusion as Thomas Campbell on these matters. He firmly believed in the gospel as a system of facts, commands and promises, as he expressed in the above statement, but he insisted that "no deduction or inference from them, however logical or true, forms any part of the gospel of Jesus Christ."

How did Smith think "opinions" in the form of "deductions" and "inferences" drawn from Scripture should affect those who hold them? Smith's answer was that "no heaven is promised to those who hold them, and no hell is threatened to those who deny them." According to him, "they do not constitute, singly or together, any item of the ancient and apostolic gospel."

Since there are so many opinions held by different Christians, how can they, Smith reasoned, ever hope to unite and be one people? His answer was a simple one: "While there is but one faith, there may be ten thousand opinions; and, hence, if Christians are ever to be one, they must be one in faith, and not in opinion." By "faith" he meant the *explicit* statements, commands, and examples found in Scripture. Like Alexander Campbell, he strongly believed that Christians must be careful in their speech. This is particularly important when it comes to how they handle their opinions. This is the only way they can hold differing opinions and at the same time be united in faith. "When certain subjects arise," he said, "even in conversation or social discussion, about which there is a contrariety of opinion and sensitiveness of feeling, speak of them in the words of the Scripture, and no offense will be given and no pride of doctrine will be encouraged. We may even come, in the end, by thus speaking the same things, to think the same things." This repeats in almost the exact words what had been written by Campbell on the pages of *The Christian Baptist* in previous years.

From such statements one must conclude that for Smith an "opinion" was the same as a "deduction." The problem that was yet to be considered in later years was whether or not it is true that no deduction from Scripture is ever to be considered a part of the faith of the gospel.

4. Alexander Campbell Again. Within five years of the address by John Smith at Lexington, Kentucky, Alexander Campbell began to write at length on the subject of *opinionism*. He was forced to treat the subject often, and in some length, because of the growing problem over opinions. In 1837 he wrote:

> There is a growing taste for *opinionism* in the ranks of the reformation. This must be squashed out or there is an end to all moral and religious improvement. It has ever been the harbinger of schism, the forerunner of all discord, and vain jangling. It has indeed been the plague of Christendom. . . . What is an opinion? Persuasion without proof, say some of our lexicographers. It is a stipulation built on probable evidence. It is neither knowledge nor faith; but in the absence of these, it is an inference, a conclusion to which the mind assents according to its information or mode of reasoning.

> An *opinionist* is one fond of opinions, especially of his own. Opinionism then is fondness of opinions. But that I may meet the exigency of the

crisis and give a proper latitude to this term, I hereby define *opinionism* to be *the liberty of propagating one's own opinions.*

Some of our correspondents suppose *opinionism*, as thus defined, to be an essential part of Christian liberty, then if any restrictions should be imposed on their benevolent efforts to propagate their opinions, they complain of an infringement of their rights.

We do not admit the right; for if this be the right of the Christian, then every man, woman and child in Christ's church has a right to propagate his or her opinions, and to complain if that right be not respected by all the Christian community. And as there is no restriction as to the number or magnitude of subjects on which opinions may be formed, there can be no limitation of the number of opinions that may be offered, adopted or propagated; and thus the whole earthly pilgrimage of the church may be occupied in the discussion of opinions.

We are therefore rationally and religiously compelled to deny any such right. *It is not the right of any one citizen of Christ's kingdom to propagate any opinion whatever, either in public assembly or private,* consequently it is not the duty of all nor of any one, to listen to an opinionist in his effort to establish his opinions. This is an important point, and we state it boldly and confidently. . . . To walk by opinions rather than faith, is effectively to make the book of God of no authority. Moreover, in the decisions of that volume, he that propagates an opinion or seeks to attach persons to it, or to himself on account of it, is a factionist in embryo, in infancy or manhood ("Opinionism — No. I," *The Millennial Harbinger*, New Series [Oct. 1837]:439-40) .

On the next page Campbell went on to show that unless we hold our opinions in this way, we will fare no better than the denominations around us:

Unless this matter is better understood it will fare with us as with Presbyterians, Methodists, Baptists and other religious communities. We shall be broken to pieces as well as they. It is owing to the patience of contradiction and the great good sense of some of our more intelligent brethren, that schisms have not already appeared amongst us under the assumption that every Christian has a right to propagate his opinions. While it is conceded that on some matters we all have liberty to form opinions, and, if asked for them, to express them, we must regard this as very different from the right to propagate our speculations, instead of practicing the precepts of the gospel (441).

Toward the end of his first article on opinionism, Campbell again pointed out what he considered to be the urgency of giving attention to this matter:

We must, I repeat it, set our faces against this course, or we will all repent it. The weakest are generally the most dogmatical, and those who know the least the most positive and overbearing, and therefore there is no convincing them. Nothing is to be hoped for from the strife of opinions; for the chorus will ever be, "My opinion is as good as thine," and "Am not I as infallible as thou?"

But we sin against the teaching of the apostles if we do not abandon this course. Paul enjoins that we "give no heed to fables" — "to endless genealogies" — that he that consents not to the doctrine which is according to godliness, is proud, self-opinionated, doting or sick about questions, and debates of words, from which comes envy, strife, railing, evil surmisings, &c. — "Avoid profane and vain babblings, oppositions of science falsely so called; which some professing have erred, not in opinion, but from the faith." He reiterates these precepts in his two epistles to Timothy: "Shun profane and vain babblings, for they will increase to more ungodliness, and their word will eat like a canker. Of this class are Hymeneus and Philetus," (men of science!). "Who concerning" opinions! nay, nay, "the *truth* have erred, saying that the resurrection is past *already*, and have *overthrown the faith of some*." This gives a key to the whole chapter of vain babblings, &c. Hence, said the Apostle, "Foolish and *untaught* questions avoid, knowing that they do gender strifes." These untaught questions are precisely questions about opinions; and that they do gender strife we do have proof (444).

Campbell had written on his distrust of deductions ten years earlier when he was still publishing *The Christian Baptist*. At that time this was his main objection to human creeds. He said the following:

Human creeds are composed of the inferences of the human understanding speculating upon the revelation of God. Such are all those now extant. The inferences drawn by the human understanding partake of all the defects of that understanding ("A Search for the ancient Order of Things, NO. II" *The Christian Baptist* [1827]:154).

Since Campbell defines "opinion" as an inference, or a conclusion, he equates opinion with implication. But the inquiring student will no doubt ask, are all implications mere opinions? Campbell does not tell us whether or not a difference should be made between what one *calls* a "true deduction" and what is *in fact* a "true deduction." When we have a true deduction from Scripture, is such a deduction (implication) binding, or is it a mere opinion that cannot be bound? This subject will be discussed in later chapters.

Chapter 20

The Problem of Differing Opinions (2): An Historical Perspective (1850-1939)

Last Half of the Nineteenth Century

1. Elijah Goodwin. A book of sermons by Elijah Goodwin titled *The Family Companion* was first published in 1856. A revised and enlarged edition appeared in 1873. The last sermon in the book was on "Christian Union" and was a study of the seven ones of Ephesians 4:1-6. Goodwin's aim was not so much to point out the areas of disagreement among those who profess to be Christians but to point out the areas of agreement among them. In his discussion of the divided state of the church in his day he ends this part of the study by affirming, "God made but one church, and Jesus prayed that it might remain one undivided and harmonious body. He has delegated to no man the right to divide his people, or to make a new church to suite himself. If any do it, they oppose the prayer of Jesus and violate the will of God" (414).

It is when he comes to discuss the "one faith" that Goodwin enters into a study of *faith and opinion*. He begins by affirming "that all the denominations that can, with any propriety, claim to be *Christian* churches, are one in faith" (417). He concedes that this may be regarded as untrue by many, but he proceeds to clarify the point by showing the difference between knowledge, faith and opinions.

> Knowledge is what we know by experience; faith is what we receive upon testimony; and opinions are deductions drawn from matters of fact that we have no testimony to establish. They may be true or they may be false. Let me illustrate: Suppose I see A kill B with a sword. I relate to the simple fact that A killed B; you believe it, and conclude he killed him

with a revolver; another supposed that the murder was committed with a dirk; a third, that it was performed with an ax.

Now, that A killed B is a matter of knowledge with me, but with you it is a matter of faith, and that the murder was committed with the instruments named in the illustrations are mere opinions, the deductions drawn by different minds from the same fact. But they are all false, for the deed was performed with a sword. Would it not be foolish for these men to fall out and quarrel about these opinions when they all believe the fact in the case?

From this illustration it is clear that all Christians cannot be one in knowledge. Some men know more than others; they have seen more; they have a more extensive experience than other men. Hence, unity in knowledge is not attainable; it is not required; for this the Savior never prayed.

Nor is it possible for all Christians to be one in opinion. Men reason differently; they view subjects from different stand-points, hence they draw different deductions, and arrive at different conclusions. These we call opinions, and in them unity is impossible while we remain in the flesh; this is not the oneness indicated in the Lord's prayer.

Still, I repeat, that notwithstanding this diversity in knowledge and opinion, all Christians are one in faith. What the Scriptures say they all believe. You cannot name a proposition in all the teaching of Christ and his holy apostles that is not believed by all who claim to be believers in Jesus Christ. They receive all as true as expressed in the words of inspiration. This is faith — evangelical faith, because it is produced by evangelical testimony. Hence the controversy is not about faith; it is about the opinions of men, good men they may be, but they have drawn different deductions from the words of inspiration, and over these they have wrangled until they have engendered the spirit of hatred and strife, rent the seamless garment of righteousness wrought out by the Lord and Savior, and clothed themselves in mere patchwork robes, composed of the opinions of men. Instead of calling the articles, of which these human creeds are composed, articles of faith, they should be denominated articles of opinion, for most of them are no more than the deductions of men. Whether they be true or false no man knows; nor does it matter whether it ever be known, for the salvation of no sinner depends on them (417-19).

After the above statement on knowledge, faith and opinion, Goodwin stated that there is agreement among religious people on five of the seven "ones" of Ephesians 4:1-6 which are essential to establish and maintain the unity for which Jesus prayed in John 17. The two "ones" over which there is much disagreement, Goodwin said, are the one baptism and one body. He pointed out, however, that there is one area in particular in which all can agree on baptism, namely, "that a believing penitent who trusts alone in Christ for salvation, is a proper subject for baptism" (420). He concluded from this fact, "then let all practice *believer's baptism* and union on this point is restored, while no conscience is violated." On infant baptism he said that those who practice it "are bound to admit that there is no command or clear precedent for the practice in the New Testament. The whole practice rests upon mere deduction, or human opinion. Then, for the sake of bleeding Zion and a bleeding Savior, let that opinion give place to the plain, unequivocal command of Christ Jesus our common Lord" (420).

Goodwin reasoned along the same lines on the action of baptism. All agree that immersion in water is scriptural. There is no dispute over this practice. We can unite upon it, but we cannot unite in the practice of affusion for all do not agree on this practice. He pointedly asks,

> Now, can not this union be affected? Come, my brother, you who practice affusion for baptism, and yet believe immersion to be valid, look at the awful effects of division among the people of God. Behold the torn, bleeding, and mangled mystical body of Christ, while thousands are stumbling over these contending parties down to everlasting ruin. Turn your eyes to Jesus, and hear him pray, *"That all may be one, that the world may believe."* O let that prayer sink down into your hearts, and move you to immediate action in behalf of union. I think I can say confidently, for all who practice immersion only, that if they as sincerely believed sprinkling to be valid baptism, as affusionists do that immersion is valid, they would, for the sake of uniting all believers according to the prayer of Christ, never immerse another person; they would universally practice affusion (421).

On the subject of the *one body*, Goodwin goes on to say, all must admit that "instead of all believers being *one* in body, they are legion." What has been the cause? He answers, "There has been a fearful departure from the apostolic order since Paul wrote to the church at Ephesus." What can be done to restore the unity of the one body according to Jesus' prayer?

> I answer, let the Bible, and the Bible alone, be adopted as the Christian's creed. What the Bible says all believe. Let opinions be held as private property, while *faith* is made the test of union. Do you say it is impossible to organize a church on the Bible alone? Perhaps not such a church as you are thinking about. I affirm that it is impossible to organize a church on any human creed *alone*. You must get the consent of the people to organize upon the creed, and then the work may be accomplished. Now, let the same agreement be entered into in reference to the Bible, and there will be no difficulty in the way of union on the Bible alone. Do any ask: Would you have men with these different opinions in the same church?

Why not? You say they all belong to the invisible Church of Christ; that they make up the one body. If this is true, why not make the union visible? As already stated, men of very different sentiments may now be found in any and every church. Many church members do not know what is in their own creed. Show them certain articles, and they will say, "I don't believe that, if it is in the creed."

If an attempt were now made in any church, formed on a human "confession of faith," to bind every member to a strict conformity to the creed, in faith and practice, it would throw the whole Church into convulsions, and result in numberless exclusions. Let the same compromise be made in reference to the Bible that is made in reference to any of the popular creeds, and all true believers in Jesus Christ can unite in the one body in an hour. Nothing essential need be given up. While all admit that a person can be a Christian without believing the items that divide them, they virtually admit that those points of difference are not essential; that they form no part of true evangelical Christianity. Why, then, hold these unessential articles as bars to fellowship? Why set at naught the prayer of the Divine Redeemer and the commands of God, and destroy the unity of the body of Christ for the sake of mere unessential opinions that have no salvation in them for any man?

. . . If men of different creeds can hold their peculiar sentiments in abeyance during a protracted union meeting, for the sake of converting sinners, why can they not continue the same course during life? If union is good for a week it is good for all time. If it gives potency to the Gospel during a meeting of a few days, what would it do if the union were perpetual? (422-24).

None should mistake this answer to mean that the unity Jesus prayed for can be brought about by allowing any and all to *teach and practice* their differing *opinions*. What is advocated here is the same as that proposed by both Thomas and Alexander Campbell, and by John Smith, and other early restoration leaders. Let all alike lay aside all their human opinions and unite upon those things clearly revealed and agreed upon by all to be a part of the faith once for all delivered to the saints. To use Goodwin's own words, "What the Bible says all believe. Let opinions be held as private property, while *faith* is made the test of union."

Again, as was true of those who went before him, Goodwin makes an opinion the same as a deduction, or a conclusion drawn from Scripture, as though all deductions from Scripture are mere human opinions. He places infant baptism in this category. But the inquiring mind might ask, is the practice of infant baptism a matter of implication or inference, or does it belong to the area of the *silence* of Scripture? If the Bible says *nothing* about it, it belongs to the silence category, not to the area of implication. This will be explained in the next chapter.

2. David Lipscomb. About 1890 or so David Lipscomp, editor of the *Gospel Advocate* for almost half a century (1866 forward), began to write extensively on the subject of unity among Christians. He was the great antagonist of the missionary society and instrumental music after these two innovations had been introduced into the work and worship of the church. In his series of articles Lipscomb was responding to another writer whom he believed was misrepresenting Campbell on the subject of opinions. In order to set the record straight, Lipscomb quoted extensively and approvingly from the writings of Alexander Campbell on the subject of unity. His articles on this subject were published in booklet form in 1916 by the McQuiddy Printing Company. The book was titled, "CHRISTIAN UNITY, How Promoted, How Destroyed. FAITH AND OPINION." Our quotations from Lipscomb are from this book.

In his articles David Lipscomb was answering the view that said that "men are to be permitted to act on their opinion, to introduce whatever their fancies or preferences desire, and to make their opinions the rule and authority for practices in the church of God — and all who differ in opinion must submit and be silent" (10). To Lipscomb this would bring havoc and ruin to the church:

> If one man's opinion, he wrote, is ground for action in church affairs, another man's is likewise, and every man's is. As we differ in opinion, then we must adopt diverse and different rules of action. And different rules of action in a church will bring conflict in action. It will necessarily produce strife and confusion and lead to division. It cannot possibly be avoided (11).

Again, Lipscomb said that

> . . . this doctrine that liberty of opinion involves the right to act on those opinions where our actions come in contact with, or affect the actions and opinions of others, is the very thing that will continually gender causes and occasions of discord and division (14).

How then must opinions be held? First he said it is well to have clear but simple definitions of the two terms involved. So on faith and opinion, Lipscomb said:

> *Faith* is a firm conviction resting upon clear and satisfactory testimony. *Opinion* is an impression resting on human judgment, without clear and

satisfactory testimony. In religion, *faith* is a conviction based upon a clear revelation of the divine will. And we must "walk by faith." That is, we are led by faith in God to do what the word of God clearly requires us to do. Whatever is clearly revealed in the word of God, is matter of faith. What is not clearly required therein is matter of opinion (9).

Lipscomb then agreed with Campbell that "opinions must be held as private property." The following illustrations from him may prove beneficial:

(1) *Aylette Rains' view that all will finally be made happy.* In other words, the belief in universal salvation. Of his view, Lipscomb said: "This was an opinion of his, without evidence, to be held as private property, not to be taught, but the things clearly taught in the Bible, seen and read of all men, were the matters of faith. These were to be taught. Rains was received into the fellowship of the church; he held his opinions as private property — did not teach them, taught what is clearly taught in the Bible, and in doing this he said his mind grew away from these opinions and he lost sight of them" (12).

(2) *Affusion for baptism.* "If a man held the opinion that men might so change under some circumstances, the ordinance of baptism, as that affusion would be acceptable to God, for baptism, let him hold the opinion as private property, let him neither practice nor teach the opinion, but practice and teach just what the Bible teaches, and in this teaching and practice of the Bible he is to be fellowshiped" (12).

(3) *Calvinism and Arminianism.* "A man might have the opinion that Calvinism is true, or Arminianism. He could hold either, or both, if it were possible, as private property, but he could not teach or enforce either on the church, or on any of its members or bring either into his teaching or into the church — to affect the faith, the actions, or the peace and harmony of the church of God" (12).

Finally, Lipscomb said of two men who hold differing opinions:

Both cannot have liberty of opinion, in the sense that they make their opinions the basis of action for themselves or for the church. One will have his opinions tyrannized over by the other. It will be none the less tyranny of opinion that a majority, great or small, imposes its opinion on the minority. One man has as much right to liberty of opinion as any other or number of others. And this doctrine that liberty of opinion involves the right to act on those opinions where our actions come in contact with, or affect the actions and opinions of others, is the very thing that will continually gender causes and occasions of discord and division (14).

So for Lipscomb a thing is of faith when it is taught plainly in the Bible: "The things taught plainly in the Bible are matters of faith" (15). Whatever does not have authority or precedent in the word of God is based on opinion. Lipscomb strongly believed that "he who introduces or maintains any practice, any service, any organization or method of work or worship, based on opinion or human judgment, introduces that which leads to division and strife, and separates man from God. 'Faith unites men to God and one another. Opinion severs them from God and one another, and is the occasion of endless strife and bitterness'" (64).

End of the Nineteenth and First Half
of the Twentieth Centuries

At the turn of the century the missionary society and instrumental music controversies were still the central issues among brethren. New faces were coming onto the scene who would continue the fight against these kinds of innovations into the work and worship of the church. Those who advocated the use of the instrument in worship were having great success, and this naturally called for the best from among those brethren who were opposed to the introduction of the instrument into the worship of the church to make strong responses. These responses always gave some consideration to the question of opinions.

1. M.C. Kurfees. One man who was quite capable of meeting the challenge was M.C. Kurfees of Louisville, Kentucky. On November 18, 1894 Kurfees preached two sermons under the title, "Walking By Faith," at the Campbell Street Church in Louisville on the subject of instrumental music in worship. The sermons were made available in tract form the next month by the Haldeman Avenue Church where Kurfees preached. The tract was kept in print as long as the church continued to exist.

These sermons on instrumental music were called for, Kurfees said, because "of the progress which instrumental music has made in the worship within recent years in our city" (Preface). The morning sermon dealt with the question of whether or not the use of the instrument in worship is authorized by Scripture. The evening sermon was on the origin of instrumental music in worship. In his evening sermon Kurfees contended that the evidence from the church historians shows that such practice was not introduced into church worship until hundreds of years after Christ. After this evidence had been presented, he then considered objections that are often made against those who oppose instrumental music in worship.

In the morning sermon he began by introducing the terms "faith" and "opinion," and pointed out how they differ from each other. The title of his sermon would require that he do this in the very outset. How does *faith* differ from *opinion*, he asked. On page six of the tract he used Romans 10:17 to show that faith comes by hearing God's word. After quoting the verse, "faith comes by hearing, and hearing by the word of God," he says: "This settles it as to how faith comes; it comes by hearing the Word of God. Accordingly, where there is no Word of God there can be no faith; and if no faith, then no walking by faith. This is not the opinion of any man or set of men; it is the unquestionable teaching of God's Word."

According to Kurfees, "where the Word of God is, there can be faith, but none beyond that. If, therefore, the Word of God says nothing concerning a given course, there can be no faith in pursuing that course . . . ." With these words he makes an argument from the *authoritative nature of SILENCE* in the latter part of this statement, when he says, "if, therefore, the Word of God *says nothing* concerning a given course, there can be no faith in pursuing that course . . ." (emphasis added).

If this is what it is to walk by faith, what is it to walk by *opinion*? Kurfees' answer is that "the word opinion signifies *what one thinks*, and in religious matters, it means what men think concerning matters on which the Bible is silent" (7). "Opinion," he says, "is what men think where the word of God does not speak," whereas faith comes by hearing the Word of God.

2. E.G. Sewell. A book titled *Gospel Lessons and Life History* by E.G. Sewell was published by the McQuiddy Printing Company in 1908. Sewell had served as co-editor of the *Gospel Advocate* with David Lipscomb for some forty years. Sewell's work with Lipscomb as co-editor of the *Advocate* was one of the reasons that led M.C. Kurfees to edit a second volume of *Questions and Answers* by Lipscomb. This time, however, answers from Sewell were also included. The first volume edited by J.W. Shepherd had included only answers to questions by David Lipscomb. In the second volume Kurfees was very complimentary of the first work, but he also expressed a wish that the book he was editing which contained additional material from Lipscomb and new material from Sewell would both "be used as companion volumes, and that they may find a welcome place in many libraries" (Preface 4).

It was, however, in the book, *Gospel Lessons and Life History*, that E.G. Sewell left with us his thinking on "Unauthorized and Ruinous Opinions," the title of one of the lessons in his book. He begins by expressing his astonishment "that there should be so many unfounded opinions rising up among those claiming to be the followers of Christ," especially, he says, when we consider "the plainness of the New Testament on all matters of faith and practice" (245). And what is an opinion? "An opinion is a notion, idea, impression, view, or judgment formed, for which there is no direct testimony or information found in the oracles of God upon which to base it." One must be careful to recognize the "vast difference between faith and opinion." "Faith," according to Sewell, "is the belief of what is stated in the word of God. Whatever the word of God plainly says should always be regarded as a matter of faith; for faith, belief, comes by hearing the word of God."

Sewell was persuaded that most of the divisions in the religious world would be avoided if men clearly recognized the difference between faith and opinion. To use his words, "if all would study the difference between faith and opinion, and would be careful to always use these words according to their legitimate meaning, and never confound their meaning by using one when the other should be used, very much of the trouble and division that now exists in the religious world might be avoided."

What lay at the root of all opinions? Ignorance. "Opinions," Sewell maintained, "are always more or less matters of ignorance. Those who form and express them do not and cannot know them to be true; for if these opinions were anywhere stated in the word of God, then they would not be matters of opinion, but of faith, for we are required to believe what the word of God says" (245-46).

How should one handle his opinions? He should handle them very carefully. Because no one can know for sure that they are true, "opinions should never be talked, taught, or argued as matters of faith. Men who hold and argue opinions are adding to the word of God. They lead people to accept and regard them as the word of God, when they are only the words of uninspired men" (246). Opinions are the "secret things" that "belong unto Jehovah our God" (Deut. 29:29). About such things not revealed in the word of God we should have no concern, and we should have nothing to do with them. Why is that? Sewell's answer was a simple one: "If we knew every truth not revealed in the word of God, these would not save us. It takes the things revealed to save. So it is a loss to men to be spending time over things not revealed, not expressed in the oracles of God."

3. H. Leo Boles. On May 2, 1939, H. Leo Boles delivered an address at the "unity meeting" being held in Indianapolis, Indiana. He titled his address, "The WAY of Unity Between 'Christian Church' and Churches of Christ." The address was published at the time in both the *Gospel Advocate* and *Christian Standard* and was also put in booklet form by the Gospel Advocate Company. In a postscript to the booklet, B.C. Goodpasture said the speech, after its publication, "created a widespread interest and called forth much favorable comment." He also quoted A.T. DeGroot, in the *Christian-Evangelist*, saying, "The strongest language employed at the conference, other than in the expected warmth of some exchanges in the open forums, came in the address of H. Leo Boles, of Nashville, Tenn."

After pointing out the common ground held by the Churches of Christ and the Christian Church, and showing that the two groups were united from 1832 to 1849 Boles got immediately to the three major "departures" that separated them, namely, the missionary society of 1849, instrumental music first introduced in 1869, and the fact that the Christian Church "has now become a denomination." On instrumental music, he pled, "Brethren, put away the organ and you will be where the pioneers first stood when the unity of God's people was enjoyed. The churches of Christ are standing now on this item where the pioneers stood before the introduction of 1859; there was unity then on this point and there can be unity now at this point when the organ is pushed aside" (*The Way of Unity* 9). He reminded brethren that he knew the attitude and convictions of the preachers and members of the churches of Christ, and though they all love unity, they are loyal to Christ and the truth of God, and there will, he insisted, be no compromise or surrender on this point.

It is when he came to discuss the "causes of separation" that Boles brought up the matter of "opinions."

> It is well to review the causes of separation, to look at the steps more closely that have been taken in the departures; then you can see more clearly the scriptural ground of union. It is noted here first that "opinion" was made equal to the word of God. There should be a clear distinction between *faith* and *opinion*. Faith is a firm conviction resting upon clear and satisfactory testimony. "Now faith is assurance of things hoped for, a conviction of things not seen." (Heb. 11:1.) We are told specifically how faith comes: . "So belief cometh of hearing, and hearing by the word of Christ." (Rom. 10:17.) This settles it as to how faith comes; it comes by hearing the word of God. Where God has not spoken, there can be no faith, for "faith cometh by hearing the word of God," and Christians, when they are loyal to God, "walk by faith, not by sight." (2 Cor. 5: 7.) Opinion is an expression based on human judgment, without clear and satisfactory testimony; the word "opinion" signifies "what one thinks," and in matters of religion it means what men think concerning matters on which the Bible is silent. The distinction between "faith" and "opinion" should be kept clear, for "whatsoever is not of faith is sin." (Rom. 14: 23.) "Whatsoever is not of faith is sin" means when we do anything as service to God not clearly required in his word, we sin. To bring things

into the service of God which are based only on opinion is to substitute opinion for faith. This substitution separates man from God and causes division among men. To substitute opinion for faith is to rebel against God; it is to put the judgments of men as our guide, and thus reject the counsel of God. Christians cannot work together in harmony with two different rules of action (11-12).

While many would challenge Boles' use of Romans 14:23 in his attempt to distinguish between faith and opinion, none can fail to understand what he meant by "opinion" when he says, "opinion is an expression based on human judgment, without clear and satisfactory testimony," or that it is "'what one thinks,' and in matters of religion it means what men think concerning matters on which the Bible is silent." In contrast to this, "faith" is based upon what God has said, not upon what he has not said. Faith, in other words, is "a firm conviction resting upon clear and satisfactory testimony." Boles insisted that faith comes from hearing the word of God, according to Romans 10:17, and he concluded by saying that "to bring things into the service of God which are based only on opinion is to substitute opinion for faith," and such "substitution separates man from God and causes division among men." When men substitute opinion for faith, to use Boles' words, that "is to rebel against God; it is to put the judgments of men as our guide, and thus reject the counsel of God. Christians cannot work together in harmony with two different rules of action."

Much was being said about the "liberty of opinion" and the "silence of Scripture." It was being argued that both of these areas give one the "right to act," or they were another way in which God authorizes a thing or an action. In response to this argument Boles, in practically the same words used by David Lipscomb, said:

If the liberty of opinion lets one put an organ in the worship, it will let another oppose that act; if acting in the "realm of silence" permits one to act for himself, it will permit every one to act for himself. If liberty in opinion will let one organize a missionary society, the same liberty of opinion will let another group of God's people oppose that society. Neither the "Christian Church" nor the churches of Christ can have the liberty of opinion, in the sense that they make their opinions the basis of action for themselves and for the church. One will have his opinions tyrannized over by the other. It will be nonetheless tyranny of opinion that a majority, great or small, imposes its opinion on the minority. One man has as much right to "liberty of opinion" as another, or any number of others. This doctrine of liberty of opinion in "the areas of silence" involves the right to act on those opinions, and our actions come in contact with the actions and opinions of others; this is the very thing that will continually gender discord and division. The slogan, "In essentials, unity; in opinions, liberty," when the opinions become the guide in work and worship of the Lord, violates the basic principles of New Testament teaching and subverts the will of God (14).

The issue of "silence" has been with us from the beginning of the Restoration Movement. This will be the subject of our next chapter.

Chapter 21

The Silence of Scripture and Implication

The first major problem that arose between those who were attempting to "restore the ancient order of things" that Alexander Campbell had proposed in his long series of articles under this title was the problem of how to determine when God has authorized a thing and when he has not. The slogan, "Let us speak where the Bible speaks and be silent where the Bible is silent," is a saying that was to be put to the test very early in the Restoration Movement. How this slogan would be interpreted came up in a difference that arose between Barton W. Stone and Alexander Campbell in the controversy over communing with the unimmersed.

Stone believed this practice was acceptable, Campbell did not. Stone's argument was that Scripture did not forbid it, therefore the practice was acceptable. Campbell responded by saying that this was not enough. He maintained that "whatever is not commanded by the Lord is human." For him there must first be authority to do something before the Lord will accept it. It was in this manner that he built his objection to communion with the unimmersed. This was an argument based on the silence of Scripture, but an argument that was the very opposite of that made by Stone on the same principle, that of silence. For Campbell there was no authority in Scripture for the practice of communing with the unimmersed, but for Stone the silence of the Scripture permitted communion with the unimmersed. Campbell believed that silence condemned the practice and Stone believed the same silence permitted it.

In addition to the silence of Scripture, there was also the question of expediency. Alexander Campbell eventually conceded that such "expedients" as church buildings were necessary. Thomas Campbell, in the *Declaration and Address*, had recognized that there might be certain "circumstantial" matters that would be "indispensably necessary to the observance of divine ordinances," but such things, he felt, should be viewed as mere "human expediency, without any pretense to a more sacred origin" (*Pioneer Sermons* 43). This statement indicates that his concern was that such matters of expediency might be introduced as having come from God by explicit authority. If this should happen, and later there should be a change in the use of them, he feared that contention and division would arise over them.

This concern of the Campbells is a reminder that the argument from "silence" and the question of "expedients" have been with us for a long time, and in one form or another the argument from silence and the question of expediency have been the basis for all the major innovations into the work and worship of the church. There has also been confusion over how silence and implication relate to one another. This confusion continues to the present day.

As early as David Lipscomb, the quotes provided in the preceding chapter have illustrated the various attempts that were made in the past to answer the arguments from silence and expediency. Those who were responding judged the subjects under discussion to be *unlawful* matters. The defense of the missionary society and the instrument of music in worship in the middle of the nineteenth century basically was an argument resting upon the silence of Scripture (whether properly or improperly defined, which we will consider below). In addition to the problem of silence, and the issue of expediency, there have also been other troublesome areas of controversy, such as how to *use* implication, if at all. These brethren do not appear to have considered whether or not expediency and implication belong to the area of silence. The reason for this may be because they never made a determined effort to define exactly how they were using the term "silence." Can we ever hope to find agreement in these areas?

So this is a subject we must consider. The first question that confronts us is, what is the meaning of the "silence" of Scripture?

The Meaning of Silence

Throughout the history of the Christian Church and the churches of Christ there have been some, like the case of Barton W. Stone from an earlier period (briefly discussed in the preceding paragraphs), who have argued that the silence of Scripture on a matter *permits*, or gives one the liberty to act. What this has meant for those who have used this argument is, if the Bible *does not forbid* a particular action, *then that action is permitted* by God. But does the silence of God on a matter give one the liberty to act? That is the issue, and the answer to the question must be determined from the Bible. What is the meaning of silence, according to Scripture? Does Bible silence permit, or does silence forbid?

1. Is Scripture Like a Constitution? We want to begin with this question because the question just raised about the meaning of silence is essentially an issue that concerns the nature of Scripture. It is not uncommon today to see those who disregard the silence of Scripture on a subject insisting that Scripture is not a constitution, but letters addressed to people with real needs, etc. From this they contend that when something is not *explicitly* mentioned in the Scriptures it means God is not concerned with that matter. "Why should one make something out of a matter about which God himself is not concerned?" we are asked. But the question begs the issue. It assumes the New Testament is a mere love letter, and it is not at all *like* a constitution. Is this true?

When making this objection, by "constitution" one usually means that the things God will accept are not all to be found in a formal 1, 2, 3 type of list. One could, however, agree that this is the case, and yet deny the conclusion that the Bible is not a constitution. One does not have to have this kind of document in order for the Bible to be a constitution. The mistake in this argument is, first, it simply is not the case that the Bible is not a constitution (and, of course, those who make this argument mean in the sense that they describe a constitution), and, second, for the Bible to be a constitution does not mean that its silence permits anything not specifically condemned. By things not specifically condemned, things like churches owning meeting houses, or having radio and television programs, or microphones, or baptistries, etc. are sometimes cited. In the words of Randy Fenter this view is stated as follows: "If the form of the New Testament is constitutional, then silence is intentional and necessarily prohibitive of anything not explicitly found in Scripture" ("Do Not Go Beyond What Is Written [2]," *Image Magazine* [September 1989]:8). To illustrate his point, Fenter cites the kinds of things listed above. The question that is raised by this argument is: If Scripture is not a constitution, does silence prohibit any thing "not explicitly found in Scripture"? This is the central issue raised by Fenter.

No one, at least to my knowledge, believes that anything "not explicitly found in Scripture" is prohibited, as Fenter claims would be the case if Scripture is a constitution. The key word in Fenter's statement is the word "explicitly." To say that if the word of God is a constitution then a thing that is not *explicitly* found in Scripture is prohibited is to overlook the fact that a thing may be authorized "implicitly" even in a constitution.

Based upon such statements, it appears that these brethren have completely renounced the place of *implication* in establishing authority for a thing or practice. The kind of things Fenter names (with the exception of colleges, which he threw into the mix; we left this out because in our judgment it does not belong in the same class as the other things in his list) are authorized by the commands to which they belong. See Question #4 in the Appendix for examples of implicit authority for the kinds of things Fenter mentions in his argument.

2. A Constitution and Implicit Authority. First, lets consider the matter of whether Scripture is a constitution. I believe the case can be made that it is proper to view the Scriptures in this way. George F. Beals makes the point that 2 Timothy 3:16-17 is enough to bring one to this conclusion:

> This passage teaches that the Scriptures contain all good works. In other words, the Bible **is** legislative, a blueprint, a constitution. So from the Scriptures one can tell what is a good work and what is not. One wonders what we are supposed to do with such instruction, if not to abide by it. So we would ask, How are the Scriptures not a set of legislations? True, the Scriptures are not **formed** throughout like Robert's *Rules of Order* or just like the United States *Constitution*. But this is merely a difference in form, not substance. One cannot correctly deduce from the form that therefore the Bible is not constitutional (a set of legislations for our lives guiding us to heaven out of love, a blueprint). From biblical **narrative** in Gospels and Acts, from **letters** like Romans, Colossians, 2 Tim and Titus one can tell what God considers acceptable behavior (good) and unacceptable behavior (sin). I invite the reader to check these and other Bible books to find examples of how this can be determined, despite Fenter's claim the Bible is not a constitution. For starters after 2 Tim 3:16-17, you may want to consider 2 Tim 1:13, 2:15, Titus 1:9, Acts 17:11, Rom 15:9, the "must" in Jn 4:24, ... *(How Implication Binds and Silence Forbids: Studies in Biblical Hermeneutics* 71, footnote 94).

Secondly, it should also be recognized that *some things are authorized by implication.* There is no contradiction between viewing the Bible as a constitution (pattern, blueprint) and also seeing it as approving some things by implicit authority. The problem some have in these areas is due to the way they define the term "silence." Some define this term in such a way as to leave no room for *implicit* authority. Fenter is a case in point. If the Scriptures are a constitution, does it follow that silence would exclude things clearly implied in Scripture? Fenter thinks so based on his definition of silence. For him "if the form of the New Testament is constitutional, then silence is intentional and necessarily prohibitive of any thing not explicitly found in Scripture." Is he right in saying that if the Bible is constitutional then all that belongs to the *non-explicit* area is prohibited? This can hardly be the case. This would leave no room at all for *implied* authority, and, as will be pointed out below, we make a mistake *when we think of Bible silence as including the implicit area.*

No doubt Fenter has a greater problem than he realizes, but basically (and we must repeat for the sake of emphasis), his problem lies in his failure to properly define silence. What does silence mean? What does silence include? Does it include things about which the Bible says *nothing* as well as those things that would be *implied?* What we really need to know is, when properly defined, is silence prohibitive? Just when do we have Bible silence?

How Silence and Implication Differ
The most thorough study of this question of silence that I have seen is the work that has been done by George F. Beals, *How Implication Binds and Silence Forbids: Studies in Biblical Hermeneutics,* quoted just before the two preceding paragraphs. The first two parts of Beals' book address the subjects of implication and silence respectively, and in particular he shows how these two things differ. We would encourage our readers to read (and even better, to *study*) this entire book, but for our limited purpose here we share with our readers a part of his treatment of *how silence differs from implication*, the subject of Chapter 10 of his book. This is a rather lengthy quote (much longer than usual), so please read through all of it. The truth is at stake here. Let the truth ring out! It will be well worth the time and effort required to work your way through what this brother says on this subject.

> As we have seen, an implicit Bible teaching (a teaching which the Bible implies, but is not specifically stated in the words of Scripture — *ww*) depends on the existence of one or more explicit Bible teachings (the very words which the Bible uses — *ww*). That is, before there can be an implicit Bible teaching there has to be something there in the Bible to do the implying. When we realize this we are well equipped to see that Bible silence is different from implication. In any body of legislation, there is silence about an action when there is nothing at all in that legislation about that action. But if one or more statements in the legislation address the action in question, explicitly or implicitly, positively or negatively, then there is something there. Then there is a passage or passages to which we can point which have to do with the action in question. And when there is something, there is not silence. Some illustrations from daily life can help us to see how implication, the subject of Part 1, differs from the silence addressed in Part 2.

Let us say there are three mothers who are going away on a trip and each leaves a shopping list for her son, as well as a certain amount of money. When we look at the first list we find the words

⟹ *Buy fruit*

These words authorize the son to purchase apples and oranges, for example. This is the case because apples and oranges, and all other kinds of fruit, are included in the term "fruit" in this sentence ("statement"). So the statement implies that the purchase of apples and oranges is authorized. This is true, even though apples and oranges themselves are not actually named in the statement.

But there is nothing in the above statement about buying a loaf of white bread — not one thing. However, we have not read the whole list yet. The mother may very well have included a statement on the list about buying white bread. If she has, this is okay: There is no conflict between such an addition and the above statement. Further, if we discover that she has not added anything about buying white bread, this too is okay: This too does not conflict with her above statement. So the statement *Buy fruit* allows the mother to add or not add *Buy white bread* without being in logical conflict with herself. And, further, we cannot tell from this statement whether or not the mother did authorize the buying of white bread. That is, the statement, *Buy fruit* has nothing to say explicitly or implicitly, positively or negatively, about such a purchase. We cannot correctly say this at this point about the whole list, but we can at this point say this correctly about the single statement *Buy fruit*.

We continue down the list and find these additions:

Buy
⟹ *meat,*
⟹ *white potato, and*
⟹ *a box of cereal.*

That's it. So we have found *nothing* in the whole list about white bread, not one thing. Thus, the first mother was *silent* about buying white bread.

Now we turn our attention to the second list. It says,

Buy
⟹ *a dozen ears of corn,*
⟹ *a dozen tomatoes,*
⟹ *a loaf of bread,*
⟹ *three T-bone steaks.*

The list does have something in it about buying white bread. It does not actually specify "white" bread. It just says "Buy a loaf of bread." But the statement includes the generic term "bread." It thus covers pumpernickel bread, wheat bread, white bread, and all other kinds of bread. So *Buy a loaf of bread* implies that this mother has authorized her son to buy a loaf of white bread. So there *is* something in this second list which has to do with buying a loaf of white bread. It is not the case that there is nothing in this list about it, unlike the first list. The first list is indeed silent about buying white bread. But this second list is not silent about it.

Now we look at the third list. It says,

Buy
⟹ *one loaf of white bread,*
⟹ *a pound of cheese,*
⟹ *a dozen eggs, and*
⟹ *hamburger.*

This list also has something in it about buying white bread. It actually says it. So this list is not silent about such a purchase.

The second and third lists differ from the first in that they are *not* silent about buying white bread, whereas the first *is* silent about it. The second and third differ from each other merely in that the second *implicitly* covers the purchase of white bread, and the third *explicitly* covers it.

It is especially important to understand the difference between the first list and the second regarding the action in question. The point is that **implication is not an instance of silence.** Implication is not nothing. But silence is nothing. Implication can occur only when there is something there to do the implying. And in the second list there is something there which does this. Namely, the statement *Buy a loaf of bread.* Thus, this list is not silent about buying white bread (any more than the third list is). Only the first list is silent about it. A body of legislation is silent on an action only when there is **nothing, zero,** in that legislation having to do with the action in question.

We might ask, What should a person do or not do when legislation, which has jurisdiction over him, is silent about an action in question? After we define Bible silence more precisely, we will concentrate on this question. But in this chapter, and in the next, we are focusing on what silence is. This is an important first step. Then we can deal better with what we are to do or not do when we have silence.

Ambiguities

See the figure on the next page. In this chapter we have illustrated two distinctions. One is that between explicit and non-explicit. The second is within the non-explicit itself, namely the distinction between implication and nothing.

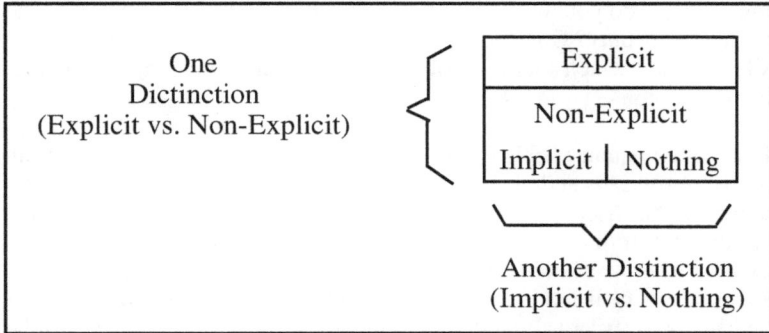

```
+----------------------------------------------------------------------+
|                                    +------------------------------+  |
|            One                  {  |          Explicit            |  |
|        Dictinction              {  +------------------------------+  |
|  (Explicit vs. Non-Explicit)    {  |        Non-Explicit          |  |
|                                 {  +----------------+-------------+  |
|                                 {  |  Implicit     |   Nothing   |  |
|                                    +------------------------------+  |
|                                        _____   _____/            |
|                                               \ /                    |
|                                    Another Distinction               |
|                                   (Implicit vs. Nothing)             |
+----------------------------------------------------------------------+
```

In material which discusses Bible silence, it has not been easy to find many authors who clearly explain and then clearly maintain these two distinctions throughout the discussion. This is especially the case with the second distinction. That is, some folks consider an implied Bible teaching to be an instance of Bible silence. This is a mistake.

The next illustration identifies the area on the figure which corresponds to each mother's shopping list.

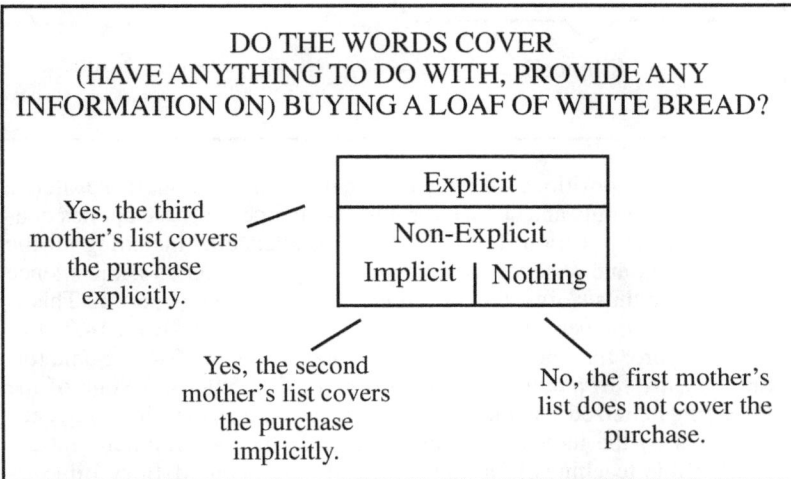

```
+----------------------------------------------------------------------+
|                     DO THE WORDS COVER                                |
|         (HAVE ANYTHING TO DO WITH, PROVIDE ANY                        |
|  INFORMATION ON) BUYING A LOAF OF WHITE BREAD?                        |
|                                                                      |
|                              +------------------------------+        |
|       Yes, the third         |          Explicit            |        |
|    mother's list covers   /  +------------------------------+        |
|       the purchase           |        Non-Explicit          |        |
|        explicitly.           +----------------+-------------+        |
|                              |  Implicit     |   Nothing   |        |
|                              +------------------------------+        |
|                          /                        \                  |
|           Yes, the second                   No, the first mother's   |
|         mother's list covers                 list does not cover the |
|            the purchase                           purchase.          |
|             implicitly.                                              |
+----------------------------------------------------------------------+
```

When we are listening to someone's explaining Bible silence, it is important that we ask him, early, what he means. If the answer is unclear, it could help if you point out first the difference between explicit and non-explicit. Then you could point out the difference between the two areas within the non-explicit. Then, almost there, you could ask, "Now, by Bible silence, do you mean (1) the entire non-explicit area (implicit and nothing)? Or, (2) do you mean the implicit area only? Or, (3) do you mean the nothing area only? Once you and he understand how he is defining Bible silence, then watch that both of you maintain this meaning throughout the discussion.

If an author equates Bible silence with the entire non-explicit area, he can easily confuse his audience and place himself in a difficult situation as he continues his discussion. Why? He then is talking about two things which are distinct from each other: implication and nothing. So he cannot now explain what we should do or not do when we have an example of Bible silence (as if he is talking about one thing). This is the case because what he can correctly say about the nothing part of the non-explicit cannot be applied consistently to implication. Let me explain this further.

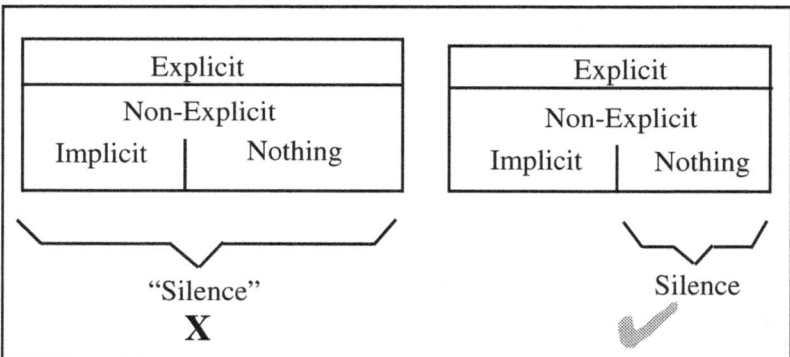

Explicit	Explicit
Non-Explicit	Non-Explicit
Implicit | Nothing	Implicit | Nothing

"Silence"
X

Silence
✔

The candidate positions we often hear in discussions about Bible silence are silence permits and silence forbids. But neither of these applies consistently to implication. Let's define Bible silence as including all the non-explicit, and observe what happens. A person claims Bible silence permits. He thus claims that all implicit Bible teachings permit. This is nonsense. Some permit: *You are permitted to eat meat* (Rom 14:2, 14). Some require: *You are required to love others* (Matt. 5:43-45). Some forbid: *You are forbidden to become drunk* (1 Cor 6:9-10). (None of the foregoing italicized statements actually occurs as is in the Bible. Yet, each is proved by the indicated Bible passage. So they are implicit, not explicit, Bible teachings.) On the other hand, someone defines Bible silence as including implication, and then claims Bible silence forbids. This too is nonsense (with this wide definition of Bible silence): Not all implicit Bible teachings forbid, as just illustrated.

(SPECIAL NOTE: At this place we have omitted the quotations of the verses cited in the above paragraph that are given in footnotes 90-92 of the book — ww)

So, defining Bible silence as including the implicit area is not a good practice. For example, it would force one to say that the Bible is silent about whether or not God loves you or me, since your name and my name are not Bible explicit. It would also force one to say that the Bible is silent about anyone today who commits homosexuality, engages in drunkenness, murders, and so forth. In fact, including implication in the meaning of silence forces one to say that the Bible is silent about **everything** any specific individual today does, because no one today is explicitly mentioned in the Bible (George F. Beals, *How Implication Binds and Silence Forbids: Studies in Biblical Hermeneutics* 63-70. Used with permission from the author — *ww*).

In light of Beals' discussion in the above paragraphs on the subjects of implication and silence, Fenter's mistake becomes obvious. But let's notice part of Beals' own response to Fenter:

First, notice he is talking about such silence forbidding *anything not explicitly found in Scripture*. So, he is referring to that area about which the Bible is not explicit. Also, notice he is talking about *anything not explicitly found in Scripture*. These words refer to the entire territory about which the Bible is not explicit. As we have mentioned [footnote 95: You may find it helpful to refer back to the figures on page 67], the non-explicit includes two areas:

(1) the implicit (that which the Bible implies), and

(2) the nothing area (that which the Bible has not addressed at all, neither implicitly nor explicitly).

So, the author, or at least his words, starts off with a double meaning of Bible silence. He starts off by defining Bible silence so broadly that it includes the two totally different hermeneutical phenomena in the non-explicit territory. Right here he has set himself up for some difficulty.

Second, from his examples we can tell that he is defining silence as including the implicit area. Here he gets himself into the trouble we warned about above. Look at some of his examples. Notice he lists radio and televison. These means of communication are not explicit in the Bible. But there is *implied* authority for their use. The instruction "preach the gospel to every creature" in Mark 16:15-16 implies some means of implementing it. Radio is a means. The instruction about providing for our own in 1 Tim 5:8 implies some means of implementing it. Repairing computers is a means. The instruction to assemble in Heb 10:25 requires some place to do it. Either rented grass or a purchased building is some place.

The instruction to partake of the fruit of the vine in 1 Cor 11:25 requires and thus implies some variety of fruit of the vine. It also requires some kind of container due to the nature of liquids, that the fruit of the vine be at some temperature, and that we be some place when we drink it. Fruit of the vine at 56 degrees F, occupying a tablespoon's volume in a modern container, consumed in a church building at 11:37 Sunday morning with the electric lights on so we can see, constitutes an instance of carrying out the Scriptural requirement. Only those specifics of a requirement which Scripture excludes are excluded. For example, consuming fruit of the vine that results in drunkenness is excluded by 1 Cor 6:6-10.

Do we not see, then, the importance of defining just what we mean by Bible silence when discussing it? And do we not see the difficulties we face when we define Bible silence in such a way that we include implied Bible teachings. In this book, *by Bible silence I am referring only to the nothing area of the non-explicit.* I do not include implication in the term silence. . . . (72-73).

Bible silence, then, is the *nothing* area. It is when the Bible says nothing about a subject (doctrine, thing, or action). It is when there is neither *explicit* nor *implicit* authority for it. Does the Bible teach us that we may find justification for something in the nothing area, or does it teach us that we are not permitted to move into the nothing area and seek justification for something in that area? This is the same as to ask, "Does Bible silence (the nothing area) permit, or does Bible silence forbid?" once Bible silence has been properly defined.

There are several passages of Scripture that clearly teach that Bible silence forbids. Colossians 3:17 shows that everything, all that we do, is to be done by the authority of Christ. This contradicts the silence permits contention. 2 Timothy 3:16-17 taken with 1 Thessalonians 5:17 does the same. Beals summarizes this latter point this way: "Now let us put the two passages together. All good works are in Scripture (2 Tim. 3:16-17). So if Scripture does not address a particular work (is silent about it), the work cannot be good. But we must *do* only what we have proven to be good (1 Th 5:21). So if we do that which is not in Scripture, where *all* good works are found, we violate 1 Th 5:21 and thus sin. In other words Bible silence forbids" (95).

Bible Silence Forbids — Illustrated from Hebrews
Several passages from the book of Hebrews may also be cited as teach-

ing that Bible silence forbids: Hebrews 1:4-5, 13; 5:1-10; 7:20-22; 7:13-14 with 8:4-5; 13:10-11. The reader should read Beals' discussion of these passages in Chapter 17 of his book (109-135). He will find here both an interesting and profitable discussion on just how each of these passages from the book of Hebrews teaches that Bible silence forbids.

Due to the restraints of space we will take a look at the first of these examples found in Hebrews 1:4-5, and then briefly consider Hebrews 7:13-14.

1. Hebrews 1:4-5. Hebrews 1:3-5 reads as follows:

> Who being the brightness of his glory, and the express image of his person, and upholding all things by the word of his power, when he had purged sins, sat down on the right hand of the Majesty on high: Being made so much better than the angels, as he hath by inheritance obtained a more excellent name than they. For unto which of the angels said he at any time, Thou art my Son, this day have I begotten thee? And again, I will be to him a Father, and he shall be to me a Son?

The method of argumentation that the writer uses in these verses for the superiority of Christ over angels follows the order of an affirmation vs. no affirmation. The word of God affirms that Christ is king, but no such affirmation is found in the word of God regarding angels. One will not read anywhere in Scripture that any angel is king. How do we know that no angel is king? Because the word of God does not affirm it. "To which of the angels did he ever say . . .?" (v. 5), the writer asks. The answer to this question is "none," of course. This is the point the writer makes by raising the question. This means that the question raised by the writer, along with the anticipated "none" answer, actually serves as an argument from silence. He affirms that Christ "sat down on the right hand of the Majesty on high" (v. 3), but regarding angels he makes no such affirmation. It is, as we said, the affirmation/no affirmation argument that is employed to make the author's point about the superiority of Christ over angels.

To show conclusively that Scripture affirms Christ's kingship, while at the same time it says absolutely *nothing* by way of affirmation about any angel being king, the Hebrew writer quotes Psalms 2:7 in verse 5. If we go back and read verse 6 of Psalms 2 with verse 7 in the same chapter, we can readily see that the writer is speaking of the time when Christ became king. Christ became Son (according to Psalms 2) when he became king, which is at the time he ascended upon high and sat down at the right hand of God.

It is important to notice that the argument is not based upon an officially worded denial such as, "*no angel* is to be accepted as king," or "an angel *shall not* serve or be acknowledged as king," etc. Rather, by making this argument the writer is telling his readers that all it takes to show that a teaching (like the subject of Heb. 1:4-5), or in other cases a thing or an action, is *not* permitted is *the absence of* an official affirmation. *An officially worded denial is not required.* What this means is, Bible silence *forbids*, and no officially worded denial is needed in order for it to do the forbidding. Let me emphasize: Bible silence does not permit, it forbids. Here is the way Beals summarizes this point:

> The passage in Hebrews that we are studying speaks of Christ as king based on what God's word **did** say about Him. But the passage does not deny kingship to angels based on this. Rather, it does so based on what God's word **did not** say about them, a lack of affirmation. This is the unauthorized area. The passage is focusing our attention one step above Bible silence and Bible-addressed prohibition. It is focusing on the Bible-unauthorized generic, telling us this forbids belief in a doctrine.
>
> Now, since when there is silence there is the absence of an affirmation, and since Heb 1:5 teaches that the absence of an affirmation forbids a doctrine, then Heb 1:5 is affirming Bible silence forbids (115-16).

The reader should consult Beals' book to understand the way he uses such terms as "unauthorized," "unauthorized area," "Bible-unauthorized area," "Bible-unauthorized generic," "Bible-addressed prohibition," etc. and how these relate to "Bible silence." One will also find considerable material by way of response to arguments made in defense of the position that Bible silence permits.

2. Hebrews 7:13-14. The last half of v. 14 reads, "of which tribe Moses spoke nothing concerning priesthood." He is speaking of the tribe of Judah from which our Lord came. In this way we are informed that Christ would not have been appointed to the Levitical priesthood because he came from another tribe than that of Levi. Of the tribe Judah Moses spoke "nothing concerning priesthood." Notice that word "nothing." On this point, Beals asks, "Nothing? What about the action concerning which the Bible teaches nothing? Can we engage in it with God's approval or not? Since Christ came from the tribe of Judah, and the referenced words of Moses said nothing about priests coming from this tribe, does this forbid? Was this adequate for concluding that, according to the law, Christ would not be a priest?" (121).

Beals then gives the Hebrew writer's own answer to this question from Hebrews 8:4-5, "for if he were on earth he would not be a priest." Why?

Because "the Levitical priests left no room for a non-Levite like Jesus to serve as a priest." Since this conclusion is based upon the *silence* of the Bible (the "nothing" area) it shows us that Bible silence (that is, when there is *nothing* to be found in the Bible about a subject) forbids.

In the next chapter we will consider the subject of expediency, including its meaning and application.

Chapter 22

Authority and the Role of Expediency

The Meaning of Expediency

The word "expediency" is a Bible term. Paul says, "All things are lawful for me; but all things are not expedient" (1 Cor. 6:12). The word "expedient" means "to help, be profitable" (Thayer 597); "to be an advantage, profitable" (Vine I:62); "help, confer a benefit, be advantageous or profitable or useful" (AG 787). Thus a thing may be right or lawful and yet not be expedient. From this passage (1 Cor. 6:12) we learn at least three things about expediency :

1. Expediency is within the realm of divine law. There must be some divine law or authority (explicit or implicit) for a practice before a thing or action can be considered an expedient, or a help in carrying out the thing or action required in the law of God.

2. Decisions about expediency involve non-essentials. No mere "aid" or "help" in carrying out some divine requirement is to be put on an equal level with the required action or thing in God's divine plan. One is required, the other is not. Whatever aid or help is used in carrying out a requirement of God, it is not a part of the requirement, but is a mere aid or help in carrying out the requirement.

3. No expediency must become an enslaving practice. In the matter of eating of meats Paul could eat all meats if he so chose, but he must keep his own appetites under control. Other things must also be taken into account. If he were to become a slave to his appetites, he would not be free in relation to them. He must maintain mastery over them and not permit them to take control, or become a master over him.

While we are not permitted to change a specific action or thing that is authorized by God, we are at liberty to change a mere aid or expedient in the carrying out of a command. For one to become enslaved to an aid or expedient would be for him to become enslaved to a mere incidental.

We may learn other things about expedients from 1 Corinthians 10:23ff. The first verse (v. 23) of this section is identical with 1 Corinthians 6:12, except the last phrase says "but all things edify not," instead of "but I will not be brought under the power of any." We may learn the following additional things about "expedients" from these verses:

4. The practice must edify. Though all things are lawful, Paul says, "all things edify not." See Romans 14:19b. So it would not be proper, nor would it be to the "advantage" of a local church, to adopt anything as a "help" that would tear down or work against this main purpose (that of edifying, or building up the members) in the carrying out of a given command. In 1 Corinthians 14:26, Paul says, "Let all things be done unto edifying."

5. The practice must be to the glory of God. Acknowledging that all that we do must be done to God's glory (1 Cor. 10:31), David Lipscomb observes that "his glory is never enhanced by our destroying his weak children to gratify ourselves. Jesus pleased not himself, but gave up all to save men and so glorify God. He is our great exemplar. We must glorify God by sacrificing self for the good of others" (*First Corinthians* 160).

6. The practice must not lead others to sin. To "offend" a brother (1 Cor. 10:32) is to cause him to sin. In the matter of eating of meats, it was to lead one to "eat with offence" (Rom. 14:20), or without the approval of his conscience. This was to "grieve" a brother, and to "destroy" him (Rom. 14:15, 20). We cannot edify a brother and destroy him at the same time. The choice of expediencies should take into account the conscience of others.

Alexander Campbell's "Expediency" Argument for Societies

Just as the area of Bible silence has proved to be a problem area for those who would "speak where the Bible speaks, and be silent where the Bible is silent," the matter of Bible expediency has also proved to be equally troublesome. As noted at the outset of the last chapter, both the Campbells, Thomas and his son Alexander, acknowledged that there is a legitimate area of "expediency," although both feared that this area would work havoc among brethren unless all were willing to hold their "opinions" to themselves. As we all know, their greatest fears came to pass. But Alexander Campbell himself was in many ways responsible for the divided outcome of the restoration cause he had helped to advance.

1. The early years. In the early days of *The Christian Baptist*, a periodical published by Alexander Campbell from 1823 to 1830, Campbell had been hard against the various kinds of societies that were so popular in his day. In the first year of publication he wrote that "the societies called churches, constituted and set in order by those ministers of the New Testament . . . were not fractured into missionary societies, Bible societies, education societies: nor did they dream of organizing such in the world" (*Christian Baptist* I [1823]:14; abbreviated *CB* from here on). He believed that such societies "robbed it (the church — ww) of its character" (*CB* I [1923]: 101-02). He insisted that "the association called the church of Jesus Christ is . . . the only institution of God left on earth to illuminate and reform the world" (*CB* I [1824]:218).

On the matter of church government, each local church, Campbell believed, "is perfectly independent of any tribunal on earth called ecclesiastical" (*CB* I [1824]: 216), and "in their church capacity alone they moved. They neither transformed themselves into any kind of association, nor did they fracture and sever themselves into divers societies" (*CB* I [1823]:14). Campbell strongly argued against the view that church organization is left to man's discretion. If this were the case, he reasoned, then no form of church government could be condemned. That being true then it would follow that the progression of church government from congregations to associations to state conventions to what would be equal to Rome or Canterbury would be allowed (*CB* V [1828]:239).

Campbell's early views about extra-congregational organizations were based solidly upon his firm conviction that the Bible is not a general charter for congregations, but a prescription of specific rules of congregational behavior and organization (see *CB* V [1828]:250ff.). He once made the point that no offender in a local church had an appeal to any tribunal (such as a council of churches) higher than the local church of which he is a member, and he affirmed that "the old book, written by the Apostles, has compelled me to hold this dogma fast" (*CB* VI [1829]:200).

2. A new era in Campbell's thinking. With the introduction of *The Millennial Harbinger* in January 1830 and the demise of *The Christian Baptist* at the end of the preceding year, it soon became clear that a change in Campbell's thinking was beginning to take place. Though he did not see that it was necessary for the Mahoning Association to dissolve as it had done just a few months before, he yet continued to oppose in the very first issue of the *Harbinger* all inter-congregational organizations. But within a year and a half of the inception of this new periodical Campbell began to defend "missionary" or "cooperative associations" as he affirmed a belief that churches in a given area (county, district, or state) had a right to meet jointly, choose officers, and co-sponsor evangelistic efforts. In his series of articles on "The Cooperation of Churches" begun in May 1831, emphasis was given to the church fulfilling its mission as the agency for the conversion of the world. Since one church could not accomplish this work by itself, all the local churches in a given district should cooperate by choosing and sending representatives to such a meeting. They could in this way "expedite" joint evangelistic effort.

The kinds of things Campbell had written against societies in *The Christian Baptist* days were certain to give him much trouble once he had made up his mind to begin to expand his thinking on church cooperation. He attempted to defend his new position by arguing that it was consistent with what he had written earlier when he was opposing the benevolent societies. He maintained he was merely opposing the abuses of such organizations; what he called their "eternal echo of the word, Money" (*MH* III [1832]:614ff.). But some of those who had read his writings on this subject on the pages of *The Christian Baptist* believed that this was not Campbell's main criticism for such organizations. They felt that he then believed they were not authorized in Scripture. His new belief was that there were scriptural grounds upon which his "cooperative system" was justified.

3. The "congregation of God" and expediency. Campbell had not opposed the Cooperation Meetings of the various districts, but his way of thinking about the matter of church cooperation was beginning to be expanded. He began to think more on a universal scale. His primary argument would be based upon his view of the universal church. He saw the church universal as being composed of the many individual *congregations* rather than individual Christians throughout the world. This "*congregation of God*," he said, "is a great community of communities" (*The Christian System* 73).Once he came to think of the church universal as being composed of congregations, he then began to notice that these local churches in various areas were divided up into "districts," such as "the churches of Galatia" (1 Cor. 16:1), etc. From this he reasoned that this is justification for these area churches to work together in "cooperative effort." For Campbell "cooperation itself is one thing, and the manner of cooperation another." Such cooperation among churches is a necessity, but the "circumstances" of Christ's kingdom was something altogether different. By "circumstances" he meant the "forms, the ways and means" of doing things. To his way of thinking the "districts" into which the local churches were divided were merely the circumstantials, accidents, ways and means of cooperation.

But for many of those who had been avid readers of *The Christian Baptist*, and who were opposed to Campbell's "plan," it was plain to them that this was wrong. For them, the church, whether universal or local, is made up of individual Christians, not local congregations, and Campbell's plan for cooperation was not simply a matter of "ways and means," but a question of organization. Those who rejected Campbell's argument, once The American Christian Missionary Society had been established in 1849, could now see that the earlier district and state conventions were only the first step toward the creation of this one central organization, through which all the churches could do their work of evangelism.

Campbell contended that even if there was no pattern for the organization through which the work of evangelism must be accomplished, no such pattern was needed. For him the "cooperative effort" was simply a matter of "expediency." He devoted a complete chapter in his book, *The Christian System*, to this subject (90-94). But how would a decision be made on something like this? In answer to this question, he said, the majority in a local church should decide on purely local matters, but in particular, "the law of expediency enacts that a majority of the seniors shall decide in all cases what is most expedient to be done in attaining any of the ends commanded in the Christian Institution, the means of which are not divinely ordained in the written laws of that institution; and that the minority shall cheerfully and conscientiously acquiesce in such decisions" (*The Christian System* 94). He was also willing to apply this same rule on a larger scale so that decisions could be made for the whole "congregation of God" in cooperative endeavors through the district churches.

One is made to wonder if Campbell had not early on decided that the majority of the brethren were in sympathy with his great desire for the churches to have a central agency or "cooperative system" for evangelizing the whole world.

About this same time Barton W. Stone was still asking, "What have the divine writers of the New Testament said representing these societies? They are all silent as the grave . . ." (*The Christian Messenger* VI [1832]:344). This was but a restatement of his position expressed in an exchange over this issue between Stone and Walter Scott in the first issue of his periodical which he began to publish in 1826. Stone never renounced his original objections to the societies as Campbell had now done. Some eight years before, as we pointed out earlier, Campbell had said, "Our objections to the missionary plan originated from the conviction that it is unauthorized in the New Testament" (*CB* I [1824]:157). His former plea, "Where is the society in the Bible?" was no longer to be heard.

Once brethren began to cry, "where is the authority for the 'cooperative plan,'" Campbell answered their demand in this way: "In all things pertaining to public interest, not of Christian faith, piety or morality, the church of Jesus Christ in its aggregate character is left free and unshackled by any apostolic authority. This is the great point which I assert as of capital importance in any great convention movement or cooperation in advancing the public interests of a common salvation" (quoted by James DeForest Murch, *Christians Only* 148).

By 1835 Campbell was so confident that his position on the new "cooperative system" was the correct one that he thought all of his brethren should accept it, and any who would not should not be used to lead in public prayer (*MH* VI [1835]:120ff.). He was happy to force his cooperative plan upon the few who were not willing to accept it.

Even though Campbell argued for his cooperation"plan" for evangelism on the grounds of expediency, he also believed that there is a pattern for it in the "district churches." It is true that he would not have described it in exactly these terms, since he did not use the word "pattern." But he did speak of his "plan" as having "apostolic sanction." By this he meant that there was specific authority for church cooperation, and the rest was simply a matter of expediency. Here are his exact words: "Any one who seeks apostolic sanctions for these views of co-operation will find ample authority in the Acts and Epistles of the Apostles" (*The Christian System* 76). He then cites several examples of what he describes as "district" churches. This was Campbell's patten for church cooperation. This much was "a part of the Christian institution," or "a part of the economy of Heaven." The manner of their cooperation was "the mere circumstantials of the Christian institution." In one long sentence, Campbell stated the case as follows: "The communion of saints, of all Christian churches — the cooperation of churches as one holy nation, a kingdom of priests, as a peculiar people in all common interests and benefits — an efficient gospel ministry, supported justly and honorably by the whole community — are matters clearly and fully taught by both apostolic precept and authority; but the forms, the ways and means by which these ends shall be attained, are left to the law of expediency" (*The Christian System* 92-93).

We must now give more attention to this "law of expediency."

Generic and Specific Action Words and What They Allow

It is generally accepted that some things are "permitted" in the worship and work of the church that are not specifically (explicitly) authorized. Sometimes such matters are discussed under the terms "generic and specific authority," and sometimes they are treated as "expedients" or "aids" in the carrying out of certain commands, both generic and specific. These are other terms used to describe *implicit* authority.

In the discussion that follows we will bring these areas of study together under one heading by considering the different kinds of "action words" that we find used in Scripture. These words, whether they are generic or specific words, authorize more than the action required in the word. We may call these "other things" expedients or aids, or we may call them "methods," but we would caution our readers to be careful in the use of these terms. We must understand the meaning of such terms and know how they are being used. Definition is important. We must take care that we use these terms properly.

We may begin this section with the following chart and summary statement (appearing under the chart) that will introduce the subject of "action words."

Words of Generic and Specific Action			
	Commands	**Methods**	
A C T I O N	GO (Matt. 28:29)	Walk Ride	GENERIC ACTION
W O R D S	BAPTIZE (Matt. 28:19)	NONE	SPECIFIC ACTION

Chart #1

Summary Explanation

A statement, command, or example that requires the performance of some act will be stated in such a way that the action word used will define the kind of action required. The action required will be either generic or specific, determined by the action word itself. If the word used is generic, as in the case of the word "go," different forms of action (methods) may be used to carry out the action required. If the action word is specific, as in the case with the word "baptize," there are no methods of carrying out the action. No *action* except that required by the word itself is authorized by the word. Any other action if it is authorized at all must be authorized elsewhere by some other passage of Scripture. But action words do, as we shall see, authorize (by implication) more than the act required by the word.

The above summary (provided under the chart) is a brief introduction to the subject of *action* words and how they authorize. One will notice that the word "baptize" does not authorize any other action, nor is there a choice of "methods" of baptizing. The action specified by the word is a specific action, that of immersing, so there is no choice regarding the kind of action that will be used in carrying out the requirement of the command. The action required is specific. This simply means that the word "baptize" is not a generic word like the word "go." There are different "methods" of going, such as riding or walking, but there are no different methods of baptizing. Please notice that the different methods of "going" are represented by other *action* words because different ways (methods) of going are just different ways one may "act" in carrying out the command to "go." They "add" nothing to the command, because walking and riding are only different forms of the same act, that of going.

Although the action word "baptize" does not have different methods of carrying out the action (Chart #1, 2nd column), the word does authorize various aids and arrangements for carrying out the specific action required in the command. None of these (listed on Chart #2, 3rd column) adds anything to the action required in the command (i.e., they do not add another action to that which is specified in the word "baptize"), so they are not additions to the command to baptize.

Also notice that while one may "go" by the use of an automobile, or a train, or a bus, an automobile or a train or bus is not a "method" of going. Riding *is* a method of going because it is one way one may choose to "act" in carrying out the command to "go." In either case (to go by auto, train, or bus) one is going by "riding." An automobile, or some other vehicle, is simply a *means* of "riding," and riding is one particular *method* of going. Notice that it is also an *action* word, which is the significant thing to notice about such a word when we are describing a "method" of carrying out an action.

So how would we classify an automobile in this illustration? Chart #2 helps explain what we mean in the "Summary Explanation" at the bottom of Chart #1 when we say, "action words authorize more than the act required by the word." By "more" we do not mean an action unless we are describing a "method" of carrying out the action specified in the command. We mean that in addition to the action specified in the action word, such words will allow (permit) some other things, because they will authorize by *implication* things such as aids and arrangements, and time and place. This is illustrated in Chart #2 below both for the command to "go" and the command to "baptize." Such things as those listed are permissible because they do not in any way violate (by addition) or change (by substitution) the "action" called for in the action words. This is the nature of action words.

Let me repeat : an automobile is not a *method* of going. This word is not an *action* word. Because it is not an action word we classify it as an "aid," or "help." It is the vehicle or *means* used in "riding." It is a *means* of carrying one to his destination, whereas "riding" is a *method* of "going."

What Action Words Allow

Generic Action	Specific Methods	Aids & Arrangements	Time & Place
	Walk	**Aids:** Shoes, cane, plane, auto	**Time:** Any time, day or hour
GO (Matt. 28:29)	**Ride**	**Arrangements:** Whole church, classes, one person	**Place:** Any place, whole world as time and resources permit
Specific Action			
BAPTIZE (Matt. 28:19)	NONE (Only the action specified is authorized)	**Aids:** Clothing, baptistry, place to dress	**Time:** Any time — any day, day or night
		Arrangements: Someone to do baptizing, classify (divide)	**Place:** Outside, inside, river, pond, baptistry

Chart #2

Such things as aids and arrangements, and time and place, belong to what we often refer to as "expedients." They are *not* examples of Bible *silence*, because they are not matters about which the Bible says *nothing*. They are authorized by *implicit* Bible authority, and when a thing is implied in a passage of Scripture, the Bible is not silent about it. Such things help or aid one in carrying out the *action* called for in the *action word* that appears in the command. We must be able to recognize, as we have said, that (1) they are not "additions" to the command, because they do not add another kind of action, and (2) they are not "substitutions" because they do not put another action in the place of the action required in the command; they simply help, or serve as an aid to one, in carrying out the action required.

In Chart #2 we have placed "auto" and "plane" under "aids" for the action word "ride," whereas in the same category we have put "shoes" and a "cane" as examples of aids for the action word "walk." We simply must apply what we have pointed out about aids or helps in carrying out an action in a given command. They are not methods of doing something, nor are they additions to or substitutions for the command. These terms do not describe actions so they cannot be another kind of action. Neither are they "methods" of carrying something out — that is, they are not *actions* of some kind; this would require another action word. An *aid* to an action that is carried out (as we are using the term "aid" in this study) is never described with another action word. What we have said here concerning aids may also be said of arrangements, and time and place.

Let us now consider the word "teach." Teach is a generic action word. Chart #3 (next page) will illustrate the difference between "methods" of teaching and other things that also would be included in this action word.

One specific *method* of teaching is to teach by "speaking" (2 Cor. 10:10-11), and another specific *method* of teaching is to teach by "writing" (2 Cor. 10:10-11). Notice that these are also *action* words. Whether one speaks or writes makes no difference. Each is simply a specific method of teaching.

To "aid" one in his speaking one might choose to use a whiteboard or a chart, or he might use a public address system. Aids in writing would include such things as a pen, paper, and ink. "Arrangements" for teaching might include a gathering of the whole church into one place (Acts 20:7), or a smaller group such as when Paul gathered the elders from Ephesus together to give them some final instructions (Acts 20:17ff.). Another arrangement for teaching by speaking might be to teach only one person at a given time. Arrangements to teach by writing could include writing to one person (1 Tim. 1:2), to a church as a whole (1 Cor. 1:2), or even to more than one church at a particular time (Gal. 1:2).

Generic Action	Specific Methods	Aids & Arrangements	Time & Place
	Speak (2 Cor. 10:10-11)	**Aids:** Whiteboard, charts, Pub. Ad. system, notes	**Time:** Any time, to whole church, smaller group
Teach (Matt. 28:20)		**Arrangements:** Whole church, small group, individual	**Place:** Any place, public or private
	Write (2 Cor. 10:11-12)	**Aids:** Pen, paper, ink, etc.	**Time:** Any time — determined by need and occasion
		Arrangements: To one individual, to a church, or several churches	**Place:** Any place, even prison

Chart #3

The "time" to teach is of course any time. One is free to choose the time just as he may choose certain aids and arrangements for teaching, whether he teaches by speaking or by writing. He may teach by speaking in either of these ways any day or hour, when the whole church is come together, or when less than a whole church is gathered. He is free to teach by writing at any time, solely to be determined by the particular need and by the occasion.

The "place" for teaching by speaking is also a matter of discretion. One may teach in this way in both public (Acts 20:20, "publicly") and private places (Acts 20:20, "and from house to house"). One may teach by letter from any place. Some of Paul's letters were written from prison, and others were written from places like Corinth, Ephesus, or some unknown place in Macedonia.

Organization vs. Teaching Arrangement

In the debate over "societies" there were some who saw no difference between separate organizations being created to do the work of the church and an orderly and systematic arrangement being used to do the same work within the framework of the local church. In the articles written in some of the papers, as well as sermons preached in some of the pulpits, no such distinction was made. Sometimes organs, societies, and "Sunday schools" were all lumped together as being without scriptural authority. As a case in point, J.W. Jackson, in his sermon "By Their Works Ye Shall Know Them," published in his book of sermons in 1902, said the following:

> Now, Paul tells us that "all Scripture is given by inspiration of God, and is profitable for doctrine, for correction, for reproof, for instruction in righteousness, that the man of God may be perfect, thoroughly furnished unto all good works." 2 Tim. 3:16-17. Jesus had said "by their fruits (works) ye shall know them." Those whom God sends will do the works of God, and we must determine their claim to be sent of God by the nature of the works done.
>
> But how am I to decide this? By charity? By the "more excellent way"? No, but by a direct appeal to God's word. I go there to find "all good works" that God has ordained that "we should walk in them" (Eph. 2:10); and by diligent search I fail to find one single line of authority for any such practice as organs in the worship, societies, mission boards, Sunday schools, *et id omne genus*. What, then, is the only legitimate conclusion? It is that such things are not of God, they are not "the works of the Father." What of those who practice them? Their claim, that they are doing God's work, is false, for God has nowhere spoken of such works, neither came they into his mind. Jer. 7:31 (*Living Words* 44).

Jackson may have been referring to Sunday school "associations," or such schools as separate organizations from the church, and may not have opposed the Sunday school as a mere teaching arrangement within the local church. David Lipscomb clearly recognized the difference between the societies that he opposed and the "Sunday school" as a systematic arrangement for teaching the Bible. He thought such a "school" was scriptural when kept within the framework of the local church as a mere mode of teaching the Bible, even though he did not think it best to use the term "Sunday school" because this was subject to much misunderstanding. In response to the question, "What is the difference, if any, between the church and Sunday school as organized bodies?" Lipscomb said the following:

> It is the privilege and duty of every Christian to use every opportunity that offers to teach the word of God to others. This teaching may be done to one alone, to a class, or to a promiscuous audience, as the qualifications of the teacher and the surroundings may suggest is best. This is all to be done in accordance with the laws of Christ, in violation of no law laid down. It is to be done in the name of Christ, as a member of his body. We cannot do a thing in the name of Christ when it is done as a member of a body not authorized by him. Christ never ordained any organization except his churches. In these, as members of his body, his children must work. No Sunday school or missionary or charitable organization outside of his church has ever been authorized. No Christian has a right to work in any of these human organizations. He must do what he does as a member of the body of Christ. Acting as a member of that body, he must do it with a proper regard for the members of that body. The elders are made the rulers to see God's laws carried out.
>
> Work ought to be done in harmony with this position of the elders. This does not mean that they should never work save as the elders direct or that they should wait for the elders to tell them before they work. Unfortunately, some get in as elders who never direct or advise work. In the church the elders should see all work is done as the Bible directs, teach the Bible, do all in the name of Christ. But when men are away from the church and opportunity offers, they should teach — teach individuals and classes — as opportunity offers. They should do it as members of the church and not as members of some human organization. Paul and Barnabas preached thus, and then reported their work to the church. It is a good example to follow. These inspired men of God honored God's church; and, notwithstanding their inspiration, they honored the elders of the churches. We would do well to follow their examples, and in all things honor the church of God, and do all that we do as members of that church, and all in the name of Christ Jesus. Then no one should work as a member of any association save the church of Christ. All should be under the direction or oversight of the elders. A Sunday school should be nothing more than the church through its members teaching the word of God (*Queries and Answers* 654-55).

In response to another question, "Is there any authority for the Sunday school?" Lipscomb's answer was given in the following words:

> There is just the same authority for teaching old and young the Bible in classes or in a school on Sunday at church as there is for preaching sermons. God requires the Bible be taught to the old and the young. He has not ordained any specific mode of teaching, but has set the example of

teaching in the public sermons by questions and answers, by reading the Scriptures to one or more or letting them read it and question them in reference to its meaning, or by simple verbal statement to one or more.

It is the duty of the church to teach children and old people who can be induced to attend the meeting. It is right to teach them in the way it can be most effectively done. We have not had a doubt for years that the most effective way of teaching people the word of God, if they will study, is to take them in classes and read and study the word of God. It is more pleasant to hear a good talker embellish and illustrate and talk about some subject than it is to study it ourselves. So it would be greatly more pleasant for a child to hear a teacher give an entertaining talk than to make him study out his lessons at school. But while it would be more pleasant, it certainly would not teach them so well or thoroughly. If our object is entertainment, the preaching of an accomplished speaker is the better; if to give knowledge of the Scriptures, the class for old and young is the better.

We become habituated to certain modes of procedure and unconsciously come to think them divine, and others to which we are not accustomed we think human innovations. We conclude this without examination. This arises from an unconscious self-sufficiency — satisfaction with self and our ways. This feeling is a great hindrance to the truth. Then Sunday schools under the direction and control of the churches are right and have just as much of divine warrant as preaching. Preaching is right. Every human being in the world ought to be preached to or taught the word of God, but both the preaching and teaching ought to be done through God's appointed agencies. His church, through its operations, unamended by man, ought to do this work. It is treason against God to say his appointments are insufficient. It is an exaltation of man above God to say the arrangements and inventions of man are more effective than God's, or that God's appointments and institutions may be improved and rendered more efficient by human additions to them.

Human organizations for preaching the word of God always subvert their object or end. They corrupt that word, nullify that word, and destroy their own ability to preach the word by depreciating it and exalting men's reason above the word of God. They, in their operations, make necessary twice the amount of money needed under divine appointments; they incite men ambitious of worldly honors and high salaries to scheme for places, position, and control in these associations. In their operations they make men stingy, illiberal, and unreliable in their contributions. They do this by substituting wrong motives for the divine ones and displacing a disposition for God's sacrifices with a love to be seen of men in their gifts.

But this is just as true of human associations to teach the Bible through Sunday schools as it is of human associations to preach the gospel by public speaking. Sunday school societies, separate and distinct from the church God, are open to every objection that missionary societies are. It is strange to see men oppose one and approve the other. Men can be found who oppose one; and then, when they can be leaders or occupy places of honor and emolument in the other, earnestly support it. The besetting sin of the world, of the religious world, in all ages has been to forget that God is wiser than man. Yet the experience of the world teaches that human inventions and devices invariably thwart their own end, over-reach their own design, and destroy that which they were builded *(sic)* to sustain. Human Sunday-school associations are no exceptions to this rule. They are built up to teach the word of God and to build up the churches. That they destroy men's respect for the one and weaken the other I have never had a doubt.

The difference in principle between the missionary societies which many in your State oppose and the Sunday school associations, in which they labor, in which they hold office, and from which they receive support, it takes one wiser than I am to see. Preaching is right; teaching the children the Bible at meeting on Sunday is right. The church, through its elder-ship, ought to see that both are done, and done in accordance with the provisions of the word of God. God's church, as he gave it, is fully com-petent to do all God's work on earth. A work that it cannot do, and do better and more effectually than any and all other institutions of earth can do, is not of God. Teach the children, by all means, the word of God, and do not destroy their respect for that word by showing you think men's institutions more effective for good than God's as set forth in his word (*Queries and Answers* 655-57).

The Bible is *silent* about the church forming other, or separate organiza-tions, for doing the work of the church, and for this reason such organiza-tions are *forbidden*. Yet such *arrangements* as Bible classes for teaching the young and old are authorized by Scripture. As the "pillar and ground of the truth" (1 Tim. 3:15), teaching the word of God is a work of the local church, and the Scriptures that place this work upon the church *implicitly* authorize the church to use various aids, helps, and arrangements for ac-complishing this work in the very best way. Lipscomb spoke plainly when he put teaching, missionary, and charitable organizations all on the same level by saying, "No Sunday school or missionary or charitable organiza-tion outside of his church has ever been authorized." Just as he said of the Sunday school, "A Sunday school should be nothing more than the church through its members teaching the word of God," the same words would equally apply to the "missionary and benevolent" work of the church that was also in his mind as he penned these words.

Expediency and the Instrumental Music Debate

From the very outset among those identified with the restoration movement the debate over instrumental music in public worship centered around the word "expediency." This also has been true of the societies. Most of those who defended the societies also defended instrumental music in worship. There were exceptions, of course, and the most notable were Moses E. Lard and J.W. McGarvey who strongly opposed the instrument but favored the societies. They did not place the two in the same category. Most of the others who defended the instrument did, however. In the exchanges between J.S. Lamar and McGarvey on the music question, Lamar said, "I still believe it and the missionary scheme being alike belong to the class of expedients, and that both are to be tested, as to the propriety of their use, by the very same principle" (*Christian Standard* 5 (April 23, 1870):132, as cited by Choate and Woodson, *Sounding Brass and Clanging Cymbals* 33).

In the early years most all of the defenders of instrumental music in worship did not argue that it was a requirement in worship, but that it was allowed as an "aid" to the voice. Some would say singing was the most important thing and it should be kept that way. W.K. Pendelton said it this way: "Let us keep music in its place, as the expression of the melody of the heart, the instrument as an aid, not the essence and end of worship" (*Millennial Harbinger* 39 [January 1868]:42, cited in *Sounding Brass and Clanging Cymbals* 27).

Some did argue from the meaning of *psallo* and *psalmos* that stringed mechanical instruments are included in the meaning of the words. The response usually was that this was not the case in the New Testament and that, if it was, then we cannot obey the command without using the instruments in worship. This would mean that every time we sing in worship without playing on a mechanical instrument of music we would violate that part of the command. Those who have argued that the instrument inheres in the Greek word *psallo* have been inconsistent in saying that it is optional, that one can use or not use the instrument in congregational worship.

Since this book is not a study of the music question, and we cannot in this work enter into a study of this subject in detail, let us now simply apply what we are studying at the moment to this subject. What would our study of action words and the matter of expediency or aids reveal to us on whether or not another kind of music is authorized by the command to sing or to make melody in our hearts? Would another kind of music be allowed as an "aid" to singing?

Take a look at the chart below. The action word is "sing." This is an action performed by the use of the vocal cords. Webster's first definition of the word sing is "1. a) to produce musical sounds or notes *with the voice*, especially in a connected series, as in *voicing* a song. b) to deliver musical selections *vocally*, especially as a professional" (*New World Dictionary of the American Language* 1361; all emphasis mine — *ww*). The English word "sing" involves sounds produced by the voice in connection with musical selections. This is also the New Testament meaning of the word "sing." Thayer says on the word *psallo*, "in the N.T. *to sing a hymn, to celebrate the praise of God in song* . . . Jas. v. 13 . . . Eph. v. 19 . . . Rom. xv.9 . . ." (675).

Generic Action	Specific Methods	Aids & Arrangements	Time & Place
Sing (Eph. 5:19)	**NONE** (Only the action specified is authorized)	**Aids:** Songbook, pitchpipe **Arrangements:** Song leader, people seated, standing, grouped for parts, etc.	**Time:** Any time, when assembled, when not assembled **Place:** Any place, church building, at home

Chart #4

The word "sing" is a *specific* action word. It involves the use of the voice, but in particular it is to utter with the voice the words of a song. It is "*speaking* to one another in psalms and hymns and spiritual songs, *singing and making melody* in your heart to the Lord" (Eph. 5:19, emphasis mine — *ww*). Notice how the terms speaking, and singing and making melody are used interchangeably in this verse. To sing is to *speak* the words of a song (psalm, hymn, or spiritual song) from the heart, and in thankfulness to God (see also Col. 3:16).

There are no "methods" of singing. There are different parts, such as soprano, tenor, alto, and bass, but not different methods of singing. To sing is "to produce musical sounds or notes *with the voice*, especially in a connected series, as in *voicing* a song." This is the act performed in singing, and the instrument used is the voice. The singers may use songbooks as an "aid," and when they do they are still just singing. No other "action" is performed by using a songbook to aid them in singing. They are still just singing. They may also use an "arrangement" whereby there is one leader and the rest are followers. They may decide that the singers will be grouped or "arranged" according to the various parts sung by the different singers.

The song leader may, or he may not, use a pitch pipe since no melody is made by using it. The "action" of singing is not changed by any of these choices, and none of these choices adds another kind of action, or another kind of music (playing). The kinds of songs listed in Ephesians 5:19 may be sung at any time, and any where: when the church is gathered, or not gathered; at home or in the church building. None of these things adds another kind of action, and none of them changes the action required in the command to "sing." They have merely to do with time and place, not action.

But "play" another kind of music on a mechanical instrument adds another king of "action" to the command to sing. "Play" is an action word, just as "sing" is an action word, and when one "plays" music he is engaging in another action that is not singing. Because it is another kind action outside of the action required by the command to sing, it is an "addition" to the command because this kind of action is not authorized. Another kind of action can never be a mere "aid" to the voice, or to singing. What is required is divine authority for this kind of action ("playing") before it can be brought into the worship.

In our final section (Part Four) we will answer some questions that will provide us an opportunity to cover some points we have not dealt with in the book that are related to our subject. This should include some areas you may have wondered about as you have been reading the book. In a case or two there will be some repetition of what has already been said in a previous chapter. In particular this will be true of what we have to say about silence and implication in this closing section of the book.

Part Four: Appendix

Now, That's a Good Question!

Appendix

Now, That's a Good Question!

Question 1: **Is it true, as often alleged, that the early restoration leaders believed that inferences or deductions should not serve as a basis for unity among Christians?** Yes, this was the position taken by most of the advocates of unity in the early years of the Restoration Movement. This can easily be demonstrated from their writings. Both Thomas and Alexander Campbell distinguish between explicit and implicit statements in Scripture. They refer to *explicit* authority by using the terms "expressly taught" and "expressly enjoined" in describing things that are taught in the very words of Scripture. Thomas Campbell believed that nothing should be bound upon Christians, nor required as terms of communion, "but what is expressly taught and enjoined on them in the word of God." Such things may be "expressly enjoined" by either "precept and precedent," or by *"their* approved example" ("Declaration and Address," in *Pioneer Sermons* 72).

For Thomas Campbell, "inferences and deductions from Scripture premises" (that is, on *implied* Bible teachings), even "when fairly inferred," he said, "may be truly called the doctrine of God's holy word, yet are they not formally binding upon the consciences of Christians farther than they see the connection, and evidently see that they are so . . ." (40). He also claimed that while "doctrinal exhibitions of the great system of Divine truths, and defensive testimonies in opposition to prevailing errors" are "highly expedient," "yet, as these must be in a certain measure the effect of human reasoning, and of course must contain much inferential truths, they ought not to be made terms of Christian communion" (41).

Alexander Campbell also rejected inferences or deductions as a basis for unity. Opinion and an inference for him are one and the same. This is also true of other early restoration leaders. An inference or implication to them was an opinion. In his articles on "opinionism" Campbell defines an opinion as "persuasion without proof," or "a stipulation built on probable evidence."

Campbell's second article on "The Restoration of the Ancient Order of Things" reveals his distrust in human creeds, and gives his reasons why such creeds can never serve as a basis for unity. "Human creeds," he says, "are composed of the inferences of the human understanding speculating upon the revelation of God. Such are all those now extant. The inferences drawn by the human understanding partake of all the defects of that understanding" (*Christian Baptist* II [1825]:154). Such conclusions, Campbell believed, "are always private property, and can never be placed upon a level with the inspired word. Subscription to them, or an acknowledgment of them, can never be rationally required as a *bond of union*" (155).

"Raccoon" John Smith was of one mind with the Campbells on this point. He says that "no deduction or inference" that one may draw from the gospel (which he said is a system of facts, commands, and promises), "however logical or true, forms any part of the gospel of Jesus Christ." He made this point in his 1832 speech on unity. He calls these kinds of deductions and inferences "opinions," as we saw in the more extensive quote given from him in Chapter 18.

Elijah Goodwin (middle nineteenth century) also equates "deduction" with "opinion," and for him no "mere deduction" can ever serve as a basis for unity among Christians. He gives infant baptism as an example. Those who practice it "are bound to admit that there is no command or clear precedent for the practice in the New Testament. The whole practice rests upon mere deduction, or human opinion. Then, for the sake of bleeding Zion and a bleeding Savior, let that opinion give place to the plain, unequivocal command of Christ Jesus our common Lord." Notice how he equates "deduction" and "human opinion" in this statement. Infant baptism is "mere deduction," he says. He does not consider whether or not there might in some cases be right deductions, and that when we have these, whether or not they are binding.

Question 2: **Were these early leaders consistent in applying this conclusion (or rule) about inferences and deductions in actual practice?** No, not exactly. And it does not appear likely that any man can take such a position and remain consistent in it very long. George F. Beals, in his book on implication and silence (cited in Chapter 21), has given some examples of how in some cases the use of implication or deduction is not merely a choice. All men use the deductive process, and when true deduction is made, then it becomes a *must* in such cases, if we are to hold true to the word of God. He demonstrates this conclusion from examples showing that some *implicit* teachings are *binding* upon us. Take a look at the following example and see if he is not right in his conclusion that certain *implicit* Bible teachings are *binding* teachings. Here is a conclusion (implication or deduction) that he says is binding upon Jason Jones, a practicing homosexual, because of what he can read in 1 Corinthians 6:9-11:

Jason Jones must stop engaging in homosexual acts to be saved.

This statement is not an *explicit* Bible teaching because these very words are not to be found anywhere in the Scriptures. Jason Jones' name, for example, is not found in the Bible. But even though his name is not to be found in this passage of Scripture, or in any other passage, it is an *implied* teaching. This means that this is a teaching that must be deduced from this (and other) passages of Scripture. This is not a conclusion that is stated in the exact words of the above statement, and yet it is a *binding* conclusion. What is said in this passage (1 Cor. 6:9-11) applies to Jason Jones and all other practicing homosexuals.

Must Jason Jones, who is engaging in homosexual acts, stop his homosexual practice in order to be saved? Where does the Bible teach that? If the Bible teaches it, how does it teach it? Does it teach it explicitly or implicitly? Where could one read these exact words in Scripture? Since it only teaches it implicitly because it is a teaching that must be *deduced* from Scripture by the use of the human mind, is this teaching a *binding* teaching even though one cannot find this conclusion in these exact words anywhere in Scripture? Do others have a right (yea, even an obligation) to bind this teaching upon Jason Jones?

How would those in the early days of the restoration movement who insisted that deductions drawn from Scripture by the human mind (a mind that is subject to all the frailties of one's understanding, and therefore prone to err in so many ways) are unreliable, have answered this question? For the sake of unity would these brethren have said that the deduction described in the example given above about Jason Jones could not be bound upon him; that such a conclusion because it is based on the deductive process must not be insisted upon?

I think not. I am persuaded that they would have said that if Jason Jones concluded that the passage of Scripture on the subject discussed in the above paragraph (1 Cor. 6:9-11)does not apply to him (perhaps reasoning that it applied to the culture to which the people of that time belonged, but not to people of our day), they would have insisted that he must cease his homosexual practice or else he would not be admitted into the fellowship of the church. They would have said that he has a right to hold such a view (that is, that 1 Cor. 6:9-11 is not binding on him today), but he must hold it as private property, meaning that he could not teach it and he could not practice it if he wanted to be admitted into the church and accepted by the church.

If someone were to ask me if this would be consistent with the statements we have quoted from these early leaders on deductions and opinions, I again would have to say, no. They would be *binding* on Jason Jones a deduction, an *implicit* Bible teaching based upon 1 Corinthians 6:9-11 and similar passages. "Racoon" John Smith said that "no deduction or inference from them (that is, from the facts, commands and promises of the gospel — *ww*), however logical or true, forms any part of the gospel of Jesus Christ." Even if it is *true*? That's what he said, but it does not appear to me that he could ever have hoped to live by this rule consistently and always in all matters as the illustration given here would indicate.

Thomas Campbell would also have had difficulty here. His view that "inferences and deductions from Scripture premises" (that is, on *implied* Bible teachings), even "when fairly inferred may be truly called the doctrine of God's holy word, yet are they not formally binding upon the consciences of Christians farther than they see the connection, and evidently see that they are so . . ." (*Pioneer Sermons* 40), is the same as that of John Smith. Would Campbell have required that Jason Jones be accepted out of consideration for his "opinion" that he should be received by the church in spite of his homosexual lifestyle? His statement that while "doctrinal exhibitions of the great system of Divine truths, and defensive testimonies in opposition to prevailing errors" are "highly expedient," and "yet, as these must be in a certain measure the effect of human reasoning, and of course must contain much inferential truths, they ought not to be made terms of Christian communion . . ." (41), if applied consistently, says that even though something is *true*, if that truth involves inferences, or human reasoning, it must not be bound upon anyone. Where would that leave him on how to treat a person like Jason Jones? If such a deduction cannot be bound upon one, even though it is true, then how could Campbell bind *his* opinion about homosexual practice upon this man? And if not on this subject, what about other *true* deductions that have been drawn on other important subjects? What about, for example, a conclusion that "for" (*eis*) in Acts 2:38 means "in order to receive," and not "because of" the remission of sins? Or, that the word "baptize" means immersion?

Alexander Campbell wrote articles on many Bible subjects in his time, and the truth of the matter is, many of the conclusions he came to and that are found in his long series of articles on "A Search for the Ancient Order of Things" were arrived at using the deductive process. Many of Campbell's writings in the *Christian Baptist* and *Millennial Harbinger* were put into a book first published in 1835, titled, *The Christian System in Reference to the Union of Christians and a Restoration of PRIMITIVE CHRISTIANITY as Plead in the Current Reformation*. The articles in this book have many conclusions that were reached through the use of deductive type reasoning. No one can go far in teaching some of the leading *truths* of the Bible without having first come to such conclusions based upon clear and indisputable evidence from the Scriptures, but not based upon *explicit* statements in the word of God.

Question 3: **Is there a difference between silence and implication? If so, what is it? Does it really matter whether or not one is able to see the difference?** We discussed in some detail the first part of this question in Chapter 21. In reading the writings of those who have written on the subject of "silence," there are times when it is difficult to know what these writers mean by the term. This is true whether one is reading early or present day writers. The same may be said on the subject of implication, and whether or not a given writer is including implication when he is discussing the subject of silence. A careful reading of the chapters on opinions (Chapters 19 and 20) will likely lead one to the conclusion that both the Campbells, John Smith, and Elijah Goodwin all used the terms "opinion" and "implication," or "deduction," to mean the same thing, but not one of them distinguishes opinions or deductions from silence.

It does not appear that the question of the "silence of Scripture" was at first carefully thought through by the early restoration leaders. The early slogan, "We speak where the Bible speaks, and we are silent where the Bible is silent" (thought by some to have been first introduced by Thomas Campbell), was yet to be tested. It took several years and the development of some issues, and the introduction of some questionable practices, for questions over its meaning to begin to be asked. We saw earlier that the controversy over communion with the unimmersed was the first critical test of the meaning of the "silence of Scripture."

In Chapter 20 we saw that both David Lipscomb and H. Leo Boles, in their booklets on unity, were responding to the argument that silence gives permission to act. These brethren insisted that when the Bible is silent on a subject like instrumental music in worship, or human societies to do the work of the church, such silence forbids; it does not permit. M.C. Kurfees (see our comments on pages 242-43) is very clear on this subject when he says, "if the Word of God says nothing concerning a given course, there can be no faith in pursuing that course . . ." (*Walking by Faith* 6). He also emphasizes the importance of respecting the silence of Scripture in his definition of opinion: "the word opinion signifies *what one thinks,* and in religious matters it means what men think regarding matters on which the Bible is silent," or "what men think where the word of God does not speak" (7).

The thoughtful reader will remember that Alexander Campbell on the matter of communion with the unimmersed contended that there must be authority for the practice before it can be accepted, and he said that the silence on the practice was not enough to permit it. In the same way, Lipscomb and Boles argued that we must have Bible authority for instrumental music in worship and human societies to do the church's work. Bible silence, they said, does not permit such practices.

It appears that through the years there has always been considerable misunderstanding on the subject of implication and silence. Just how do these two subjects relate to one another? Do they refer to the same thing? We can grant that they do at least have one thing in common: *they both belong to the non-explicit area.* But if we have *implicit* authority for something, does that mean that the Bible is *silent* about it? This is an important question in light of how some are using the term "silence" today. There can be little doubt that this is how the term is used in much of the writing that is being done in our own time, and from the writings of the early restoration leaders one would think that this also is how they used the term.

We would encourage our readers to read George F. Beals' excellent treatment of this subject, found on pages 63-70 of his book, a section that we quoted in Chapter 21. Though both implication and silence belong to the non-explicit category, they differ in that silence belongs to the *nothing* area of the non-explicit category, whereas implication is in an area to itself (the implicit area) in the same non-explicit category. Confusion exists and a lot of problems arise when implication is put into the silence area of the non-explicit category.

We will repeat here the example cited by Beals (p. 70f. of his book). It illustrates this problem well. He offers a quote from Randy Fenter where he lists things like the ownership of church property, radio and television programs, microphones, and baptistries, and places them in the area of the silence of Scripture, saying, "silence simply means that the particular issue under discussion was not addressed in those God-given letters." In Fenter's view, the Bible is not a constitution because if it were "then," according to him, "silence is intentional and necessarily prohibitive of anything not explicitly found in Scripture." Is this true? Is the Bible constitutional, and, if it is, is it *silent* about such things as radio and television programs, microphones, baptistries, etc.? Yes, the Bible is constitutional, as we have argued earlier in this book, but no, the Bible is not silent about matters of this kind. These things are authorized by *implicit* authority, and where there is implicit authority for something, the Bible is not silent about it. Note the following:

Television and radio programs are authorized by Matthew 28:18-20 and Mark 16:15-16, because some *means* of communicating the gospel is implied.

Microphones are authorized by Mark 16:15, because such an aid is implied when it is needed so that one might be heard when the gospel is preached.

Church property is authorized by Hebrews 10:25, because to assemble implies that a place for such gatherings be provided, whether such a place is owned or rented by the church.

Baptistries are authorized by Mark 16:16, because the command to baptize implies a *place*, or one might say, a *container* that can hold enough water to immerse a person in water.

Now, it is also true that similar means or aids are also authorized in any constitution for the carrying out of the work of the government, or any agency that has a constitution. Fenter is confusing Bible silence with implication by making silence include the implicit area. Or stated in another way, he is making "silence" refer to the whole "non-explicit" area, which it does not (see Beals 66-70). It is this very mistake that creates a lot of problems for him, and for any others who confuse the implicit and silence (the *nothing* area) areas by making Bible silence include the whole non-explicit category.

Question 4: **Does silence give one the liberty to act? Does it set one free so that he is at liberty to do as he pleases with regard to the teaching or action under consideration?** No, but this is the general, though mistaken, view regarding the subject of silence. When the Bible is silent on a teaching or action (says *nothing* about it) it does not permit, it forbids. Remember, we are *not* talking about *implication* here. We are talking about silence, and silence is not implication, as we were pointing out in answer to the previous question. This is the mistake Randy Fenter was making when he talked about the Bible being silent about church property, television and radio programs, baptisteries, etc. The Bible is not silent when there is something in the Bible about a matter, even when that something is something *implied.*

Question 5: **Why has the plan for unity that was advocated by the early restoration leaders, whereby every brother would simply hold his opinions to himself as private property and not teach or practice them, not worked?** Most likely agree that the plan for unity that was proposed was a good plan. Yet, as restoration history has demonstrated, for various reasons brethren simply have not always been willing to work the plan. Alexander Campbell himself made a deliberate decision not to adhere strictly to it when he chose to bring the readers of his magazine, *The Millennial Harbinger*, to his own conclusion about church cooperation. We saw in an earlier chapter that he argued for the acceptance of his cooperation "plan" on the basis of expediency. Campbell argued that the majority should rule in such matters, and all others should accept the decision of the majority.

The problem with Campbell's approach was that the minority would not always agree that what was being offered as an expedient is *in fact* a mere expedient. Campbell's decision that when others (a small minority) did not submit to his decision that the society was a mere *expedient* (or, only the *form*, the *way* and the *means*, as he described it) by which the end of church cooperation would be attained should not be called on to lead public prayer was a sure way to divide the church over this issue. It appears that Campbell had come to the place where he was now willing to leave behind all those who did not go along with him in his conclusion on this subject. In other words, Campbell was willing to divide the church over his "cooperation plan" since apparently only a small minority would not go along with him.

But others have done the same thing over other differences that have arisen since the first major division over the missionary society. This was the procedure that was used in the controversy over instrumental music from 1869 on, and the same procedure was used when the difference arose over the sponsoring church arrangement and the church support of human institutions in the middle of the twentieth century. And what about the controversy over women teachers, and Bible classes, and using more than one container in serving the Lord's supper? It appears that each of us at one time or another has been on the side of the majority over some issue and has been willing to see a division result over that issue when the protest came from a small minority.

There is no easy solution to this problem. Each has the responsibility of learning how an action or thing is authorized as an expedient and when it is not. We must come to know the difference between an "aid" and an addition. This involves a correct understanding of the meaning of silence (that silence forbids and does not permit) when it comes to the interpretation of Scripture. It is also important that one recognizes that silence and implication are not the same.

Question 6: **Doesn't the fact that brethren have not agreed over these kinds of matters through the years illustrate the point that people are not able to understand the Bible alike?** No, I would not go that far with it. It is a matter of record that we *have not* understood Bible teaching on these subjects in the same way. But that is not the same thing as to say that we *cannot* come to the same understanding on these subjects. I believe that we can, and that we should. Certainly the fault is not with the Bible. I believe the preachers have been right through the years in preaching that the Bible is a book that can be understood, and that if it is understood at all, it is understood alike.

But, I also am willing to grant that some Bible subjects are much more difficult to understand than others. Surely all of us would agree that the subject of how to establish Bible authority, or how to know when a thing is permitted, required or forbidden, is no easy matter. Yet, just because it is difficult does not justify our failure to give to it the time that it requires in order to come to understand the subject. Once we understand this subject, then we are required to make the kinds of *applications* to our *practice* that our new knowledge would require of us. This is not easy either. In fact, this perhaps is the hardest part. Alexander Campbell in later years conceded that he had no idea, once he began to lay out the *principles* upon which "a restoration of the ancient order of things" would take place, just how much havoc those *principles* would make upon his *opinions*. Here is how he describes it:

> We were not, indeed, at first apprized of the havoc which our *principles* would make upon our *opinions*. We soon, however, found our principles and opinions at war on some points; and the question immediately arose, *Whether shall we sacrifice our principles to our opinions, or our opinions to our principles?* We need not say that we were compelled to the latter, judging that our principles were better than our opinions. Hence, since we put to sea on board this bottom, we have been compelled to throw overboard some opinions once as dear to us as they are not to those who never thought of the difference between principle and opinion.

> Some of those opinions (as the most delicate and tender buds are soonest blighted by the frost) immediately withered, under the first application of our principles. Infant baptism and infant sprinkling, with all infantile

imbecility, immediately expired in our minds, soon as the *Bible alone* was made the only measure and standard of faith and duty. . . . (Preface, *The Christian System* 9-10).

Is Campbell saying here that in the early years his belief in infant baptism and infant sprinkling "withered" once he came to respect the authoritative nature of the *silence of Scripture*? That appears to be exactly what he is saying. Once the *Bible alone* came to be his "only measure and standard of faith and duty," he realized that the Bible had *nothing* to say about those subjects, and therefore the practice of infant baptism and infant sprinkling were *forbidden*. *That* is the true meaning of Bible *silence*!

Why then was Campbell not able to make the same application on the subject of "organization" when it came to the question of church cooperation? In my reading of Campbell, it appears to me that he did at first (at least in theory) make the same application to "organization" that he later made to infant baptism and infant sprinkling. It is true, as some thought at the time, that Campbell appears to have been inconsistent in supporting the Cooperation Meeting in those early days. "How could he do this in light of his own writings at that time?" they asked. Of local churches he had said, "in their church capacity alone they moved. They neither transformed themselves into any kind of association, nor did they fracture and sever themselves into divers societies" (*CB* I [1823]:14). During these early years he had rejected the idea that church organization was left to man's discretion, and because he believed the Bible offered a prescription of specific rules of congregational behavior and organization, extra-congregational organizations were not allowed (*CB* V [1828]:250ff.). Was not this an argument from the silence of the Scripture, insisting that because the Bible says nothing about extra-congregational organizations, they are therefore forbidden?

It may be that Alexander Campbell's thinking about church cooperation was influenced more than he realized by his great desire to see the restoration cause grow at a much faster pace than what he was witnessing at the time. He may also have been influenced a great deal in his thinking by the fact that brethren in general seemed to want some way for all the churches to cooperate in evangelizing the world. It is easy for one's thinking to become clouded by what he *wants* to see accomplished. It is a dangerous practice to first want something and then to go to the Scriptures to seek justification for it. When we do that we will find something in Scripture in favor of it almost every time.

Question 7: **What are "change agents" in the church that some are writing so much about today? Is there any real need to be concerned**

about them? Certainly if I felt there was no real need to be concerned about what are being called "change agents" in the church today, you would not be reading this book. This book is an attempt to respond to some of the things that are being taught by these change agents. Other books have been written for the same purpose, each having its own approach and emphasis. Some of these books our readers should know about are as follows (in chronological order by date of publication):

Thompson, Bert. *Is Genesis Myth? The Shocking Story of the Teaching of Evolution at Abilene Christian University.* Montgomery, AL. Apologetics Press, 1984.

Highers, Alan. *How Do You Spell F(f)ellowship?* Henderson, TN. Privately published, 1985.

Moffatt, Jerry, editor. *The Current Digression I.* Austin, TX: Firm Foundation Publishing House, 1987.

Moffatt, Jerry, editor. *The Current Digression II.* Austin, TX. Firm Foundation Publishing House, 1988.

Jividen, Jimmy. *Koinonia: A Place of Tough and Tender Love.* Nashville: Gospel Advocate Co, 1989.

Music, Goebel. *Behold the Pattern.* Colleyville, TX. Goebel Music Publications, 1991.

Bales, James D. *The Church in Transition — To What?* Searcy, AR. Privately published, 1992.

Woodson, William. *Change Agents and Churches of Christ.* Athens, AL. School of Bible Emphasis, 1994.

Cates, Curtis A., editor. *Heaven's Imperatives or Man's Innovations: Shall We Restructure the Church of Christ?* Memphis, TN. Memphis School of Preaching, 1995.

Miller, Dave. *Piloting the Strait: A Guidebook for Assessing Change in Churches of Christ.* Pulaski, TN. Sain Publications, 1996.

Beals, George F. *How Implication Binds and Silence Forbids: Studies in Biblical Hermeneutics.* Ann Arbor, MI. PC Publications, 1998.

Wilhelm, Jack. *Contemporary Concerns of Christians*. Florence, AL. Cox Creek Bookhouse, 1999.

The third book from the end of this list, that of Dave Miller, *Piloting the Strait*, is the most comprehensive and up-to-date of the books in the list, and it should be required reading for all those who want to be familiar with what is happening in the church today. He covers the subject of "change agents" from top to bottom, including the roots, fuel, and mechanism (the "new hermeneutic") of change in the church, as well as all the specifics of the changes that are taking place. Miller also offers a reasonable response to the leading arguments made by the leaders in this movement. All elders and gospel preachers in the church should read this book.

The next-to-the-last book in the list, that by George F. Beals, *How Implication Binds and Silence Forbids: Studies in Biblical Hermeneutics*, is *must* reading for those interested in the subject of biblical interpretation. Every gospel preacher in the Lord's church should *study* this book, and preach the truths that are to be found in it on the subject of the silence of the Scriptures and implication.

Those who have come this far in reading my book do not need to have the meaning of a change agent specifically drawn out for them. They have seen an example of a change agent at work in the church in the person of Cecil Hook, and his book, *Free in Christ*. But to give the reader a feel for what is now taking place in many churches, just take a look at this list of the *specifics of change* dealt with in Dave Miller's book (181-390):

The Assault on Worship
New Preaching Style
Church Music
Lifting Up Hands
Hand-clapping
Drama and Dramatic Reading
Female Leadership
Religious Holidays
Dedicating Babies
The Lord's Supper
Variety in Assembly Formats (Sunday Night Cluster Groups, Children's
    Worship, "Contemporary" Services)
Embracing Denominationalism (Fellowship, Grace, Unity, Baptism)
The Authority of Elders
Moral Issues (Homosexuality, Divorce and Remarriage, Abortion, Lot-
    tery, Modesty)
The Holy Spirit

Question 8: **Is it true that some of these change agents teach that one is saved by faith only?** Yes. This has been documented in some of the books in the above list. Several of those who are well known among the change agents, including men like Rubel Shelly and Max Lucado, have indicated a belief in the denominational doctrine of salvation by faith only. I found the following statement from Max Lucado in his book, *When Christ Comes* (106). He is discussing the subject of rewards and points out that none of us "has ever done one work to enhance the finished work of the cross." True, we do not contribute to the *ground* of our salvation, either from our past sins or our final salvation in heaven. But Lucado, in describing our salvation in heaven, goes on to quote these words from Donald Bloesch: "We are accepted into heaven on the basis of faith alone, but we are adorned in heaven on the basis of the fruits of our faith."

That's good Baptist doctrine, but it is not Bible truth. Lucado makes no attempt to harmonize the above statement with James 2:14ff. where James describes our faith and works in connection with our salvation in heaven. In verse 14 James asks, "For what doth it profit, my brethren, though a man say he has faith, and have not works? Can faith save him?" Note how this verse ends. It ends with the question, can faith *save* him? *Save* him? Yes, that's what James asks. He is talking about the kind of faith that *saves*, not the faith that rewards one in heaven. So whatever James teaches on the subject of faith and works in this chapter, keep in mind that he is talking about salvation, or what kind of faith will *save*, not how one will be rewarded once he is in heaven.

What faith is it that will *not save* a man? The faith he has just described; faith without works. Again, pay particular attention to how James asks his question. "Can the kind of faith (faith without works) he has just described *save* him?" he asks. Therefore, his question is, "Will faith *only* save him, or must it be faith plus works that saves a man?" That is James' question.

His answer is a straightforward answer: faith *without works* will *not* save a man. Only faith *with works* will save him. But Lucado says that faith *with* works will *not* get a man into *heaven*; faith *only* does that for him. Let me repeat: According to Lucado, it takes faith *only* to get a person into heaven, or to *save* him. Now who is right about that, James or Max Lucado? James goes on to say, "Ye see then how that by works a man is justified, and not by faith only" (v. 24)! Notice how he uses the word "justified" here. He isn't talking about rewards in heaven. He is talking about justification, how a man will be saved in heaven. That's what Lucado is talking about when he quotes Donald Bloesch, and Bloesch says that one will be saved in heaven by "faith only"! James says the exact opposite of what Max Lucado says on this subject.

Question 9: **Are these same men saying that water baptism has nothing to do with man's salvation from his past sins?** Again, the answer is yes. Because of his erroneous doctrine on the subject of salvation by faith only, Lucado also has come to put baptism in the category of what one does *after* he becomes a Christian. We would expect this from a Baptist preacher, which again shows that this is the place to which Max Lucado has come. By his teaching he belongs with the Baptists. If you ask, "Are you sure Lucado believes water baptism is for the Christian and not for the alien sinner?" the answer is yes. E. Claude Gardner recently said the following to Max Lucado: "In your interview with the *Christian Chronicle*, you declare that baptism is an act of obedience showing one has been saved by faith only. The article states:

> Once a person admits sin and trusts Christ for salvation, a step must be taken to proclaim to heaven and earth that he/she is a follower of Christ. Baptism is that step. Baptism is the initial and immediate step of obedience and worship by the one who has declared his/her faith to others.
>
> This is the denominational plan of salvation and not the Bible. Where in the Bible is this plan delineated by precept and example?" ("Questions That Should Be Asked of Max Lucado," 117, *Firm Foundation* [Dec. 2002]: 17).

Lucado believes in the "sinner's prayer" that has been used by denominational preachers through the years. Gardner gives the following prayer from Lucado's book, *He Did This Just For You* (50):

> Would you let him save you? This is the most important decision you will ever make. Why don't you give your heart to him right now? *Admit* your need. *Agree* with his work. *Accept* his gift. Go to God in prayer and tell him, *I am a sinner in need of grace. I believe that Jesus died for me on the cross. I accept your offer of salvation.* It's a simple prayer with eternal results.

A very similar denominational plea was made by Lucado in a sermon of his heard over station KJAK in Lubbock, Texas in December of 1996:

> God will make you worthy and the invitation is for you. And all you have to do is call him Father. Just call him Father. Just turn your heart to him even right now as I am speaking. Call him your Father and your Father will respond. Why don't you do that? 'Father, I give my heart to you. I

give you my sins. I give you my fears. I give you my whole life. I accept
the gift of your Son on the cross for my sins. And I ask you, Father, to
receive me as your child. Through Jesus I pray. Amen."

Is any more proof needed? In what he teaches on the subject of salvation, Lucado makes himself into a good Baptist because he teaches Baptist
doctrine, and he comes very close to admitting it. He may be preaching for
a so-called "Church of Christ" in San Antonio, Texas, but he is *not* a *gospel*
preacher. E. Claude Gardner quotes him as saying in an interview with the
Baptist Standard, "But I really don't consider myself a Church of Christ
minister. . . . I think I would be a good Baptist." He should have said, "I *am*
a good Baptist," because Lucado preaches the Baptist plan of salvation as
well as any Baptist preacher ever did.

Question 10: **When one teaches that baptism is necessary for salvation, isn't he saying that men are earning their salvation, since baptism is a work, and we cannot be saved by works?** We don't need to
worry about earning our salvation, nor should we be fearful that in our
obedience to the gospel we will be adding something to the death of Christ.
If Christ had been concerned about that he would not have *required*, as he
did through Peter in Acts 2:38, that one repent and be baptized *for the
remissions of sins*. This is what the Bible elsewhere describes as *obeying*
the gospel *in order to* be saved. We know that one must obey the gospel in
order to be saved because Paul says that the Lord will come "in flaming
fire taking vengeance on them that know not God and obey not the gospel
of our Lord Jesus Christ" (2 Thess. 1:8). This shows that, if one is to be
saved, he must *obey* the gospel. If *obedience* to the gospel is not a *requirement* put upon man by God *in order that he might be saved*, what would
you call it? Since it is a requirement, and a requirement is something man
must DO, is such obedience a *work*, and if a work, is it a work of faith (1
Thess. 1:3; Jas. 2:14-26; Gal. 5:6) and therefore not meritorious, or is it a
work of human merit?

The same may be asked of repentance. What about repentance? Is this
something that man does, or will the change agents in the church now say
that this is a work that God does for man by a direct working of the Holy
Spirit upon the heart of man? Will these men now say that repentance is the
work of regeneration as it is defined by our Calvinist friends, and that it is
a miracle of the new birth wrought in man by God, and not something man
does? The only reason the Calvinists ever came to define repentance in this
way was so they could avoid the problem of saying that any "work" whatsoever on man's part is involved in his being saved. Come, now, ye (change
agents) who are so set on changing the church of Christ into a sectarian

body, what say ye about repentance? Is it something man does, or will you with the Calvinists make repentance a work wrought by God through the Holy Spirit in the human heart? If you say it is something man does, then is it a work? Is it a human work? Since this is how you are describing baptism, why would not repentance which is also done by man be the same, a human work, and therefore meritorious ?

Question 11: **How can one claim that man is saved by faith and works and not contradict the Bible's claim that one is saved by grace?** Max Lucado has a problem with how to reconcile grace with a faith that works, just as all change agents in the church are having a problem with this matter. Rubel Shelly, for example, says "our salvation arises only and entirely from grace . . . . It is entirely of grace through faith . . . ," and yet he fails to explain how a thing can be "entirely" by grace (one thing) and at the same time be "entirely of grace through faith" (two things)! How can salvation be "entirely" of one thing and at the same time be "entirely" of two things? These men are no better at untangling their contradictory positions on the subject of salvation by faith only than our denominational friends have been through the years.

How can one like Lucado say our *rewards* in heaven will be *on the basis of works* if he is fearful of any and all kinds of merit systems? Will we *earn* by *human* works our rewards in heaven? James says we will even be "saved" or "justified" by a faith that works, Max Lucado to the contrary notwithstanding! But Lucado certainly does not mean that one will *earn* his salvation (or his rewards in heaven, for that matter) in heaven, does he? Lucado must agree that there is no human *merit* involved in works of faith, or else he could not say that Christians will be rewarded in heaven on the basis of works. Meritorious works, Max? If not, how would you describe these *works* of faith that bring us rewards in heaven?

When faith works in such a way that God is pleased, it is a "faith working through love" (Gal. 5:6). We have nothing to boast about when we do something through faith; something that God himself has commanded. When we are obeying something God commands, the fact that it is a response being made in faith is enough to show that it is not an act of merit. Such a response of faith is an act of surrender, a giving up of one's own will in the matter; it is an acknowledgment that we cannot accomplish the thing we are seeking (whether it is salvation or rewards) on our own. In an act of obedience to something God has commanded, man in obeying is in that very act turning to God and making an appeal to God for mercy. In the matter of salvation, he is acknowledging that God's provision for his sins is Jesus Christ, and that he is God's only answer to the sin problem.

Even in our baptism into Christ for the remission of sins, our faith is in "the operation of God" who raised up Jesus Christ from the dead (Col. 2:12). Our trust is in what God is doing for us (forgiving our trespasses, v. 13), not in what we are doing in being "buried with him in baptism" (v. 12a). Neither the act of obedience, nor the baptism itself is the object of our faith, but rather it is faith in "the operation God," or trust in what God is doing for us at that time.

R.L. Whiteside makes the following observations in his commentary on Romans:

> An effort is sometimes made to explain Paul and James by saying that Paul was talking of justification of an alien sinner, and James, about the justification of a Christian. It is argued that an alien sinner must be justified by faith only, in order that it may be by grace, and that if the sinner has to perform any conditions, his salvation is of works and not of grace. But what about the Christian? It is strange that these super-exegetes do not see that if works of faith destroy grace, then the works which they say a Christian must perform to be justified destroys all grace from the life of a Christian. Tell us ye super-exegetes, how according to your judgment, there can be any grace in the justification of a Christian by works.
>
> But the theory that Paul's argument (in Romans 4:4-5 — ww) eliminates all conditions from the salvation of a sinner not only contradicts James, but Paul also. If all works are eliminated, faith itself is eliminated, for it is a work. "They said therefore unto him, What must we do, that we may work the works of God? Jesus answered and said unto them, This is the work of God, that ye believe on him whom he hath sent" (John 6:28, 29). And Paul tells us emphatically that eternal life is granted to those who "by patience in well-doing seek for glory and honor and incorruption" (Rom. 2:6, 7). To seek by patience in well-doing requires human effort. Again: "But thanks be to God that, whereas ye were servants of sin, ye became obedient from the heart to that form of teaching whereunto ye were delivered; and being made free from sin, ye became servants of righteousness" (Rom. 6:17, 18). They obeyed from the heart. That means that their faith expressed itself in obedience to God. By this obedience they were made free from sin. Here again is human effort (*A New Commentary on Paul's Letter to the Saints at Rome* 96-7).

Question 12: **What is "unity in diversity"? Is this a scriptural expression? How much diversity can there be in the body of Christ and there yet be only "one body"?** The expression "unity in diversity" does not appear in the Bible, yet within certain limits the thought conveyed by these words expresses a true biblical concept. We found some illustrations of the kinds of diversity that can exist in the body of Christ (even in a local church) in our first chapter, titled "One Body Yet Many Members." The Bible describes the church as a diversified unit. In the church at Corinth Paul found different nationalities, social classes, and gifts. Yet in spite of this kind of diversity there was unity of origin, and unity of heritage. There is also unity of relationship, each member being united to Christ as head, and as long as each member maintains this contact with the head, there is also cohesiveness of the body because each member provides benefit to all the other members (see pp. 6-7).

Some have been frightened away from using the expression "unity-in-diversity" themselves because it has been so grossly misused by others. But just because a term is misused does not mean that the term should no longer be used by us. My denominational friends misuse the word "conversion," but I go right on using the term the way it is used in the Bible. Others misuse the word "prayer" when they teach the "praying through" system of salvation, but the word has a legitimate use in Scripture and I refuse to stop using the term just because others are misusing it. These may not be the best examples, but the reader can see the point.

It is the abuse that is made of the expression "unity in diversity" that should concern us, not whether or not the expression can be scripturally used. Cecil Hook, for example, charges that where brethren have gotten off track is due to

> a legal approach to the Scriptures and justification. According to this line of thinking, since salvation depends upon rightly keeping of law, each point of law must be known and practiced in detail. Unity and fellowship are based on total doctrinal agreement, ruling out any thought of unity in diversity. This mentality will continue to emphasize differences and force those distinctions into dividing issues (*Free in Christ* 9).

Following this statement Hook then gives a list of one hundred things about which brethren have differed and says, "We have continued in congregational fellowship while disagreeing on these many points; thus our very practice has been inconsistent with our denial of unity in diversity" (9).

I will grant that for those who refuse to admit that the terms "unity in diversity" properly describe the condition of the church as it actually is today cannot be consistent in their view. We have had, and will continue to have, diversity in the way Hook claims in this statement. We would expect this kind of diversity among an intelligent and free-thinking people. The issue is not whether or not there are many different points of view held by different people on a number of Bible subjects. The issue is, how can we hold differing points of view and yet remain united?

Yet not all the differences in his list of one hundred items are equal. Some of the things in the list are bound to be more troublesome for some people than others. Some involve moral issues (abortion, serving in the military during times of war when lives are taken, remarriage of a divorced person, modesty in dress, social drinking, dancing, etc.), while others involve collective action and in some cases would call for all members to participate (those things involving the collection, such as the use of the church building for secular purposes, fellowship halls, support of colleges from the treasury, church benevolence, operation of church hospitals). Some other things in the list involve what is done in the assembly of the church and would also involve all the members, either by direct participation, or by indirect participation by being present as the activities are being engaged in (special group singing such as choruses, choirs, and quartets, and solo singing, or applauding in the assembly, lifting hands while singing, singing as the emblems are passed).

The kinds of things we have just listed in the above paragraph are things that cause real problems in local churches. The separate list of eleven items (given on page 13 of his book) over which Hook says he has known of cases where churches have divided are described by him as things over which

> we have become hair-splitters serving a God of quibbles. Sincerely, but being either ignorant or intellectually dishonest, we have twisted and mis-applied Scriptures to support our contentions. We have become fixed in the tracks of dogmatism. God's purposes in His directives have been over-shadowed by emphasis on lawful requirements. Binding incidental details often has become more important than the love without which we cannot be bound together. Doctrine, instead of the Savior, has become our center. The binding of scruples has limited the liberties of others. We have not trusted others with the freedom which Christ gives. We have become judgmental and exclusive and have given ourselves a name to distinguish ourselves from others. God's grace has been limited to our achievement. We continue not only to divide but also to prevent the only true unity. Unless we change our perspective, we shall continue on this ill-fated course (*Free in Christ* 13-14).

Just how one can be sincere and at the same time intellectually dishonest, Hook fails to explain. But that's how he describes the "hair-splitters serving a God of quibbles," which of course in his view is a fitting portrayal of all except him and those with whom he is identified. So at the outset of his book we see Cecil Hook, and all those who are with him, standing alone among his brethren as those who are the intellectually honest, and they could never be guilty of twisting and misapplying Scripture! Only the "hair-splitters serving a God of quibbles" could ever be guilty of that crime.

And who are the "hair splitters" who are either "ignorant or intellectually dishonest," and who twist and misapply Scriptures to support their contentions? All those who will not give him and his the "freedom" or the "right" he is pleading for to *teach and practice* all of the 111 items he lists on pages 11-13 of his book. Yet, the truth of the matter is, there has never been a man who is more able to twist and pervert Scriptures in defense of what he claims is his "right" to teach and practice any and everything he wants, than this man. And all the while he could not call any of us a "false teacher" (since his only criterion for a *true* teacher is sincerity) because he begins by crediting all of us as being "sincere" — even if we are "ignorant" and "intellectually dishonest"!

Hook's point about "directives" and "lawful requirements" in the above quote has been thoroughly dealt with in earlier chapters of this book. He is simply laying down here what is to be the central thrust of his book. No one believes that a Christian should bind incidental details, and they certainly should not put the binding of incidental details above love for God, or as being more important than love that binds Christians together. But, at the same time, those who are more conservative in their interpretation of Scripture are going to continue to believe that many of the things in this list are not mere "incidental details," and that when Jesus said, "if you love me, keep my commandments," he is saying that commandments are "lawful requirements" and not simply "love directives." John says, "And this is love, that we walk after his commandments . . ." (1 John 2:6a).

Exactly what our true standing is in relation to Christ is not simply a matter of choosing between doctrine and the Savior, nor is our standing to be determined by whether we give more emphasis to the Savior than we give to doctrine. The question to be answered is, can one truly let Christ be his center without having a proper respect for his doctrine or teaching? How can one ignore or deliberately disregard *any* teaching of Christ and keep Christ as Savior at the center of his life?

We come to a restatement of Hook's real purpose in writing his book, when he says, "The binding of scruples has limited the liberties of others. We have not trusted others with the freedom which Christ gives." The "binding of scruples"! Everything in Hook's list of the 111 items is a scruple to him. What he really is saying is that *as long as he can have his way* on these 111 items (actually, other things could be added to the list, such as a plurality of elders in a local church, since he does not believe there is a pattern for this practice in the N.T.) we can have unity. But in those passages where Paul is discussing such matters (incidentals and scruples) he usually emphasizes the need for *the denial of one's rights* in order that there might be unity (Phil. 2:1-11). He never insists on himself or any other brother having his way on such matters in order that unity might prevail. He went in the exact opposite direction and argued that brethren must deny their own personal rights for the sake of unity.

On the other hand, when the great doctrinal issue over the law arose, and some maintained that certain requirements of the law should be bound upon Christians, Paul insisted that the binding of these requirements is to deny the freedom (from the law) one enjoys in Christ. Such matters are not mere incidental details and scruples. When one turns back to the law, he reasoned, they are severed from Christ, and have fallen from grace (see Gal. 5:1-6).

Whatever the difference in teaching and practice may be between two brethren, how can one man be free to teach and practice the kinds of things given in this list and another not be free to oppose such teaching and practice? The person who does not believe that a certain teaching and practice are right has every "right" to oppose that teaching and practice. This is why early restoration leaders maintained that in such areas each must hold his views as private property if unity is to be maintained.

Do you suppose, as Hook suggests in this statement, that our real problem is that "we have not trusted others with the freedom which Christ gives"? If that is our problem, then Paul must have been guilty of making the same mistake. He did not allow people to teach and practice just anything they wanted to teach and practice. The same may be said of Jesus. And if "we have become judgmental and exclusive," so was Jesus and so was Paul. Jesus said to certain Jews of his day, "And in vain do they worship me, teaching as doctrines the commandments of men" (Matt. 15:9), and he said he hated the doctrine of the Nicolaitans (Rev. 2:15). Paul would have nothing of the teaching of Hymenaeus and Philetus because "concerning the truth," he said, "they have erred, saying that the resurrection is past already; and overthrow the faith of some" (2 Tim. 2:17-18). Were Jesus and Paul being judgmental in these matters? Were they being exclusive? You can count on it. They were indeed being both judgmental and exclusive, and so must we.

Do you suppose Jesus and Paul had this problem? Did they not trust others with the freedom that Christ either would give or had given to them? Of course not. It was not a matter of whether or not they trusted others with his freedom, and that is not our major problem today. Our problem has more to do with those who do not understand the meaning of Christ's freedom; they are not properly defining it. If the unity that Christ advocated and prayed for is to ever be created, and then maintained, freedom cannot be license. Jesus never taught that freedom is the license to teach and practice just anything one wants to teach and practice.

On the statement that we "have given ourselves a name to distinguish ourselves from others," see the next question.

Hook says that "God's grace has been limited to our achievement." On the surface this statement appears to mean that man's obedience is not required in order for one to be a recipient of God's grace. Yet, we suspect this is not what he means in any absolute sense. But if this is what he means, just how do you suppose he would attempt to prove this statement from the Bible? Try he may, but prove it he never shall! By "achievement" Hook may mean perfect obedience. If this is what he means, then of course none of us believes anyone shall be saved on the basis of perfect obedience. Anyone who lives perfectly does not need God's grace.

Grace is available to the sinner (both the alien sinner, and the Christian who sins), but not unconditionally. God's grace has appeared to all men bringing salvation (Tit. 2:11), but only those who obey the gospel of God (2 Thess. 1:7-9; 1 Pet. 4:17; Mark 16:16; Acts 2:38) and continue faithful to him (1 Cor. 15:58; Matt. 25:21, 23; Col. 1:23) will be saved. Do you suppose Hook would say that "work out you own salvation with fear and trembling" (Phil. 2:12) involves any "achievement" on man's part? Or, we might ask, what about the alien sinner? Has God "limited his grace to achievement" for him? We know he is saved by God's grace, but as Hook concedes in his book, there are certain conditions involved. Does this mean God's grace for him is limited to achievement because there are conditions? The answer he gives here should say something about how God's grace is made available to the Christian. It is certainly not unconditional.

Hook thinks he has the answer to (or should we say, plan for) "the only true unity," and that all who are not with him are preventing it. And what is his answer? From the way he writes, he appears to be saying that we should let him, and those with him, have their way! Isn't he saying, "Just back off and let me and those who are in agreement with me do as we want (in both teaching and practice) on all 111 items in my list on pages 9-13 of my book, and we can have unity." That and that alone, according to Cecil Hook, will produce "the only true unity"! And why should we do that? Maybe it's because, as he said earlier in this chapter, we are either "ignorant" or "intellectually dishonest," even though we are sincere!

Perhaps another reason Hook thinks we should all adopt his plan for "the only true unity" is because he has the only sound hermeneutic: love that is the only effective motive for our actions, love that fulfills the intent of all other laws, love that lifts us above efforts of legal justification, and love that transcends any sense of duty. We have dealt with these points and his enlargement upon them in some detail in chapters 7 through 17 of this book.

Question 13: **Does Christ's church have a specific and exclusive name?** When I first read Hook's statement that "we have given ourselves a name to distinguish ourselves from others," I was made to wonder, just what do you suppose Cecil Hook would suggest about "the name"? Wouldn't it be interesting to see what "name" is in front of the building where he meets with others to carry on assembly matters? In view of his criticism one might wonder if he could approve of having any designation there at all.

I am inclined to agree with Hook on this subject because I realize that having some way to distinguish ourselves from others does in fact place us at a distinct disadvantage, but, on the other hand, to fail to be identified in some way also has its drawbacks. And I also seriously doubt that any group of Christians who have put the designation "Church of Christ" in front of their building have done so *wanting* to denominationalize the church. It may be that this practice tends to have this effect, but the decision to put this or some other scriptural designation in front of the building is a judgment call to be decided by each local church.

Paul had no problem describing the various local churches he referred to in Romans 16:16 as "the churches of Christ," so why should it disturb us to see local churches of Christ designating themselves as a "church of Christ"? If Hook wants to call the church where he lives "the church of the Beavertons," since he lives in Beaverton, Oregon, or "the church of God which is at Beaverton," or "the church of Christ," it makes no difference to me. When the article "the" is placed before the term "church of Christ," no one in that group of Christians really believes that particular local church is the whole body of Christ, and they don't mean to suggest that their local membership constitutes the whole body by having that description on display in front of their building. All these terms, and others we find in the

New Testament are scriptural ways of identifying a local church that belongs to God and to Jesus Christ.

No, Christ's church, either universal or local, does not have a specific and exclusive name. There are several descriptive terms used in the New Testament to describe the Lord's church, and any of these will serve a local church well in identifying itself. Each group of Christians in a particular area can make that decision for themselves.

Those who insist on a need to adopt a new name sometime choose a name that makes it appear that "all denominations are welcome here." To identify a local church as "the community church," for example, not only shows total disrespect for the terms God himself has used to describe local churches, but those who use this name appear to have the same desire in their choice as the denominations. They are announcing by their name that they welcome into their number any in the denominations regardless of what they teach and practice.

Question 14: **How are brethren in a local church to work together and be at peace when some in the church know very little of the Bible and others are much more advanced in knowledge?** Knowledge is important, and in many ways it is an asset to the one who possesses it; but it also may have its downside depending on how one handles it. It may cause one to become "puffed up": "Now concerning things offered to idols: We know that we all have knowledge. Knowledge puffs up, but love edifies. And if anyone thinks that he knows anything, he knows nothing yet as he ought to know. But if anyone loves God, this one is known by Him" (1 Cor. 8:1-3, NKJV). In the class of things being discussed in this chapter (eating meat sacrificed to an idol in a pagan temple) Paul shows that knowledge does indeed matter, but there are also times when lack of knowledge is better. If one does not know that meat he is eating has been offered to an idol in a heathen temple, he cannot associate it in his mind with an idol and become guilty of sin. Had it not mattered whether or not one had this knowledge Paul would not have instructed these brethren to ask no questions when purchasing meat in the market place (1 Cor. 10:25). When one does not know that an idol is nothing, and/or he does not know that food does not commend one to God, Paul says he cannot eat meat that may or may not have been offered to an idol without becoming defiled in conscience (v. 7). However, those who have knowledge that an idol is nothing and food does not commend one to God are not to exercise their right (liberty) to eat such meat when it will cause their brother to eat it against his conscience (1 Cor. 10:28-33). The strong (those who have knowledge) are to support the weak (those who do not have such knowledge) by foregoing their liberty in such cases.

Whatever the reason may be, whether one has *true* knowledge (knowledge that is from God) in those things that are essential makes a difference with God. If this were not the case, many New Testament passages would have no meaning. Why would it matter, for example, "how" men hear or "what" they hear if God is not concerned about what man believes, teaches and practices? Jesus warned, "take heed how ye hear" (Luke 8:18), and "take heed what ye hear" (Mark 4:24). It is failure in these two areas that causes men to turn away from the truth (2 Tim. 4:4; Tit. 1:14).

There could of course be many factors involved when one fails here, but clearly Paul was concerned that immaturity in knowledge is one of them, and this is why he often urges Christians to grow in knowledge. The most familiar passage that comes from Paul and that is linked with the subject of moving on to maturity is his discussion in Ephesians 4:13f. The gifts that have been given to the church (v. 11) are "for the perfecting of the saints, for the work of the ministry, for the edifying of the body of Christ" (v. 12). This "edifying" of the body is intended to bring each saint "to the knowledge of the Son of God, unto a perfect man, unto the measure of the stature of the fulness of Christ" (v. 13). Why is Paul concerned about whether or not this work of bringing each member to this level of maturity is successful? Because as long as there are those in the body who are yet "children" there is the risk that these members will from their lack of knowledge be "tossed to and fro, and carried about with every wind of doctrine, by the sleight of men, and cunning craftiness, whereby they lie in wait to deceive" (v. 14).

Knowledge is necessary to understanding, and we are commanded to understand the will of the Lord (Eph. 5:17). Without knowledge we would not have been able to escape the pollutions of the world in the first place (2 Pet. 2:20). At one time God's people in the Old Testament period were destroyed for lack of knowledge (Hosea 4:6), and the same will also happen in our day if we fail to teach the truth of God, or if people reject true knowledge, which is the same as to reject the truth of God. Only the truth will make one free (John 8:31-32). Correct knowledge is necessary to acceptable obedience. This is what makes growth in knowledge so important and necessary. Peter warns against those who are unlearned and unstable, because not only do they misuse those things hard to be understood in Paul's letters, but they also "wrest other scriptures, unto their own destruction" (2 Pet. 3:17). He goes on to show in the last two verses of his letter how prior knowledge goes a long way toward protecting Christians from error, but it is no guarantee that they will not be led astray: "Ye therefore, beloved, seeing ye know these things before, beware lest ye also, being led away with the error of the wicked, fall from your own steadfastness. But grow in grace, and in the knowledge of our Lord and Saviour Jesus Christ. To him be glory both now and for ever. Amen" (2 Pet. 3:17-18).

Clearly many of the differences that exist among brethren with regard to knowledge are not threats to the unity of the body. Brethren may and have come to different conclusions about the meaning of certain Bible passages and yet continue to remain together and work together with brethren in a given local church without any one of the number in that local church feeling that he can no longer continue to be a member there because of these differences in knowledge. Division among brethren does not result from brethren *holding* different opinions, but from brethren failing to hold (as private property) the opinions they have about different matters. The *propagation* of opinions (by either teaching them, or by the practice of them, or by both) is what causes division.

Question 15: **Can you illustrate this last point that you just made, i.e., the propagation or practice of an opinion, or a particular point of view, always runs the risk of causing division in a local church?** Yes, I believe I can illustrate this point, and what I will say about the case I will use could equally be applied to other differing opinions. One brother (#1), we will say, concludes from his study of the passages on divorce that there is no justification whatsoever for one Christian to divorce another Christian for any cause except where there has been sexual infidelity on the part of one of the partners in a marriage. In such a case the innocent party may put away the guilty party. Another brother (#2) comes to the conclusion that there are certain circumstances where one Christian may divorce another Christian. This may be either when an unbeliever abandons a Christian woman, per 1 Corinthians 7:15, or when a brother or sister for some unspecified reason puts a marriage partner away, per 1 Corinthians 7:10-11. Both of these cases would be where there has been no sexual infidelity on the part of either partner in the marriage relationship. Brother #1 and brother #2 may have friendly exchanges over this subject whenever a passage of Scripture that deals with the subject of divorce comes up in a Bible class. Neither of these brethren is persistent in his point of view to the point of causing division in the local church over this subject.

But let's say that one day a brother or sister in that local church divorces his/her marriage partner for some cause other than fornication. When this happens it no longer is simply a difference of opinion being "held" by these two brethren. As brother #1 sees it, the very thing he thinks is a sin now has become a *practice* in the local church where he is a member. Does this matter? It most certainly does matter to brother #1. Did it matter that his brother "held" a different opinion on the subject of divorce? Yes, it mattered, but so long as he held it as private property and did not promote his view and did not practice it, he could tolerate it. For him the different points of view that once were held between them are now a case of sin being tolerated in the church. This practice will no doubt become a point of contention and it may eventually become a cause for division in that local church.

Question 16: **What do people mean when they say that Christians are united in the faith but they are divided in matters of faith?** This is the "unity in diversity" argument. Those who use this kind of language usually make the gospel vs. doctrine argument. They contend that the gospel is for unbelievers, but doctrine is for believers. All must agree in gospel but not in doctrine. Hook gives one chapter in his book *Free in Christ* to "Gospel and Doctrine" (59-64). His basic argument is that allowance must be made for people to grow:

> New creatures in Christ who are saved and in fellowship must be fed, confirmed, and matured so they will continue in fellowship and salvation. From the point of spiritual birth there will be diversity in disciples in knowledge, understanding, strength, ability, and maturity. Their justification is in being made right by an act of grace, not because they are right in all things. They are in the right because they are in Christ who is their righteousness, though they may not be right in all matters of faith.

I suppose that one will find general agreement among all followers of Christ on this point. At least up to the place where it is taken in the above quote. But this statement of the matter does not cover the entire ground. Those who make this argument carry it far beyond this point. They are pleading that each brother and sister allow all others to teach and practice whatever they believe on any given point.

Even as one grows in knowledge he will most certainly find areas of disagreement among those with whom he associates in the church. The question that then arises is, what exactly will be the basis of fellowship between them? Can they hold different points of view and still be in fellowship with one another? Certainly. But they will continue in fellowship with one another only so long as they continue to be *united* in their *teaching* and united in their *practice.* When brethren begin to teach and practice different things that pertain to united action, they will eventually separate and go their different ways. This will be the necessary consequence if they both insist on teaching and practicing their particular points of view. If they wish to remain together and continue to worship and work as one in a local church, it will be necessary for both of them to lay aside their differences and no longer teach and practice them. This is the only way they can remain united in their teaching and practice.

Cecil Hook makes an unbelievable statement as he concludes his discussion on the subject of gospel and doctrine. He says, "Fellowship is established when the element of the word called *the gospel* is believed and obeyed. Fellowship is sustained with God and man by following the other *teachings* of the word" (64). This statement affirms the exact opposite of the very point Hook has been attempting to make in his chapter "Gospel and Doctrine." According to him gospel and teachings are two different bodies of truth. The former is for alien sinners, the latter for brethren. The gospel is what brings one into fellowship with God, but doctrine or teachings do not establish, nor do they sustain one's standing in relation to God. According to Hook, and other "unity in diversity" advocates, even though those who have come into Christ "may not be right in all matters of faith," "they are walking in the light, continually cleansed, and in fellowship (1 John 1:5-10)" (63-64).

But the last sentence in the first quote given above denies that this is the case. It affirms that "fellowship is sustained with God and man by following the other *teachings* of the word." Did Cecil Hook mean to say that? That fellowship is *"**sustained** . . . by following the other **teachings** of the word"*? Is this what he meant to say, or do you suppose he would like to take it back?

Why should one practice tolerance in the area of doctrine, the tolerance Hook has been advocating throughout his book, if fellowship with God and man is sustained by following the other *teachings* (doctrine) of the word? Hook is in a quandary here. On the one hand he says that all these differences in doctrine are taken care of by God. To use his words, "they are walking in the light, continually cleansed, and in fellowship (1 John 1:5-10)." But on the other hand, "fellowship is sustained . . . by *following* the other *teachings* (not gospel — ww) of the word." In the first statement it reads like one is in fellowship when he is not following the teachings, but in the other statement fellowship is sustained by following the *teachings* of God's word.

One who does not abide in the doctrine (teaching of) Christ (2 John 9) does not have God. See our discussion of this passage in Chapter 6.

Bibliography

Greek Sources

Arndt, William and William F. Gingrich. *A Greek-English Lexicon of the New Testament and other Early Christian Literature.* Chicago: University of Chicago Press, 1957.

Thayer, Joseph Henry. *Greek-English Lexicon of the New Testament.* Grand Rapids: Zondervan Publishing House, 1965.

Trench, Richard Chenevix. *Synonyms of the New Testament.* Reprint of the 9th ed. of 1880. Grand Rapids: Wm. B. Eerdamns Publishing Company, 1973.

Vine, W.E. *An Expository Dictionary of New Testament Words.* 4 vols. in one. Westwood, NJ: Fleming H. Revell Co., 1952.

Periodical and Other Articles

Bassett, Don. "Our Daily Life As Worship." *Christianity Magazine* III 1(January 1986): 21.

Brown, T. Pierce. "Worship." *Firm Foundation* 98 (April 21, 1981): 246, 251.

Campbell, Alexander. "A Restoration of the Ancient Order of Things" Nos. 1-5; *The Christian Baptist* II (1825-26), Nos. 6-13; *The Christian Baptist* III (1826), and Nos. 14-19; *The Christian Baptist* IV (1826-27).

____. "Opinionism — No. I" *The Millennial Harbinger, New Series* (October 1837): 439-44.

Fenter, Randy. "Do Not Go Beyond What Is Written (2)." *Image Magazine* (September 1989): 9.

Gardner, E. Claude. "Questions That Should Be Asked of Max Lucado." *Firm Foundation* 117 (December 2002): 17.

Green, Ken. *South End Expounder Bulletin* V 12 (March 23, 1970: 1-4.

Harrell, David Edwin. "The Bounds of Christian Unity (3)." *Christianity Magazine* V (April 1988): 102-03.

Jackson, Wayne. "The Weekly Observance of the Lord's Supper." *Christian Courier / Web Edition* (Archives) 4.

Malherbe, Abraham J. "The Unity of the Church in Paul." *Restoration Quarterly* II 4 (1958): 187-96.

McGarvey, J.W. "Immersion in the Holy Spirit." *Lard's Quarterly* I 4 (June 1864): 428-42.

Needham, James P. *PSD Bulletin* XI 6 (February 1979): 2-4.

Roberts, J. W. "Instrumental EN in the New Testament." *Restoration Quarterly* IV 3 (1962): 143-46.

Smith, G.V. "False Prophecy." *The International Standard Bible Encyclopedia*. Vol. 3 of 4 volumes. Fully revised. General ed. Geoffrey W. Bromiley. N. T. ed. Everett F. Harrison. Grand Rapids: William B. Eerdmans Publishing Company, 1986. Pp. 984-86.

Wright, John J. "Worship Will Not Fit into a Pigeonhole." *Firm Foundation* 97 (N 25, 1980): 755.

Books and Booklets

Bales, James D. *Wore Unto You?* Paragould, AR: College Bookstore & Press, n.d.

Beals, George F. *How Implication Binds and Silence Forbids: Studies in Biblical Hermeneutics*. Ann Arbor, MI: PC Publications, 1998.

Best, Ernest. *One Body in Christ*. London: S.P. C. K., 1955.

Boles, H. Leo. *The Way of UNITY Between "CHRISTIAN CHURCH" AND CHURCHES OF CHRIST*. Nashville: Gospel Advocate Company, 1939.

Campbell, Alexander. *The Christian System*. Salem, NH: Ayer Company, Publishers, Inc., 1988 reprint.

Campbell, Thomas. "Declaration and Address of the Christian Association of Washington, Penn." (1809). *Pioneer Sermons and Addresses*: pp. 14-104. Compiled by F.L. Rowe. Cincinnati: F.L. Rowe, Publisher, 1908.

Ferguson, Everett. *Early Christians Speak: Faith and Life in the First Three Centuries*. Austin, TX: Sweet Publishing Company, 1971.

Franklin, Benjamin. *The Gospel Preacher: A Book of Twenty-One Sermons* II. Nashville: Gospel Advocate Company, 1954.

Goodwin, Elijah. *The Family Companion: or A Book of Sermons on Various Subjects, Both Doctrinal and Practical*. Cincinnati: Bosworth, chase & Hall, Publishers, 1873.

Hook, Cecil. *Free in Christ*. First published 1984, revised in 1995. Beaverton, OR: Privately published, 1998.

Kurfees, M.C. *Walking by Faith*. Louisville: Haldeman Avenue Church, 1894.

Lipscomb, David. *CHRISTIAN UNITY, How Promoted, How Destroyed, FAITH AND OPINION*. Nashville: McQuiddy Printing Company, 1916.

Loshe, Eduard. *The New Testament Environment*. Trans. by John E. Steely. Nashville: Abingdon, 1976.

Metzger, Bruce M. *The New Testament: Its Background, Growth, and Content*. 2nd ed. enlarged. Nashville, Abingdon Press, 1983.

Mosheim, John Lawrence von. *Institutes of Ecclesiastical History, Ancient and Modern, in Four Books*. Vol I., 3 colume set. Tarns. fromthe Latin by James Murdock with added notes. 3rd revised and enlarged edition.

New York: Harper & Brothers, 1847.

Murch, James DeForest. *Christians Only: A History of the Restoration Movement.* Cincinnati: Standard Publishing, 1962.

Murray, John. *Principles of Conduct.* Grand Rapids: Wm. B. Eerdmans Publishing Co., 1957.

Phillips, H.E. *Scriptural Elders and Deacons.* Gainesville, FL: Phillips Publications, 1959.

Robinson, John A.T. *The Body.* Studies in Biblical Theology. No. 5. London: SCM Press Ltd., 1963.

Sewell, E.G. *Gospel Lessons and Life History.* Nashville: McQuiddy Printing Company,1908.

Thomas, J.D. *Harmonizing Hermeneutics: Applying the Bible to Contemporary Life.* Nashville: Gospel Advocate Co., 1991.

Williams, David J. *Paul's Metaphors: Their Context and Character.* Peabody, MA: Hendrickson Publishers, 1999.

Williams, John A. *Life of Elder John Smith.* Cincinnati: R.W. Carroll & Co., 1870.

Commentaries

Alexander, Joseph Addison. *The Gospel According to Matthew.* Thornapple Commentaries. First published in 1860. Grand Rapids: Baker Book House, 1980 reprint.

Arnold, Albert N., and D.B. Ford. *Commentary on the Epistle to the Romans.* An American Commentary on the New Testament. Ed. by Alvah Hovey. Philadelphia: The American Baptist Publication Society, 1889.

Broadus, John A. *Commentary on the Gospel of Matthew.* An American Commentry on the New Testament. Ed. by Alvah Hovey. Valley Forge, PA: The American Baptist Publication Society, 1886.

Brooke, A.E. *A Critical and Exegetical Commentary on the Johnine Epistles.* The International Critical Commentary. Eds. C.A. Briggs, Samuel R. Driver and Alfred Plummer. New York: Charles Scribner's Sons, 1912.

Brown, Raymond. *Christ Above All: The Message of Hebrews.* Dowers Grove, IL: InterVarsity Press, 1982.

Bruce, F.F. *Philippians.* New International Biblical Commentary. New Testament ed., W. Ward Gasque. Peabody, MA: Hendrickson Publishers, 1983.

Carson, D.A. *The Gospel According to John.* Grand Rapids: William B. Eerdmans Publishing Company, 1991.

Cottrell, Jack. *The College Press NIV Commentary: Romans*, Volume I. Eds. Jack Cottrell and Tony Ash. Joplin, MO: College Press Publishing Company, 1996

Edwards, Thomas Charles. *A Commentary on the First Epistle to the*

Corinthians. First published in 1885. Minneapolis: Klock & Klock Publisers, 1979 reprint.

Ellicott, Charles J. *St. Paul's First Letter to the Corinthians, With A Critical and Grammatical Commentary*. First published in 1887. Minneapolis: The James Family Christian Publishers, n.d.

Faulkes, Francis. *The Letter of Paul to the Ephesians: An Introduction and Commentary.*Tyndale New Testament Commentaries. Revised edition. General ed. Leon Morris. Grand Rapids: William B. Eerdmans Publishing company, 1989.

Godet, Frederic L. *Commentary on the First Epistle of St. Paul to the Corinthians*. 2 vols. Trans. by A. Cusin. Grand Rapids: Zondervan Publishing House, 1957 reprint.

Hailey, Homer. *A Commentary on Isaiah with Emphasis on the Messianic Hope*. Grand Rapids: Baker Book House, 1985.

____. *A Commentary on the Minor Prophets*. Grand Rapids: Baker Book House, 1972.

Hamilton, Clinton. *Truth Commentaries: The Book of Romans*. Edited by Mike Willis. Bowling Green, KY: Guardian of Truth Foundation, 1998.

Hendriksen, William. *New Testament Commentary: Exposition of Paul's Epistle to the Romans II*. Grand Rapids: Baker book House, 1981.

____. *New Testament Commentary: Exposition of the Gospel According to John I*. Grand Rapids: Baker Book House, 1953.

Hughes, Philip E. *Paul's Second Epistle to the Corinthians*. The New International Commentary on the New Testament. Grand Rapids: Wm. B. Eerdmans Publishing Co., 1962.

Jeremiah, David. *Turning Toward Joy*. Wheaton, IL: Victor Press, 1992.

Kistemaker, Simon J. *New Testament Commentary: Exposition of the Epistles of James and the Epistles of John*. Grand Rapids: Baker Book House, 1986.

Lea, Thomas D. and Hayne P. Griffin, Jr. "1, 2 Timothy Titus." *The New American Commentary*. Vol. 34. General ed. David S. Dockery. Nashville: Broadman Press, 1992.

Lenski, R.C.H. *The Interpretation of St. Paul's Epistle to the Hebrews and the Epistle of James*. Minneapolis: Augsburg Publishing House, 1963.

____. *The Interpretation of St. Paul's Epistle to the Romans*. Columbus: Wartburg Press, 1960.

____. *The Interpretation of St. Paul's Epistle to the Colossians, to the Thessalonians, to Timothy, to Titus, and to Philemon*. Minneapolis: Wartburg Press, 1964.

Lipscomb, David and J.W. Shepherd. *Ephesians, Philippians and Colossians*. New Testament Commentaries Vol. IV. Nashville: Gospel Advocate Company, 1984.

MacArthur, John. *The MacArthur New Testament Commentary: Matthew*

8-15. Chicago: Moody Press, 1987.

McGarvey, J.W. *A Commentary on Acts of Apostles*. Eighth original edition. Nashville: Gospel Advocate Company, 1983 printing.

McGarvey, J.W. and Philip Y. Pendleton. *Thessalonians, Corinthians, Galatians and Romans*. Delight, AR: gospel Light Publishing Company, n.d.

Meyer, Heinrich August Wilhelm. *The Epistles to the Philippians and Colossians*. Trans. by John C. Moore and rev. and ed. by William P. Dickson. Edinburg: T. and T. Clark, 1879.

Moule, Handley C.G. *Philippian Studies: Lessons in Faith and Love*. London: Pickering & Ingles Ltd., n.d.

Murray, John. *The Epistle to the Romans*. 2 volumes in one. Grand Rapids: Wm. B. Eerdmans Publishing Co., 1979.

Plummer, Alfred. *The Gospel According John*. The Cambridge Bible for Schools and Colleges. Cambridge: At the University Press, 1923.

Polhill, John B. "Acts." *The New American Commentary*. Vol. 26. General ed. David S. Dockery. Nashville: Broadman Press, 1992.

Robertson, A.T. *Paul's Joy in Christ: Studies in Philippians*. Rev. and ed. by W. C. Strickland. Nashville: Broadman Press, n.d.

Salmond, S.D.F. "The Epistle to the Ephesians." *The Expositor's Greek Testament*. 5 vols. Grand Rapids: William B. Eerdmans Publishing Co., 1952.

Vincent, Marvin R. *Epistles to the Philippians and to Philemon*. The International Critical Commentary. Edited by Samuel R. Driver, Alfred Plummer, and Charles A. Briggs. Edinburg: T. and T. Clark, 1955..

Weaver, Walton. *Truth Commentaries: The Books of Philippians and Colossians*. Edited by Mike Willis. Bowling Green, KY: Guardian of Truth Foundation, 1996.

Whiteside, Robertson L. *A New Commentary on Paul's Letter to the Saints At Rome*. 8th ed. Denton, TX: Privately published by Miss Inys Whiteside, 1982.

www.ingramcontent.com/pod-product-compliance
Lightning Source LLC
Chambersburg PA
CBHW021216090426
42740CB00006B/245